Saving Souls, Serving Society

Saving Souls, Serving Society

Understanding the Faith Factor in Church-Based Social Ministry

HEIDI ROLLAND UNRUH *and*
RONALD J. SIDER

UNIVERSITY PRESS

2005

OXFORD
UNIVERSITY PRESS

Oxford University Press, Inc., publishes works that further
Oxford University's objective of excellence
in research, scholarship, and education.

Oxford   New York
Auckland   Cape Town   Dar es Salaam   Hong Kong   Karachi
Kuala Lumpur   Madrid   Melbourne   Mexico City   Nairobi
New Delhi   Shanghai   Taipei   Toronto

With offices in
Argentina   Austria   Brazil   Chile   Czech Republic   France   Greece
Guatemala   Hungary   Italy   Japan   Poland   Portugal   Singapore
South Korea   Switzerland   Thailand   Turkey   Ukraine   Vietnam

Published by Oxford University Press, Inc.
198 Madison Avenue, New York, New York 10016

www.oup.com

Oxford is a registered trademark of Oxford University Press

Library of Congress Cataloging-in-Publication Data
Unruh, Heidi Rolland.
Saving souls, serving society : understanding the faith factor in church-based social
ministry / Heidi Rolland Unruh and Ronald J. Sider.
    p. cm.
Includes bibliographical references and index.
ISBN-13 978-0-19-516155-7
ISBN 0-19-516155-6
1. Christian sociology. 2. Missions—Theory. 3. Evangelistic work. 4. Church and
social problems. 5. Christian charities. I. Sider, Ronald J. II. Title.
BT738.R655 2005   2005008223
261.8'32—dc22

9 8 7 6 5 4 3 2 1

Printed in the United States of America
on acid-free paper

During the work on this book, my sons Maurice and Jacob entered our family, and my mother Kit departed from her earthly family. This book is dedicated to them.
— *Heidi Unruh*

Acknowledgments

We owe a special debt to many people and organizations who made this research project and book possible. The Congregations, Community Outreach, and Leadership Development Project could not have been undertaken without the funding support extended by The Lilly Endowment and the John Templeton Foundation. We gratefully acknowledge the work of the team of researchers who conducted the fieldwork in the churches (Averil Clarke, Joan Hoppe-Spink, Paula McCosh, Kesha Moore, Timothy Nelson, Jill Witmer Sinha, and Gaynor Yancey), whose careful data-gathering and insightful field notes, reports, and team discussions provided the foundation for our analysis. Dr. Paul Light, as data analyst and project consultant, played a key role; Dr. Don Haider-Markel at the University of Kansas also provided helpful data analysis services. We were also aided and encouraged by input from evaluators Dr. Katie Day and Dr. Harold Dean Trulear, an advisory council of local religious leaders, a consulting council of professionals in the field of congregational studies, and consultations with researchers at the Center for Social and Religious Research at Hartford Seminary, particularly Dr. Adair Lummis and Dr. Nancy Ammerman. We note that the opinions expressed in this book are those of the authors and do not necessarily reflect the views of the foundations, researchers, or consultants who supported our work.

This book benefitted from its development in the context of a dynamic research environment. Our insights were enriched and enlarged by the work of many others. Discussions with colleagues at the University of Pennsylvania, Baylor University, the Hudson Institute, and the Roundtable on Religion and Social Welfare Policy were particularly beneficial. "As iron sharpens iron, so one person sharpens another" (Proverbs 27:17). In keeping with this proverb, our views on faith-based initiatives were broadened and refined by our participation in two dialogues with leaders from religious, civic, and policy advocacy organizations with a diverse range of views: In Good Faith: A Dialogue on Government Funding of Faith-Based Social Services (Heidi), and the Working Group on Human Needs and Faith-Based and Community Initiatives (Ron).

Our editors at Oxford have been more than gracious. We thank the *Review of Religious Research* and the *Nonprofit and Voluntary Sector Quarterly* for allowing us to include our journal articles as chapters. We are grateful to Meg Cox for improving the manuscript with her discerning editorial eye. We also thank Eastern University for providing a home for the project, and particularly Ron's indomitable assistant Naomi Miller.

I, Heidi, express my deep gratitude to my family for their enduring "faith, hope, and love" in supporting this project through a season of change in our lives. My husband's wise assurances encouraged me not only to complete my work, but to do so with conviction and joy.

Finally, we extend our appreciation to all the wonderful congregations, pastors, and ministry leaders who participated in this research. We hope others may be as inspired by their vision, faith, witness, courage, and compassion as we have been.

Contents

PART IV   Saving Souls and Serving Society

PART I

Church-Based Social Ministry

I

Introduction

Church-Based Social Ministry in Context

The meal was spread on a table at the front of the room at Koinonia Christian Community Church of God in Christ, buffet style: barbecued turkey wings and baked chicken, mixed vegetables, potato salad, rice and gravy, corn bread and white bread, donuts, bananas, and juice. Hungry people deserve a good home-cooked meal, said the wife of pastor Jerome Simmons:[1] "something you would feed to people you invited to your home for dinner." Before the food was served, Rev. Simmons led a brief worship service, in which he shared his dramatic testimony. "I was born again behind a bar, outside where I used to go to get drunk . . ." He acknowledged that many African Americans like himself feel disenfranchised by American Christianity, but he emphasized, "Jesus is *not* white!" Closing the service with a prayer, Rev. Simmons invited his listeners to join in a prayer for salvation. As volunteers served the food, Rev. Simmons also stood in line to receive a plate and sat at the table, eating and talking with the other guests. "Come to church on Sunday!" he urged as they left.

The Pre-Work program at Centro Nueva Creación, a nonprofit founded by Nueva Creación Lutheran Church, hired inner-city preteens to work in community service projects. Youth cultivated a garden in an empty lot, helped with the church's summer day camp, maintained the church and community center, painted flowers over graffiti at local playgrounds, and ran a small snack food business. The program taught values such as conflict resolution, integrity, and forgiveness. Participants also learned how to become community advocates. On a field trip, their van got stuck behind a garbage truck in an upscale neighborhood. The youth were surprised to see the sanitation work-ers place the cans back at the curb and pick up garbage that they dropped, instead of throwing the cans into the street and leaving spilled garbage behind. This gave the pastor an opportunity to lead a discussion of why this does *not* happen in their own neighborhood, and what they might do to foster change. The youth also learned to integrate faith with service, through regular group prayers and discussions on spiritual topics. When asked what the program taught them about God, one girl responded: "When we help people, we're doing something God wants us to do."

Facing emergency needs, Dedra, a struggling single mother of three, ap-proached the Germantown Avenue Crisis Ministry for help. The ministry was born two and a half years after the passage of welfare reform, when a dozen congregations in the community realized that they could not keep up with the steadily increasing requests for emergency assistance. They pooled their re-sources to hire a part-time social worker, and set up a system of referrals. The ministry served about a hundred people each month, far more than the churches could do working by themselves. For Dedra, the ministry provided food vouchers, subsidies for her children to attend church camp, and a paid internship at one of the churches while she attended Temple University. The internship led to a job paying $30,000. Dedra planned to volunteer for the Crisis Ministry's support group for women. "I just want people in my situation to know that with prayer and support, they can make it too," she said (John-Hall 1999b).

The pastor of an African American church in a struggling neighborhood stood before the delegates from the fifty or so congregations belonging to the Philadelphia Interfaith Action coalition to give his report on the progress of Nehemiah Homes. This public-private collaborative venture had brought af-fordable, owner-occupied housing to almost a hundred families. A slide show juxtaposed the clusters of tidy new Nehemiah homes with the blighted district targeted for the next phase of development, posing two different visions of the city: hope versus despair, renewal versus devastation. Drawing inspiration from Nehemiah, the biblical prophet who led the rebuilding of Jerusalem, the speaker called the assembly to continued support with the reminder that "God's blessings usually come through people." He vowed that Philadelphia Interfaith Action would hold the mayor accountable for the full 1,000 units they had been promised.

Stories such as these have become familiar, thanks to political controver-sies and unprecedented media attention that have thrust the community-serving work of religious organizations, particularly congregations,[2] into the limelight. "Faith-based" has become such a common qualifier for "social serv-ices" that it is easy to assume that this adjective has well-defined content. But we have much yet to learn about religious social action programs, particularly in relation to their spiritual dynamics. This book aims to provide a preliminary map of this oft-visited yet uncharted terrain.

The Breadth and Depth of Congregational Social Ministry

A cluster of studies have significantly contributed to our understanding of the faith community's involvement in public life.[3] Together these studies reveal complex but consistent patterns of data on the proportion of congregations offering social services, the congregational characteristics associated with social activism, the range and depth of services provided, and the partnerships and resources that make them possible.

Congregation-Based Social Services

Indisputably, the great majority of congregations engage in efforts to improve the well-being of those outside their membership. Findings from national studies on the percentage of congregations that sponsor social services range from 57% (Chaves 1999) to 80% (Roozen and Dudley 2001) to 87% (Hodgkinson and Weitzman 1993).[4] The norm of congregational involvement appears to be intensified in a concentrated urban milieu. In Washington, D.C., for example, 95% of congregations were found to provide some type of service (Printz 1998). Cnaan and Boddie's (2001) census of Philadelphia faith communities (described in more detail in the next chapter) discovered social service programs in 88% of congregations. According to a seven-city study by Cnaan et al. (2002), congregational programs serve an average of 142.3 nonmembers each month. About half of church members volunteer through their congregations, and about half of this time is channeled into activities that reach beyond the church membership (Hodgkinson and Weitzman 1993). The prolific involvement of congregations in the human service arena leads Cnaan and Boddie to conclude: "From mentoring programs for children to feeding the hungry, congregations are the most visible and frequent community institution to which people in need apply" (2001, 575).

The impressive breadth of congregation-based social services, however, does not appear to be matched in depth. Most congregation-sponsored programs provide a limited commodity to meet urgent or one-time needs, such as food, clothing or emergency financial assistance (Scott 2002). Baggett laments "a tendency among congregations to focus primarily on projects that are short-term, small-scale, and ameliorative rather than those that are ongoing, extensive, and directed at the underlying causes of social problems" (2002, 432). Moreover, churches tend to balk at serving particularly disenfranchised populations, such as welfare recipients and persons with AIDS (Grettenberger

2001). Chaves (2001) finds that the resources congregations dedicate to service projects are thin: only 6% of congregations commit a staff person at least quarter time to social programs, and direct congregational expenditures on social service programs is only about 3% of their average budget.[5] Chaves concludes, "Although most congregations do some sort of social service activity, only a small minority actively and intensively engage in such activity" (2001, 124). Rather, congregational social action "typically involves mobilizing small numbers of volunteers to conduct relatively well-defined, periodic tasks" (125–26).

The picture of congregational activity is complex in part because congregations have, as Baggett puts it, a "constitutively double-edged" nature (2002, 430). Congregations are not, first and foremost, social service organizations. Most congregations say they exist primarily to promote "the spiritual well-being of their members" through worship and opportunities for spiritual growth, followed by "fellowship," or cultivating a caring community of fellow believers (Ammerman 2001; see also Garland 1992 and Clerkin and Grønbjerg 2003). Some congregations may place social activism and outreach to persons outside the membership on equal footing with the nurture and care of members, but none have this as their sole charter. On the one hand, this makes the level of outreach sustained by congregations all the more remarkable. On the other, their nature as voluntary associations means that congregations must always balance the resources, needs, inclinations, and aversions of their membership with the impulse for charitable involvement. A congregation's commitment to social ministry will always stand in dynamic tension with the other facets of its mission. Thus the character of congregational involvement in the community service arena is pervasive but bounded.

In part because of congregations' multifaceted mission and limited resources for outreach, a significant portion of their social action is done through collaborations (Wineberg 1992; Chang et al. 1994; Rogers and Ronsheim 1998; Wuthnow 2000; Ammerman 2001). A church is only one strand of the "dense and complex web of connection in every community" (Ammerman 2001) that includes other congregations, faith-based and secular nonprofit agencies, governmental entities, civic groups, and businesses. The average congregation forges a cooperative relationship with six other organizations, particularly those that provide direct services (food, clothing, and shelter) or educational, health, and cultural services to the community (Ammerman 2001). Congregations supply funds, material goods (food, clothing, furniture, etc.), volunteers, and meeting space to outside groups. In addition, 16% paid dues to an association or belonged to a coalition that advocated or lobbied on their behalf (Saxon-Harrold et al. 2000). In return, congregations often rely on nonprofit agencies to coordinate programs, manage funds and volunteers, give and take client referrals, supply information and technical expertise, serve as liaisons with secular funders, and provide legitimacy or visibility for the congregation's efforts. Church-state collaboration, including nonfinancial cooperative arrange-ments, is a small but growing piece of this web of connectivity (Griener 2000; Green and Sherman 2002). These patterns of activity suggest that congrega-tions fulfill a critical role in supporting and supplementing other players in the social service arena.[6]

What type of congregation is most likely to be involved in social projects? Because there is broad agreement among American congregations about the norm of compassionate outreach, the presence of some form of charitable ministry cuts across most congregational types (Mock 1992; Becker 1999; Cnaan, Wineburg, and Boddie 1999). However, some characteristics correlate with more prevalent or extensive public engagement. In general, mainline Protestant, more theologically liberal congregations have been the most active in providing services and working collaboratively with other organizations. A congregation's involvement is also influenced by its available resources: its budget, size, and facilities. The largest 10% of congregations account for more than half of all the money spent by congregations on social services (Chaves 1999). Ministry context is another factor. Congregations located in low-income neighborhoods tend toward more social service activity than those in higher-income neighborhoods. The choice to engage in public ministry is often a response to a neighborhood that is experiencing change (Ammerman 1997a). The disposition of church leaders toward public ministry is another influential factor, as clergy are most often responsible for initiating, selecting, and sus-taining congregational involvement (Billingsley 1999; Cnaan et al. 2002; Day 2002). A typical profile of the most active church is a large, middle-class, main-line Protestant congregation located in a poor or transitioning neighborhood (Chaves 1999; Ammerman 2001; Chaves and Tsitsos 2001; Parks and Quern 2001; Cnaan, Boddie, and Yancey 2003).

Cnaan and Boddie (2001) found that African American congregations in Philadelphia were slightly more likely to offer community-serving programs, and offered a slightly higher average number of programs (2.4 versus 2.25 programs), than non-black congregations. Other research indicates that African American congregations may not be more likely to sponsor social ministry programs in general, but they may be more involved in particular social con-cerns such as education and mentoring (Chaves and Higgins 1992; Boddie 2003; Tsitsos 2003). African American churches, particularly large, well-established congregations, are also more likely than Anglo churches to participate in economic and community development as well as community organizing (Vidal 2001; Warren and Wood 2001; Scott 2002). The significance of the material aid, economic empowerment, and political advocacy sponsored by black churches is indisputable, owing in part to the uniquely situated role of the black church as the foremost economic and social institution within the African American community.[7]

Putting all this research into context, Cnaan, Boddie, and Yancey (2003,

115) caution against reducing congregational involvement to statistical variables.

> Given that most congregations are involved in at least one social ser-
> vice program, the distinction between the high performers and the
> low performers is not mediated by budget, size, membership, or
> theology. Rather, it is mediated by the congregation's commitment
> to faith-based action and a tradition of congregational care.

While internal and external conditions can affect the likelihood that a congregation will act on its social impulses, faith-based activism ultimately draws
from more intangible sources that cannot be explained solely in terms of other
variables.

Indirect Contributions of Congregations to Public Life

Looking only at the formal programs that congregations sponsor or support
yields an incomplete picture of their contribution to the public good. Congregations indirectly enhance the lives of individuals and communities in at least
four other ways.

First, beyond the charitable activities of congregations as corporate entities,
individual members disproportionately contribute to the social welfare of their
communities. The members of congregations contribute substantial amounts
of time and money to programs outside the congregation, both secular and
religious, which meet human need. Church members are significantly more
likely than nonmembers to report being active in their communities, and
stronger attachment to a congregation correlates with higher volunteer participation. Regular attenders are also more likely to embrace civic activities such
as voting and membership in civic groups. Similar patterns hold true for charitable giving. Moreover, church attendance appears to foster altruistic values
and informal acts of compassion, such as helping a homeless person. Congregations empower and inspire members to embody norms of social responsibility as they go about their day-to-day lives.[8]

Second, charity often begins at home: Congregations serve as support networks for their own members in need, leading to the redistribution of resources within the congregation and the capitalization of external resources
through networking and referrals. As "caring communities" (Wuthnow 2004,
64), congregations provide material aid, counseling, and emotional encouragement to their members.[9] An emphasis on mutual care can become exclusive, eclipsing concerns beyond the congregation. However, in congregations
with concentrations of low-income members, the distinction between internal
care and community service becomes blurred. As the congregation helps members to care for their own families, they contribute to a safer and more stable
community.

Third, congregations provide a forum for educating and mobilizing members to interact with social concerns. Congregations equip members with awareness, information, and skills by addressing current issues from a religious perspective in sermons and Sunday school classes; offering special study groups on concerns such as housing or racism; training members in community organizing; hosting community meetings; taking a stand on a social or political issue; maintaining bulletin boards on local and world affairs; and distributing literature from advocacy groups such as Bread for the World. More broadly, through religious education, congregations "nurture moral values that help humanize capitalism and give moral direction to democracy" (Reichley 1983, 359; see also Jeavons 1994 and Cnaan et al. 2002).

Finally, religious commitment boosts personal well-being, which has a spill-over effect on a community. Byron Johnson's review of hundreds of studies confirms "a striking correspondence between religiosity and general health and well being" (Johnson 2002; see also Fagan 1996 and Cnaan, Wineburg, and Boddie 1999). Church attendance, as one of the measures of religiosity, correlates with better health, positive psychological adjustment, more stable family life, higher educational outcomes, and reduced risk factors. Church involvement has been identified as one of the most important factors among black males in high-poverty neighborhoods who escape the destructive cycle of gangs, drugs, and delinquency (Freeman 1986; Johnson et al. 2000). One study even suggests that having church-going neighbors can diminish the likelihood of negative behaviors among at-risk youth (Case and Katz 1991).

Thus, while congregations' organized social action commitments tend to be shallow, the contribution of congregations to the public good cannot be measured only in terms of direct interventions. Overall, among American congregations, social concerns are seldom wholly absent but also seldom central; they are pursued indirectly, individually, and informally as much as through organized, corporate means; and they are addressed largely through collaborations with other entities. These qualities of congregational compassion have a taken-for-granted nature that bridges the variety of expressions of religion in public life.

Sociopolitical Context

Four aspects of the broader sociopolitical context have particular implications for studying the spiritual dimension of congregational outreach: devolution, faith-based initiatives, changing norms of religion in public life, and ambivalence toward proselytizing.

Devolution and Remoralization

Reverend Donna Jones, pastor of Cookman United Methodist Church, defends her belief that churches should be involved in welfare reform:

> The government has decided to divest from it, and the government has stated, "We're looking to the church." I believe that if we don't pick it up, the government does not have any intent of picking it up again. The church used to be the resource for social service. The government picked it up in between, and they're saying, "Here, take it back." Historically, it's been one of the things that the church has done and, I believe, we do it well. . . . I believe we honestly offer the power of God and I don't believe that the government can.

Her explanation highlights the motif of devolution, part of the discourse on the changing relationships among various actors in the social welfare arena. *Devolution* refers to the decentralization of the social safety net and the transfer of social responsibilities to the private sector, a trend that Cnaan, Wineburg, and Boddie (1999) call a "newer deal"—reversing the New Deal welfare policies that emerged from the Depression and reached their political apex in the 1960s. The movement toward devolution gained momentum in the 1980s with a resurgence of local community-minded social strategies, supported by the policies and rhetoric of President Ronald Reagan. The most notable achievement of this movement was the welfare reform legislation of 1996, signed into law by President Bill Clinton, reflecting the mainstream consensus on this political philosophy. This legislation "devolved" welfare responsibility to the states through block grants, ending federal welfare entitlements, and encouraged grassroots faith-based social services through the provision known as charitable choice. Devolution became a principal tenet of President George W. Bush's "compassionate conservatism."

As Rev. Jones's quote illustrates, devolution is more than public policy; it is a sociopolitical narrative—a way of constructing America's social history. An influential book by Marvin Olasky, *The Tragedy of American Compassion* (1992), sets out this history. Olasky emphasizes the religious origins of antipoverty efforts, lauding nineteenth century benevolence for being local, personal, and morally discerning. These qualities were sacrificed, according to this narrative, by the creeping influence of secularism in social work, and the expansion of the bureaucratic welfare state. The advent of New Deal welfare programs allegedly undermined the faith community's response to poverty in two ways: firstly by making private charitable efforts irrelevant with the federalization of aid, and secondly by marginalizing moral approaches to benevolence with the philosophy of entitlement. Thus follows the claim for government to "give back" responsibility for the poor to the private (and presumably, more often than not, religious) charitable sector. As Rev. Jerome Simmons put it, "What the government has been trying to do for years, the church should have been doing it. That's the job of the church."

A foundational assumption of the movement toward devolution is that the impersonal and inflexible nature of government, especially the federal government, renders it incapable of waging an effective war against poverty. A corollary assumption is that private-sector efforts, particularly faith-based ones, are inherently more effective and can mobilize resources with greater efficiency. Moreover, advocates of devolution often envision public and private realms as being in competition, so that growth in one arena comes at the expense of the other. As former senator Dan Coats argues, government undermined mediating institutions "when we usurped so much of their authority and so many of their resources, over such a long period of time" (Streeter 2001). Another basic assumption of devolution is that public life is best conducted at the local level. Federal and state governments need to step aside in order to allow communities to devise solutions to their own problems (Woodson 1998; Goldsmith 2002). Devolution has thus fit seamlessly with experimentations with privatization and with calls for the renewal of civil society (see Eberly and Streeter 2002; Dionne 1998).

Some advocates of devolution additionally call for the *remoralization* of American charity (Loconte 1998; Olasky 2000; Streeter 2001). According to conservative commentator Chuck Colson, "If assistance is to make a longterm difference, it has to come with moral strings attached. It involves making people learn how to behave responsibly." This position asserts that secular welfare may temporarily meet material needs but produces little lasting change. Olasky's narrative (1992) attributes this to the New Deal's philosophy of "demoralization," which ascribed social problems solely to structural causes. "It soon became customary to argue that only the federal government had the potential power to create a socioeconomic environment that would save all" (220–21). As a result, moral concerns and tests to sort out the "deserving poor" were abandoned in favor of a social-scientific approach to welfare and a doctrine of benefit entitlement.

Remoralization, in practice, thus entails a personal, value-laden approach to social-service delivery, such as that presumably offered by congregations and other grassroots faith-based organizations. Remoralization reintroduces the tenets that charitable aid should promote moral values, hold persons accountable for choices that have negative economic consequences, require persons to take responsibility for their own recovery, and uphold familial and community networks as the first lines of assistance. The title and substance of the 1996 welfare law—the *"Personal Responsibility* and Work Opportunity Reconciliation Act"—highlights these themes. President Bush has also highlighted the moral dimensions of social policy through initiatives designed to promote marriage and sexual abstinence, which often involve collaboration with faith-based groups.

Aside from the implications of devolution and remoralization for social welfare, these movements have had the effect of politicizing faith-based services as a battlefield in a broader ideological and cultural clash.[10] It should be noted, however, that not all advocates of devolution emphasize remoralization. Conversely, some interject a moral dimension into discussions of welfare policy without ascribing poverty to moral failures or downplaying government's role (see Wallis 2001). This is the stand taken by Rev. Donna Jones. "I believe the church is here to enable government to do a better job by incorporating and infusing Christian principles," she says, but adds a warning: "The danger that we have is that the church will take on everything, and abdicate the government from any responsibility in social service."

A modification to the devolution narrative is suggested by Stephen Monsma's examination (1996) of the changing role of religion in social services. Monsma argues that as government expanded into fields of social activity already occupied by nonprofits, many of them religious, it did not smother private benevolence. Rather, the rise of the welfare state led to a complicated pattern of shared public and private efforts, sometimes parallel, other times overlapping. This coexistence has engendered a system that John DiIulio (quoting Don Kettl) calls "government by proxy," in which government carries out its public agenda *through* private and quasi-public institutions (DiIulio and Bennett 1997). This has generated new forms of direct collaboration and indirect influence. Religious providers have become an integral link in the public social safety net, while government's presence is felt through the regulation, licensing, and financing of many private organizations.

This theme of collaboration thus appears to be the latest stage in the historical arc of social welfare—from the 1960s era of entitlement and elevation of government's role in fighting poverty, to the 1980s trend of depreciating government and reemphasizing the role of the private sector, to the rising prominence of public-private partnerships in the mid-1990s.

Faith-Based Initiatives

The term *charitable choice* was first coined in reference to Section 104 of the 1996 welfare reform law.[11] This provision established the unprecedented rule that government was not to take an organization's religious status into account when awarding public funds for social services. Up to this point, eligibility for government funding had been ostensibly guided by the "pervasively sectarian" standard, which ruled that congregations and other organizations with religious purposes at their core were ineligible for public dollars.[12] Slowly and unevenly, state welfare departments began to revise their funding guidelines and open the doors to faith-based service providers. It took the media and policy analysts several years to catch on to the implications of this innovation.

In one of his first official actions as president, George W. Bush accelerated the momentum for faith-based partnerships by establishing the White House Office on Faith-Based and Community Initiatives (OFBCI). OFBCI was charged with identifying and eliminating administrative hurdles to equitable faith-based participation in federal government programs, and with providing a liaison for religious groups interested in public funding. The Bush administration has also sought to advance the goal of leveling the playing field for faith-based services through new legislation, with limited success (see Unruh 2002).[13] Although attention to faith-based initiatives has been mitigated by foreign-policy concerns, as President Bush entered his second term of office he reaffirmed his commitment "to change the culture permanently so faith-based and community organizations will be welcome in the grant-making process of government" (Farris 2005).

These measures have triggered a firestorm of debate.[14] The public discourse has clustered around three areas of disputation: constitutional (is government funding of faith-based groups legal?), pragmatic (is it good for society?), and ecclesiastic (is it good for the church?). Many contend that government funding of religious institutions—particularly congregations—violates the First Amendment's prohibition against the establishment of religion and threatens the religious freedom of clients who receive services from faith-based providers (Davis and Hankins 1999; Eilperin 2001). Others argue on pragmatic grounds that the initiative may not succeed in expanding the efficacy and scope of human services (Chaves 2001; Wineburg 2001; Farnsley 2003). Some religious groups, such as the Baptist Joint Committee and the American Jewish Committee, oppose charitable choice for its potentially negative consequences for the faith community—pitting religious groups against one another in competition for public funds, muffling the prophetic voice of the church, and creating dependency on government (Rogers 1999). Somewhat unexpectedly, voices of protest have also arisen from the conservative Christian wing, charging that the initiative does not go far enough in protecting faith-based providers' religious autonomy (Milbank and Edsall 2001).

Supporters of the faith-based initiative, including ourselves, likewise argue its merit on legal, pragmatic, and ecclesiastic grounds.[15] Advocates contend that charitable choice offers a necessary corrective to decades of governmental bias against faith-based organizations, particularly evangelical ones, and restores the constitutionally protected religious autonomy of religious groups. Proponents also point to evidence for the efficacy and efficiency of faith-based social services as incentive for government to partner with the religious community. Countering ecclesiastic concerns, advocates claim that faith-based initiatives allow churches and other religious groups to guard their religious integrity while enhancing their capacity to carry out their mission. (See Monsma 1996; Esbeck 1997; Loconte 1998; Sherman 2000; Glenn 2000; Sider and Unruh 2000 and 2001.)

One of the focal points of the debate has been concerns over proselytizing with public funds (see Sider and Unruh 2001). Americans instinctively resist the notion of a government-funded, church-based job training program pressuring beneficiaries to convert to Christianity. The 1996 charitable choice provision actually prohibits the use of government money to fund the direct transmission of religious ideas: "No funds provided directly to institutions or organizations to provide services and administer programs under [this provision] shall be expended for sectarian worship, instruction, or proselytization." Significantly, however, charitable choice does not explicitly rule out using private funds for separate, optional religious activities, and White House guidelines have indicated the permissibility of these arrangements. Nor do restrictions on religious activities apply in the case of vouchers or other indirect funding mechanisms, where a beneficiary, rather than the government, chooses the provider. These gray areas are the subject of ongoing clarification and conflict (White House Office 2003).

The National Congregations Study, conducted in 1998, provides a baseline measurement of congregational interest and involvement in government funding (Chaves 1999). While 11% of congregations relied on outside funding for their social service programs, only 3% received funds from the government. Other studies have found similarly low levels of congregational use of public funds (Printz 1998; Cnaan and Boddie 2001).[16] Congregational *interest* in public funding, however, has run significantly higher: 36% of congregations in the National Congregations Study (Chaves 1999) and 61% in the Philadelphia census (Cnaan and Boddie 2001) indicated openness to pursuing government funding for their social service programs. (In comparison, 16% of congregations in the National Congregations Study had a policy *against* seeking government support.) As Chaves points out, even if only a fraction of this substantial minority received public funds it would represent a major shift in church-state relations.

Given this level of interest, have faith-based initiatives made a difference in congregations' access to federal resources for human services?[17] According to White House figures, about 10% of federal grants, totaling about $2 billion, were awarded to faith-based organizations in fiscal year 2004 (Farris 2005). A 2002 Hudson Institute study of charitable choice implementation in 15 states documented 726 contracts with faith-based entities, 22% of which were congregations, involving a wide range of services. Although contracts with congregations tended to be small (70% under $50,000), they do represent new funding opportunities, as 90% of the congregations began collaborating with government only after the passage of charitable choice in 1996 (Green and Sherman 2002). On the other hand, the competitive access of many grassroots religious organizations is limited by their lack of experience and administrative capacity (Farnsley 2001; Wineburg 2001). In sum, it appears that congregations (particularly African American churches), along with other smaller, grassroots religious organizations, now have a limited but growing presence in the public-funding arena. The extent of these partnerships will be constrained, however, by limits in organizational capacity, by religious groups' openness to government funding, and by potential legal and legislative challenges to faith-based initiatives.

Changing Attitudes Toward Religion's Role in Society

When David Larson was in medical school in the 1970s, he was informed that becoming a good psychiatrist entailed setting aside his religious beliefs. Later, as a research psychiatrist at the National Institute of Mental Health, he documented the bias against the inclusion of religious variables in research on social indicators, despite the fact that where faith was taken into account it had a generally positive impact (see citations in Fagan 1996). This indifference, or even antipathy, toward religion pervaded the realms of medicine, the media, and the academy for decades (see Carter 1993). Professional social work norms elevated an objective, nonjudgmental approach, stripped of the passionate religiosity that attended the birth of the movement (Hugen 1994; Cnaan, Wineburg, and Boddie 1999; Glenn 2000). In *The Naked Public Square* (1984), Richard John Neuhaus argued that religion had become marginalized from public life, relegated to a shrinking arena of private affairs.

In 1996, Bill Moyers depicted a changed ethos: "Religion is breaking out all over." The last 15 years have seen a remarkable transition in public attitudes toward faith. Scholarship has slowly begun to make up for its neglect of the role of religion in society (see D. H. Smith 1983; C. Smith 1996). As a fellow at Harvard's new Center for the Study of Values in Public Life, Jim Wallis described the overwhelming response to a series of discussions of faith and social concerns: "Something was certainly happening, and, even at Harvard, it began to feel a little like a movement" (2001, 330). Religious topics began appearing regularly in secular media outlets, as coverage of the charitable-choice debate led to an explosion of media interest. The index of news articles related to religion and society on the Web site of the Roundtable on Religion and Social Welfare Policy (www.religionandsocialpolicy.org) now contains hundreds of references.

Religion has also gained increasing prominence as a factor in social policy. Although "religious" came to be associated with "the Right" during the 1980s, policymakers began to pay more attention to the religious roots of progressive politics as well (C. Smith 1996; Parker 2000; Wallis 2005). Discussions of the role of personal faith in political formation have become not only accepted but expected from political leaders. In 2000, both presidential candidates vied to be seen as "faith friendly" and promised to support partnerships with faith-based organizations. Three-fourths of citizens believe that congregations contribute significantly to solving America's social problems (Pew Forum 2002).

Most Americans do not want government simply to turn welfare over to the churches, but they do want government to heed the perspective of religious voices and work with the strengths of the religious community.

These changes have accompanied a resurgence of popular interest in spirituality (though not necessarily church attendance), driven in part by the cultural dislocations generated by postmodernity. As minister-journalist Roy Larson commented: "Our secular, scientific, rational world view is coming apart because it doesn't capture the wholeness of reality." America is on a "quest for spiritual meaning" (Galloway 1994). This hunger for wholeness and transcendence has been reflected in the appeal of religious offerings in popular media. Following the terrorist attacks of September 11 and subsequent military interventions, the search for religious meaning and ballast in an uncertain world has gained greater urgency. In a November 2001 poll, an unprecedented 78% of citizens said that religion's influence is increasing in American life—almost twice the typical response of past years (Pew Forum 2002). Growing openness to the spiritual dimension of human existence is also evident in the practice of medicine, psychiatry, and social work (Cnaan, Wineburg, and Boddie 1999; Hodge 2001; Hugen and Scales 2002). But these new dynamics are constrained by norms of appropriate religious expression, as discussed below.

Ambivalence Toward Proselytizing

Speaking in support of faith-based ministries at a church in January 2004, President Bush affirmed, "Problems that seem impossible to solve, can be solved. There is the miracle of salvation that is real, that is tangible, that is available for all to see. . . . Miracles happen as a result of the love of the Almighty." As evidence, the President pointed wryly to his own salvation experience. "I quit drinking because I changed my heart. I guess I was a one-man faith-based program." Reverend Donna Jones, who helped Cookman United Methodist Church launch a welfare-to-work ministry, also believes in the miracle of conversion. "The gospel is liberating," she says, "and we're dealing with people who need to experience that freedom and hope." A student in the program speaks to this experience: "If I had God in my life before, it would have helped me more toward my education. It leaves you more at peace."

Political science professor Francis Moran is less sanguine about faith-based services. "Suppose you're not of the faith" and you seek services from a religious organization, he cautions. "They could make it uncomfortable for you. It would be a way to subtly coerce people into accepting the faith" (Scott 2004). The director of a faith-based organization in the Ozarks is similarly wary of religious coercion. "We respect a person's dignity," he says. "Our philosophy is not to impose something as sacred as spirituality at a time of vulnerability." A client of the program agrees: "It's insulting if they try to tell you their way is right" (Chong et al. 2003).

These quotes illustrate two competing voices in the discourse on faith-based social ministries. One side (including some who are not themselves religious) looks to the transforming potential of religious faith to bring moral order, hope, and a sense of purpose to the lives of struggling individuals. They assert that faith changes people's lives, makes them more whole persons and responsible citizens, and thus strengthens the social order. The other side (including some who consider themselves religious) voices a pervasive norm that considers proselytizing offensive or even harmful to the social order. Whether or not faith "works," they argue that it is wrong to impose one's faith on others, especially when those others are at their most vulnerable.

As discussed above, concerns about faith-based groups using public funds to proselytize have appeared on center stage in the debates over charitable choice. At root, these concerns are as much cultural as they are constitutional. While the great majority of Americans profess to be religious, the nature of American religious life tends toward a "vaguely privatized and weakly integrated faith" (Roozen, McKinney, and Roof 1995). The mainstream of religious culture that runs through many varieties of religious expression reflects contemporary values: it is largely individualistic, experiential, pluralistic, tolerant, and open-ended (Bellah et al. 1985; Wolfe 2003). Proselytizing stands in tension with two key themes in American religious thought identified by Hart (1992): *voluntarism*, or the right of individuals to self-determination and, by extension, to freedom from external religious influence; and *universalism*, or the essential equality of all persons and, by extension, of all personal religious beliefs.

Voluntarism is closely aligned to the cherished notion of a zone of personal privacy, which evangelistic encounters are perceived to violate. "I am very uncomfortable going up to somebody and asking them details about their spiritual life," confesses a member of Media Presbyterian Church. "How would you feel if somebody came up and asked you intimate details about your sex life? Same thing, just as private. 'None of your business, leave me alone' is your proper response." Many associate proselytizing with the use of "cajolery, bribery, undue pressure, or intimidation, subtly or openly, to bring about a seeming conversion," as declared by the World Council of Churches in 1961 (cited in Wilson 2000, 3). These concerns are magnified in the context of social services to vulnerable populations who may not be in a position to defend their right to religious self-determination.

Evangelism also runs counter to the tenet of universalism, which views moral and doctrinal absolutes with suspicion. An evangelical invitation to saving faith derives from an authoritative claim about the uniqueness of Christ that many find restrictive and exclusive (Martin 1969). Wolfe's (1998) study of suburban attitudes toward religion reveals a tendency to interpret energetic public expressions of religion or appeals for conversion as distasteful displays of extremism and intolerance (see also Coleman 2001; Cuddihy 1978). In the aftermath of the 9/11 attacks by Islamic terrorists, the nation has become particularly sensitive to extremism in the name of religion. In an interview on National Public Radio, for example, Episcopal pastor Marianne Wells Borg suggested that the way to avert religious violence is for the world's religions to maintain a hands-off respect. "We can celebrate the particularities of our faith tradition but that does not suggest exclusivity or absolutism. Evangelism today is not about conversion. It's about learning from one another."

Even evangelicals are ambivalent toward evangelism. A near-unanimity among conservative Christians about sharing faith in principle is not borne out in practice. Among the 92% of evangelicals who believe Christians should try to change society, 91% said "converting people to Jesus Christ" was a very important strategy for accomplishing this goal. Yet only 32% of evangelicals reported telling others how to become a Christian "a lot" in the previous two years (C. Smith 1998, 38, 40). Evangelical researcher George Barna observes: "Almost every church leader assents to the importance of evangelism and a desire to have a church that takes the promotion of the gospel seriously. But a comparative handful of those churches carry out their stated evangelistic intention with true passion, urgency, diligence and joy" (1995, 89). Structural impediments to personal faith sharing, such as the decline of "neighborliness" and the frenetic pace of modern life, rob evangelicals of opportunities for in-depth spiritual conversations. Wolfe notes the result: "Churches that take on an evangelical mission can be of two minds as they confront the realities of living in a culture that goes out of its way to tame strong forms of faith" (2003, 195).

Thus two of the prevailing trends described above—remoralization and openness to religion in the public square—have come into tension with a deep-seated cultural resistance to promoting religious change in others. The norms against proselytizing and making religiously grounded moral judgments are codified in professional social work practice and reinforced by public- and private-sector funders. This places religious service providers in an ironic bind. Despite a growing scholarly appreciation of the positive corollaries of personal faith and the public courting of faith-laden approaches to social services, the actual process of encouraging beneficiaries to embrace a new faith remains countercultural. According to a 2001 survey by the Pew Research Center (www .people-press.org), the general concept of government funding of faith-based organizations enjoyed the support of 75% of respondents. When respondents were asked about funding for "groups that encourage religious conversion," however, the favor rating dropped to 32% (see Wuthnow 2004).

Americans want religious groups to bring the resources of their faith to bear on social problems, but not if it involves overtly encouraging others to embrace that faith. While many agree that people's lives are better off when they find God and abide by Judeo-Christian moral teachings, Americans generally resist the idea of telling another person what to believe or how to live.

Even evangelicals, the ones most motivated to witness to their faith, struggle to carry out this obligation against the tide of prevailing culture and the complexities of modern life.

Implications of the Sociopolitical Context

These trends have significance for understanding the religious dynamics of faith-based social services explored in this book in several ways. First, our research observed congregations during a dynamic period of shifting patterns in the relationship between religion and public life. The emerging receptivity to the civic role of religion has fostered new opportunities for churches and encouraged creative experimentation with public-private collaboration, but has also generated uncertainties and conflict. Government agencies have been reaching out with unprecedented openness to churches and other religious groups, while renegotiating the rules and norms for churches' public engagement. Similar opportunities have been expanding for church collaborations with nongovernmental entities, such as initiatives launched by secular foundations in the Philadelphia area that welcomed faith-based applicants.

The pastors in our study sometimes remarked on a new-found sense of permission to approach the public table as equals. As Rev. Jones noted, "The church is there to help the government understand that it is not the be-all and end-all, . . . that they do not have all the answers." But she was wary of a fine line between being valued and being used. Richard Kyerematen, pastor of Germantown Church of the Brethren, shared this concern:

> I don't think that the city, and for that matter the state, is really prepared to work with churches. I think that they're looking for people to do their dirty work for them—they see there's going to be a big crisis and they think that the churches are the most established organizations that can deal with some of the crises.

For churches engaged in public ministry, the trade-off for being no longer marginalized by the secular community is the risk of being misunderstood and manipulated. These changing patterns of relationships, and the opportunities and dangers they represent, have encouraged churches to reassess their own outreach strategies.

Secondly, the experiences of the churches we studied demonstrates the material impact of government's increased willingness to work with churches, but also indicates a mismatch between some of the rhetoric and the grassroots reality.[18] Eight of the churches relied on direct government support for programs run by the church or by a nonprofit affiliated with the church, particularly food aid. Several other church programs received indirect government support, such as day care subsidies. The political changes did stimulate some new collaborative activity; most notably, Cookman decided to apply for state funding only after learning about the protections guaranteed by charitable choice. Most of the collaborations, however, predated charitable choice. Long before it became controversial, these churches, like many other faith-based organizations, were tapping government resources to carry out social ministry objectives (Monsma 1996). Moreover, a majority of the churches we studied cooperated with governmental entities in more informal ways, such as by "adopting" public schools. These illustrate how church-state partnerships cannot be reduced to a simple bilateral transaction, but rather represent a complex set of interactions between churches with multifaceted agendas and multilayered public institutions (see Wuthnow 2000; Dionne and Chen 2001).

Third, these evolving patterns have cast a spotlight on the uniquely *religious* contribution that congregations bring to the civic table. The discourse on remoralization and the faith-based initiative highlights the presumed connections among spirituality, moral behaviors, and positive social outcomes. Faith-based programs are said to deliver services "in a qualitatively different manner, one that addresses matters of the heart by drawing on spiritual and moral resources that are beyond the competence of government" (Luis Lugo, quoted in Glenn 2000, 241). Changing attitudes toward religion in the public square have made it more possible to bring these claims into the realms of scholarly scrutiny and professional social work practice. In a new way, religious faith is being objectified (and some fear, commodified) outside the religious community, not merely as the sum of other social forces but as an independent variable in its own right (see Stark 2000; C. Smith 1996).

These developments are making it possible to study religious social activism and to apply this knowledge to social policy in more focused ways. This dynamic context invites a fresh appraisal of conventional interpretations of religion's public role, and a new conceptual framework for interpreting churches' orientations to mission. In particular, new language is needed to describe the "faith factor" that has meaning outside of the religious community, but that does not reduce faith to a product of other social variables or an agent of social outcomes. This task calls for holding two perspectives on faith-based outreach in tension: one framework highlights its cultural embeddedness and instrumental social value, while the other views it as an arena for the expression of transcendent, transformational beliefs.

Overview of the Book

This book aims to serve as a guide to the exploration of the religious dynamics of church-based community ministries. Part I provides an overview of the terrain. Chapter 2 introduces the churches and their outreach and presents new typologies for church-based social action and evangelism derived from the study. Chapter 3 presents eight case studies that illustrate the diverse ways that churches engage the social and spiritual needs of their communities.

Part II explores the spiritual nature of faith-based social outreach. What is particularly *religious* about the social programs we studied, beyond the fact of their church affiliation? Chapter 4 examines the subjective dimension of religion as it gives meaning to acts of social care, while the following chapter catalogues the overtly religious elements that may be integrated into social action programs. Chapter 6 draws on concepts from the previous chapters to construct a typology of the religious characteristics of organizations and programs.

Although studies of churches' public involvement typically refer to *evangelistic* and *activist* as mutually exclusive orientations, our observations as well as those of many others present a more complex picture. Part III considers the range of ways that churches put their faith in action, beginning with an explication of five mission orientations that describe how churches engage their context through social action and/or witness. Chapter 8 examines the factors influencing churches' selection and application of a particular mission orientation, including a historical perspective on the relationship between evangelism and social action in American Protestantism. Chapter 9 explores in more depth the characteristics of outreach in churches that promote conversions as well as social compassion.

Part IV reflects on the role, potential, and limitations of churches' contributions to public welfare. Chapter 10 scrutinizes the relationship between spiritual dynamics and social outcomes, unpacking the claims for the efficacy of faith-based programs. Chapter 11 assesses the relationship between religious capital and social capital, particularly for churches with an emphasis on evangelism. The final chapter considers the implications of our analysis for faith-based initiatives, for research on faith-based organizations, and for religious social activism.

Understanding the Faith Factor

The religious dynamics of church-based social services are the subject of conflicting expectations. It is hoped that the religious community will be able to solve entrenched social problems by harnessing the transformational power of faith; it is feared that religious programs will coerce clients into conversions. It is hoped that providing faith-based organizations greater access to resources will expand the social safety net; it is feared that such policies will crumble the wall of separation between church and state and erode the autonomy of religious institutions. It is hoped that faith can strengthen caregivers' motivation for service and their empathetic kindness toward those they serve; it is feared that religious people will display intolerance toward prospective staff and clients who do not share their beliefs. It is hoped that congregations will embrace vulnerable persons, providing them with a supportive "family" and ongoing spiritual nurture; it is feared that churches will reduce social services to a manipulative inducement for people to join their religious group. It is hoped that a faith-based approach will encourage people in need to become more responsible, healthy, and self-reliant members of families and communities; it is feared that faith-based programs will become co-opted by and complicit with an unjust system that uses the language of personal responsibility to camouflage society's abandonment of the poor.

How can churches fulfill these hopeful expectations while avoiding the pitfalls? To navigate the tensions, we need more precise ways of thinking and speaking about religion's role in civic life. This book aims to help by mapping the largely unexplored terrain of the religious contours of churches' public engagement.[19] We still have much to learn about the *faith* in faith-based social services, and particularly about the intersection of witness and compassion. Many scholars and social advocates are unfamiliar—or even uncomfortable—with themes associated with evangelism. For a segment of churches, however, the commitment to serving society is intertwined with the desire to lead people to salvation. A better understanding of the connection between spiritual and social care can equip policy makers, scholars, and practitioners to respond wisely to the unique opportunities posed by faith-based social action.

2

The Churches and
Their Ministries

This chapter introduces the fifteen churches that were studied in depth, and places them into their local context. (A brief description of each of the churches, with a list of each one's outreach programs, is provided in appendix 1; more detailed profiles of eight selected churches are presented in chapter 3.) The second part of this chapter defines the key terms *social ministry* and *evangelism*. We present typologies for church-based social action and evangelism derived from the study, and provide an overview of the ministries sponsored by the churches.

The Churches in Context

One of the most difficult tasks in our research was narrowing the field to fifteen case studies. Potential churches were identified through a referential sample, in which Philadelphia area religious leaders, denominational offices, and faith-based social service agencies were asked to name Protestant churches that were actively involved in community outreach. We expected that this process would generate 75 or so names, with overlapping referrals pointing out the leading outreach churches. We were pleasantly surprised when our 23 sources recommended a list of 126 churches. Only five churches shared referrals from three or more people.[1] While this outpouring of referrals complicated our selection task, it also highlighted the remarkable abundance of churches in the Philadelphia region that are actively involved in their communities.[2] Our experience suggests that in the local religious ecology there are few stellar churches with a luminous reputation for outreach. Rather, there blooms a field of churches doing good work, most without widespread recognition.

The census of Philadelphia congregations and their social programs by Cnaan and Boddie (2001) confirms this impression.[3] (For the sake of comparisons, we note that four of the churches we studied were outside the city: two were in Philadelphia suburbs, one in the nearby city of Chester, and one about an hour from Philadelphia in Mt. Holly, New Jersey.) In the Philadelphia ministry census, 88% of congregations reported at least one organized social program. Each congregation-sponsored program served an average of sixty-three non-church-members. The primary beneficiaries served by congregation-sponsored social programs were children and youth, families, and low-income persons, along with the community at large. An average of sixteen members per congregation participated in social service activities as staff or volunteers, along with nine volunteers from outside the congregation. A conservative estimate of the annual replacement value of the services provided by all Philadelphia congregations totaled a staggering $246,901,440. In Philadelphia, the authors conclude, "congregations not only serve others in the community but also do something to feed a civic culture that increases citizen involvement and enhances the quality of life in most communities" (2001, 571).

Given this strong local norm of congregational involvement, the churches in our sample were thus not unusual merely for addressing social needs, but for the amount and breadth of their activity. The fifteen case-study churches sponsored a total of 158 local social outreach ministries, or an average of 10.5 each, well above the average number of 2.41 programs per congregation recorded in the Philadelphia census.[4]

Our selection of cases aimed to maximize diversity across a range of demographic, geographic, organizational, pastoral, and theological factors, as well as the number and type of programs sponsored by the church. Table 2.1 lays out key characteristics of the case-study churches, while table 2.2. profiles their members. Thirteen of the churches came from twelve denominations (five mainline, four evangelical, and three historic black denominations), plus two churches were nondenominational. Congregational size ranged from forty to four thousand members. The majority (nine) of the churches were African American, along with four Anglo congregations and two with mixed Hispanic/Anglo membership. Nine of the churches were located in inner-city areas. The remaining churches were in downtown, metropolitan (non-inner-city urban), or suburban locations. The age of the churches fell into a wide range. Five of the churches had celebrated their ministry centennial, led by Tenth Presbyterian Church with 170 years; Koinonia Christian Community Church (also the smallest congregation) had existed just three years. Pastoral tenure also varied significantly, from four to thirty-three years. The churches also had mixed financial health (not shown). Five of the churches were facing financial diffi-

TABLE 2.1 Case Study Churches: Church Profiles

Church[a]	Denomination	Size[b] (members/ attenders)	Ethnicity	Location	Age (years)	Pastoral tenure (years)
Bethel Temple Community Bible Church	Independent	250	Hispanic, Anglo	inner city	9	11 & 7[f]
Central Baptist Church	Baptist (ABC)	260/180	Anglo	suburb	101	6 & 3[f]
Christian Stronghold Baptist Church	Baptist (Independent)	4,090/1,700	Black	inner city	22	33
Church of the Advocate	Episcopalian	150/60	Black	inner city	102	9
Cookman United Methodist Church	United Methodist	50	Black	inner city	26[c]	6
Faith Assembly of God	Assembly of God	100	Black	inner city	9	18
First Presbyterian Church	Presbyterian Church U.S.A.	700/500	Anglo	downtown	156	26
Germantown Church of the Brethren	Church of the Brethren	70/90	Black	metro[d]	10[c]	10
Koinonia Christian Community Church of God in Christ	Church of God in Christ	40/30	Black	inner city	6	6
Life in Christ Cathedral of Faith	Independent	300	Black	inner city	13	13
Media Presbyterian Church	Presbyterian Church U.S.A.	880/400	Anglo	suburb	150	4
New Covenant Church of Philadelphia	Church of God, Anderson	3,500/2,300	Black	metro[d]	17	17
Iglesia Luterana Nueva Creación / New Creation Lutheran Church	Evangelical Lutheran Church of America	200/75	Hispanic, Anglo	inner city	5	5
Tenth Memorial Baptist Church	National Baptist/American Baptist	1,500/600	Black	inner city	84	25
Tenth Presbyterian Church	Presbyterian Church in America	1,100/1,150	Anglo[e]	downtown	170	32

a. All data is recorded as of 1999.
b. Membership records were not available or reliable in some churches. Where a single figure is given, this represents average church attendance.
c. Cookman and Germantown were "reborn" after a period of closure. Cookman was originally founded in 1881, Germantown in 1723; both churches closed their doors for a period in the 1960s. The age given is for the more recent congregation.
d. Metro means a non-inner-city urban residential area.
e. Tenth Presbyterian Church is the most diverse non-Hispanic church in the study, with a congregation that is 84% Anglo, 9% Black, and 7% Asian.
f. Bethel Temple and Central Baptist were led by co-pastors.

TABLE 2.2. Case Study Churches: Member Profiles

Church	Residence[a]	Primary age groups[b]	Education[c]	Professional[d] (percent)	Theology[e]
Bethel Temple	local	<25, 26–40	medium	15	conservative
Central Baptist	semi	41–55, >56	high	39	liberal
Christian Stronghold	semi	26–40, 41–55	high	33	conservative
Church of the Advocate	local	>56	medium	<20	liberal
Cookman	local	26–40	low	<20	moderate
Faith Assembly of God	local	26–40	low	<20	conservative
First Presbyterian	local	41–55, >56	high	34	moderate
Germantown	local	26–40	medium	<20	conservative
Koinonia	local	<25	low	<20	conservative
Life in Christ	local	26–40	medium	20	conservative
Media Presbyterian	semi	>56	high	39	moderate
New Covenant	commuter	41–55	high	32	conservative
Nueva Creación	local	<25	low	<20	liberal
Tenth Memorial	semi	41–55, >56	medium	11	conservative
Tenth Presbyterian	commuter	26–40	high	56	conservative

a. Residence of members: local = majority live in immediate neighborhood (within 15 minutes), semi-local = majority live in nearby neighborhoods (within $1/2$ hour), commuter = significant minority (over 15%) live more than a half hour away.

b. Member age: primary age group = 25 and under, 26–40, 41–55, 56 and over.

c. Education: low = less than 50% have had at least some college education; medium = 50%–75% have some college; high = over 75% have some college.

d. Professional: Percentage reporting their occupation as professional or executive/management. At several of the churches, the sample size is too small to report a reliable percentage, but the proportion of professionals is estimated to be under 20% in each of these churches.

e. Theology: based on two survey questions—liberal = the Bible is not literally true, and everyone or all true believers are saved; moderate = the Bible is inspired but not literal, and only the born-again are saved; conservative = the Bible is to be taken literally, and only those who have been born again are saved.

culties, as reported by the pastors; five said their finances were adequate; and five reported finances in good or excellent condition.

Where members live in relation to the church is a salient dynamic. We classified nine of the churches as local, meaning that a majority of attendees lived within fifteen minutes of the church, according to our congregational surveys.[5] (Of course, in a city of neighborhoods like Philadelphia, fifteen minutes can take a resident across significant class and ethnic boundaries.) In the four semi-local congregations, the majority of attendees lived within half an hour of the church, while in the two commuter churches, over 15% of attendees drove over half an hour to worship.

Church members' place in the life cycle influences their availability for volunteer projects and openness to new ministry ideas (Cnaan et al. 2002; Boddie 2003). Three of the churches were youth-oriented churches, meaning a primary age group was twenty-five or under. Four were older churches, in which people over fifty-five constituted a primary age group. Another factor with significance for a congregation's outreach is education (Chaves and Tsitsos 2001). In six of the churches (including all the Anglo churches), over 75%

of survey respondents had some college education; at four inner-city churches, less than half the membership had some college education (though two of these were churches in which a large slice of respondents were not yet of college age).

We grouped congregations theologically depending on the pastor's response to two questions about "the way most members of your congregation view the Bible" and "the way most members of your congregation view salvation."[6] Conservative views (the Bible is to be taken literally, and only those who have been born again are saved) were cited as the majority in nine of the congregations. The two PC USA and the United Methodist churches took the moderate stance that the Bible is inspired but not literal, and only the born-again are saved. We identified three churches as liberal for the response that the Bible is not literally true, and that everyone or all true believers are saved. While these indicators—and the labels themselves—are imperfect gauges of a congregation's total theological package, they are useful in locating these churches in the universe of other studies that have used them (see Dixon, Jones, and Lowery 1992).

How do our case studies fit into the larger picture of Philadelphia churches? According to the congregational census, in Philadelphia, as in our sample, the majority (54.9%) of congregations are African American, with Anglo and Hispanic congregations constituting 26.2% and 5.3%, respectively. Residency patterns relative to church location in our sample appear similar to the distribution for other Philadelphia churches. The average age of Philadelphia congregations, fifty years, is close to our churches' average. Over half the congregations in Philadelphia have budgets under $100,000, and nearly a third have budgets under $50,000. Here, too, our churches appear to fit the range. The main difference is that the two megachurches raise the average church membership in our small sample higher than the citywide average of 346.

It may also be helpful to consider our sample against the more narrow frame of congregations that are socially active.[7] Factors relevant to congregational involvement include resources, size, ethnicity, member age, church age, theology, educational attainment, leadership, and location (see the helpful literature review by Scott 2002; also Cnaan et al. 2002). Our sample's bias toward African American congregations in distressed urban neighborhoods appears appropriate to capture the higher level of social needs and commitments of this group (Cnaan and Boddie 2001; Boddie 2003). Overall, the case-study churches appear to reflect the diversity of congregations in the Philadelphia region in general, but tend to be more theologically conservative, smaller, and poorer than the typical portrait of a socially active congregation. Since conservative churches are presumably more likely to incorporate religious content into social service programs, this weighting of our sample was helpful in enriching the range of religious dynamics to observe.

Social Ministry

We use two key terms throughout the book: *social ministry* and *evangelism*. A careful definition of each is important.

What Is Social Ministry?

Social ministry refers to any corporate effort of the church to influence society or improve quality of life beyond the church's membership. *Social action, social activism,* and *social outreach* are here interchangeable terms.[8] Our usage of the terms *outreach* or *community outreach* is meant to be inclusive of ministries that are either social or evangelistic in nature. Church-sponsored social ministries may take a variety of organizational forms, including loosely configured arrangements, formally organized programs under the control of the church, and separately incorporated nonprofits affiliated with the church. Churches frequently sponsor ministries in collaboration with other organizations, including religious, private secular, and public entities.

While it might seem that inventorying social ministries would be the easiest part of the study, we encountered more ambiguity than we expected. Ministries that had been reported on the initial pastoral survey disappeared when we actually went to observe them, and, conversely, after spending six months with a church we would discover a program that no one had told us about.[9] Some congregations carried out social service activities informally, never elevating them to the status of a "program." In other cases, the pastor was involved in community development activities that the congregation knew little about. Collaborative projects introduced another area of ambiguity: Does attending steering committee meetings for a housing project and putting a line in the church budget constitute a social ministry?

We developed a set of rules for counting social programs. We did not count special holiday donations (such as Thanksgiving baskets), financial support for denominational social programs, independent programs that met on the church's property (like AA), or occasional benevolence (as in the provision of emergency rent money).[10] These are important community-serving activities but do not reach "program" status. We also did not count benevolence directed out of the country; programs that, in principle, were open to the community but almost exclusively served church members in actual practice (like some churches' youth activities); or programs that had tangential social benefits but were largely evangelistic in content (like leading worship services in a prison). All these disclaimers serve as a reminder that the true social impact of churches is far greater than the sum of their programs.

Although we focus on activism directed outside the church, it should be noted that ministries targeting internal needs can also have a significant social impact, particularly in congregations that embrace people of lower economic status. For example, New Covenant Church fights unemployment in its midst by printing a "help wanted" list of open positions in members' places of employment. The Blessings and Needs ministry at Life in Christ facilitates sharing within the congregation by matching needs with donated goods and services. Mutual aid programs such as these serve as a first line of defense for church members and prevent them from having to turn to other sources of aid (Taylor and Chatters 1988; Ellison and George 1994; Ellor, Netting, and Thibault 1999). In a congregation that "constantly reaches beyond those who regularly give, to bring in those who constantly need" (Livezay 2000, 102), the line between social ministry and mutual aid becomes blurred.

Important ministry also takes place outside of structured social programs, through informal acts of compassion (Cnaan, Boddie, and Yancey 2003; Harris 1995). Reverend Joel Van Dyke described Bethel Temple's simple food ministry: "There is no program, but we get a lot of extra food from the food bank. . . . We give it to people who we know who need it." At Life in Christ, Dickie Robbins and his wife welcomed two at–risk children from the community into their home and raised them as their own, and have encouraged church members to do the same. A woman came to First Presbyterian Church during the week looking for a church office volunteer who had told her about a potential job opening. When the volunteer discovered that the woman lacked transportation, she put down the envelopes she was stuffing and offered to take her to fill out a job application. A strictly programmatic approach misses the ways that church members personally intervene to address others' needs.

Four Social Ministry Types

Four basic categories emerged from our catalogue of the churches' social ministries: relief services, personal development, community development, and systemic change (Sider, Olson, and Unruh 2002, 86).

- *Relief services* (giving a hungry person a fish) involves directly supplying food, clothing, or housing to someone in need.
- *Personal development* (teaching a person to fish) seeks to empower individuals to improve their physical, emotional, intellectual, relational, or social status.
- *Community development* (giving people fishing equipment) renews the building blocks of a healthy community, such as housing, jobs, health care, and education.
- *Systemic change* (helping everybody get fair access to the fish pond) means transforming unjust political, economic, environmental, or cultural systems.

Programs of relief tend to be short-term and oriented toward emergency or one-time needs, while personal development ministries typically involve multiple, more extensive interactions with beneficiaries. Amy Sherman (2000, 33) describes this as the difference between "commodity-based benevolence" versus "relational benevolence." McRoberts (2003, 101) refers to the socializing function of personal development ministries as "activities that prepare individuals for participation in broader social worlds." These ministries have an undercurrent of empowerment that transcends the immediate provision of tangible aid such as food and clothing. Community development ministries address the economic and social needs that affect a neighborhood on a broader scale, and tend to result in the creation or restoration of institutions (such as schools, community centers, or health clinics) that provide long-term benefits to the community. Community development projects may or may not involve direct interactions with persons in need. Systemic change efforts involve strategic, often long-range actions that may be undertaken on behalf of causes or needy groups (as in lobbying), or may involve affected persons as change agents (as in community organizing). Ministries of community development and systemic change are often collaborative, bringing neighborhood residents and organizations together around a common goal. While community development projects directly remedy or replace failing community functions, systemic change initiatives work to hold government or other power brokers accountable for their community responsibilities.[11]

The case studies provide examples of each ministry type in the arena of health:

- *Relief services*: a temporary mobile health clinic that provides free immunizations and other services to residents in an impoverished neighborhood for several weeks during the summer (Tenth Presbyterian Church).
- *Personal development:* Overeaters Anonymous and other support groups that encourage people to reduce health risks by changing lifestyle habits (First Presbyterian Church).
- *Community development:* a handicap-accessible gym that gives wheelchair-bound crime victims a place to exercise (Bethel Temple).
- *Systemic change:* well-publicized interventions by Philadelphia Interfaith Action, a community-organizing coalition, to pressure the City of Philadelphia to protect residents of the Logan neighborhood from the health risks posed by contaminated soil (Church of the Advocate and Nueva Creación Lutheran Church).

A way to visualize the relationship between these four categories is presented in table 2.3. The columns represent the locus of ministry activity: Does the ministry provide services to individuals (or their immediate family unit), or does the ministry address social need on a structural, corporate level

TABLE 2.3 Types of Social Ministries

Nature of benefit	Focus of action	
	Individual *a person or family unit*	Corporate *a geographic/political area* *or social structure*
Direct *Benefit addresses mani-* *festations of need*	Relief services	Community development
Indirect *Benefit addresses factors* *underlying the need*	Personal development	Systemic change

(whether neighborhoods; ethnic groups; institutions such as schools or credit unions; or social structures such as the healthcare or justice system)? The rows represent the nature of the service provided in relation to the need. How does the benefit provided by the ministry address a presenting social concern? Relief and community development both take the *direct* form of response to a need. Richard Smith of Faith Assembly of God describes this as a "felt-need" approach: "If people come to the door saying they are hungry, we feed them. So we have the food ministry. If someone needs a house, we get housing. People need jobs, so we build a relationship with people who can get them jobs." In comparison, what we have labeled *indirect* forms of social ministry (personal development and systemic change) address the underlying, often intangible reasons for the socioeconomic need. This is illustrated by the way a Presbyterian pastor justifies the church's strategy of personal development: "Our main concern is that there's no hope. There's no hope because they're unemployed. They're unemployed because they're uneducated." Materials for the community organizing coalition COPE point to the "ethic of power and justice" as their central resource for systemic change. Direct ministries redistribute needed goods and services; indirect ministries work with information, skills, and power.

Distribution of Social Ministry Types

It is not always possible to sort out the proportions of the four types proposed here from existing studies of congregation-based social programs that use different categories. It is clear, however, that ministries to individuals (relief and personal development), particularly ministries responding to short-term needs, predominate over ministries addressing problems on a structural, corporate level (community development and systemic change).[12] Overall, congregation-based services tend toward relief along with some forms of developmental assistance, especially to youth (Scott 2002). The Faith Communities Today study reports that cash, food, and clothing assistance were the three most common forms of community ministry (claimed by 88%, 85%, and 60% of congregations, respectively); personal development programs were claimed by about a third of congregations (Roozen and Dudley 2001). Philadelphia exhibits a similar pattern, according to the congregational census (Cnaan and Boddie 2001). The most common programs, offered by more than a third of the congregations, were food pantries, summer day camps, recreational programs for children and teens, and clothing closets. Systemic change ministries were the least prevalent, with no program of this type sustained by more than 15% of congregations. Black congregations in Philadelphia not only supported a slightly higher number of programs on average but were also more likely to sponsor personal development ministries.

Table 2.4 presents the distribution of social ministries among the fifteen congregations in our study, alongside the number of evangelistic programs. The specific programs of each church are listed in appendix 1. The fifteen churches sponsored a total of 158 social ministries: 62 personal development ministries (39.2%), 44 relief services (27.8%), 38 community development programs (24.1%), and 14 systemic change ministries (8.9%). Nine churches had ministries in all four categories; none had ministries limited to a single type.

TABLE 2.4 Case Study Churches: Outreach Profiles

	Number of programs						
Church	Relief services	Personal development	Community development	Systemic change	Total social action	Evangelism	Outreach priority[a]
Bethel Temple	3	5	5	0	13	5	E
Central Baptist	2	2	1	4	9	0	S
Christian Stronghold	2	6	5	1	14	8	E
Church of the Advocate	3	4	2	1	10	1	S
Cookman	4	3	0	0	7	5	B
Faith Assembly of God	3	5	1	0	9	5	B
First Presbyterian	4	5	5	2	16	6	B
Germantown	5	5	4	1	15	8	B
Koinonia	4	3	0	0	7	4	E
Life in Christ	2	3	4	1	10	6	B
Media Presbyterian	4	4	2	1	11	5	B
New Covenant	2	2	0	0	4	8	E
Nueva Creación	2	6	4	1	13	5	B
Tenth Memorial	1	4	5	2	12	3	B
Tenth Presbyterian	3	5	0	0	8	10	B
Totals	44	62	38	14	158	79	

a. Outreach priority: E = evangelism, S = social ministries, B = gives about equal priority to both (based on survey question, "Would you say that overall, your church currently places a higher priority on . . .").

All sponsored some form of relief and personal development, and four sponsored *only* these individualistic ministries.

The most common programs identified in the Philadelphia census—food programs, clothing closets, and programs for youth—were also among the programs with the highest frequency in our sample. Almost half of the programs of relief in our study were food-related (offered by thirteen of the fifteen churches). Relief ministries were commonly targeted to persons who were homeless or had emergency housing needs. Other relief services included one-time health-related ministries (such as health fairs), pregnancy centers, thrift stores, and staff social workers who handled aid distribution and referrals. The most prevalent forms of personal development were youth recreation or mentoring, provided by nine of the churches. Eight churches offered summer camps. Another significant developmental ministry area was substance abuse treatment, with seven churches offering recovery groups or rehabilitation homes. Other forms of personal development included counseling, support groups, job training, educational and tutoring programs, and general-interest seminars on topics such as parenting or credit management.

The most prevalent forms of community development related to housing and education. Eight of the churches engaged in housing repair and construction (including senior housing). Six churches "adopted" public schools, meaning they supported the schools in various symbolic and practical ways. A third of the churches participated in community development coalitions. Other development programs included economic development initiatives and general community improvement projects, such as tending a community garden. Systemic change efforts addressed concerns at the national, citywide, and neighborhood level, and took on causes at all points of the political spectrum. Central Baptist Church urged members to pressure Congress to strengthen environmental protection laws and increase funding for AIDS research; First Presbyterian Church pushed the state and county governments and local banks to uphold fair housing policies and community reinvestment practices; Christian Stronghold Baptist Church lobbied the city to reject benefits for same-sex couples and to block the liquor license of a local business. Five of the fourteen systemic change ministries involved community organizing collaboratives, including Philadelphia Interfaith Action. PIA, founded on the Industrial Areas Foundation model, is known for its sometimes confrontational but often effective tactics. Six of the churches had no involvement in systemic change.

These cases are not to be taken as representative of churches in general (much less all religious congregations), because our sample only included churches that were exceptionally active, with an average of 10.5 ministries per church. Because we selected churches for a balance of ministries, the distribution of social programs among these fifteen churches probably underrepresents relief and exaggerates the presence of other types of programs. Housing repair and construction, substance abuse recovery programs, and community organizing/lobbying activities in particular are over-represented in our sample relative to the Philadelphia congregational census data. Having a greater number and variety of social programs exposed our study to more forms of religious program activity than we would have encountered in a strictly representative sample.

Judging a church's activity solely by the number of ministries can be misleading, as programs vary widely in the amount of time and resources dedicated by the church. One program may entail daily activity by a dozen volunteers; another may involve only a few volunteers once a month. However, the number of ministries does say something about the types of needs perceived by these fifteen churches and the patterns of their preferred response. For example, even among these very active churches, systemic change is clearly not a preferred form of ministry. This concurs with the observation by Cnaan et al. that in comparison with six other cities they studied, "Philadelphia congregations provide many support services to individuals and families but do not engage in social change issues" (2002, 78).

Coming face to face with need can play a signal role in the development of a church's social ministries (Cnaan et al. 2002). However, different churches have different ways of responding to the needs they confront. Discovering a homeless man on the Tenth Presbyterian Church steps, for example, became the catalyst for personal development ministries that encourage homeless persons to change their lives. Desperate requests for shelter prompted Life in Christ to procure housing units for emergency use and low-cost rentals. Responding to the death of a church member, which was related to inadequate housing, Tenth Memorial Church has supported a series of community-development collaboratives to build apartments for low-income seniors, replace deteriorating housing with new homes, and promote home ownership. The prevalence of homelessness in its North Philadelphia community is one reason Church of the Advocate participates in Philadelphia Interfaith Action, seeking systemic change. Faced with similar social concerns, why do churches develop different patterns of social ministry in response? Researchers like Dudley and Van Eck (1992) and Mock (1992) have concluded that linear factors cannot predict which churches will develop social ministries. Based on our study, we add that the *types* of social ministry to emerge at a given church also defy easy prediction.

Evangelism

What Is Evangelism?

By *evangelism*, we mean sharing the gospel (the Christian message about salvation) by word and deed with people not actively affiliated with Christian faith, with the intention that they will choose to accept and follow Jesus Christ and join a church community for ongoing discipleship (see Sider, Olson, and Unruh 2002).

We acknowledge that this definition incorporates conservative theological assumptions not shared by all the churches that we studied. Fr. Isaac Miller, rector of Church of the Advocate, said he rejected "the standard textbook definition of evangelism," describing evangelism in terms of faithfully carrying out the work of compassion and justice. At Central Baptist Church, one member explained, "Evangelism is how the marginalized person calls you and you respond to that call." Another Central member commented that "the words of the faith that smack of the old traditional meaning of evangelism would be a mine field." While alternative understandings of evangelism have more internal validity for these congregations, we adopted the above definition as common usage for our research purposes.

Evangelism is distinct but inseparable from *discipleship*, or the growth process of education and nurture in the faith. Discipleship-oriented evangelism attends not only to those who do not call themselves Christians, but also to disaffiliated Christians seeking to be reconnected with their faith. Important concepts related to evangelism are *spiritual renewal* or *recommitment* (i.e., when people rededicate themselves to Christ and church participation after an absence). We use the broad term *spiritual nurture* to cover the range of ways in which people (including those who already call themselves religious) are encouraged to embrace a more committed, vibrant faith. Ministries may involve spiritual nurture without being specifically evangelistic, or even specifically Christian. The fruit of this process is what Lockhart (2003, 507) terms "religious internal status transformations," or a change in how people "think of themselves and are perceived by others" in their spiritual condition or identity.

Our definition concludes with the words *and join a church community for ongoing discipleship*. After studying religious beliefs and behavior in the United States, Wuthnow concluded that "religious inclinations make very little difference unless a person becomes involved in some kind of organized religious community" (Wuthnow 1991, 13). Evangelism is not the same as promoting a privatized spirituality disconnected from organized religious bodies, though such forms of spirituality have been gaining ascendancy. On the other hand, while evangelism is congruent with membership recruitment, they are not synonymous. Inviting unchurched people to worship services is a common form of evangelism, but congregations also often court people who are already Christians looking for a new church home. In the market model of voluntary association (Warner 1993), this form of new member recruitment is analogous to encouraging consumers to switch brands. Evangelism means opening a previously untapped market. Recruitment activities such as mailing church brochures to new residents in the community, placing church ads in local newspapers, or following up with visitors to the church may have evangelistic side benefits, but our study does not count them as evangelism.

This definition leaves room for diversity on several key points. Churches disagree on whether "getting saved" is an event or a process. Theologically conservative churches typically emphasize making a decision for Christ, a point in time that marks a "before" and "after." The climax of evangelism is a definitive conversion experience, accompanied by a public declaration of faith. Other theological streams understand salvation as a gradual process of a growing awareness of God's presence in one's life and a deepening commitment to living in the way that God intends. In this context, the goal of evangelism is "to create opportunities for people to take their next logical step in their relationship with God," according to a staff member at First Presbyterian Church. Another point of diversity is the evangelistic message—the content of the gospel being communicated through evangelism. Some churches highlight the promise of deliverance from sin through Christ's sacrificial death and resurrection; others, the sense of meaning and purpose endowed by a personal relationship with the Creator; others, the invitation to join a redemptive community that carries forward God's work of justice and peace in the world. Christians also vary in the role they ascribe to Jesus in the evangelistic message. Churches agree that Jesus is *a way* to salvation, but some (like Central Baptist and Nueva Creación) question whether Christ is *the way*.

There is also significant variety in the ways churches practice evangelism. We identify nine main methods of local evangelism (excluding global mission projects), organized by the nature of the relationship or activity that provides the context for the evangelistic encounter (Sider, Olson, and Unruh 2002):

1. *Network evangelism* involves evangelistic contacts within one's natural relational networks (friends, family, co-workers, etc.). Example: sharing your testimony with a neighbor.
2. *Contact evangelism* entails making intentional personal contact with people for the purpose of evangelism where little or no prior relationship existed. Example: distributing tracts door-to-door.
3. *Sanctuary evangelism* includes evangelistic interactions in the context of regular church activities. Example: offering "seeker"-friendly worship services.
4. *Target group evangelism* reaches out to a particular population or group, often at an off-site location. Example: leading worship services at a public housing complex.
5. *Service evangelism* entails evangelistic interactions in the context of social ministries. Example: offering a devotional before a soup kitchen meal.
6. *Youth evangelism* includes activities designed to reach unchurched children and teenagers. Example: presenting a gospel message at a youth rally.

7. *Special event evangelism* occurs at special events to which non-Christians are invited. Example: sponsoring an evangelistic crusade.
8. *Media evangelism* involves evangelistic communications via broadcast media (television, radio, Internet). Example: producing a radio program that answers callers' questions about Christianity.
9. *Prayer evangelism* entails praying for people to embrace the Christian faith (with or without their knowledge). Example: "prayer-walking" through a neighborhood.

Life in Christ employs each of these evangelistic strategies. Bishop Dickie Robbins teaches periodic classes on personal *network* evangelism, and regularly encourages members to invite friends and family to church. Following a strategy of *contact* evangelism, a male evangelism team distributes tracts to men on street corners. Church functions frequently close with altar calls (*sanctuary* evangelism), in which attenders are given an opportunity to respond to evangelistic exhortations by stepping forward or raising a hand. *Target groups* for evangelistic focus include outreach to prisoners and residents of local homeless shelters. The church appeals to *youth* through rallies and other special activities. One goal of the Music and Fine Arts Ministry is to perform at *special events* designed to engage people with an evangelistic message. *Prayer* is considered so essential to evangelistic efforts that Bishop Robbins once required church leaders to sign up for weekly sessions of prayer for the church's witness. *Service* evangelism is pervasive in Life in Christ's relief and personal development ministries; for example, the Drug Free program features prayer, religious teachings, and explicit invitations to salvation.

All of the examples above involve explicit verbal communication of a religious message. Many of these evangelistic methods have an implicit variant, in which the gospel is modeled through actions that draw people to Christ without an overt verbal component. A member of a Presbyterian church articulates her rationale for this more implicit, existential approach: "People can know what you believe by who you are and what you do, not necessarily by preaching to them." An implicit form of network evangelism, for example, is to try to conduct yourself in such a way that people who know you will see something different about you and attribute it to your faith (what some call *lifestyle evangelism*). An evangelistic intent may be implicitly present in special events such as performances of sacred music. One implicit version of service evangelism is what Steve Sjogren (1993) labels *servant evangelism*, or enacting symbolic gestures of God's love for people through simple acts of kindness or token gifts. On a churchwide level there is an implicitly evangelistic dimension to being known in the community for compassionate care of the needy or for taking a biblical stand against injustice or immorality.

In general, when we refer to evangelism in this book, we are referring to the explicit variety. In some sense, *any* activity or quality associated with the Christian life is implicitly evangelistic. Indeed, some church members informed us, followers of Christ are supposed to make their whole lives a witness, showing their faith by their works (James 2:18). However, if we defined evangelism so broadly as to include displaying a godly character or serving others in Christ's name, then we would not have conceptual leverage for examining the relationship between sharing good news and doing good works. Our definition of evangelism thus specifies sharing the gospel by word *and* deed. Deeds alone do have valid evangelistic ramifications, but our references to evangelism assume an intentional verbal component.

Evangelism Programs in the Case Studies

Table 2.4 above lists the number of evangelism programs sponsored by each church. Only one church—Central Baptist—had no overt evangelistic activities. At the other end of the spectrum, four churches (Christian Stronghold, Germantown, New Covenant, and Tenth Presbyterian) sponsored eight or more evangelism programs. As with social ministries, however, the raw number of programs is not necessarily an indicator of the priority attached to evangelism; Bethel Temple only lists five programs, but it pours considerable energy into them, besides injecting an evangelistic flavor into almost everything else it does.

Aside from network and service evangelism, we counted seventy-nine evangelism programs in all.[13] This figure by no means captures the full witness of these churches. Most of the churches employed some form of service evangelism, but, in order to be consistent, we counted any programs with a significant service or developmental aspect to them as social programs, not evangelism. (Service evangelism will be examined in more depth in chapter 5.) Our count of evangelism programs also does not include network evangelism, because this most often took place informally and individually, rather than as a distinct program. Several churches did encourage network evangelism by designating a particular Sunday as a target date to invite newcomers to church. Seven churches offered training in evangelism, largely directed at helping members share the gospel with family and acquaintances.

Table 2.5 shows the distribution of evangelism program types. The most common form of evangelistic outreach, with eleven of the fifteen churches sponsoring twenty-six programs in all, was target group evangelism. Nine of the churches had outreach to prisoners or their families. Nursing home visitation was another common ministry.[14] Other target sites included homeless shelters, a public housing complex, college campuses, and a mall. Target group evangelism was particularly favored by the Anglo churches, accounting for 43% of their evangelism program activity. One possible reason for the popularity of targeted ministry is that its narrow focus makes it easier to organize activities

TABLE 2.5 Number of
Evangelism Programs by Type

Contact Evangelism	15
Youth Evangelism	9
Sanctuary Evangelism	9
Special Event Evangelism	14
Target Group Evangelism	26
Media Evangelism	2
Prayer Evangelism	4
Total	79

and sustain volunteer motivation. Many of these programs originated with a lay person or small group with a "burden" for a given population. This affinity for an evangelistic target audience sometimes overlaps with or gives rise to a sense of calling to meet the social needs of that group.

Contact evangelism, sponsored by twelve of the churches, was the second most common type. This is the most public form of evangelism, in many cases literally taking the gospel to the streets as church members canvass door-to-door, hand out tracts or token gifts to passers-by, or preach on street corners. (See McRoberts 2003 for an insightful analysis of "the street" as an arena for public witness.) Contact evangelism has different meanings in different settings. Street witnessing is a fairly accepted feature of the urban drama; twice when the New Covenant tract distribution team arrived at a street corner, they found other church groups evangelizing there already. The two Anglo churches with contact ministries—Media Presbyterian and First Presbyterian—practice a less confrontational version, such as offering free water with accompanying tracts at a street fair.

Ministries in the other evangelistic categories reveal the variety of means employed to share the Christian message. Seven of the churches sponsored revivals or participated in citywide crusades. Other special events included street festivals (a block party with a religious theme), movies, dramas, and concerts attached to a presentation of the gospel. Sanctuary evangelism programs featured Bible studies and special worship services designed to reach unchurched folks. In several cases these were appended to a meal or food giveaway. Two churches (Cookman United Methodist and Media Presbyterian), representing quite different social locations, utilized the Alpha program—a series of meals, presentations, and small group discussions introducing Christianity. While almost every church had a youth group, about half of the churches made an intentional effort to attract youth beyond the church's membership. Four churches organized times of prayer focused on the spiritual needs of non-Christians; at Cookman this took the form of walking prayerfully through the church's neighborhood. Two churches broadcast radio programs.

This overview of the churches' evangelistic efforts is important because an interest in social outreach often eclipses attention to evangelistic activity, despite the fact that both represent public extensions of a church's mission. An exclusive focus on social programs trivializes the emphasis that the churches themselves may place on evangelism, as evidenced by the number and breadth of programs sponsored by this group of socially active congregations. Later chapters will look more closely at the range of ways their evangelistic intentions intersected with their social outreach.

Closing Observations: Evangelism and Social Action

Table 2.4 identifies the outreach priority cited by each church on the congregational survey: evangelism, social action, or an equal emphasis on both. Two churches gave priority to social action; not surprisingly, these had the fewest overtly evangelistic ministries. But the reverse is decidedly not true. The four churches that prioritized evangelism sponsored an average of 9.5 social ministries each—not as high as the overall average 10.5 ministries, but still a rather significant level of activity. Moreover, the churches that emphasized both forms of outreach sponsored nearly as many evangelism programs on average as churches that gave priority to evangelism alone (5.9 versus 6.3 ministries). These findings are not necessarily representative beyond our sample, because we deliberately overselected churches active in both spiritual and social outreach. Nevertheless, within this group of churches it is clear that evangelism and social action are not exclusive ministry realms, and that a strong emphasis on evangelism does not preclude a church from investing in the social well-being of its community. On the other hand, a strong emphasis on social action sometimes exists wholly apart from evangelism.

Having clear definitions of evangelism and social action makes it possible to examine these features of American congregational life more carefully—as long as these definitions take into account that they are to some extent artificial constructs. When the church members we interviewed discussed their church's ministry they were rarely concerned with the fine distinctions that we developed. Their conception of mission did not necessarily distinguish between informal acts of compassion or witness and organized outreach programs. Some did not even draw a line between witness and service, but viewed both activities simply as ways of sharing God's love. Moreover, it is important to consider outreach within the perspective of a church's broader sense of mission. Each church's internal landscape of activities, goals, and priorities provides a unique context for its commitments to evangelism and social action.

3

Case Studies of Faith in Action

In the hallway at Central Baptist Church, a prominent display shares the stories of several persons in the Baptist tradition who exemplify the church's mission.[1] One such hero is Maria Cristina Gomez, union activist in San Salvador, whose "senseless murder . . . is a reminder of why this church expresses its active solidarity with the poor, oppressed, and forgotten in Central America and throughout the Third World." Another profile is Jitsuo Morikowa, a formerly interned Japanese American who promoted the teachings of the social gospel. Each Sunday School classroom bears the name of one of these leaders in the faith, a reminder that the purpose of discipleship is to follow Christ into costly service. By telling these stories, Central Baptist attaches names and faces to the ideals that are preached and taught each week.

Likewise, stories about churches and their ministries present a valuable window onto an understanding of faith in action. The following chapters will offer a new vocabulary for describing the role of faith in relation to community activism, and lay out conceptual models for capturing the variety of forms of this relationship. Types and models do not exist in the abstract, however. They are only useful to the extent they describe what we encounter in the living world. This chapter highlights eight of the churches we studied, focusing on the way these churches define their mission, particularly in terms of the relationship between social action and evangelism, and put their ministry beliefs into action.

As a complement to these stories, tables 3.1 through 3.3 present survey data on the congregations' priorities, motivations, and beliefs

TABLE 3.1 Phrases That Most Describe the Church

Church	Top three phrases selected as very much describing the church[a] (percentage selecting each phrase)		
Bethel Temple	evangelistic (87)	compassionate (63)	community partner (60)
Central Baptist	compassionate (58)	social change agent (45)	empowering (45)
Christian Stronghold	evangelistic (86)	empowering (85)	respected (82)
First Presbyterian	community partner (57)	compassionate (48)	respected (47)
Life in Christ	empowering (72)	compassionate (69)	community partner (67)
Media Presbyterian	community partner (57)	respected (54)	compassionate (53)
New Covenant	empowering (81)	respected (76)	evangelistic (67)
Tenth Presbyterian	traditional (67)	respected (67)	evangelistic (39)

a. Respondents were given a list of phrases and asked to indicate how much each phrase described their church. The percentage saying this phrase very much describes the church is given in parentheses.

TABLE 3.2 Mission Priorities of the Church

Church	The church gives priority to . . . (percent selecting each option)					
	Care of members	Outreach to non-members	Both about equally	Social ministries	Evangelism	Both about equally
Bethel Temple (N = 62)	12.7	25.4	61.9	4.8	46.0	49.2
Central Baptist (N = 142)	46.4	3.6	50.0	87.1	0.0	12.9
Christian Stronghold (N = 620)	29.1	4.0	66.8	2.0	60.9	37.1
First Presbyterian (N = 193)	27.8	15.0	57.2	33.9	10.1	56.1
Life in Christ (N = 120)	16.7	13.2	70.2	8.0	43.4	48.7
Media Presbyterian (N = 226)	24.8	9.6	65.6	17.9	15.6	66.5
New Covenant (N = 311)	31.7	8.4	59.9	6.0	53.5	40.5
Tenth Presbyterian (N = 227)	39.9	9.2	50.9	17.3	31.4	51.4

TABLE 3.3 Reasons for Outreach

Church	Reasons for ministering to others through outreach[a] (percent saying extremely important)			
	Show compassion	Make society more just	Bring persons to Christ	Bring persons to church
Bethel Temple	74	33	57	18
Central Baptist	68	59	4	2
Christian Stronghold	76	41	54	35
First Presbyterian	58	20	27	9
Life in Christ	82	40	64	30
Media Presbyterian	69	27	31	13
New Covenant	77	38	62	26
Tenth Presbyterian	66	15	46	7

a. The question asked, "Why do you minister to others? For each of the following reasons, please circle a number between 1 and 5 showing how important it is for your involvement in outreach, with 1 being 'extremely important.'"

TABLE 3.4 Acts of Evangelism, Compassion, and Civic Involvement

Church	Talked about your faith with a non-Christian[a]	Helped lead someone to accept Christ[a]	Gave food, clothing, or money to someone in need[a]	Provided transportation or child care[a]	Volunteered for a charity outside the church[b]	Involved in community organizing or political action group[b]
Bethel Temple	86	48	81	74	42	28
Central Baptist	50	11	70	61	68	49
Christian Stronghold	90	57	80	74	44	20
First Presbyterian	62	21	69	51	64	34
Life in Christ	90	60	85	78	48	33
Media Presbyterian	56	23	78	54	69	24
New Covenant	93	65	88	80	55	31
Tenth Presbyterian	76	21	65	49	50	15

a. Percentage saying they did this often or sometimes in the past year.
b. Percentage saying they did this at least a few times a year.

relevant to outreach ministry. Table 3.4 shows rates of actual practices of evangelism, informal acts of compassion, and civic involvement reported by congregants. (For additional information on the churches and their ministries, see the tables in chapter 2 and also appendix 1.)

Central Baptist Church

"One of the things that's exciting to me about Central Baptist Church," declares Rev. Marcus Pomeroy in a sermon, "is that we're not normal!" A medium-sized Anglo congregation in a trendy Philadelphia suburb, Central revels in its legacy as a haven for radical social activists and theological nonconformists. Despite considerable theological diversity—epitomized by a sermon entitled "Wider Is Better"—church members share a remarkable degree of consensus around the ideal of social justice.

Central has a history of moving from principled concern over a social issue to sacrificial engagement. After the assassination of Martin Luther King Jr. and the subsequent urban tumult, some of the members put forward a risky proposal: Mortgage the church property for $100,000, and use the money to address the crisis. After four hours of debate, the Martin Luther King Jr. Memorial Fund was established, and the fund poured resources into a host of programs in the African American community. In 1984, criticism of U.S. policies toward Central America led the church to become an underground sanctuary for political refugees. Several church members were arrested for their involvement. When teenagers broke into the church and used the gas stove for heat, initial concerns about the security of the building gave way to a call to address the human need. The incident propelled Central to join the Main Line Interfaith

Hospitality Network (IHN), a consortium of churches that provide shelter to homeless families on a rotating basis. In 1992, an American Baptist resolution on the immorality of homosexuality sparked a dialogue at Central that led to the church adopting a controversial "Welcoming and Affirming" stance toward gays and lesbians. The coordinator of a ministry that provides support and advocacy on behalf of homosexuals comments, "I view our church in a coming out process, just like gays go through."

Such bold actions are fueled by a strong, shared sense of identity: "The people of Central are activists," as one member puts it. Central's mission identity is unmistakable from the moment one enters the church, from the stained glass windows adorned with symbols of peace and justice to the bulletin boards reserved for information about social concerns and service opportunities. The membership covenant concludes with a dedication to mission: "We covenant as individuals and as a congregation to work with others toward peace, justice and the wholeness of God's creation." Central members take this covenant seriously: over 60% of the congregation are involved in an outreach program, the highest level of involvement in our study. Co-pastor Marcia Bailey reports that many members say they chose the church "because of what they had heard or what they had seen about the social justice work that this church does." On the other hand, reflects co-pastor Marcus Pomeroy, the congregation has lost potential members who were not ready to reach the "threshold" of commitment to its mission.

Central's ministries are organized into nine lay-led mission groups, each with the stated goal "to reach out beyond ourselves with God's love." The role of the pastors is to empower and coordinate the members as they pursue various expressions of the core ministry vision. Even children are drawn into this vision. In the Children's Conversation portion of one Sunday service, the speaker led a kid's-eye review of the church's ministries:

> Habitat for Humanity, right. And IHN. . . . Having [homeless persons] eat here and have a place to live. And going to El Salvador and helping those people grow food and learn how to build. . . . There are ways that our church gets involved in helping people that are always getting picked on. . . . The Undoing Racism group is one. . . . CBC Concerned [support for homosexuals] is another group. . . . And we also get involved in writing to government to work toward our country not participating in the fighting that other countries are doing.

Besides having the highest number of systemic change ministries, Central leads the case-study churches in its principled embrace of social justice. Central members are by far more likely than those at any other church to claim that "helping make society more just" is a motive for their outreach involvement, to agree that poverty is "due to social, economic, and political factors" (as opposed to personal failings), and to identify "actively seeking social and economic justice" as an essential quality of the good Christian life.

Another area of broad agreement among Central members is an aversion to evangelism. "We are not trying to convince anyone," says one member. "We never have been a church out saving people by word." Among the case-study congregations, Central members are by far the least likely to describe their church as "evangelistic" (selected by only 6%), to claim that conversion will help poor people escape poverty, to be motivated to outreach by the hope of "bringing persons served to Christian faith," or to value "seeking to bring others to faith in Jesus Christ" as an essential characteristic of the Christian life. Central sponsors no corporate evangelism ministries, and individual members are also the least likely to engage in evangelistic acts. Only one of the ministry leaders we interviewed expressed a desire to help ministry beneficiaries grow spiritually; others said this would, in fact, be inappropriate.

The culture of Central, with its values of inclusivity and respect for all beliefs, recoils at anything that smacks of fundamentalism. Distaste for the idea of imposing beliefs on others is amplified by ambivalence about their own beliefs. The congregation is divided on whether faith in Christ is a requisite for personal salvation, and even on the meaning of salvation. Says one ministry leader, "If a spiritual community is based around Christ, that is okay, but it is not a necessity." Faith is understood less as a doctrine or a decision than as an evolving process. Members thus express uncertainty of what they would be evangelizing people *into*. Rather, the prevalent belief that Jesus may be encountered in "the least of these" turns the traditional notion of evangelism on its head. Instead of urging others to seek Christ, Christians are to seek solidarity with the poor in order to find Christ. As one member explains, "Evangelism is how the marginalized person calls you and you respond to that call."

Despite their resistance to overt evangelism, members do evince concern for the spiritual life of people outside the church. The majority agree that churches should care *both* for people's "spiritual well-being" and for their "social and emotional well-being." An almost equal majority, however, believe that the way to share God's love is by "demonstrating it with caring actions" rather than "telling people about Jesus." Spiritual well-being is promoted implicitly, by deed rather than by word. Evangelism, asserts one member, "does not mean that you are a fisher of men, like we've been taught. If you are a good role model, people will be drawn to you." The member who coordinates IHN volunteers offers her own definition: "Evangelism is showing God's love through example. We show our faith in God through our kindness to others."

Media Presbyterian Church

On the video commemorating Media Presbyterian Church's 150th anniversary in 2000, a long-time member reflected, "There is a spirit here in this church that will keep on bringing new members in, a lively program that will serve the people and do what Christ wants us to do—which is to reach out into the world and serve those who are in need and broadcast the good news to everyone." As his comments indicate, Media's vitality is linked to its sense of mission. In true Presbyterian fashion, pastor Bill Borror often preaches on the theme of being "predestined for ministry." The purpose of the church, he says, "is to be an instrument for redemption."

The church's redemptive impact on society is mediated primarily through "incarnational ministry," or "God's people fleshing out the truth of the gospel," according to Rev. Borror. This means drawing members to become personally engaged in service, not simply to donate money from a distance (though the church does this as well—fully a third of its budget goes to mission work far and near). In 1998 a Faith In Action Committee was formed with the goal of involving at least half the congregation in hands-on ministry. Church volunteers support an array of relief and development projects: summer day camps for inner-city kids, home repairs for elderly and low-income households, a food pantry, mentoring children of single parents, reading to students at an urban Christian elementary school, visiting "throw-away parents" in nursing homes. Several service projects have been undertaken in partnership with Life in Christ Cathedral of Faith, an inner-city church profiled later in this chapter. A highlight of the church's outreach calendar is the annual Habitat for Humanity "blitz-build" in rural North Carolina. In 1999, about 150 churchgoers spent a week of their summer vacation laboring together to build an entire home for a low-income family, from the foundation up.

While many of the church's service projects transport members out of their suburban context into high-poverty areas, Media Presbyterian has also become attuned to the hidden poverty of the suburbs, regularly answering urgent requests for food, rent money, or medicine. The church sponsors several support groups, such as for divorcees and for families grieving a death. The church also confronts what Rev. Borror calls "the fragmentation of the youth culture" in middle class families. In one year, their community reeled from the death of five high school students in an auto accident, several youth suicides (the youngest in sixth grade), and a murder. In response, Rev. Borror and Media's youth pastor became unofficial chaplains for the community, working with the school district and with grieving families.

"This congregation has embraced the idea of hands-on ministry in a much more radical way, more quickly than I anticipated," remarks Rev. Borror. A significant factor in the church's ability to mobilize its membership has been an emphasis on the benefits of active service for the spiritual life of those who serve. This was underscored by the hiring of an associate pastor responsible for both outreach and congregational care. "I think we should be working with the poor," says Rev. Borror. "But my chief concern, as a pastor, is [that] that will help my people love God and love Christ more." Aiding people in need presents members with an opportunity to express and strengthen their faith. In particular, according to the survey, Media's compassionate service is animated by gratitude to God and to the church. In a congregation filled with busy professionals, volunteering also often reflects a personal quest for a deeper sense of meaning and connection.

Unlike their embrace of service, members display ambivalence toward evangelism. "The word *evangelism* kind of unnerves me," confesses the chair of the Evangelism and Outreach committee. "When you say evangelism, people think, 'Holy Roller.' I think it's intimidating." When she gives her definition of evangelism, she is quick to add: "It's not preaching at people . . . It's interacting with people in a way that shows them God's love." A difference between Media and Central Baptist is that Media members accept that they are *supposed* to evangelize even though they may be uncomfortable with it. Over three-fourths of survey respondents believe that "seeking to bring others to faith" is an essential or very important aspect of the Christian life. Two-thirds of respondents believe that Media gives about equal priority to evangelism and to social action. The Outreach and Evangelism Committee has struggled to find ways to close the gap between the theological mandate for evangelism and the reluctance of members to put it into practice.

The primary mode of faith-sharing has been network evangelism. Reverend Borror preached: "Evangelism is to take place in your neighborhoods, the PTA, the soccer fields, the workplace." Low-key approaches are preferred, such as forming friendships with non-Christians, talking about one's religious experiences rather than emphasizing doctrine, and inviting acquaintances to "Bring-a-Friend Sunday." The evangelism training curriculum stresses that the gospel is to be modeled through a lifestyle of caring actions: "Ninety percent of evangelism is love" (quoting Petersen 1980). Members are encouraged to identify themselves as Christians, show caring, and respond in spiritually substantive ways as relational openings arise.

A variety of service projects facilitate network evangelism by offering non-"churchy" activities to which members can invite their friends. While Media's social ministries rarely involve overt evangelistic appeals, members believe that social service offers tangible evidence of their faith to the surrounding skeptical culture. The chair of the Faith in Action Committee comments, "People think that all churches do is condemn and complain about people, so they like to hear about a church that is doing good." Faith-based community involvement is enough of a rarity in Media's context to generate publicity for their activism. The church's ministries have prompted newspaper articles with titles like

"Practicing What Jesus Preached: Habitat Volunteers Help Needy Family Get a Home." Media's reputation has attracted new members seeking affiliation with a compassionate congregation.

In many ways Media fits Ammerman's (1997b) description of a "Golden Rule congregation." Members tend to center their religious life around civic duty and family values; express their faith in practical rather than theological terms; place a high premium on children's ministries; faithfully devote themselves to acts of community service; and feel uncomfortable with outreach that challenges the status quo, whether in the form of social justice advocacy or aggressive evangelism. "We're pretty normal people who are just trying to do the right thing," remarks a member. Yet the congregation has been accepting a push from the leadership to be both more intentionally evangelistic within their social network and more actively engaged in addressing social needs outside their network. These ministry goals are harmonized by the confidence that acts of compassion quietly cultivate the field for an eventual spiritual harvest. "You have to believe that if you plant the seeds, something will happen sooner or later," reflects a deacon. "That's our job, I guess—to plant seeds of goodness."

Life in Christ Cathedral of Faith

When Dickie Robbins left his impoverished hometown of Chester for a college education and a better future, he had no intention of returning. Ten years later, however, he and his wife sensed a compelling call from God to address the problems in Chester that had made him want to leave. They moved back to the inner city and founded a church. They began preaching the gospel on corners where drugs were sold and in public housing developments, and soon their congregation included an expanding circle of converted addicts. The rehabilitation ministry, Drug Free, was so successful and the resulting growth of the congregation so explosive that the congregation became known as "the druggie church on Third Street." In 1998 the congregation moved to a larger building and took a new name that reflected Bishop Robbins' expansive vision: Life in Christ Cathedral of Faith.[2]

"Holistic ministry is properly balancing evangelism and social justice," declares Bishop Robbins. The city of Chester provides a desperately relevant context for putting this principle into action. In 1998, nearly three-quarters of households had annual incomes under $10,000, the school district ranked dead last in the state of Pennsylvania, the child mortality rate was the highest in the state, and the city government earned the dubious honor of being voted one of the ten most corrupt in America. The city is a dumping ground for the rest of the suburban, mostly Anglo county, with waste treatment facilities almost literally in residents' back yards. Faced with the community's complex, interlocking problems, Life in Christ has taken a multifaceted approach.

Relief services are a central focus because of the constant stream of requests for emergency assistance, from both within and outside the congregation. "I had people coming to me in the middle of the winter, women with children saying we don't have a place to stay and the shelters are full," says Bishop Robbins. A nonprofit arm of the church owns two homes and thirteen apartments, some of which are reserved for emergency housing and some rented at a discount. After discovering that no one served food to Chester's homeless population on Sunday, the church organized L.I.F.E. (Love In Feeding Everyone), which feeds up to seventy-five people weekly at open-air sites.

Beyond material deprivation, states Bishop Robbins, "Poverty is a mentality." The church's personal development ministries challenge that mentality through substance abuse rehabilitation, education, youth mentoring, and financial counseling. A foundational premise of Life in Christ's social ministry is that internal and external problems form a vicious cycle. To interrupt the cycle, the church complements its ministries of personal development with projects aimed at rebuilding the community. The Life in Christ Economic Development Corporation creates opportunities for entrepreneurship, coordinates housing rehabilitation, and also generates income for the church's ministries through rental properties. As an alternative to the failing school system, the church started a private elementary school.[3] Life in Christ also participates in several local community development collaborations.

Bishop Robbins, a political conservative, believes that systemic change plays a crucial role in community revitalization. He founded the Political Involvement Ministry to inform and organize congregational action on local concerns, such as "dumping" waste treatment facilities in low-income African American neighborhoods. "We really do battle in the political area because [these issues] directly affect a person's quality of life, and in many cases their ability to live." Robbins also exercises influence on behalf of the church by participating in public and nonprofit boards that develop social policies, such as a Chester environmental action committee. "I can't wait until the wagon's fixed," he says of his activism. "I should be a part of fixing it." Yet Life in Christ does not emphasize social justice as an abstract theological concept. Only 8% of respondents identified "a more just society" as an important factor in helping people escape poverty. While the word respondents say most describes the church is *empowering*, one of the least selected phrases is *makes social change happen*.

Life in Christ teaches that empowerment comes ultimately through spiritual change. A church elder declares, "For every spiritual truth, there is a natural parallel." This axiom captures the church's Pentecostal belief in a direct connection between spiritual and material realities. Accordingly, Life in Christ's spirituality has a practical cast. Sermons often touch on practical topics like health, financial stewardship, and home ownership. Social and spiritual dimensions of well-being constitute overlapping facets of the overall goal of the "abundant life." Most of the church's social ministries have an explicitly religious character: budget counseling is based on biblical teachings, for example, and the provision of emergency housing often comes with the expectation of church attendance. According to the majority of respondents, evangelism entails *both* verbally sharing the gospel and demonstrating God's love through caring acts. Consistent with this belief, Life in Christ members reported the second highest score of acts of evangelism of the eight churches profiled here, and the highest score of acts of compassion. Active evangelism is seen as vital to the church's mission of empowering the community, a point emphasized in sermons and evangelism training classes.

Social ministries are also vital to the church's success in evangelism, as they offer a point of contact between the church and potential new members. Bishop Robbins explains this outreach strategy: "You don't expect a fish to just come and jump into the boat! You throw out a net. . . . We look at the outreach as casting a net. Once we get people into the net we gently draw them in to what we consider the local church to be—a lifeboat." Most of the church's current lay leadership and up to a third of the congregation were drawn in through the church's Drug Free ministry. Focusing on neighborhood outreach has yielded a membership that is poor in resources and skills (fewer than a third have college degrees) but high in empathy and compassion. "When there is a need, rather than join in the complaints, we create an alternative," says Bishop Robbins. "God sent me here to transform a community. And that is what we are doing."

First Presbyterian Church of Mt. Holly

A brochure describes the origins of Homes of Hope, one of First Presbyterian Church's oldest social programs: "The congregation was responding to the deteriorating neighborhood within sight of the church. They were faced with the decision of whether to improve it or move out of it, and chose to stay and get involved." This choice to take a stand with its surroundings in downtown Mt. Holly, a small city in New Jersey, altered First Presbyterian's missional direction. "I didn't realize the full ramifications that was going to bring into my life," reflects a member who volunteered to refurbish the first abandoned home and later became director of Homes of Hope. He paid a visit to Millard Fuller, the founder of Habitat for Humanity, and caught what he calls "Habititis"—a vision for changing the lives of poor families. Since its founding in 1979, Homes of Hope has rehabilitated or constructed over twenty housing units and has provided low-cost rental housing for more than one hundred families.

As middle-class Caucasians working with low-income tenants from diverse backgrounds, First Presbyterian members have been challenged to confront their stereotypes. "My parents had parents who taught them the good disciplines in life," reflects the director, "so they didn't have to struggle with some of the things that our people are struggling with." Tenants' emotional and spiritual needs helped provide the impetus for founding a counseling program, called The Well. Other church ministries emerged, such as free lunches, health screenings, and various support groups, providing a network of service. To meet the immediate needs of homeless families, First Presbyterian joined their area's Interfaith Hospitality Network. Together with a Baptist church, First Presbyterian established a Christian retirement center, after a long-time member had to move away from Mt. Holly in search of affordable elder housing.

First Presbyterian's concern for housing leads the church to look beyond the needs of individual families to the broader social forces affecting housing availability. When activists protested the county's failure to provide short-term housing assistance by pitching a "tent city" on the courthouse lawn, senior pastor Jim Kraft joined other local pastors at the courthouse, waiting to be arrested. (A compromise was reached that averted their arrests.) In another instance, Homes of Hope sued the town of Mt. Holly to challenge a restrictive zoning ordinance. This led to a New Jersey Supreme Court decision that has expanded affordable housing for low-income and disabled persons. To increase its impact, First Presbyterian helped launch the Affordable Housing Coalition of Burlington County. The coalition shares information and helps agencies access development resources, as well as holding local government and banks accountable for fair housing policies and community reinvestment. First Presbyterian also aspires to change attitudes about having the "wrong kinds of people" as neighbors through their involvement with Continuing the Dream, an interfaith racial reconciliation ministry.

In part because of its multilayered approach to social needs, First Presbyterian has the highest number of programs among the churches in our study. To maintain this level of involvement, First Presbyterian has created an effective system for connecting church members with ministry. Interviews with new members probe the skills, experiences, and interests they can bring to service. A staff member with the title of director of servant development maintains a database of this information, along with each member's service record in the church and community. Bulletin inserts, announcement boards, newsletter articles and personal appeals keep volunteer opportunities before the congregation. Not surprisingly, *compassionate* and *community partner* are words congregants are most likely to use to describe their church.

Alongside social ministry, evangelism is a core feature of the church's identity and mission, emphasized in sermons, newsletters, and discipleship classes. The welcome letter to first-time visitors underscores both areas of mission: "Besides our concern to share faith in Christ with our neighbors, we are very active in trying to meet some of the social concerns of the needy and hurting in our community." About an equal number of survey responders consider sharing faith and showing compassion to be essential features of the Christian life. Members of First Presbyterian, as at Media Presbyterian, prefer a low-key approach to evangelism. The church discontinued its involvement in "Evangelism Explosion," a structured program of door-to-door canvassing, because members felt it was too confrontational. Pastoral staff use the term *pre-evangelism* to describe their strategy of offering activities for nonchurchgoers that foster a connection with the congregation and signal the church's availability to meet their spiritual and social needs. Such activities include First Focus educational seminars and an arts camp for youth. The associate pastor for outreach explains the evangelistic intent of these services: "We build up a rapport with them. Then the evangelistic moment of saying, 'This is who Jesus is—would you like to enter that kind of relationship with him?' . . . that makes sense to them."

This approach is reflected in their most ambitious evangelistic outreach, the Burlington Mall Ministry. Conceived of as a mission outpost in a "cathedral of consumption," the rented space creates an inviting atmosphere for weary mall shoppers to browse Christian literature, share prayer requests, talk with the volunteer host, or just sit. A brochure explains the ministry's rationale: "In obedience to Jesus' example and his command to go and make disciples (Matt. 28:19), we are heading to the marketplace nearest to us to share this saving message with hurting and hungering people. . . . While our desire is to be clearly evangelistic, programs will reach out to the multifaceted needs of people." Program offerings to meet these needs include seminars, children's activities, health screenings, a beginners' Bible study, and a variety of support groups. A "Weigh Down Workshop," for example, "takes the focus from whatever 'weighs you down' spiritually and refocuses you on God." Food court coupons are distributed to down-and-out visitors.

The integration of spiritual care with efforts to address people's "multifaceted needs" is evident in most of First Presbyterian's social ministries. The Well provides counseling with a "Christian base," meaning that prayer, biblical teachings, and church attendance are offered (though not required) as resources for clients. The crisis pregnancy center founded with the church's support provides incentives for women to attend church and invites women to pray with staff. A Christian tract is tucked into each basket of food or bag of school supplies distributed by the church. One of the three free lunches each week incorporates prayer and a worship service following the meal, called Bread and Bible. The church's leadership is also attuned to the evangelistic implications of service ministries for volunteers from outside the church. For example, one woman joined First Presbyterian after her daughter, whose employer supplied the Community Luncheon with food, suggested that she help out with the program.

Reverend Kraft exhorted in a newsletter, "The church has done evangelism and the church has done social ministry—but not always together. We must get excited about the whole gospel to minister to whole persons." The majority of survey respondents give equal importance to people's social well-being and their spiritual well-being, and believe that God's love is made evident equally in caring actions and in telling people about Jesus. Yet members disagree whether social ministries are appropriate venues for sharing the gospel; only a fourth of respondents say bringing beneficiaries to faith is an extremely important motivation for outreach. One lay leader who oversees the distribution of holiday baskets declares, "I don't personally do what I do as a way of evangelizing." The position of the pastorate, however, is that segregating social and spiritual dimensions of care inadequately represents "the whole gospel." Reverend Kraft explains: "I want to reach the whole person. Human beings don't live by bread alone, but by the Word and ministry of God. . . . I think we're only doing part of the job if we don't introduce people to Christ. I don't want what we do to be strictly seen as social services."

Christian Stronghold Baptist Church

Located on a busy thoroughfare in a poor, largely African American section of Philadelphia, the barbed-wire fence encircling the parking lot of Christian Stronghold Baptist Church literally presents a "stronghold" against the neighborhood banes of drugs, crime, and prostitution. "We offer solutions to many problems with faith," the church informs first-time visitors. The church's pragmatic, family-centered, community-minded character boosts its continued growth, with an average weekly adult attendance of 1,700. The economically diverse congregation draws a mix of local residents and commuters from other Philadelphia neighborhoods. Christian Stronghold divides its attention between the urgent needs of its immediate neighborhood and issues affecting African Americans across the economic spectrum, such as single-parent households and lack of quality education.

A key axiom of Christian Stronghold's ministry, expressed by an associate pastor, is that "Success comes from knowing God's word and applying it." The primary focus of social ministry is personal development: mentoring, counseling, tutoring, promoting home-ownership, teaching literacy, and encouraging debt reduction. Personal development ministries present the information and skills needed for social advancement from a biblical perspective. The Christian Research and Development Institute, established by the church's founder and senior pastor Dr. Willie Richardson, produces resources such as a "Success

Planning Journal" to help people achieve personal goals. The theme of education for empowerment runs through much of the church's internal nurture and community outreach. Christian Stronghold's purpose in publishing a community newspaper, for example, is "to open up people's minds to new things that would help to uplift them spiritually so that they would be able to achieve."

Alongside the emphasis on developing individuals, Christian Stronghold is also invested in community development, using the church's size and prominent reputation to influence local change. Christian Stronghold has participated in two faith-based housing coalitions that together have built or renovated more than four hundred homes. Other projects have involved negotiations to bring a decent supermarket into the neighborhood, a job placement collaborative, and plans for a new recreational center. The church also created a Community Action Council "to be the salt and light from a biblical perspective" on salient civic and political matters. Actions undertaken by the council include "adopting" the local elementary school, lobbying to upgrade a public bus stop near the church, registering members to vote, testifying to city council against condom distribution in public schools and benefits to same-sex partners, and blocking the liquor license of a nearby business. Such interventions seek to bring dysfunctional social realities into conformity with God's will, as expressed in the Scriptures.

Addressing social concerns in the name of Jesus has inherent merit, says Rev. Richardson, but following Jesus' example entails sharing faith as well. People who have had their material needs met without an explicit evangelistic encounter, he explains, "came to eat the appetizer and never got the rest of the menu." Thus, according to Rev. Richardson, "Everything we do is an evangelistic outreach in nature. Every opportunity we have, we witness to people." Ideally, the act of providing a service creates an arena for church members to verbalize the gospel and draw beneficiaries into the congregation. While most social ministries do not require participation in religious activities in order to receive aid, they do have a distinctively Christian character. At church-sponsored health fairs, for example, doctors blend spiritual and medical advice, telling patients not only about exercise and proper nutrition, but also "that your body is the temple of the Holy Spirit and that you have a responsibility to be a steward of it," according to an associate pastor. In the counseling program, church counselors "establish the salvation of the person" and, if necessary, "present the salvation message." If you use the church's food pantry, says a ministry leader, "before you walk out of here with that brown bag, somebody's gonna share the Lord with you."

In addition to the integration of explicit spiritual messages into social ministry, Christian Stronghold employs a range of other evangelistic strategies. A strong emphasis on network evangelism encourages people to reach those within their relational circle, particularly family members. The church conducts well-organized campaigns of telephone and door-to-door evangelism, which target the area immediately around the church and members' own neighborhoods. Most worship services end with an altar call, inviting rededication to active church membership alongside first-time professions of faith. The church hosts special events, like Family Day and Men's Breakfasts, designed to bring new people into the church where they can hear an evangelistic message. Church volunteers print and distribute a community newspaper with articles covering local events, useful information, and a biblical perspective on social and moral issues, along with an invitation to attend Christian Stronghold.

"Everybody who is saved has been called to witness and to bring someone to Christ," declares a ministry leader. Nearly 80% of survey respondents consider sharing faith with others to be an essential quality of the Christian life (about twice the percentage who say taking care of the needy is essential). Members put this directive into practice. One quarter of the congregation reported participating in a structured evangelistic ministry. More than three-fourths of respondents reported that they often or sometimes talked about their beliefs with non-Christians, invited someone to church, or led at least one person to Christian faith in the past year. Reverend Richardson rallies this strong participation in evangelistic outreach through persistent teachings on the importance of evangelism and thorough training. Not surprisingly, the word most identified as describing the church is *evangelistic*, followed closely by *empowering*.

The interweaving of evangelism and empowerment is evident in Christian Stronghold's response to welfare reform. "When the state and city stopped welfare programs, people came out of the woodwork," says the director of educational services. The church began offering classes to help people earn their high school equivalency certificate. The director describes how these GED classes incorporate a spiritual dimension:

> We open up with prayer, and every opportunity we have we witness
> to people. . . . Our purpose is to help them with their education.
> With that in mind, when the opportunity arises, we turn the conver-
> sation to Christ. . . . We have opportunities within the lesson plan to
> discuss the way God would have them handle the situation. . . . You
> have to rely on the Holy Spirit to bring back into remembrance all
> you have studied. If you rely on God to help you, it makes it much
> easier.

Students are invited, but not required, to attend church services; one year, about a third of the nonmembers in the class ended up joining Christian Stronghold. The ministry director waives the $25 class fee for students who cannot afford it. His explanation for doing so illustrates the church's "trickle up" approach to transforming a community by means of educating and empowering individuals: "When they say, 'Why did you do that?' I will say, 'This is our community.' And if you get your GED and get a job, that will help the community."

Bethel Temple Community Bible Church

Joel Van Dyke, co-pastor of Bethel Temple, stood up at a congregational meeting to announce that after a year-long process, the church had a new mission statement: "Discipling our members, evangelizing our neighborhood, and revitalizing our community in the name of Jesus Christ." By way of explanation, he remarked, "In the last ten to fifteen years, conservative, evangelical churches like us have become part of a movement . . . to develop the communities they minister to without losing the centrality of the gospel of Jesus Christ."

Founded in 1912, the original Bethel congregation was known for its annual parades through the Kensington community of Philadelphia to drum up new members, and, at its zenith, it taught several hundred children in rotating Sunday school classes. After World War II, Kensington followed the path of many American urban neighborhoods: the flourishing manufacturing economy gradually failed, and the landscape became marred with husks of abandoned factories, boarded rowhomes, and weed-filled lots. As the composition of the neighborhood shifted from working-class Anglos to lower-class Latinos, Bethel's interest in outreach waned. In 1990 the dwindling church relocated to an Anglo enclave in a different part of the city, and turned over the building to pastor Luis Centeno, a Puerto Rican local. The reborn Latino-Anglo congregation changed its name from Bethel Temple Independent Bible Church to Bethel Temple *Community* Bible Church. A colorful cross atop the church, created from reclaimed refuse, projects a powerful symbol of the hope Bethel offers its community.

The legacy of the original Bethel persists in the church's strong affirmation of evangelism. Sermons, song lyrics, banners, and an annual missions conference reinforce the mandate to reach people with the gospel. According to a ministry leader, "The primary, number one mission for Christians is to tell other people about Christ, and I think we have a lot of different options of how to do it." These options include programs of open-air evangelistic preaching and tract distribution, which engaged the participation of about half of survey respondents. Service evangelism is another option that is central to the church's outreach strategy. Reverend Van Dyke describes social service as "a tool the church can use to present the gospel in a holistic fashion." Most social ministries incorporate an explicitly evangelistic dimension, often in the form of informal dialogues about spiritual concerns. Outreach ministries to youth, substance abusers, and single moms allow time for "hanging out," creating an environment where trust can develop and spiritual conversations can naturally evolve.

Reverend Centeno explains that what sets Bethel apart from other evangelistic groups is its attentiveness to social needs: "Unlike the Mormons and the Jehovah's Witnesses that are just all over the place around here, we only go [door-to-door] when we have something to give to people. . . . So they know that we are a church that's not trying to get from the community, but [is] there to give." The urgent and deep-seated needs of their target population make demonstrations of social compassion a relevant and winsome evangelistic strategy. As a ministry leader asserts, "Just to verbally proclaim to somebody, 'Just believe in Jesus, he'll love you,' isn't enough. You have to be able to show that."

While the congregation has a reputation for informality and spontaneity, Bethel's approach to social ministry has been growing more intentional and organized. The church created a new position, director of economic and community development, and added several programs, including a computer lab, an after-school program, and vocational training in graphic arts. While all of these activities have a spiritual character, Bethel's organizational chart places some ministries under the heading of "evangelism" and others under "community revitalization," depending on whether their main objective is to nurture faith (such as the summer day camp) or to meet a social need (such as the after-school tutoring program). The director of community development explains: "The gospel has to be in everything we do, but certain things we're not doing because we want to share the gospel in the sense of verbally proclaiming or evangelizing. We're doing it because people need it. If you love people, you do those things."

Bethel's social ministries emphasize relief and personal development. This individualistic orientation reflects their belief, articulated at a missions conference, that the gospel "recreates people from the inside out, and it can recreate a city from the inside out as people are changed, one by one." In recent years, Bethel has begun to expand its vision to include structural change. Church leaders observed that as people in their neighborhood became Christians and improved their lives, they tended to move away, draining the church and the community of stable, responsible families. To counteract this trend, Bethel has defined a goal of visibly improving the quality of life in the area around the church so that people will choose to stay. Church leaders are expected to set an example by living in the neighborhood, instead of safer or higher-status locations. Experiencing firsthand the injustices faced by residents and negotiating with the city over abandoned properties has led some leaders to consider more political forms of involvement. The director of community development voices his hope that as people "take pride in their houses and their possessions and their ownership and their block and care for one another—then differences will be made. People will start saying no to the injustices."

Tenth Presbyterian Church

Half a century ago, when Tenth Presbyterian Church faced the decision of whether to follow the trail of so many other conservative white urban churches out to the suburbs, Tenth took a definitive stand with its setting in the heart of downtown Philadelphia.[4] A current associate pastor recalled this commitment in a letter to the congregation: "We believe that the gospel is for the whole city. . . . Our concern for urban issues arises out of our biblical and theological emphasis, not in spite of it." This posture of openness to the community is reflected in the statement which appears prominently in church materials declaring that, to any and all, "this church opens wide her doors and offers her welcome in the name of the Lord Jesus Christ." Through its outreach ministries, the church literally opens its doors to people on the social margins.

After a prayer meeting on a cold night in 1982, several Tenth Presbyterian members were stopped short by the sight of a homeless man huddled on the church steps. One member turned to another and said, "We need to do something about that." After consulting with the deacons, a group of members decided to start providing meals for the growing homeless population in the area. From that modest beginning, ACTS (Active Compassion Through Service) has evolved into a diverse set of ministries that involves about 20% of a congregation of over a thousand members. ACTS services include free meals, after-school tutoring, nursing home visitation, outreach to homeless persons, a worship service for people with HIV/AIDS, single-parent/divorce support groups, and a racial reconciliation group.[5] According to the ACTS mission statement, a common goal for each ministry is "the total transformation of individuals in the name of Jesus. [ACTS] seeks to be a prophetic witness of Christ's love to those who suffer from spiritual and physical poverty."

In keeping with the evangelistic thrust of this mission, ACTS ministries emphasize personal development grounded in spiritual transformation. A leader of the ACTS tutoring program for youth at a housing project remarks that he has a problem with ministries "that simply want to look at the living conditions of people and don't want to give the gospel of Jesus Christ. I think the reason you're helping them has to be known to them." Verbal communication of the gospel is essential, because "If they will not hear, how will they believe?" Thus, tutoring sessions begin with a Bible study. At the same time, the ministry leader asserts, putting the gospel into action through service gives credence to the verbal witness. "We want [youth] to understand that the reason that we are there . . . is because [the] Bible that we teach is so real to us that we believe it means living it out." For ACTS volunteers, he continues, living out the Bible means caring for students as whole persons—"making sure that you get good grades, or you learn how to read better, or maybe you need a shoulder to lean on, or someone to talk to."

Tenth has the highest number of evangelism programs (ten) of the churches in the study; seven of these are target-group ministries to specific populations, including college students, Jews, seniors, homosexuals, and international students. Twice as many survey respondents say that bringing others to faith is an essential quality of the Christian life as those who say the same about caring for the sick and needy. Respondents are more likely to talk about their faith with non-Christians than to assist someone in need or to volunteer for a charity outside the church. The church's fundamental dedication to evangelism has roots in its conservative denomination, the Presbyterian Church in America, which promotes biblical inerrancy and the propagation of orthodox faith.[6] The embrace of social ministry represents a relatively late chapter in the church's 170-year history, as Tenth Presbyterian has come to define itself as an urban church with a mission to "reach the city with the Gospel through word and deed." In the experience of David Apple, the director of ACTS ministries, moving from word alone to word *and* deed has required first "converting those who call themselves believers."

Raised in an activist Jewish family, David Apple spoke at civil rights rallies while still in high school. He recounts his salvation experience: "I was saved in a small, black church, through the witness of former drug addicts, recovering alcoholics, former prostitutes, and people who had nothing physically, but showed me that they had everything because of Jesus Christ." Influenced by their example, and by struggles he faced in his own life, he says, "My calling, my passion, is to be available to God to help the poor." He became a social worker with the welfare department but chafed at the restrictions against sharing his faith. In 1988 he joined Tenth Presbyterian Church as director of ACTS, and began mobilizing the congregation to expand their involvement in social concerns.

"Conversion is not only a change of mind or heart as far as a person's convictions and relationship to God are concerned," Dr. Apple writes, "but also a commitment to join what is understood to be God's program of change for the world" (1994, 19). This change agenda is "incarnational," meaning that it is characterized by spiritually transforming personal relationships with those in need: "Just as Jesus became a servant of others, washing others' feet, . . . not being afraid to come alongside people who are hurting, not being afraid of coming alongside someone who may smell—we're called to be advocates, to come alongside and be available." Tenth Presbyterian's outreach to homeless persons strives to emulate this model. At the monthly Community Dinner, about 120 guests are served family-style beside church members who share the meal and the dinner conversation. Church volunteers meet regularly to pray for the material and spiritual needs of homeless beneficiaries. Volunteers also work with homeless individuals, not as case managers but as friends—providing referrals to other service agencies, informal counseling, and invitations to participate in church activities, such as a weekly Bible study designed for "street people," accompanied by a simple meal.

For Tenth Presbyterian, sharing the gospel is a goal of social ministry, and social change is a goal of sharing the gospel. "The bottom line is that our guests, as well as us sinners, need the salvation that's found only in Jesus Christ," Dr. Apple explains. "But in order to establish relationships and trust, so that we can present the gospel, we need to meet the need at hand."

New Covenant Church of Philadelphia

New Covenant, a large African American congregation, occupies a capacious and well-maintained campus in a historic, mostly Anglo urban neighborhood. Its far-flung membership gives credence to its expansive motto of "Touching Philadelphia and Beyond." New Covenant's doctrinal statement declares that Christians are sent by Christ into the world "to be witnesses of His saving grace and that their primary purpose in life should be to glorify God by obedience to our Lord Jesus Christ's command to preach the Gospel to every creature." One way that the church fulfils this purpose is through its home-based Vacation Bible School (VBS) program, in which "great care has been taken to make the Gospel message clear," according to the manual. In the summer of 1997, 110 VBS groups met in locations around the Philadelphia metropolitan area, enrolling over one thousand youth. This decentralized format demanded significant congregational participation, but allowed the church to evangelize far more children.

This explicit and energetic focus on evangelism pervades the church's ministries. In addition to VBS, evangelistic efforts include the distribution of evangelistic tracts on street corners; PowerHouse, a youth-oriented program held in the community center of a low-income neighborhood; occasional evangelistic events featuring Christian musicians and sports celebrities; and twice-monthly worship services at a prison. Ministries keep statistics on how many people are witnessed to and how many "decisions for Christ" are made. Additionally, the church emphasizes network evangelism, the primary vehicle being the extensive system of neighborhood-based cell groups called NetCare—an acronym for "Network of Evangelistic Teams Contacting And Relating to Everyone." New Covenant also joined Lighthouses of Prayer, a national program that encourages families to pray for and evangelize their neighbors.

New Covenant has the second highest number of evangelism programs among our case study churches (second to Tenth Presbyterian), and the fewest social ministries directed outside the congregation. Two of the four social ministries sponsored by New Covenant have an overtly evangelistic intent. Christians United Against Addictions (CUAA) was developed as a Christocentric alternative to Alcoholics Anonymous. CUAA provides a curriculum for recovery groups meeting in churches and homes throughout the Philadelphia area. If non-Christians join a group, "Automatically we introduce them to Christ," says the program's founder. "My personality is that I have to talk about Jesus. That is the personality of the congregation too." Richard Allen Ministries (RAM) began as a rally to introduce the services of CUAA to the residents of Richard Allen Homes, which then had a reputation as the worst housing project in Philadelphia. RAM expanded to include the provision of food, clothing, and children's activities, usually in the context of evangelistic activities such as distribution of Christian literature, Christian concerts, and a worship service at the community center. Over time, the focus of the ministry shifted from short-term relief to more developmental efforts such as a Computer Learning Center. The director began organizing residents around community concerns such as health and public safety. However, the closure of most of the housing project for renovations has put RAM on indefinite hold.

From the lack of programmatic focus on social ministry, one might expect New Covenant members to attach a low priority to social concerns. According to the member survey, however, this is not the case. Showing compassion to needy individuals was selected as an extremely important outreach motivation by more respondents than the desire to bring people to Christ. Respondents were nearly as likely to have provided aid to someone in need as to have talked about their faith with a non-Christian. Although the majority say the church prioritizes evangelism over social ministry, respondents are about equally likely to describe their church as *compassionate* as to describe it as *evangelistic*. The majority affirm that the way to share God's love with people includes caring actions, not only verbally witnessing about Christ. The new member manual calls members "to minister to the physical, social and spiritual needs of those around us."

The seeming discrepancy between New Covenant's social consciousness and its dominant focus on evangelism is clarified by its mission statement: "Reaching and empowering individuals to fulfill God's victorious and prosperous plan for their lives, for their families, and for their communities, through the Lord Jesus Christ." *Empowering* is a central theme at New Covenant, the primary word selected by survey respondents to describe the church. The concept of empowerment encompasses spiritual, physical, relational, and financial prosperity that is rooted in spiritual wholeness, as changes in attitudes and behavior free people from internal barriers to well-being. Evangelism is a priority because this individual empowerment is understood to precede change at the community level. A lay leader explains that social change "takes one heart at a time"; as individuals receive Christ, this produces "a snowball effect on their families, their street." A focus on evangelism thus reflects a strategic investment of resources. Founding paster Milton Grannum remarks: "Community development is not possible unless people are reaching levels of whole-ness. . . . So I don't apologize for putting the spiritual dimension first—it *has* to come first." Social concern is mediated through evangelism and discipleship.

New Covenant's emphasis on individual empowerment does not mean that the church blames poverty on individuals. A quarter of respondents se-lected "better personal morals or lifestyle" as a solution to poverty, in contrast to the nearly three-quarters who selected "a good education and a decent job." At the same time, only 8% say that the task of the church is to work to change society, versus 60% who say the church's role is to change individuals. The lack of attention to social justice on a structural level is not rooted in a lack of compassion or blindness to social issues but, rather, in a deep pessimism about the potential for sociopolitical reform coupled with a belief in the potential of regenerated individuals for prosperity.

This was illustrated by a sermon in which Bishop Grannum harshly crit-icized Supreme Court Justice Clarence Thomas for voting to dismantle affir-mative action. Yet even within an unjust system, he preached, Christians can experience an inner, spiritual empowerment that eventually influences their external circumstances. People "can stop you in the street because your car looks too good or because they don't like the color of the person who's driving the new car. . . . But no one can take away what is in you. It's called empow-erment." The church does not confront racial injustice directly, but frees in-dividuals from the internalized limitations of a racist society. This empower-ment is presented as a quiet, even subversive form of activism. "You will still have to live with the system on your back," Rev. Grannum's sermon continued, but, empowered by Jesus, "you will defy the system."

The parlaying of spiritual conversion into socioeconomic uplift, according to the New Covenant vision, requires diligent discipleship in the context of a supportive church community. In addition to teaching about the biblical path to empowerment, the church offers members significant opportunities for per-sonal and entrepreneurial advancement, including marriage and family sem-inars, financial counseling, leadership development training, job placement services, and a business incubator. The NetCare system of small groups en-courages members to share resources and advancement opportunities with one another. The church provides members a social safety net and equips them to participate wholesomely in society, then charges them with bringing others into the church's circle of care through evangelism.[7]

Conclusion: Mobilizing a Commitment to Faith in Action

Despite the variety in their expressions of ministry, the churches we studied also share striking similarities. The first is a remarkable commitment to the world beyond the walls of the church. Each church instills in its members the belief that being a good Christian means reaching out in mission—though exactly what that mission entails varies considerably. As David Apple of Tenth Presbyterian Church puts it, authentic faith entails "a commitment to join what is understood to be God's program of change for the world" (1994, 19). These churches may conceive of "God's program of change" differently, but they all invest significant resources and energy into bringing it about. The focus on outreach gives these churches a sense of having a unique identity and a compelling reason for their existence. *Traditional* is a word that few congregants selected to describe their church.

A related similarity is the ability of these congregations to mobilize members around their mission. Most often, this comes about through the persistent efforts of pastors who embody, communicate, and advocate for the vision. However a church defines its mission, its execution depends on the ability of leaders to move the congregation to principled affirmation and organized action. As Christian Stronghold Baptist Church instructs its new members, "We're a serving church. If you are going to be a part of this ministry you need to understand we are here to serve, not just to get saved."

PART II

Toward a New
Vocabulary of Faith

4

Perceptions of Spiritual Meaning in Faith-Based Social Action

"I don't look at it as a job. I look at it as a ministry." A woman on staff with a welfare-to-work program at Cookman United Methodist Church shared this comment when explaining why she persevered with a difficult job under less-than-ideal working conditions. But what makes preparing single mothers to gain economic self-sufficiency a ministry? What spiritual meanings do people of faith invest in acts of social care? What is it that gives their work religious significance?

Some meanings derived from social activism are shared by secular and religious folks alike. These include the personal rewards of helping others, such as the good feeling that accompanies altruism; civic values such as good citizenship, fairness, and justice; and guilt or a sense of obligation related to one's good fortune. Each of these may be consistent with a religious ethic without being given a specifically religious interpretation. My ideal of compassion might lead me to volunteer for Habitat for Humanity whether or not I believe in God. But if I am inspired by Jesus' example of self-sacrificial compassion, or if I believe that helping to build homes is God's will for my life, my volunteering takes on an added layer of spiritual meaning.

Humans are "meaning-craving creatures" (C. Smith 1996, 5). People have an elemental hunger to know that their life is guided by something and counts for something beyond self-gratification. Very often they turn to religion to satisfy this longing for self-transcendent meaning (Bellah et al. 1985; Fowler 1991; Hadden 1995; Roof 1996). That which provides meaning is the primal material with which we define our identity, make sense of our experiences, order our priorities, make choices, enter into relationships, and impart values.[1] This concept of spiritual meaning, applied to social ministry, includes but is broader than motivation. Certainly faith has the potential to motivate people to ministry, though such potential is not always realized (Wuthnow 1991 and 1997). Besides influencing the choice of whether to become involved in social action, faith also helps to shape how people define their involvement (e.g., as *ministry* versus *social work*), how they interpret the outcomes of social involvement (e.g., as furthering the kingdom of God versus promoting the American dream), the priority they assign to various social concerns, the spiritual benefits they hope to gain or confer on others through their involvement, and the role of this involvement in forging or fulfilling their personal identity.

The ascription of these multiple layers of spiritual meaning to social ministry is part of the larger religious enterprise that Peter Berger refers to as "world-building." Berger describes religion as "the audacious attempt to conceive of the entire universe as being humanly significant." Rather than accepting things and events at face value, people "pour out meaning into reality" (1967, 28). Though theists and existentialists may debate whether this meaning is revealed by God or created by humans, caring for others is wired into the religious worldview of many people of faith, regardless of how it comes to be so. Acts of compassion and justice, while not sacred in the same way as baptism or the Lord's Supper, may be part of the system of religious significance that orders all of life in relation to the divine and finds expression through these sacred acts.

Those who study social action sometimes regard these religious dynamics like the dark side of the moon. While they know there is more there than meets the eye, they question whether what they cannot see is relevant to what is plainly visible. For those whose primary interest is in social outcomes, it is easy to overlook this mysterious region except as a prop for the bright face of the benefits of faith-based ministry. But understanding faith-based social action entails taking seriously the meanings that people of faith pour into their actions. In his classic *Varieties of Religious Experience*, William James (1902) admonishes: "To describe the world with all the various feelings of the individual pinch of destiny, all the various spiritual attitudes, left out of the description . . . would be something like offering a printed bill of fare as the equivalent for a solid meal" (500). Max Weber writes similarly that, to understand religious acts, one must take into account what they mean to the actor: "The external courses of religious behavior are so diverse that an understanding of this behavior can only be achieved from the viewpoint of the subjective experiences, notion, and purposes of the individuals concerned—in short, from the viewpoint of the religious behavior's 'meaning'" (1963, 1). The next chapter explores the diverse "external courses of religious behavior" that may be associated with faith-based social action. This chapter takes up the range of internal, subjective viewpoints and meanings that individuals invest in this ministry.

Specifically, we consider the question: For people of faith, what makes participation in social ministry *religious* behavior? We map out four broad domains of subjective spiritual meaning attached to social action, particularly among Protestant Christians.[2] The religious character of social action may be *dutiful, empowered, devotional,* or *evangelistic.* In these four modes of meaning, religion provides the mandate for social action, divine agency is seen to be at work through human efforts toward social change, participation in social ministry reflects or enhances the participant's inner spiritual state, and social ministry is intended to open others to new spiritual realities.

Dutiful Ministry: Faith as a Mandate for Social Action

We must practice justice toward one another in order to take care of
God's business on earth . . . as it is in Heaven. (Apple 1994, 17)

A woman who attends Nueva Creación Lutheran Church explained in an interview why she works for an agency that aids immigrants: "Social change comes from an understanding that we are children of God, and that this is not the way God wants things. . . . I became a human rights activist because of my relationship with God—I knew God would not want these things to happen." Her sense of a spiritual mandate gives meaning to her work for social change. As her quote illuminates, this mandate rests on three specifically religious axioms. The first is that God has a plan for the way things *ought* to be. The speaker's sense of "ought-ness" is derived from "an understanding that we are children of God," or the belief that human beings have innate, God-given dignity and rights. A corollary axiom is that the condition of the world does not conform to "the way God wants things." In this speaker's experience, the worth of immigrants in God's eyes contrasts with how immigrants are actually treated. The third axiom is that violations of God's plan call for Christians to respond by taking action. When Christians know that "God would not want these things to happen," their "relationship with God" demands that they get involved in the solution. Dissonance between the biblical vision and actual social realities creates a "holy discontent" (Frenchak 1996, 25) that fuels the imagination and the will for action.

Religious people do not necessarily feel a greater obligation to respond to social needs, and religious obligations do not necessarily generate the most active involvement (Wuthnow 1991). Many people follow the same trajectory without a religious motivation. They see a need that violates their sense of how the world ought to be, and they are moved to take restorative action. But when this determination to act takes place in dialogue with a perception of God's designs and expectations, spiritual meaning adds a layer of depth to the discernment of what is, what could be, and what Christians ought to do about it. A sense of duty to a religious mandate may not be *more* meaningful than secular motivations, but it is *uniquely* meaningful.

The church members we interviewed had different ways of interpreting this duty, guided by different spiritually rooted ideals of the way things ought to be. A compelling spiritual vision may be developed in two dimensions: the personal and the corporate. On the personal level, the vision looks beyond individuals' current state of dysfunction and distress to their God-given worth and potential. "Helping people become the person God wants them to be" was the response of a deacon at First Presbyterian Church when asked about the meaning of social ministry. The corporate level of vision focuses on God's design for the communal life, institutions, or culture of the local community and the broader society. A sermon by Marcia Bailey, co-pastor of Central Baptist Church, challenged members "to imagine the possibility of justice. To imagine the landscape of economic equality. To view with God's heart the interconnectedness of God's global community." Doing what God requires in the world, she preached, requires Christians "to see the big picture of what might be there."

Given their perception that reality falls far short of God's vision for individuals or communities, the corollary for many socially active Christians is that God has enlisted them to do something about it. Bill Borror, pastor of Media Presbyterian Church, voiced this theme emphatically: "God is very clear about wanting us to address the needs of the poor and to comfort those who are hurting." The authority for this religious mandate derives from various sources. Here we highlight five: scriptural commands, Jesus' example, the perception of Christians as instruments of God's work on earth, the interpretation of social problems as spiritual evil, and a sense of personal calling.

The first oft-cited source for social engagement is scriptural commands. A volunteer at Faith Assembly of God summarized the simple logic of this belief: "We're to be a church that's run according to the Word. The Word says that we're to feed the hungry and that we're to clothe the naked." Volunteering for the food and clothing ministry of her church was meaningful, for her, as a way of complying with this scriptural mandate. Many interviewees cited the "Great Commandment" to love your neighbor as yourself (Luke 10:27). The director of Homes of Hope at First Presbyterian Church drew on multiple biblical sources to explain his sense of a theological mandate for community development:

> Isaiah . . . talks about what kind of a fast is to loose the bonds of oppression, to provide the hungry with food, the homeless with shel-

ter. Nehemiah's great conversion [happened] when he was advised by someone who came to Jerusalem and said, 'The city's in ruins, there's no housing.' And he went back and rebuilt the city. And Jesus's words in Matthew 25:40, "If you've done it unto the least of these my brothers, you've done it unto me."

Appropriating these texts gives the director's work of providing affordable housing a spiritual cast, even though the connection is not made explicit in the day-to-day operation of the ministry.

Another commonly cited source of spiritual authority for ministry is Jesus' example. Repeatedly when we probed into why people were involved in social ministry, we were told, in essence, that caring for others was the answer to the popularized question, "What would Jesus do?" A deacon from Media Presbyterian Church gave this explanation:

> Many times when I've delivered food or visited someone after they lost a family member, they will say, "Why are you doing this?" We were providing material needs for a domestic abuse agency in Media—totally material aid, to a totally social service agency. I said, "We're doing this because this is what Jesus did when he was here."

To this interviewee, what set her charitable work apart from the services provided by this secular domestic abuse agency was her conscious imitation of Christ. A similar idea was expressed by the director of Germantown Ecumenical Ministries, which ran an after-school program with minimal religious content at Germantown Church of the Brethren. Explaining the ministry's educational philosophy, he remarked, "You teach them. That's what Jesus did. He taught. He taught people and that's what we need to do." Elevating Jesus as a role model gives participation in social ministry spiritual meaning, even when the program is "totally material" or nonsectarian.

A third source of religious authority for social action is the perception that Christians serve as instruments of God on earth. The 1997 Media Presbyterian Church mission committee report quoted sixteenth-century theologian St. Theresa of Avila to reinforce the importance of local outreach:

> Christ has no body on earth but yours,
> No hands but yours,
> No feet but yours,
> Yours are the eyes through which Christ's compassion is to look out
>   to the world;
> Yours are the feet with which He is to go about doing good;
> Yours are the hands with which He is to bless men now.

The idea that God relies on people to carry out God's work in the world is at once emboldening and humbling. "I'm just human hands for a program that is God's," acknowledged the volunteer coordinator from Central Baptist Church for the Interfaith Hospitality Network. Seeing her activism as an extension of God's own agenda was meaningful to her because it infused the social service with a higher purpose.

The religious imperative of social ministry can also draw on the interpretation of social problems as manifestations of spiritual evil. As David Apple, ministry leader at Tenth Presbyterian Church, asserted: "Poverty is the work of the devil. The function of God's people is the destruction of that work. The church must therefore bring about the end of poverty" (1994, 17). Within this framework, social ministry takes on the character of a crusade. Christians United Against Addictions, a program sponsored by New Covenant, described its work as "spiritual warfare" against the demonic forces that enslave addicts. Other ministries focused on the evil powers substantiated in societal structures that keep people poor. Philadelphia Interfaith Action (PIA), a coalition of congregations organized for social change, frequently used religious language in confronting those in power for failing to uphold their civic responsibilities. By doing so, they overlaid their protest actions with inferences of the righteous wrath of God.

Finally, the sense of duty to a religious mandate may take the form of a personal calling. A speaker at a PIA meeting issued a plea for volunteers for PIA's job-creation efforts. He challenged the assembled delegates: When they heard God summoning them, in the words of Isaiah 6:8: "Who will go?," they should imitate the prophet's response: "Here I am. Send me!" In our interviews, some church ministry leaders reported hearing directly from God that they were being "sent" to participate in a social ministry. Perhaps the most dramatic example came from Central Baptist Church. A member reported having a dream in which God spoke to her, saying: "Feed my sheep." Later, her spiritual mentor told her that many Albanians and South Americans were coming into the community and that they needed to be taught English. Convinced that God was calling her, she responded by starting a program at Central Baptist to teach English as a second language.

Many of those we interviewed expressed the conviction that they were involved in social action because they knew, in one way or another, that God wanted them to do so. They refused to accept the status quo because they believed that God intends something better for individuals and communities. This belief infused their acts of caring with spiritual meaning, although the religious framework might not be explicitly transparent in their ministry. David Apple urged, "We must practice justice toward one another in order to take care of God's business on earth." According to those who share this perspective, seeking justice and showing compassion are, ultimately, God's business.

By participating in faith-based ministries, these believers are not just doing good works—they are doing God's work.

Empowered Ministry: Faith as an Agent of Social Change

When the Lord is in it, it works. (Lay leader, Christian Stronghold Baptist Church)

People of faith involved in social action often see God as the agent of change in individuals, neighborhoods, and society as a whole. Like yeast in dough, God's active presence in social ministries is perceived to expand their impact in a way that transcends the actual social intervention. A divine force is seen to be at work through the compassionate commitments of God's people, giving their work spiritual meaning.

Illustrating this mode of meaning, a lay leader at Christian Stronghold remarked in reference to the church's efforts to encourage home ownership: "When the Lord is in it, it works." Some interviewees claimed that the spiritual transformation of beneficiaries is what makes faith-based ministry "work." This perspective is particularly associated with the personal development program type, which aims to help people overcome internal barriers to empowerment. Other interviewees gave God the credit whenever people were helped, whether the beneficiaries realized God's hand in it or not. In their view, when ministry works—when people experience a better quality of life, when economic or political structures become more equitable—then the Lord must be in it. This latter understanding of divine agency can thus imbue social action with religious meaning even when it is undertaken in a seemingly secular manner.

People of faith also describe turning to spiritual sources to carry out ministry in ways above and beyond their own natural competency. "Act in the power of the God we serve!" urged Fr. Isaac Miller, rector of Church of the Advocate, to a gathering of PIA delegates. For the leader of Christian Stronghold's counseling ministry, acting in God's power entails relying on the Bible and on prayer. When clients present a problem that stumps the counselor, "It's at that moment you really, even while you're listening to them, just start praying for the Holy Spirit to give you wisdom in what to do in the next second." This faith in God's leading enhances counselors' confidence that their efforts will bear fruit. This is not to say that they rely *only* on prayers for the Holy Spirit's guidance to get them through a session. In order to participate in the ministry, counselors undergo at least two years of training, and they are instructed to refer truly difficult cases to professional therapists. But, as this counselor's remarks indicate, they perceive God's Spirit reinforcing their human expertise.

Divine agency is also credited with extending the scope and vitality of human compassion. "The Spirit within us is what and how we were able to get as far as we have come," attested a ministry leader at Church of the Advocate. A community leader who has labored for a decade on development projects alongside Germantown Church of the Brethren similarly credited God as the source of her stamina:

> I tell Pastor [Richard Kyerematen] all the time that he and I work so hard . . . and this church congregation works so hard. I said, "You know, I oftentimes think, where do we get the energy?" And his word all the time to me is, "You know God don't get tired of giving you blessings, and giving you strength, and giving you courage, and giving you good thoughts for your community."

Other interviewees acknowledged God's hand in prodding them into action despite an innate tendency toward selfishness and passivity. One such remark came from a woman who directs social ministries at a large African American church in inner-city Philadelphia. "We volunteer because we know Christ is going to make the difference. If I didn't think . . . that Christ would not meet me here to address every one of these needs, honey, I would be somewhere in Hawaii, just enjoying myself." She laughed. "It overwhelms you in the natural. But when I walk out my door and I know that the Lord has a purpose today, and he wants to touch a life today, I get in a hurry, so I don't miss him." Faith that God was working purposefully through her made her efforts "in the natural" seem meaningful, even exciting.

At Nueva Creación, hope in God's empowering agency was expressed on a grander scale. "Jesus brings *shalom*, which is the restoration of the whole creation," proclaimed Patrick Cabello Hansel. Their community garden serves not only as a source of fresh vegetables but as a living symbol of this promised restoration in the midst of urban decay. Reverend Cabello Hansel drew on the metaphor of a garden to describe the significance of his church's investment in the community: "God is going to transform the world, and we plant little seeds of that, and the church is a gardener. . . . And it's a long process, but I do believe that transformation's coming, and it's coming here." For Rev. Cabello Hansel, social ministry has value and meaning beyond its immediate outcomes as a demonstration plot for God's larger restorative work.

Reverend Marcia Bailey eloquently sounded this confident motif relevant to Central Baptist Church's work for economic justice: "It's God's vision, and with God's love and God's power and God's promise it will happen. . . . If we hold fast to God, then the little we do will be increased beyond anything that we can dream or imagine." This belief in the potency of God's vision for change invigorates the congregation's struggle for social justice.

Devotional Ministry: Social Action and the Spiritual Life
of the Self

*The best way to disciple in the way of Jesus Christ is to have Christians
involved in hands-on ministry. (Rev. Bill Borror, Media Presbyterian
Church)*

Media Presbyterian Church began an annual tradition of sending a group to
North Carolina to "blitz-build" a Habitat for Humanity home for a poor family.
In 1998 about 150 members made the trip. During the Sunday worship service
after their return, participants talked about their experience. One person after
another stood up to share how they had gone with the desire to help someone
else, but, to their surprise, had themselves discovered new spiritual truths and
grown closer to God. Their involvement was more meaningful because of the
religious affect uniquely associated with service (cf. Hugen et al. 2003; Dudley
2002; Bartkowski and Regis 2001; Becker and Dhingra 2001; Jeavons 1994).

Social action can connect with the religious experience of the activist in
several ways. First, social ministry gains a devotional quality through the belief
that compassionate acts open a sacred space where one may find God. A newspaper article about Media's work in the inner city of Chester quoted Rev. Borror: "By doing something visible [to help others] we encounter the invisible—
the spiritual. We believe that you encounter God by loving your neighbor; you
encounter Christ in the eyes of the poor" (Hardy 2001). Here, Rev. Borror was
alluding to the parable of the sheep and the goats in Matthew 25:31–46, in
which Jesus tells those who have labored to provide for the needy that whatever
they have done to "the least of these," they have actually done to him. This
parable surfaced in many of our interviews. One member of Nueva Creación
extended this concept to whole communities, describing how the church ap-
proached its neighborhood "not bringing the presence of God, but more discovering the presence of God that is already here." In this light, community
development takes on the character of a spiritual quest. This approach can
breathe energy and meaning into service by ennobling both the caring act and
those who receive care. No act is too menial to be offered in devotion to Christ,
no person or neighborhood too derelict to host God's presence.

For David Apple, ministry leader at Tenth Presbyterian Church, the spiritual heart of social ministry goes beyond providing services to *being* a Christian
servant. Dr. Apple explained that having the character of a servant means "to
know that God is in charge of our time and our resources and our valuables
. . . To give all those things to God, for his service." The spiritual meaning may
be located not just in actions, but also in the attitude one brings to social
ministry—the affirmation of a life that is dedicated to God and is thus available
to others. In the words of a "Deacon Highlights" column in the Media Pres-

byterian Church newsletter, meeting needs is a way to "show others who rules our lives."

This religious perspective both transforms service into a devotional act and can be transformative to those who act with devotion. Participants in social ministry may believe not only that they encounter Christ in the poor, but that the encounter makes them more like Christ. By serving God in service to the vulnerable, preached co-pastor Marcus Pomeroy at Central Baptist Church, "something is released that makes me freer. More whole and more holy." Interviewees credited their involvement in social action with amplifying desirable spiritual attributes, such as reliance on God, humility, kindness, empathy, patience, and prayerfulness. Ministry experiences also confronted people with their spiritual flaws such as materialism, prejudice, laziness, and the idolatry of comfort. The pastor of a Reformed church said she had come to see the homeless persons whom her church aided as her congregation's spiritual tutors: "We have to serve in order to become Christian. . . . These men remind us that we can't solve problems on our own, that we need God." For this pastor, participation in social ministry had a sacramental quality. One may discover aspects of faith and connect with God *uniquely* through ministry among the poor.

Social ministry provides not only an arena for spiritual illumination but also a symbolic syntax for the expression of religious ideas. A Presbyterian pastor involved with Bread for the World linked advocacy with celebration of Jesus' resurrection: "Easter calls us to act in hope . . . Every letter we write, every action we take as Bread for the World members proclaims, 'Christ is risen!' "[3] For Luisa Cabello Hansel of Nueva Creación, the church's work of cleaning parks and painting over graffiti is one way they worship God the creator, bringing to light "the hand of God, how creative is God, how beautiful is what God creates." Through social ministry, Christians embody their interpretation of God's attributes and actions in the world.

Gratitude to God also links social involvement with spiritual life (see Park and Smith 2000). The First Presbyterian Church "ministry opportunities" brochure displays the motto: "Served By Christ We Serve." The community outreach of First Presbyterian members is prefaced and permeated by their awareness of being beneficiaries of Christ's ministry. Social action can also reflect appreciation for God-given material abundance. "I am middle class," observed a Central Baptist volunteer for Habitat for Humanity. "My family never suffered, tangibly, in any sense. In gratitude, I do this because I have lots and I can afford to do it." Others speak of gratitude for God's deliverance through times of hardship. A woman on staff at a Christian crisis pregnancy center explained why she worked there: "My sister was in a crisis pregnancy, I was in a crisis pregnancy, so I can relate. I had an abortion; my sister had a baby. So it's a very personal thing. I know the forgiveness God has given, and I've gotten healed from that, but I would never want anyone to go through it." Her work acquired spiritual meaning in connection with her own experience of trauma and spiritual healing.

The sacrificial commitment of social involvement is also made meaningful by the anticipation of God's future rewards for faithful service. The director of the private school at Christian Stronghold Baptist Church, for example, said she encourages her staff with the words, "Blessings are on the other side of obedience." According to rational theory explanations for altruism, people choose to give up something of value—money, time, comfort, autonomy—in order to gain something of greater worth (Wuthnow 1991). In a religious framework, this equation takes into account the promise of spiritual blessings both now and in the afterlife.

Evangelistic Ministry: Social Action and the Spiritual Life of Others

> *Commit today to invest your time, talent, and treasure in meeting the felt needs of your "neighbors" and God will open doors for you to speak of the soul's need of the Savior. (First Presbyterian Church newsletter)*

For many practitioners, social ministry is intended to have spiritual outcomes as well as material benefits. "Many people come to us who are not Christians and who don't understand why we do this," said a Media Presbyterian Church member who distributes donated household items to needy families. "You can't make people understand, but you can say, 'We do this as a representation of Christ's love.'" Faith-based social service provision may be animated by the expectation that the experience of receiving care—and, by proxy, "Christ's love"—can foster a new level of awareness of or responsiveness to spiritual realities. For some volunteers, the meaning of social ministry lies in the message that it is intended to send, implicitly or explicitly, to beneficiaries: Jesus loves you, God's Spirit can transform your life, you have worth in God's eyes, you are welcome at this church.

This communication of religious meaning may take place via four different tracks: *implicit spiritual nurture,* in which social ministry wordlessly demonstrates religious truths to beneficiaries; *altruism evangelism,* in which social action improves the community's perception of the church or Christianity; *pre-evangelism,* in which social ministry provides a context for building relationships with non-Christians and issuing invitations to more explicitly religious events; and *integrated evangelism,* in which social service deliberately creates openings for sharing the gospel to beneficiaries.

Many believe that acts of compassion *implicitly* convey religious messages that can serve as a catalyst for beneficiaries' spiritual healing or moral renewal. Some interviewees expect this spiritual dynamic to take place as beneficiaries make the connection between the material aid and its faith-based providers. A leader of a support group for grandparents raising children sponsored by the Church of the Advocate presumed that if these families "know that this group is associated with the church, then they'll know that God works." Others point to the quality of the relationships between caregivers and beneficiaries as the primary carrier of religious significance. In this view, treating beneficiaries with compassion, dignity, and respect has profound spiritual implications. Others ascribe an inherently spiritual quality to the act of social care itself, as an embodiment of God's love and restorative power. As the director of a nonprofit founded by Church of the Advocate mused, "Eventually, somewhere in the world, somebody is coming to the church, or being saved or coming to Christ, because somebody who was of Christ helped them." The religious meaning of social activism, in this view, lies in its potential to unleash spiritual forces that can change a person's heart even without overt religious suasion.

Luisa Cabello Hansel of Nueva Creación brought her artistic talents to bear in organizing youth to paint over graffiti around their neighborhood. She reflected on her rationale for this activity:

> One of the more aggressive ways that people express themselves, their anger, their dissatisfactions, is through graffiti. . . . [Painting] flowers, and butterflies, signs of hope, to me is giving the children a message that life can be better than what they used to see. In my opinion this is absolutely part of our spiritual life.

Just as graffiti is a visible symbol of a despondent inner landscape, according to Luisa Hansel, a change in the physical environment can trigger a renewal of the spirit. Although they were not traditional religious images, she trusted the cheerful murals to speak for themselves to inspire hope in a better future. Her husband Patrick described such efforts as a sign of "the incarnation—that a new creation is here in Christ through Christ's people." The incarnation provides a metaphor for the implicit spiritual meaning of social ministry: like ineffable God taking on corporeal human form, social action enfleshes the intangible essence of the gospel, providing material testimony to intangible spiritual realities.

A second way that community outreach may be seen to enlarge a church's spiritual circle of influence is through *altruism evangelism*. Like implicit spiritual nurture, altruism evangelism looks to the potential of compassionate acts to demonstrate a spiritual message. But here the focus is not the beneficiaries of ministry, but the people who watch from the sidelines—residents of the church's neighborhood, nonchurched volunteers and ministry partners, and members of church volunteers' social networks. Seeking to enhance the appeal of their message in the marketplace of ideas, religious social activists perceive that "the best and perhaps the only way to get these [religious] ideas taken seriously is to *demonstrate* their validity" (Jeavons 1994, 55). By modeling an alternative to the narcissism and negativity of the surrounding culture, social ministry participants hope to upgrade popular perceptions of the church or of Christianity.

For example, after Media Presbyterian Church participated in a well-publicized Habitat for Humanity project, a lay leader described what he hoped would come of it:

> The people that read about it in the newspaper know that we are from a church and they know that we are doing what Jesus taught us to do. . . . When we did our blitz build we got attention and that was good, because [the pastor] was on television talking about why we were doing it. . . . I just hope somebody watched that newscast that may be frustrated with [televangelists] and said, "Hey, maybe all these Christians aren't such bad people after all."

For this leader, the significance of Media's work with Habitat extended beyond the home that the church built to the image of Christianity that the ministry was helping to refurbish. His ultimate goal for the church's service projects is that they lead to evangelistic encounters. "Tell people, tell your neighbors, tell your friends, tell your coworkers what you're doing, and they'll ask you why you're doing it," he advises Media members who participate in outreach. "It's a good opportunity to witness."

The third major track is *pre-evangelism*, a term gleaned from interviews at First Presbyterian Church of Mt. Holly. Pre-evangelism refers to social involvement that paves the way for opportunities to present the gospel more explicitly with beneficiaries. At First Presbyterian, this takes the form of First Focus seminars on topics of mental, physical, or relational health, such as family life or back care. Although the seminars do not feature an explicitly religious message, ministry leaders explain that they create a point of contact with community residents who might never otherwise visit the church. Ministry leaders hope that people who benefit from the seminars might respond to the invitation to attend worship services, and to turn to the church in a time of crisis. To church leaders, the social significance of these pre-evangelistic seminars is enhanced by their potential to fertilize a future evangelistic harvest.

Facilitating relationships of caring and trust with persons in need is an important way that practitioners may see their ministry involvement as pre-evangelism. A staff worker at Bethel Temple Community Bible Church explained his approach to youth outreach: "Just building the relationship is what counts the most. . . . Not forcing Jesus into it, but showing his love and being an example." In his experience, engaging in recreational, educational, and mentoring activities with a young person forged a bond that would eventually open the doors to a spiritual dialogue. The prospect of gaining a hearing for his faith was an assumed undercurrent of his investment into the emotional and developmental needs of youth.

Finally, some practitioners promote the spiritual impact of social ministry through *integrated evangelism*, or service evangelism that directly incorporates religious messages and activities into the provision of aid. Unlike implicit spiritual nurture, integrated evangelism emphasizes proclaiming the gospel as well as demonstrating it. A lay leader at First Presbyterian Church explained: "A lot of people do good—Boy Scouts or Good Samaritans or whatever—but we need to have a verbal witness too, in saying why we're doing things." In her perspective, explicit evangelism is what sets the church's ministry apart from secular efforts to "do good." Joel Van Dyke, co-pastor of Bethel Temple, described social ministries as "a tool the church can use to present the gospel in a holistic fashion. So you present the gospel by providing a house for somebody. You present the gospel by providing emergency aid." When Rev. Van Dyke looked at the church's community ministries, he saw the provision of housing and emergency relief as only part of the picture. The significance of these ministries lay equally in the provision of a vehicle for the presentation of the gospel. Such a view does not diminish the importance of material aid, but it alters the church's perception of the meaning of this aid. This is evident in the way Bethel labeled its drug program an "addictions discipleship center." Reverend Van Dyke explained, "We stay away from the word rehab because that's not really what we are doing. We aren't [rehabilitating] them, we are discipling addicts."

Parallels between Social Ministry and Evangelism

One discovery that arises from this survey of the spiritual meanings invested in social action is that they are analogous to the meanings supporting evangelism. Interviewees drew on similar concepts, even similar language, to describe the significance of sharing their faith as they did for addressing social needs: God commands us to evangelize; God enables us to do evangelism and brings about the outcomes; witnessing to others enriches our own faith and expresses our gratitude and obedience to God; and (of course) evangelism can enhance the spiritual life of beneficiaries.

Church members discussed evangelism as a mandate grounded, like social ministry, in Scripture, Jesus' example, and in the exhortation voiced by Rev. Lou Centeno that "you are God's vessel, God's instrument." For one ministry leader at Christian Stronghold, the "bottom line" for evangelism is that "we know that that is what we have been instructed to do" by the Bible. Asked about the reason Christian Stronghold engaged in social ministry, Rev. Willie Richardson stated, "Jesus says that they will see our good works and will glorify [God]." A ministry leader at Tenth Presbyterian used similar language to describe the "ultimate goal" of evangelism: "To bring people to worship God and glorify him." Both evangelism and social action can derive from the understanding that God directs Christians to express their faith actively in the world in order to bring about God's design for humanity and, ultimately, to give God the glory.

The theme of God's agency provides another area of common language. A ministry leader at Christian Stronghold explained her confidence in their evangelistic efforts by ascribing their outcomes to God. "We as Christians . . . cannot save people. We can only invite them to open their minds to a knowledge of Jesus and plant the seeds—the harvest comes from the Holy Spirit." Luisa Cabello Hansel drew on similar organic growth imagery in assessing the long-term impact of their work with youth in the community. Faith requires that they plant the seed and trust that God is working through their efforts, she said, even though the process remains mysterious—like a plant growing under the ground.

Both social ministry and evangelism may be linked to personal spirituality. In a sermon at Life in Christ, Dickie Robbins insisted that "the only way to serve God is through serving people." Christians express their gratitude to God through compassionate ministry to those on the margins of society. "God died for us and lives through us. What does he get out of it? For us to serve the ones he cares so much for." A lay leader at Life in Christ expressed a parallel conception of the relationship between personal faith and evangelism. "Sharing the gospel increases your faith. It draws you closer to God. It keeps you constantly reminded of what Christ has done in your own life. . . . It keeps your heart humble."

Leaders at two very different congregations pointed to gratitude to God as an underlying current of both social ministry and evangelism. When the researcher asked a lay leader at Germantown Church of the Brethren what motivated him to get involved with the church's full slate of community outreach, he responded, "For me, that's the easiest one you asked all day!" He continued, "It's my opportunity to express my gratitude back to my Savior for the love he has expressed to me and the salvation of my soul and the forgiveness of my sins." A staff member at First Presbyterian used similar language in describing why she participates in an evangelism ministry. "I realized that God had done so much for me and I really wanted to share it with all the people around me, so I became part of our Outreach Evangelism program in the church."

These pairings tell us that whether they are reflecting on social ministry or on evangelism, practitioners of religious outreach draw from the same well of religious ideas. Christian faith generally teaches that we should be gratefully obedient to God, that stepping out to act on our beliefs helps us grow in our faith, and that we have to trust the results of our efforts to God. This also suggests that the motivations for service and witness may be mutually reinforcing.

Relationships between the Modes of Meaning

The modes of spiritual meaning, summarized in figure 4.1, are not mutually exclusive. A congregation might agree in principle that each of these areas are important, even though not every theme appears in the rhetoric and practice of its ministry. These four themes are building blocks that faith-based organizations or individual volunteers can assemble in various ways to construct a meaningful experience of social action (Hart 1992). It is the selection and combination of meanings that gives a faith-based ministry its distinctive character. "Though we force no religious observance on those we serve, we are a community of faith and that is the call of faith that inspires us," states a Church of the Advocate brochure. Advocate emphasizes the theme of dutiful ministry while distancing itself from evangelistic ministry. At Media Presbyterian Church, Rev. Borror also highlights the religious mandate for their ministry, while downplaying the motif of spiritual empowerment for social outcomes: "We work with the poor because that is who Jesus is and what he calls us to do, not because we are going to be successful."

An example of how ministries blend meanings comes from the Christian Anti-Drug Dependency Coalition (CADDC), a consortium of church-sponsored substance abuse programs organized by the pastor of Germantown Church of the Brethren. CADDC's mission statement sounds the theme of dutiful ministry: "Challenging the Church to mobilize its spiritual, human, and financial resources to stem the tide of the drug epidemic." The empowered and evangelistic ministry motifs are front and center in its ministry philosophy: "The restoration and solidification of recovering addicts' relationships with their Maker through Jesus Christ is the key to unlocking each person's potential to

---

FIGURE 4.1 Perceptions of Spiritual Meaning in Social Services

1. Dutiful ministry: God mandates involvement in social ministry.
The spiritual meaning centers around the misalignment between social realities and God's will, and the duty of people of faith to work toward different social conditions.

2. Empowered ministry: God is an empowering agent of social change.
The spiritual meaning centers around God's activity in the world, through people of faith, that brings about different social conditions.

3. Devotional ministry: Social ministry enhances or expresses the spiritual life of the participant.
The spiritual meaning centers around the personal religious experiences associated with involvement in social action.

4. Evangelistic ministry: Social ministry enhances the spiritual life of others.
The spiritual meaning centers around intended spiritual outcomes for the beneficiary or the broader community.

---

live in total and permanent victory." The devotional aspect of social ministry is absent from descriptions of this program.

A contrasting blend of meaning modes is illustrated by New Community Corporation, an extensive community development nonprofit in Newark, New Jersey (Linder 2001, 156). The founder, William Linder, affirms that faith is deeply rooted in the organization's history and purpose: "Without its religious center, NCC would not exist." Linder describes "three interrelated and indispensable dimensions of religion" in their work of community development:

> As a source of community, religion answers the question, "Who are we?" NCC's answer is that we are God's people. We find our identity not merely in our separate selves, but in the fact that we belong to one another and to God. As a source of vision, religion answers the question, "Where are we going?" NCC's answer is that we are on a prophetic journey in a direction that God's design has revealed. As a source of empowerment, religion answers the question, "How is God's design to be fulfilled?" NCC believes that the way to reach our goals is to struggle for justice and reconciliation in ways that strengthen and call upon those who most need God's love and His gifts. Our organizational mission and strategy thus combines all three elements and articulates the centrality of religion to our work: "To help residents of inner cities improve the quality of their lives so that they reflect their God-given dignity and personal achievements."

The three questions correspond neatly to three of the modes of spiritual meaning. The way NCC defines its identity highlights the devotional aspect of ministry, in amplifying participants' sense of belonging to God and to a community of faith. The second and third questions—"Where are we going?" and "How is God's design to be fulfilled?"—illustrate the dimensions of faith as visionary mandate and empowering agent. Although the organizational mission is not overtly evangelistic, it includes the intention that beneficiaries realize their "God-given dignity," an expression of implicit spiritual nurture.

For both CADDC and NCC, faith is meaningfully related to the program's goals of social change. However, this relationship takes on a quite different cast depending on whether it entails explicitly promoting spiritual transformation in beneficiaries. NCC affirms that God's power works through those who struggle prophetically for justice in accordance with God's revealed design. Their faithful efforts can implicitly convey to "those who most need God's love" a sense of their God-given dignity. CADDC, in contrast, explicitly encourages addicts to strengthen their relationship with Christ as the "key" to their victory over addiction. For NCC, the main role of faith is that it leads people into a journey of social action; for CADDC, the role of faith is that it produces social outcomes by fostering spiritual transformation.

Examining the religious meanings attached to social action thus helps us understand how faith-based programs are different from one another and what they share in common. It is striking from the examples presented in this chapter that churches share spiritual meanings across boundaries of denomination, race, class, and other delimiting characteristics. While the churches in our sample were quite diverse, they drew on a similar pool of religious concepts in describing what their social ministry meant to them. On the other hand, as the contrast between NCC and CADDC illustrates, these shared meanings are embedded in the broader mission and identity of a religious organization in distinctive ways.

This analysis helps us understand the ambiguity often clouding the discourse on faith-based social ministry. By saying its service is faith-based, one group may mean primarily that its caring religious staff demonstrates God's love to beneficiaries. Another may view faith-based service as a vehicle for explicit evangelism. Being faith-based to another group may mean that they look to God for their motivation and strength to serve. Yet another may emphasize the personal spiritual fulfillment they derive from social engagement. For all of these groups, the work of feeding the hungry or building affordable housing has a transcendent significance, but they interpret that significance differently. Because of the diversity of spiritual meanings associated with social activism, people may speak the same language but mean quite different things.

Conclusion: Secular Actions, Sacred Meanings?

Religion in its broadest sense embraces "solutions to questions of ultimate meaning" which presume the existence of a supernatural power involved with the natural world (Stark and Bainbridge 1979, 119). In this sense, any aspect of social action based on postulates of ultimate meaning of a supernatural order (such as the belief that God commands people to feed the hungry) has religious significance. This includes activities that on the surface appear secular (such as serving a hot meal to someone in need), in which the religious dimension is not intrinsic to the action itself but lies in the meaning attached to it. While faith-based and secular activism often look similar in terms of the goods or services provided, they may be shaped by significant differences in what this involvement *means* to activists—what motivates them to participate, how they define the need, what spiritual outcomes they are hoping for, what they believe makes their work effective, and how it is fulfilling to them personally.

For a religious volunteer, a bag of groceries offered to a hungry family may also be a gesture of grateful worship offered privately to God. Organizing a protest against government policy may be an act of spiritual warfare against the evil powers that sustain systemic injustice. These meanings are hidden to observers, unless they are explicitly disclosed. Similarly, a ministry's spiritual impact on beneficiaries may not be readily apparent. An associate pastor at

First Presbyterian Church described how the church's community luncheon affected a homeless man who regularly attended:

> He says nothing to no one. . . . You have no idea what's getting
> through to [him]. . . . I don't know if anything will happen in spiri-
> tual terms with him but I have to believe in a bigger picture of
> God's economy that something spiritual is happening just by [his]
> feeling that "This is a safe place for me to go. . . . Nobody is going to
> hurt me here."

Despite the man's impassivity, the pastor trusted that God was moving in his life simply through the experience of feeling valued and safe. By its very nature, religion is concerned with what cannot be seen except through the eyes of faith. This makes religion a sometimes uneasy partner with the current trend toward objective documentation and quantitative evaluation of results.

Social ministry has a dual nature as both socioeconomic transaction and spiritual venture. It is "faith in action," as captured by the name of the com-mittee for local mission at Media Presbyterian Church. Christians disagree over the extent to which others must acknowledge the role of faith to appreciate the action. The visionary Catholic activist Dorothy Day held that Christian social service cannot be properly understood without attention to the spiritual life that animates it. "We feed the hungry, yes," she said. "We try to shelter the homeless and give them clothes, but there is strong faith at work; we pray. If an outsider who comes to visit us doesn't pay attention to our praying and what that means, then he'll miss the whole point" (quoted in Forest 1995, 22). In contrast, Boston pastor Rev. Eugene Rivers—a man of equally strong and active faith—once insisted that the point is whether faith-based services pro-duce public goods, not how religious particularities influence this process. "For us, at the end of the day, serving the needs of the poor is the priority. And that's not about religion, it's about results" (Rivers 2001, 95).

Providers of faith-based services also disagree whether beneficiaries should be made explicitly aware of the religious dynamics underlying the aid they receive. Programs that emphasize themes of empowered or evangelistic min-istry tend to verbalize the spiritual truths that can transform people's social status or spiritual condition. This viewpoint is represented by a staff member at Christian Stronghold: "Everything we do is evangelism in nature. . . . You look at the outreach in our community, and you say, 'Well, how is that reaching people for Christ?' People become very curious why you are helping them. It gives us an opportunity to change the conversation to Christ." Unless the con-versation is directed to Christ, this leader implies, a central spiritual meaning of this service may be lost. In contrast, for programs that emphasize themes of dutiful or devotional ministry, the locus of the spiritual meaning is internal to those who engage in social action—whether the stirring of their social con-science in response to God's call to justice and compassion, or the enrichment of their own spiritual life through activism. These private meanings do not depend on public disclosure. In fact, for some, the devotional quality of their service may be compromised by calling attention to religious motives.

Good works which are ostensibly secular may be saturated with personal religious significance, even when the religious meanings attached to these public acts remain implicit and privately held. Yet for some, the significance of Christian social activism is not wholly fulfilled unless the spiritual dimension of this action is explicitly articulated. The divergence between these two positions is at the heart of much of the debate over the proper role of religious expression in faith-based social services. The next chapter examines the ways that a spiritual dimension may be publicly expressed in social ministry.

5

Religious Elements of Faith-Based Social Programs

As previous chapters have suggested, service evangelism reflects the intention that social programs convey a religious message and provide spiritual care to those served. This chapter[1] examines the ways that specifically religious content may be incorporated into the methodology and program design of social ministries.

Categories of Religious Program Elements

Religious elements of social service programs are activities or messages that serve to create a religious environment, convey religious values, communicate religious beliefs to beneficiaries, engage beneficiaries in religious rituals, or bring spiritual resources to bear on social problems. Jeavons refers to this religious program content as the use of *spiritual technologies* in the production of social benefits (1998). While behind-the-scenes organizational dynamics such as religious preferences in staff selection can have a significant impact on a program's religious nature, the focus here is limited to activities and attributes that may be directly encountered by beneficiaries. This narrower model allows for a more detailed exploration of religious program content.

Religious program elements, as defined here, are *explicitly* religious in nature. They include activities and verbal messages which are, on their surface, intrinsically religious. This is not to negate the importance of other program dynamics that *implicitly* convey religious identity and meaning, as discussed in the previous chapter.

Implicit religious elements include program content derived from religious teachings (without explicitly stating the source), religious beliefs that motivate the service of staff and volunteers, religious values that foster attitudes of care and respect for beneficiaries, the intention that the program serve as an expression of God's love and justice, and the desire of staff and volunteers to grow closer to God through acts of compassion (see Jeavons 1994). A program may be infused with these types of implicit, nonverbal qualities while outwardly appearing similar to programs with no faith affiliation. Unless the connection to religion is made explicit, beneficiaries may experience a faith-based program without awareness of its basis in faith.

The differentiation made here between implicit and explicit religious features draws on the distinction that some make between the terms *spiritual* and *religious*. (We have not made this distinction in our use of these terms, but the analysis is helpful.) Canda defines the former as the "basic human drive for meaning, purpose, and moral relatedness among people, with the universe, and with the ground of our being," and the latter as an "institutionally patterned system of beliefs, values, and rituals" (1989, 573; also Sherwood 1998). In this sense, aspects of a social service program (such as convictions which motivate staff) may have a *spiritual* dimension without finding specifically *religious* expression (Ressler 2002). As the last chapter pointed out, the act of serving a meal, for example, may be a profound spiritual experience for the server, yet might not be interpreted as a religious activity by the one being served. Conversely, activities which are unmistakably religious, such as prayer, may or may not carry spiritual meaning for participants. This chapter focuses on programmatic features that are self-evidently *religious*.[2]

Thus defined, religious program elements fall into nine basic categories:

1. Religious references in program self-descriptions
2. Objects with religious associations in the program environment
3. Invitations to a religious service or activity
4. Prayer
5. Use of sacred texts
6. Worship
7. Sharing of personal testimonies
8. Religious teachings or discussions
9. Invitations to a personal commitment to faith or spiritual renewal.

Table 5.1 provides an example of each category of religious element from the fifteen case studies.

The first category involves the self-identification of a program as religious in descriptive materials, such as mission statements, program brochures, or the name of the program. The brochure for Transitional Journey, a welfare-to-work program of Cookman United Methodist Church, presented its identity as a "Christ-Centered Job Development Program."[3] References to religion may

TABLE 5.1 Religious Elements of Social Service Delivery

Type	Examples
Religious self-descriptions	• Including in the Jobs Partnership mission statement the goal of helping persons experience "wholeness through relationship with Jesus Christ" (Koinonia/Germantown) • Naming a youth mentoring program G.O.D. (Generation of Destiny) (Life in Christ)
Religious objects in the program environment	• Having posters with religious themes in the space where the GED class meets (Tenth Memorial) • Playing Christian music in the background at a pregnancy center (First Presbyterian)
Invitation to religious service/activity	• Inviting parents of children in the after-school program to attend church services (Nueva Creación) • Distributing flyers listing church ministries and special events along with food bags (Faith)
Prayer	• Saying Grace before a soup kitchen meal (Advocate) • Asking people who receive health services if they would like prayer for any other personal needs (Bethel/Tenth Presbyterian)
Use of sacred texts	• Quoting the Bible in Jobs Partnership materials and classes (Koinonia/Germantown) • Starting youth tutoring sessions with a Bible study (Tenth Presbyterian)
Worship	• Singing religious songs with guests at a soup kitchen after the meal (Media) • Starting the day at a church-based elementary school with "praise and worship" time (Christian Stronghold)
Personal testimony	• Giving your faith testimony at a drug rehab support group (Life in Christ) • Sharing with homeless persons how prayer has helped you through stressful times (Central Baptist)
Religious teaching/discussion	• Teaching classes on spiritual topics (e.g., "How to Live the Christian Life") in a substance abuse recovery program (Faith) • Holding informal religious discussions with youth in the context of educational/recreational activities (Bethel)
Invitation to personal faith commitment	• Preaching evangelistic sermons and handing out tracts in conjunction with food and clothing give-aways (New Covenant) • Encouraging a resident in a transitional living program for ex-offenders to turn to God for help changing her life (Cookman)

Source: Unruh 2004

take the form of allusions to a biblical image or story, such as the Nehemiah Homes project supported by a coalition of churches, named after the prophet who led the rebuilding of Jerusalem. Interestingly, very few of the programs in our sample had self-evidently religious names. Nor did a lack of religious language in the mission statement always indicate the absence of other religious elements. As Ebaugh et al. (2003) discovered in their research, about a quarter of organizations that call themselves faith-based do not include religious references in their statement of purpose.

The second category is the presence of objects with religious associations in the program space. Objects come in several forms: sacred images or icons, such as a cross, a menorah, or paintings of scenes from religious history; verbal messages, such as a plaque of the Ten Commandments or a poster featuring a Bible verse such as "All things are possible with God—Mark 10:27"; and religious music played in the background, as an auditory rather than visual "object." The program space itself also may be considered a religious object if its main function is for sacred purposes, such as a worship sanctuary. The Transitional Journey handbook instructed students in the decorum befitting the program's setting: "Please remember we are located in a church. Always wear appropriate undergarments; please do not wear clothing that is very tight; please do not wear clothing that is revealing. . . ." For some programs, the presence of religious objects is an incidental byproduct of being housed in a church. Other programs intentionally use religious objects to craft a religious environment as an aid in nurturing the faith of beneficiaries. For instance, staff may place religious reading material in a waiting room for beneficiaries to read or take home.

The third type of religious element, invitation to a religious event or resource, serves as a bridge between social service delivery and activities of a specifically religious nature. Invitations may come in oral or printed form, separately or bundled with other items or information given to beneficiaries (such as a calendar of church events tucked into a food bag), and in various degrees of intensity—from *informing* to *encouraging* to *coercing*. When Central Baptist Church hosted homeless families for a week at a time as part of the Interfaith Hospitality Network, guests were told that they were welcome to attend Sunday worship services, but no special effort was made to follow up on the invitation. Cookman United Methodist Church staff often went a step further, as a former resident of a transitional housing program for recovering substance abusers described: staff "invited us to Bible Study, and if we didn't have a ride, they would sometimes give us car fare and invite us along to special activities." The event to which beneficiaries are invited may be part of the sponsoring church's regular activities (e.g., worship services, youth group, etc.), or it may be an event designed specifically for beneficiaries. An example of the latter comes from a welfare-to-work program in a church where we conducted a supplemental interview. The government-funded program curriculum was secular—but, said the pastor, "the lunch break is a whole other ball game!" Clients were invited to a free lunch funded by the church, during which the pastor led a Bible study.

The fourth religious programmatic element is prayer: prayer *for* beneficiaries, whether spontaneously in response to personal needs that beneficiaries share with staff, or as a regular part of a counseling or educational session; prayer *alongside* beneficiaries, as in a prayer before a meal or at the opening of a program; and prayer *by* beneficiaries, as, for example, in the Transitional Journey self-esteem class, which gave students the option of volunteering to lead a prayer at the start of class. Prayers may be improvised or liturgical, and may function to express gratitude, appeal for divine intervention or blessing, invite personal or social change, empower and guide caregivers, or communicate religious messages indirectly to beneficiaries. A staff member at First Presbyterian's counseling center observed that beneficiaries often agreed to prayer even when they turned down an explicitly Christian approach to counseling: "No one has ever said they don't want to pray with me."

The fifth religious element involves the use of material from a sacred text (e.g., the Bible), quoted or cited in conversations or printed materials, either with commentary or standing alone, presented to beneficiaries or studied interactively with beneficiaries. Sacred texts invoke an authority outside the speaker to shed light on the social need at hand, to offer comfort or guidance, to assert a moral principle, or to call attention to a spiritual need. The welcome page of the Transitional Journey handbook, for example, set an optimistic tone by expounding on a passage from the New Testament:

> Philippians 4:13 says, "I can do all things through Christ which
> strengtheneth me." We believe that if both you as students, and we
> as staff, keep our hearts and minds focused on the Lord Jesus
> Christ, through Him, we will indeed be able to do all things.

Worship is the sixth category. Singing, liturgy, and religious ritual are common features of worship services. Worship services certainly may also include other religious elements—prayer, the reading of sacred texts, religious teachings—but they further have the unique purpose of directing praise and reverence toward God, or sharing expressions of faith in God. As an example, Transitional Journey's curriculum included an optional weekly worship service. The church also held a baptism service in conjunction with the first graduation ceremony for several women who had become Christians in the course of the program.

The use of testimonies, the seventh type of religious programmatic element, means sharing faith from personal experience, often highlighting the role that one's faith has played in helping with needs similar to those of beneficiaries. A Transitional Journey staff member brought her life experience as a sight-disabled, former welfare recipient into her work with the students:

> Because I've been there . . . is why we can relate to them. But we
> can also say you don't have to stay there. And that's what I say to
> my ladies all the time. Folk will say to me because of my vision,
> "How do you do that?" "Me and God. Every day. . . . Didn't I tell you
> I was a child of the King?"

Testimonials speak of faith in the subjective, stopping short of directing to listeners what *they* should believe, though that message may be implied. This is often perceived as an important distinction, as expressed by a volunteer at the Interfaith Hospitality Network program for homeless families at Central Baptist Church: "It is appropriate to say, 'When I am stressed I light candles and meditate, or I pray and give my burden to God.' But it is not appropriate to say, 'Let me tell you about Jesus.'"

Religious teachings, the eighth category, are more propositional, presenting truth-claims of a religious nature. Use of religious narratives also falls in this category, such as referring to the story of Jesus multiplying the loaves and fishes to reassure someone in financial distress of God's provision. Religious instruction may overlap with the use of sacred texts, but is a broader category because teachings may invoke general biblical principles rather than referencing specific citations. Often teaching is done in a formal setting such as a sermon, devotional, counseling session, or class. Religious teachings can take place more informally as well, as when a Transitional Journey client dropped by the office in a time of personal crisis and staff workers assured her of God's enduring love. Regardless of whether religious content is part of the official curriculum, staff have many opportunities to interject religious teachings: when beneficiaries raise a question with theological implications, ask for advice, or share their own faith perspective; when a beneficiary's behavior or attitude contradict the religious values of the program; or when tragedy strikes a beneficiary's family, community, or nation. A lay leader at Germantown Church of the Brethren described how religious teachings entered into their summer camp for inner-city youth:

> Our counselors are from the church, and we talked a lot in our staff training that they should feel free to use their nurturing occasions to help the children to understand biblical principles. There were numerous opportunities on the playground . . . where kids would be asking about some situations that they were going through, and we had the opportunity to point them to the principles that Christ taught in the Scriptures.

Besides these informal occasions, he noted that the "virtue" class that was part of the curriculum often sparked a religious discussion.

Religious teachings can come in several forms—conversations, printed materials, videos—but they have in common the verbal communication of religious ideas. The purpose of religious discussion can be to instruct listeners in particular religious doctrines (e.g., the divinity of Christ), or it may be to present information relevant to the social service from a religious perspective (Jeavons 1998). An example of the latter comes from the Transitional Journey brochure, which stated:

> What is God's vision for your life?
> 1. To build confidence and self esteem through the world of work.
> 2. To become independent and self-reliant.

3. To help you progress from transition to transformation.
4. To help you on your journey as you discern God's vision for your life.

Items 1–3 in the above list are not religious doctrines, but they are linked to religion by being framed as "God's vision for your life." Thus church-based programs can blur the line between secular and sacred by attaching concepts which are not, on their face, religious (such as confidence and self-esteem) to religious precepts (such as God's having a plan for your life). On the other hand, transmitting religiously derived values (such as honesty or respect for authority) without identifying their religious roots does not constitute explicitly religious instruction.

The final category, an invitation to personal faith commitment, moves from presenting religious truth-claims to asking beneficiaries to respond to these claims. This category, particularly in evangelical contexts, corresponds most closely with what many would mean by "proselytizing." The line between religious instruction and proselytizing is sometimes a nuanced one, but the key distinction is whether the religious discussion is brought to the personal level and framed in terms of a decision. This element involves laying out a set of beliefs or course of action intended to lead the beneficiary to a spiritually transforming experience. This may take several forms—a one-time act of conversion, a rededication to the faith, a commitment to change one's behavior or lifestyle in response to religious teachings, or an experience of spiritual renewal in a more general sense. The optional Transitional Journey spirituality class encouraged students to personalize the religious instruction. In one session, students read a workbook chapter called "Salvation," which included this exhortation:

> What are some ways you "miss the mark" with your family, your friends, your relationship with God? Have you confessed your mark-missing nature to God and asked God to come into your heart and direct your life? Do you feel you understand what it means to be able to say, "I've been saved by grace"? (Dunn 1998, 28)

The class instructor complemented the text by giving students an opportunity to ask Christ for salvation.

Descriptive Variables across Religious Elements

The above categories delimit the range of activities or expressions of an explicitly religious nature in the context of social service provision. These religious programmatic elements are further distinguished by a set of seven descriptive variables. The categories frame the *what* of religious program content;

these variables depict *how* this content is presented. Religious elements that fall into the same category can be encountered by beneficiaries in quite different ways. The first two variables address the relationship of religious elements to the overall design of the social service program. The next five describe the manner or style in which religious elements are manifest.

First, religious elements may or may not be *mandatory*. (It should be noted that this variable, like the other six, will not apply to every type of element—it does not make sense, for example, to ask whether the religious content in self-descriptive materials is mandatory.) Some programs mandate only that beneficiaries be present for the religious component, while others require them to play a more active role. When guests at Tenth Presbyterian Church's Community Dinner were asked to sit through a prayer before the meal, they were not compelled to participate personally in the act of prayer so much as to be present for it. In contrast, Faith Assembly of God's transitional housing program for recovering addicts required residents to spend time praying and reading the Bible, give their testimony in evangelistic open-air services, meet with a spiritual counselor, fast, and engage in other acts of personal religious devotion. In the programs we observed, as these two examples illustrate, mandatory religious dynamics typically involved either a one-time or minor benefit like a free meal, or an intensive program of personal change like substance abuse recovery in which religious transformation is seen as integral to the social outcome. Mandatory religious activity also often appeared in programs for children, such as day care and summer camp, which had Christian education as part of their purpose.

Second, religious elements vary in their *relationship to the structure of the social service program*. This relationship can take three basic forms. A religious element may be integrated into the formal program design as a planned, routine part of the program. A religious element can occur regularly as a separate and supplemental segment of the program, outside the bounds of activities directly related to social service provision. Or an element can occur informally, having a more spontaneous or relational quality. The food ministry of Faith Assembly of God incorporated all three forms. The church provided clothing and bags of groceries to low-income households three days a week, and served a hot lunch twice a week. Before staff began handing out food bags, they would invite those present to join hands in a "prayer circle." Requests were shared, and then a staff person prayed. While optional, the prayer circle was a formal, routine element of the food bag program. After the food bag distribution hours and before a hot lunch was served, a worship service was held in the sanctuary upstairs. The worship service was separate and supplemental to the food bag program, removed in time and space from the social aid; those who received groceries were invited to attend, but many did not. Informal religious elements were also an important aspect of the food ministry. Conversations with people who came for food often led to prayer and religious discussions, particularly when people arrived in distress. Encouraging evangelistic relationships was, in fact, an overt goal of the food program, illustrating that informal religious elements, while unscheduled, are not necessarily unintentional.

The third variable is the *relevance* of religious inputs to the social service benefit provided by the program (Jeavons 1998). This variable does not examine the impact of religion on outcomes—that is a separate matter—but rather the *topicality* of the religious content. In some cases, the religious content is directly pertinent to the desired benefit, as in a teen pregnancy prevention program that teaches the Judeo-Christian moral basis for abstinence. In other cases, the relevance of the religious component is more indirect. Reverend Donna Jones, the pastor of Cookman United Methodist Church, explains one way that religious teachings help women make a successful transition from welfare:

> The Sisters of Faith curriculum that we use is trying to build that inner strength, so that when the stressors come, people have some tools that they can use to manage the stress. . . . It's that curriculum that is going to sustain them when the kid is sick, the boss is calling, they have to work overtime, and they have to take the third shift.[4]

For the most part, the religious content of Transitional Journey did not relate directly to learning computer skills or preparing for a job; rather, its stated role was to help beneficiaries build the inner resources to apply these social benefits more effectively.

Fourth, religious elements vary in the *specificity* of the beliefs and values they express. Do elements convey a specific set of religious beliefs rooted in a particular religious tradition, or do they affirm "faith" in a more general sense? In the Transitional Journey program, this distinction was evident between the self-esteem class (which was mandatory), and the Sisters of Faith spirituality class (which was optional). The self-esteem class drew on religiously rooted concepts such as humanity's God-endowed dignity. However, the texts and teachings were not specific to Christianity, and they were not designed to lead students to embrace one particular faith. The class encouraged beneficiaries to develop their spiritual side, but left open how they defined spirituality. The material in the Sisters of Faith class, in contrast, taught explicitly evangelical Christian doctrine. The instructor articulated the hope that students would experience spiritual renewal through a profession of faith in Christ.

A fifth factor is that religious elements can be *corporate* or *individual;* that is, they can involve interactions with beneficiaries either as a group or one-on-one. At one church's hot meal program, two approaches to presenting the Christian gospel came into conflict. One lay leader favored preaching a sermon to all the dinner guests as they ate. The pastor preferred having volunteers sit around the dinner tables to engage beneficiaries in conversation on religious topics one-on-one. The leaders agreed on the content of the religious message, but disputed the most appropriate method for presenting it. This illustration points to a common pattern observed in the churches of formal corporate religious elements and informal individual elements. At Tenth Presbyterian Church, religious elements that were built into the structure of social pro-grams—prayer before meals, Bible studies at youth tutoring, invitations to church services at English classes for foreign students—tended to be addressed to beneficiaries as a group. At the same time, volunteers were encouraged to develop personal relationships with beneficiaries that could lead to spontane-ous one-on-one evangelistic interactions.

The sixth variable is the *frequency* of religious elements. Youth events at Bethel Temple Community Bible Church almost always incorporated a reli-gious presentation, while Germantown Church of the Brethren's Youth Nights featured religious discussion topics on an occasional basis. Religiously themed posters were conspicuous at Christian Stronghold Baptist Church's day care, but only a few were displayed at the day care at Central Baptist Church. The grandparents-as-parents support group at Church of the Advocate opened meetings regularly with prayer; a similar support group at Media Presbyterian Church included prayer only when a crisis situation arose.

Finally, a religious element may be encountered in varying degrees of *intensity*. Intensity derives from the prominence of the religious aspect (print-ing a Scripture passage in small type on a certificate of literacy training com-pletion versus using the Bible as a literacy textbook), the degree of intentionality or personal involvement that program staff invest into the religious activity (displaying flyers announcing a Bible study on a bulletin board in program space versus personally inviting beneficiaries to the study), or the extent to which the program encourages beneficiaries to participate in the religious ex-perience (talking about the value of prayer versus asking a beneficiary if he or she would like to pray with you now). Other variables can also contribute to intensity; elements which are mandatory, faith-specific, one-on-one, or fre-quent may be perceived as being more intense.

Religious Integration Strategies

As indicated by the previous two sections on the categories of religious ele-ments and their descriptive variables, social service programs face a range of options for what religious content will be included in the program and how it will be presented. The analysis now moves to a closer consideration of the ways that social service programs may incorporate this religious content. The first two variables described above address whether religious elements are man-datory and how they are related to the overall program structure. These two variables have particular salience for the role of religion in social service program design. Permutations of these two variables are used to construct a typology of five integration strategies: implicit, invitational, relational, integrated-optional, and mandatory. These strategies are not mutually exclusive; a program may combine various strategies, though one may best capture its flavor. Churches may also employ multiple strategies for different programs.

As table 5.2 shows,[5] the strategy types are organized by three questions: Is explicit religious content significantly present in the program, or is the religious dimension mainly expressed implicitly through the organizational culture or the motivations and caring actions of staff? Are explicit religious elements part of the planned or routine program design, or is religious content limited to informal interactions with personnel, or to activities that take place outside the official program parameters? And are religious elements mandatory, or can beneficiaries opt out of participation? Each strategy is considered below in more detail.

The first strategy, *implicit,* describes programs in which explicit religious programmatic elements are not significantly present (i.e., the program may have a religious name, or take place in a sacred space, but incorporates few or no explicitly religious activities or messages). This strategy corresponds with the concept of implicit spiritual nurture discussed in the previous chapter. Religion is implicitly modeled rather than overtly expressed in the context of social service delivery. The program may be based on religious principles, and staff may be motivated and guided by faith, but religious elements are not incorporated into the program. Efforts to do so may, in fact, be considered

TABLE 5.2 Strategies for Integrating Religious Elements into a Social Service Program

| Strategy | Are explicitly religious program elements . . . | | |
	Substantially present?	Part of the planned program design?	Mandatory?
Implicit	No	No	No
Invitational	Yes, in the form of invitations to outside religious activities	No in the service provision; Yes in religious activities outside the program parameters	No
Relational	Yes, in the form of informal interactions with staff	No in the service provision; Yes in intentionally cultivated relationships	No
Integrated-Optional	Yes, unless clients decline to participate in religious activities	Yes	No
Mandatory	Yes	Yes	Yes

Sources: Sider, Olson, and Unruh (2002); Unruh (2004)

inappropriate. The Interfaith Hospitality Network discouraged participating congregations from seeking to influence the religious beliefs of the homeless families they hosted. The IHN coordinator for Central Baptist Church explained, "Evangelism is showing God's love through example. We show our faith in God through our kindness to others. We are very careful not to push people about anything concerning their faith."

In the second, *invitational* strategy, beneficiaries are extended the opportunity to connect with religious resources or events outside the parameters of the social service program, including spiritual counseling (such as with a chaplain), regular church activities (such as Sunday worship services), special events (such as an Easter pageant), or religious activities offered in conjunction with the social service (such as a Bible study after program hours). Similar invitations may be extended to unchurched volunteers. These invitational elements are distinct from the program's service methodology, though they may be an important part of the church's plan of evangelism. Church-state restraints led Bethel Temple Community Bible Church to employ an invitational strategy in its outreach to the public middle school across the street. When church staff were invited by the school to conduct workshops on teamwork and problem-solving, they avoided overt religious expressions. Personal invitations and word of mouth, however, drew students into faith-centered youth activities held at the church or on school grounds after hours.

The third strategy is *relational*. In this strategy, beneficiaries encounter explicitly religious elements through informal interactions with staff or volunteers. In the context of relationships, program personnel may share their faith testimony, offer a religious perspective on social problems, discuss spiritual concerns, and encourage beneficiaries to make religious commitments. Such relational encounters may occur spontaneously through the initiative of individual staff, or they may be more systematically encouraged by the program's leadership. The previous chapter described the First Focus seminars offered by First Presbyterian Church. While the seminars did not overtly address religion, fostering evangelistic relationships between church and community members was part and parcel of their purpose, as an associate pastor explained:

> The idea is to get folks to walk inside of our building, meet some
> other Christians, find out that they're normal folks just like them.
> . . . We build up a rapport with them. Then, the evangelistic moment
> of saying, "This is who Jesus is, would you like to enter that kind of
> a relationship with him, this is how you could do that"—then it
> makes sense to them.

Because the goal of both invitational and relational strategies is to lay a foundation for more overt opportunities to present the gospel, together these correspond to the mode of expressing faith called *pre-evangelism*, introduced in chapter 4. A program may employ invitational and relational strategies to complement more formally integrated religious elements. In other cases, these pre-evangelistic elements may be pervasive in a program in which faith otherwise has little overt presence.

The fourth strategy is labeled *integrated-optional*. As implied by *integrated*, religious elements are intentionally woven into the structure of service provision. The program has an unmistakably religious character. However, as indicated by *optional*, beneficiaries may opt out of participating in explicitly religious activities or teachings. Transitional Journey provided a good illustration of this type, with a clear Christian self-identification and a curriculum that included optional religious content. The handbook stated in bold letters:

- Please note that the spiritual component of this program is NOT MANDATORY. You do not have to participate in prayer, Sisters of Faith or the Friday [worship] Service.
- If you choose not to participate, another spiritual or non-spiritual activity will be provided.

Students entering the program signed waivers saying that they were aware of its Christian nature and of their right to opt out of religious activities. A number of students—including several Muslims—availed themselves of this right, substituting educational activities, such as practicing in the computer lab, during time scheduled for religious activities. Transitional Journey's opt-out policy was mandated by the state because the program received public funds. Other programs make religious elements optional out of their own sense of what is appropriate or realistic for their clientele.

The final type of strategy is *mandatory*. As in the optional type, significant religious elements form an integral part of the program design, but here beneficiaries' participation in religious activities is required. (Both mandatory and integrated-optional strategies correspond to the concept of *integrated evangelism* described in the last chapter.) Conversion or a meaningful spiritual experience may be a central goal of the program. Mandatory strategies are often associated with a one-time or minor benefit, such as the Thanksgiving food baskets distributed by Germantown Church of the Brethren. A Germantown staff member described their decision to make this an evangelistic event:

How to determine who gets one hundred boxes of food in your community is somewhat of a challenge. . . . This past year we decided, since this was not government-donated food, this was donated food from the church, that we certainly had the right to require that recipients [first] attend a worship service. . . . That's an example of how we are trying to connect the physical with the spiritual.

In this example, the mandatory religious participation was not directly relevant to the benefit. In other cases, the religious elements are embedded in the methodology for meeting the social need. Jobs Partnership of Philadelphia, which the pastors of Germantown and Koinonia helped to organize, blended employment services (a life skills and work-readiness training class, and job placement upon graduation) with religious elements (a "Keys to Work" Bible study, prayer teams, and post-placement support from a Christian mentor). These spiritual components were seen as crucial to the process of overcoming internal barriers to successful employment. Full participation in the religious as well as the more "secular" aspects of the program was thus required.

Conclusion

This chapter proposes an inductively derived exploratory model for analyzing the explicitly religious components of faith-based social service delivery.[6] This model has three layers: religious elements (what religious content is present in the program), descriptive variables (the manner in which this content is presented), and integrative strategies (how these elements are incorporated into service delivery). Beyond potentially helping researchers measure the *amount* of religiosity in a program (e.g., by constructing a scale based on variables such as the number, frequency, and intensity of religious elements), this model also calls attention to the *type* of religiosity expressed in the program, in terms of the variety of combinations of religious elements, variables, and integration strategies. This conceptual framework, once empirically tested and refined, may help advance our understanding of what faith-based programs do and how they do it, and how they view the role of religion in the process. It could also have practical applications in helping social ministries assess and communicate their own religious identity.

Studies of faith-based social services are just beginning to clarify the prevalence and types of religious elements in faith-based programs. Some of the existing research indicates that the level of religious activity involving beneficiaries is far from trivial, at least in certain social service fields. Monsma (1996), for example, found that among religiously based child-service agencies, 71% had "religious symbols/pictures in facilities," 70% made "informal references to religious ideas by staff with clients," 64% had "spoken prayers at meals," and 33% would actively "encourage religious commitments by clients." Among faith-based organizations contracting with government, Green and Sherman (2002) found that half made supplemental religious programming available to beneficiaries; a third integrated explicitly religious content in programs, but made participation optional; and a fourth regularly asked clients if they would like to join in religious activities outside of the program. Case studies of faith-based nonprofits that serve substance abusers (Bicknese 1999), the unemployed (Lockhart 2003), and the homeless (Goggin and Orth 2002) describe extensive integration of religious content in some programs.

On the other hand, Cnaan et al.'s study of congregation-based social services noted few attempts to infuse services with religious teachings and practices (2002). Seley and Wolpert's study (2003) of service providers in New York City observed that faith-based organizations preferred an implicit religious character to "religious particularism"; a study of faith-based coalitions by Pipes and Ebaugh (2002) came to a similar conclusion. A study of faith-based groups serving the homeless in Houston (Ebaugh et al. 2003) found that certain religious elements are favored over others: while 84% incorporated religious language into self-descriptive materials, and the use of prayer and the distribution of religious material were common, the more intensive religious elements such as encouraging faith commitments were relatively rare.

The factors that influence a program's selection of integration strategies are both broadly cultural and program specific. The broader factors inhibiting an integrated or mandatory approach include "professional norms, concerns about religious diversity and tolerance, and the lack of longer-term or communal relationships" (Wuthnow 2004, 285).[7] Faith-based organizations are subject to isomorphic pressures that reinforce secular program models (Smith and Sosin 2001, Wuthnow 2004). Programs are also influenced by specific circumstances of funding, sponsorship, personnel, and client constituency. The decision to accept funds from government or secular foundations can deter some religious elements and strategies while favoring others. Charitable choice legislation expressly permits religious self-identifications and objects with religious meaning in the program environment, while prohibiting worship, religious instruction, and proselytizing. Subsequent executive guidelines (White House 2003) have allowed an invitational or optional strategy in which religious elements are clearly segregated from the government-funded portions of the program in time and space. Dependence on funds and staff from an evangelistically oriented congregation or denomination, on the other hand, increases the likelihood of explicit religious components. The mandatory religious character of substance-abuse support groups sponsored by New Covenant is driven by the program's founder, who asserts: "My personality is [such] that I have to talk about Jesus. That is the personality of the congregation too." Religious dynamics thus represent a balance between forces of culture, theology, personality, and practical necessity. The prevalence of the implicit approach among faith-based programs owes in part to its presenting the path of least resistance along these multiple lines of tension.

We need to develop a more complete portrait of how faith-based programs manifest their faith in the context of service provision. This question is one facet of the broader issue of how faith-based organizations define and express their religious identity, to be explored in the next chapter.

6

A Typology of Faith-Based Organizations and Programs

The Need for a Typology

What is a faith-based organization? Consider the following mission statements:

> To fulfill the will of God for this ministry by letting our Christian light shine before men so they may see the good works and glorify our Father in heaven (Matthew 5:16). (Koinonia Christian Community Church of God in Christ)

> To minister to the born again recovering substance abuser. . . . To help group members become rooted and grounded through the teaching of the Word of God, and to prepare them for Spiritual Warfare. (Christians United Against Addictions, sponsored by New Covenant Church)

> To help individuals and families experience the fullness of their lives and be whole. (Lafiya Family Services Center, affiliated with Germantown Church of the Brethren)

> To befriend, equip, and employ some of Philadelphia's neediest residents, empowering them towards becoming productive community members and experiencing whole-ness through relationship with Jesus Christ. (Jobs Partnership of Philadelphia)

To strengthen families by restoring to public life civic virtue and the Judeo-Christian ethic essential for the well-being of our society and city. (Urban Family Council, supported by Tenth Presbyterian Church)

A nonprofit, ecumenical Christian organization dedicated to eliminating substandard housing and homelessness worldwide and to making adequate, affordable shelter a matter of conscience and action. (Habitat for Humanity International)

Each of these organizations is connected to a faith community and is committed to some form of social involvement. But there the similarities end. The statements represent a spectrum of entities: a church, a church-sponsored program, a nonprofit affiliated with a church, a coalition of churches, a local nonprofit, and a worldwide organization. They also represent different ways and degrees of incorporating religion: helping families "experience the fullness of their lives and be whole" versus "experiencing wholeness through relationship with Jesus Christ." The purpose of each reflects a different blend of spiritual and social concerns: One organization has the genteel goal of restoring "civic virtue and the Judeo-Christian ethic," another seeks to glorify God through good works, another aims to prepare recovering addicts for "spiritual warfare."

These mission statements underscore the diversity and complexity of the social work sponsored by the religious community. The reductionistic vocabulary of the debates over faith-based initiatives has failed to reflect these complex realities. The catch-all term *faith-based organizations* confuses and divides because people hold conflicting conceptions of what it means to be faith-based (Jeavons 1997). Some interpret the term to include the broadest possible swath of agencies with any and all connection to religion, while others reserve it for agencies that are religious in a particular sense. No simple definition takes into account that each of the above organizations is faith-based in a different way.

This lack of clarity creates problems for studying and making policies regarding religious social services. The lack of clear analytical categories hampers comparative research on the effectiveness of service programs. Studies of the nonprofit sector that do not carefully distinguish the religious characteristics of their sample may end up overstating, understating, or misstating the role of faith in program outcomes. They may also miss the relationship between particular religious characteristics and other key variables (such as resource level or administrative capacity).

This undifferentiated language also clouds the cultivation of sound public policy. The proposition of funding faith-based organizations is taken to mean different things—to some the core issue is funding small, grassroots nonprofits; others focus on the prospect of allocating public money to congregations; others point to established service agencies like Catholic Charities that have long received government aid. Advocates and opponents often end up talking past one another rather than engaging the substantive issues. This closes doors to constructive and creative policy-making. One-size-fits-all language yields one-size-fits-all policies; what we need now is a whole wardrobe of options.

This chapter[1] proposes a typology that organizes entities based on their religious nature, building on the ideas and definitions developed in the previous chapters. It is significant that our typology was embraced and refined by a group seeking common-ground solutions to this critical challenge (Working Group 2002 and 2003).[2] All sides to the questions raised by faith-based initiatives stand to benefit from the enhanced clarity and precision such a model can bring.

Review of Classification Efforts

While there are many classification schemes for organizations in general, several scholars have developed taxonomic models specific to faith-based organizations.[3]

Monsma has identified a list of religious attributes and practices incorporated by social welfare and educational institutions and ranked FBOs (faith-based organizations) as high, medium, or low on a Religious Practices Scale (Monsma 1996). In a later study, Monsma (2002) uses the scale to differentiate between *faith-based/integrated* and *faith-based/segmented* welfare-to-work programs. Faith-based/integrated programs incorporate religious elements into welfare-related services; faith-based/segmented programs keep religious activities separate from their social services.

Jeavons (1998) suggests seven dimensions for defining an organization as *religious*, drawing on applied organizational theory:

1. organizational self-identity;
2. selection of organizational participants (staff, volunteers, funders and clients);
3. sources of funds and volunteers;
4. goals, products, and services (including "spiritual technologies");
5. information processing and decision making (e.g., reliance on prayer and religious precepts for guidance);
6. the development and distribution of organizational power; and
7. organizational fields, including program partners.

For each dimension, an organization may be placed along a spectrum from least to most religious.

Smith and Sosin (2001) adopt an institutional analysis to understand the ways that service organizations are "coupled" with faith (i.e., how they are connected with denominations or other religious groups, and the relationship of this coupling to the structure of service delivery). Religious coupling may be described by three main dimensions. *Resource dependency* indicates the proportion of financing and staff from religious sources. *Authority* refers to the bureaucratic or normative control that religious agencies hold over an organization (e.g., through formal affiliation). *Organizational culture* describes interactions with religious influences in relation to secular influences such as professional associations; these shape the worldview assumptions governing service methodologies. Organizations can be placed along a continuum from high to low coupling in each of these areas.

Goggin and Orth (2002, 51) draw on the above works to develop a Faith Integration Scale that measures the extent to which social service programs incorporate elements of religious identity or practice. Items on the scale are organized under five headings:

> Organizational factors include the structural characteristics of the FBO itself. The administrative factor focuses on the mission, management, and staffing practices of the organization. Environmental factors include the physical characteristics of the facilities in which FBO services and programs are provided. Funding factors concern the distribution of financial resources that FBOs receive from secular and religious sources. Finally, the programmatic factors focus on specific religious components of FBO activities/services, and the extent to which these components are mandatory or voluntary in nature.

Recognizing that faith traditions express their religiosity in different ways, this scale assesses the relevance of commonly identified religious practices to the faith tradition of the FBO. In this way, only practices that are germane to a given religious tradition are taken into account.

These works have contributed significantly to the taxonomic task. While each model takes a different approach to examining and defining the faith dimension of nonprofits, they share several themes. One motif is the concept of religious integration—the notion that religion is not an independent attribute but a dynamic that is incorporated into the organization in a variety of ways and intensities. A related theme is the challenge of designing a measure of religious integration that applies across different faith traditions. Somehow, a classification system must indicate the role of religion in an organization in a way that is neutral to the content of that religion. Another commonality in the literature is the recognition that the question of whether an organization is faith-based cannot be adequately answered with a simple "yes" or "no." The faith-nature of organizations is multidimensional, requiring a range of types.

The typology presented here builds on these common themes, assigning labels to categories that represent meaningful and measurable ranges of religious integration. The typology draws on an established set of organizational dynamics and religious elements to construct a model of the ways that religion is manifest in a social service or educational organization. The typology also takes into account the distinction in the literature between institutional and behavioral manifestations of religion. Some classification systems focus on organizational attributes such as resources, governance, and staffing; others focus on the inclusion of religious practices in program methodologies. Both emphases are important to our typology, but remain distinct considerations.

Explanatory Notes

Before describing this typology of religious characteristics, five explanatory notes are needed to clarify its organization and limitations.

First, like the analysis of religious elements in the previous chapter, this typology focuses on the tangible and overt rather than the subjective and implicit aspects of religion. It primarily engages religion as it is expressed in observable and explicit phenomena like language, symbols, policies, and activities. This typology does not fully reflect the depth of religious meanings attached to social action explored in chapter 4, such as personal convictions about compassion and justice that motivate service work. We thus emphasize that the typology is *not* a tool to characterize a group or program as being more or less religious in the sense of being animated by a set of beliefs. An organization in any of the types may be deeply religious in this sense, if the individuals who work there infuse their vocation with their private spiritual commitments. An organization need not be faith-based to provide an arena for people to live out their faith. This distinction has implications for public policy. Those who debate faith-based initiatives seldom question whether devout individuals who see their service as faith-acts may work for a publicly funded program. They do, however, challenge whether a preference for staff who are devout may be explicitly codified in a publicly-funded organization's hiring policies.

Some religious streams express their religiosity in more tangibly evident ways than others (Goggin and Orth 2002). Some faith traditions, for example, emphasize verbalizing their beliefs to beneficiaries of social services; others consider overt faith-sharing in the context of service provision to be inappropriate. This chapter, like the preceding one, refers to "explicitly religious" program content to identify liturgical, devotional, and proselytizing activities or messages which are, on their surface, intrinsically religious (such as prayer, study of sacred texts, or discussions of religious doctrine). This terminology is not meant to imply that such content is inherently more "faith"-ful. As previous chapters have pointed out, a program may outwardly appear secular, yet be rooted in religious convictions and nonverbally embody a religious message.

A second explanatory note concerns the division of the typology into two sections: characteristics of organizations and characteristics of programs or projects. The organizational section focuses on features related to administration, personnel, sponsorship, and resources; the program/project section focuses on the integration of religious elements into service provision. This division reflects the fact that an organization may run a program that has a different set of religious characteristics than the organization. For example, a faith-centered organization may run a program that is faith-affiliated in nature, or a secular organization such as a hospital might operate a 12–step addiction treatment program with ties to a religious group. Moreover, an organization may run several different programs, each falling into a different category. One reason for this is that organizations and programs are sensitive to different pressures, influences, and patterns of institutional change. An organization is more likely to accept funding that restricts the religious characteristics of a particular program than funding that alters the religious nature of the overall organization. The nature of religious expression in different programs within an organization may be influenced by different sets of professional standards brought to bear on these programs. Thus, to get an accurate picture it is often necessary to consider the organization as a whole and each of its programs separately.

Third, this model focuses on social service organizations and programs. The term *social service* is meant to encompass relief, personal development, and community development, using the categories laid out in the second chapter. Social services provide aid or skills to individuals or improve the general quality of life of a community, covering a broad range of ministries: food pantries, elder care, substance abuse counseling, job training, immigration assistance, day care, housing rehabilitation, GED instruction, after school tutoring, private schools, medical clinics, etc. The typology was not designed with community organizing or social change projects in mind (such as groups based on the Industrial Areas Foundation model). Lobbying and advocacy programs do not typically entail direct interactions with beneficiaries (except potentially as participants in community organizing) and thus involve different patterns of integrating religious elements and connecting religious content with outcomes. The work of classifying these types of programs is beyond the scope of this chapter, though there may be significant parallels.

It should fourthly be noted that this typology does not cover every important organizational or programmatic attribute. Additional classification systems are needed to capture other variations among faith-based agencies with significance for research and policy-making, such as structure, purpose, capacity, and context (Yanay 1985; Lampkin, Romeo, and Finnin 2001; Working Group 2002). In particular, we need language that recognizes differences between such distinct organizational forms as ecumenical coalitions like Interfaith Hospitality Network, denominational or sectarian organizations like Jewish Family and Children's Services, independent nonprofits like Teen Challenge, and congregation-sponsored programs like soup kitchens (Cnaan 1999).

Finally, this typology, like any typology, is inherently limited. Life is more complex than can be depicted on a chart. A typology is meant to capture general trends, while the reality is that many organizations and programs will fall in the gray area between the types, or combine elements of different categories. The categories should be viewed as points along a spectrum rather than discrete archetypes (Jeavons 1998).

Types of Faith-Based Organizations and Programs

The typology of religious characteristics includes five categories of faith-based organizations or programs, in addition to the secular type. The categories are summarized below.

In *faith-permeated* organizations, the connection with religious faith is evident at all levels of mission, staffing, governance, and support. Faith-permeated programs extensively integrate explicitly religious content. The religious dimension is part of the program's methodology and believed to be essential to the program's effectiveness. Therefore, participation in religious elements or a religious affiliation is often a prerequisite for access to benefits.

Faith-centered organizations were founded for a religious purpose, remain strongly connected with the religious community through funding sources and affiliation, and require most of the governing board and key staff to share the organization's faith commitments. Faith-centered programs incorporate explicitly religious elements but are designed so that participants can readily opt out of religious activities and still benefit from the program.

Faith-affiliated organizations retain some of the influence of their religious founders (such as in their mission statement), but typically look beyond the faith community for staffing and support. They do not require personnel to affirm religious beliefs or practices, with the possible exception of some board and executive leaders. While faith-affiliated programs incorporate little or no explicitly religious content, they may affirm faith in a general way, make spiritual resources available to participants, and encourage spiritual nurture through nonverbal acts of compassion and care.

Faith-background organizations tend to look and act secular, though they may have a historical tie to a faith tradition. While religious beliefs may motivate some personnel, faith commitments are not considered in the selection of the staff or board. Faith-background programs have no explicitly religious content, aside from their possible location in a religious setting, and do not expect religious experience to contribute to program outcomes.

Faith-secular partnerships present a special case in which a secular (or faith-background) entity joins with one or more congregations or other explicitly religious organizations. This type of organizational arrangement is typically secular in its administration, but relies on the religious partners for volunteer

TABLE 6.1 Typology of Religious Characteristics of Social Service Organizations and Programs

Characteristic	Faith-Permeated	Faith-Centered	Faith-Affiliated	Faith-Background	Faith-Secular Partnership	Secular
I. Characteristics of Organizations						
1. *Mission statement and other self-descriptive texts*	Include explicitly religious references	Include explicitly religious references	Religious references may be either explicit or implicit	May have implicit references to religion (e.g., references to "values")	No explicit reference to religion in mission statement of the partnership or the secular partner, but religion may be explicit in mission of faith partners	No religious content
2. *Founding*	By religious group or for religious purpose	By religious group or for religious purpose	By religious group or for religious purpose	May have historic tie to a religious group, but connection is no longer strong	Faith partners founded by religious group or for religious purpose; no reference to religious identity of founders of the secular partner; founders of the partnership may or may not be religious	No reference to religious identity of founders
3. *Affiliated with a religious entity?*	Yes	Yes	Often	Sometimes	May have dual religious/secular affiliation	No
4. *Selection of controlling board*	Explicitly religious; may be a) self-perpetuating board with explicit religious criteria or b) board elected by a religious body	Explicitly or implicitly religious; may be a) self-perpetuating board with explicit or implicit religious criteria for all or most members or b) board elected by a religious body	Some, but not all, board members may be required or expected to have a particular faith or ecclesiastical commitment	Board might have been explicitly religious at one time, but now selected with little or no consideration of board members' faith commitment	Board selection typically controlled by secular partner, with little or no consideration of faith commitment of board members; input from faith partners	Faith commitment of board members not a factor

5. *Selection of senior management*	Faith or ecclesiastical commitment an explicit prerequisite	Faith or ecclesiastical commitment an explicit or implicit prerequisite	Normally (perhaps by unwritten expectation) share the organization's religious orientation, but explicit religious criteria may be considered improper	Religious selection criteria considered irrelevant or improper	Required to respect, but not necessarily to share faith of religious partners	Religious selection criteria considered improper
6. *Selection of other staff*	Faith commitment is important at all staff levels; most or all staff share organization's religious orientation, with faith an explicit factor in hiring decisions	Faith commitment may be an explicit selection factor for jobs involving religion, but may be less important in other positions	Staff expected to respect but not necessarily share the religious orientation of the organization; religious beliefs motivate self-selection of some staff/volunteers	Little or no consideration of faith commitment of any staff; religious beliefs may motivate self-selection of some staff/volunteers	Staff expected to respect but not necessarily to share faith of religious partners	Religious criteria for selection of any staff considered improper
7. *Organized religious practices of personnel*	Religious practices play a significant role in the functioning of the organization; personnel are expected or required to participate	Religious practices often play a significant role in the functioning of the organization; personnel may be expected to participate	Religious practices are optional and not extensive	Religious practices are rare and peripheral to the organization	Faith partners may sponsor voluntary religious practices; secular partners do not	No organized religious practices
8. *Cultivation of financial support and nonfinancial resources*	Intentional cultivation of support from religious community; policy of refusing funds that would undermine religious mission/identity	Intentional cultivation of support from religious community; may have policy of refusing funds that would undermine religious mission/identity	May cultivate volunteer and in-kind support from religious community	May or may not cultivate support from religious community	Significant cultivation of volunteer and in-kind support from faith partners	Little cultivation of support from religious community

(continued)

TABLE 6.1 (*continued*)

II. Characteristics of Programs/Projects

Characteristic	Faith-Permeated	Faith-Centered	Faith-Affiliated	Faith-Background	Faith-Secular Partnership	Secular
1. *Religious environment*	Usually	Usually	Often	Sometimes	Sometimes (program administration is usually located in a secular environment, while program activities may be located in a religious environment)	No
2. *Explicitly religious content of program*	Includes explicitly religious, mandatory content integrated into the program; beneficiaries are expected to participate in religious activities and discussions	Includes explicitly religious teachings and activities that may be segregated from provision of care; beneficiaries may opt not to participate in religious program elements; beneficiaries may also be invited to outside religious activities, or discuss religious ideas informally	The religious aspect is primarily implicit in acts of compassion and care; program includes little (and entirely optional) or no explicitly religious content; practitioners may invite beneficiaries to outside religious activities, or discuss religious ideas informally	No explicitly religious content; religious materials or resources may be available to beneficiaries who seek them out; the religious component is seen primarily in the motivation of individual personnel	No explicitly religious content in program activities designed by secular partners; faith partners sometimes supplement with optional religious resources and activities	No religious content

	Mandatory	Integrated-optional, invitational, or relational	Invitational, relational, or implicit	Implicit	Implicit, invitational, or relational	None
3. Main strategy for integrating explicitly religious elements with other program components (see Table 5.2)	Mandatory (engagement with religious content is required of beneficiaries)	Integrated-optional, invitational, or relational (engagement of beneficiaries with religious content is optional, or takes place in activities outside program parameters and/or informal relationships with practitioners)	Invitational, relational, or implicit (engagement of beneficiaries with religious content takes place only in activities outside program parameters and/or informal relationships with practitioners)	Implicit (beneficiaries only encounter religious content if they seek it out)	Implicit, invitational, or relational, depending on staff/volunteers of the faith partners	None
4. Expected connection between religious elements and desired outcomes	Expectation of explicitly religious experience or change, and belief that this is essential or significant to desired outcomes	Strong hope for explicitly religious experience or change, and belief that this significantly contributes to social well-being though is not necessary to receive the expected program benefit	Little expectation that explicitly religious experience or change is essential for desired outcomes; some believe caring acts have an implicit spiritual impact that contributes to social well-being	No expectation that religious experience or change is needed for desired outcomes	No expectation that religious experience or change is needed for desired outcomes, but the faith of volunteers from religious partners is expected to add value to the program	No expectation of religious change or experience

Source: Working Group (2002, 2003); Sider and Unruh (2004)

and in-kind support. Leaders and staff respect but do not necessarily share the faith of the religious partners. The programming typically does not integrate explicitly religious content, though volunteers and staff may offer supplemental religious resources and activities. The faith of the religious partners is considered a program asset whether or not it is expressed explicitly. As this category indicates, social service projects often entail a set of complex institutional relationships rather than a solitary entity (Ammerman 2001; Wuthnow 2000).

Secular organizations have no reference to religion in their mission or founding history, and regard it improper to consider religious commitments as a factor in hiring and governance. Secular programs include no religious content.

Religious Organizational Characteristics

The typology classifies organizations based on eight characteristics, and programs based on four characteristics. Below we briefly describe these religious characteristics (see the rows in table 6.1) and why each is salient to the faith classification.

Organizational Characteristics

There are eight organizational characteristics in four broad categories: identity (mission statement, founding, and affiliation), personnel (controlling board, senior management, and other staff), support, and the religious practices of personnel.

   1. *Mission statement*: The first characteristic concerns the extent to which a mission (or "purpose" or "vision") statement or other self-descriptive document uses religious language in defining the organization's identity and purpose (see Ebaugh et al. 2003 for a detailed definition of *religious language*). The mission statement can act as a "screen" to attract or filter out personnel and funders based on their identification with the expressed religious values (Smith and Sosin 2001). In the faith-permeated and faith-centered (and some faith-affiliated) types, the mission statement usually includes explicitly religious language, such as references to Christ or the Bible. In the faith-background (and sometimes faith-affiliated) type, the language may be indirectly religious, referring to values such as justice or mercy grounded in a religious heritage. Religious language may also be found in other self-descriptive statements, such as the text in program brochures.

2. *Founding*: This characteristic examines the connection with a religious heritage in an organization's past and the continuing relevance of this heritage. Many social service and educational organizations have their roots in a religious movement, though the ongoing influence of religion on these organizations has been variable (Demerath et al. 1998). In the first three types, the religious founding is still a part of the organization's ongoing identity. Faith-background organizations may have been founded by a religious group, but the link has since been dissolved. Many hospitals, for example, were established by a religious denomination but have no remaining official ties to the founding group, except possibly in their name. The faith-secular partnership type may have originated from either the secular or the faith-based arena.

3. *Affiliation*: If the organization is currently affiliated with another agency, is that agency religious? It should be noted that not all organizations have an external affiliation, and so this characteristic may not apply to every case. Affiliation is here defined as a close relationship with another entity (not necessarily the founding entity) that provides legal sponsorship, administration, or key resources. This relationship may be governed by official documents such as bylaws, or it may be more informal. Affiliation with a religious entity affects the influence of religious authority on the organization's actions (Smith and Sosin 2001). The affiliation, if any, of an organization in the first two types is almost always with a self-evidently religious entity such as a congregation or denomination.

4. *Controlling board*: This characteristic examines the role of religious identity in the selection of board members. Is a particular religious orientation a requirement for board members? In the first two types, an intentionally religious board is created either by the inclusion of religious criteria in guidelines for board member eligibility (such as membership in a denomination), or by the direct selection of board members by a religious entity. Faith-affiliated agencies typically set aside a certain portion of board positions (whether by rule or by tradition) for persons of faith. This is often the case for nonprofits initiated by a religious organization that have since been broadened to encourage greater ownership by members of the community (Schneider 1999 details an example). In the remaining types, the faith of board members has little or no influence on their selection.

5. *Senior management*: Executive leadership plays a critical role in guiding the course and character of an organization. As with the board, the first two types make a particular faith commitment a requirement for senior staff. This could mean adherence to a set of beliefs, membership in a particular denomination, and/or demonstration of a life-

style consistent with the agency's religious convictions. In faith-affiliated organizations, senior management often do share in the faith tradition of the agency, but this may not be an explicit requirement. Management of a faith-secular partnership is required to have respect for, but not necessarily to share their religious partners' faith. In a secular organization, and in many faith-background organizations, consideration of a candidate's faith commitments is considered not only irrelevant but improper.

6. *Other staff.* The admissibility of religious criteria in staff hiring has long been a hotly contested legal issue (Stronks 1995; Esbeck, Carlson-Thies, and Sider 2004). Court rulings have distinguished between staff positions that are integral to the religious mission of the organization, and positions that fulfill primarily secular functions. In a faith-permeated organization, faith is viewed as an important quality for all staff. Faith-centered organizations may consider religious criteria to be more relevant for certain positions, such as those that directly involve religious program components or interactions with beneficiaries. In the next two types, the organization's religious heritage may factor into the self-selection of staff with faith commitments, but religion is seldom an official requirement. Thus faith-affiliated and faith-background organizations may have many staff members for whom faith was an important factor in their decision to apply to work for the agency, but not in the agency's decision to hire them. Faith-secular partnerships often draw significantly on the faith community for volunteers, without taking faith into account in their decisions regarding paid staff.

7. *Personnel religious practices:* In the first two types, staff, volunteers, and/or board members typically participate together in organized religious practices (not involving clients), such as prayer, chapel services, or the study of Scriptures. This category can also include codes of conduct (e.g., governing sexuality and consumption of alcohol) that are explicitly grounded in religion. Such shared activities and norms may play a significant role in how the organization makes decisions (e.g., by seeking God's guidance through prayer at board meetings), cultivates staff unity and morale, shapes its organizational culture, and explicates the relationship of faith to service (Jeavons 1994 and 1998). Faith-permeated organizations may require staff participation in religious activities. In faith-affiliated agencies, if personnel engage in religious practices, they are not as critical to decision-making or as integrated into organizational routines. In faith-secular partnerships, the religious partners may institute religious practices, but they are not central to the operations of the partnership.

8. *Support:* This characteristic includes both financial support and nonfi-

nancial resources, such as space, volunteer time, and in-kind donations (food, clothes, equipment, etc.). Faith-permeated and faith-
centered organizations intentionally target appeals for support to the
faith community (though not necessarily *exclusively* to the faith community), and appeals include explicitly religious references; secular
organizations, in contrast, seldom specifically recruit support from religious sources. The other types vary in how intentional they are
about cultivating donors and volunteers from the religious community. Faith-secular partnerships tend to turn to the faith community
particularly for nonfinancial support. Moreover, faith-permeated and
some faith-centered organizations often have a policy of rejecting
funding sources, such as United Way, that would restrict their religious nature.

Religious Program Characteristics

The four program characteristics examine religious dynamics in the service
environment and in the program content, the integration of religious elements
into program activities, and the expected connection between religious elements and desired outcomes.

1. *Religious environment*: Does the program take place in a building
   whose main function is for religious purposes, such as a church? Are
   objects with religious meaning present in the program space, such as
   a cross, a list of the Ten Commandments, or a poster featuring a Bible verse? A religious environment can also be suggested by religious
   references in a program's name (such as Exodus Ministries or Philadelphia College of the Bible). In the case of faith-secular partnership
   programs, the program activities may take place in a religious space
   while the administration may occur in a secular environment.
2. *Program content*: Are any of the religious elements described in the
   previous chapter (beyond religious references in program self-
   descriptions and a religious program environment) present in the
   content of the service program? These spiritual technologies may include prayer, worship, study of sacred texts, religious teachings and
   testimonies, and invitations to religious activities or faith commitments. Religious elements are an important component of the first
   two program types, though they are more segregated from service
   provision in faith-centered programs. Faith-affiliated programs, corresponding to the group Elliott (2005, 14) describes as *faith unspoken*,
   do not involve explicitly religious content, but may respond to client-
   initiated requests by offering spiritual resources outside of program
   parameters. In faith-secular partnerships, the core program activities

involve no explicitly religious content; the faith partners may add supplemental religious resources and activities.

3. *Integration of religious components*: This characteristic examines how
   service beneficiaries are likely to encounter religion in the context of
   the program, referring to the five general integration strategies defined in the previous chapter (see table 5.2): implicit, invitational, relational, integrated-optional, and mandatory. The strategy types are
   organized by three questions: First, is the religious dimension explicit
   (and typically verbal, as in prayers and sermons), or is it solely implicit (e.g., in the motivations and caring actions of staff)? Second, is
   explicitly religious content part of the planned or routine program design (e.g., in regular times set aside for devotionals), or does religious
   exposure occur primarily in activities that take place outside the official program, or through informal relationships? Finally, are explicitly
   religious elements mandatory, or can beneficiaries opt out of participation? These strategies are not mutually exclusive, but each program
   type is associated with one or more typical modalities. In faith-secular
   partnerships, the faith partners determine the strategy within the parameters of what the secular partner will allow.

4. *Expected connection between religious elements and desired outcomes*:
   This characteristic looks at the expected connection between spiritual
   technologies and the social product (e.g., job placement or a high
   school diploma; see chapter 10). Faith-permeated and faith-centered
   programs intend for beneficiaries to have a meaningful, transformational spiritual experience through their encounter with explicitly religious content. The methodology of faith-permeated programs is
   shaped by the belief that religious outcomes, such as conversion or
   joining a church, are essential or significant to the desired social outcome. In faith-centered programs, spiritual renewal is believed to
   contribute to social well-being but is not necessary for beneficiaries to
   receive the expected social service. Faith-affiliated programs do not
   consider explicitly religious interventions to be integral to social service outcomes. They may, however, be shaped by a belief that acts of
   compassion by people of faith can in themselves serve as a catalyst
   for spiritual healing or personal transformation. The remaining types
   have little or no expectation that beneficiaries will have a religious experience that will impact the outcomes of the program.

Examples

The following examples of organizations and programs are taken from the
fifteen case studies. The organizations are separately incorporated nonprofits

either founded by a church or affiliated with the church in some way. The programs are nonincorporated ministries, dependent on the church for staffing, funds, or administration. The variety illustrates how the same type of organization—a church—can be associated with a range of faith-based program categories.

Faith-permeated

ORGANIZATION. Christian Stronghold Baptist Church places a high priority on education. The church founded and provided space for two educational organizations: The Creative World Learning Center provided affordable day care for 110 children, and the Christian Stronghold Learning Academy offered biblically-based private schooling for 29 children in kindergarten to second grade. Prayer, Bible teachings, and worship services formed an integral part of the curriculum. The Academy required that at least one parent of each student be a practicing church member, though not necessarily from Christian Stronghold. Aside from student fees, funding came largely from church support and religious donors. Board members were also members of the church; the pastor chaired the board. The organizations preferred but did not require staff to be Christians, and expected staff to endorse the spiritual mission of the organization and to share regular times of prayer and biblical training. The director of the Center and Academy, a committed Christian, saw herself as an evangelist, and left a lucrative corporate position to come to Christian Stronghold in order "do [God's] work while in his setting."

PROGRAM. The Men's Redirection Center, a ministry of Faith Assembly of God, provided up to six men recovering from substance abuse with housing and life skills training. In Phase I, the program prepared residents for independent living with basic skills like cleaning, cooking, getting a driver's license, and time management. Their days were highly structured, with time set aside for prayer and Bible reading in the morning; several worship services during the week; volunteer work for various church ministries; and classes on spiritual topics such as "Temptation," "Growing in Faith," and "How to Live the Christian Life," adapted from the Teen Challenge curriculum. Twice a week, the men fasted (abstained from eating for religious reasons) until dinnertime, and once a week they participated in evangelistic street outreach. Participation in these religious activities was considered essential to the recovery process. After six to nine months, graduates could move on to the Phase II home and work at an outside job. While less structured, spiritual development remained at the heart of the program. Residents were expected to maintain an active personal spiritual life and involvement in church ministries.

Faith-centered

ORGANIZATION. Lafiya Family Counseling Services was founded in 1992 through the initiative of an "urban missionary" on staff with Germantown Church of the Brethren. The organization rented space from a property owned by the church. Lafiya provided individual and family counseling, an after-school program and summer camp located at the church, and other youth activities. Lafiya's mission statement, quoted at the beginning of the chapter, lacked overtly religious language. Though not all staff were Christians, both core staff positions were filled by members of the church. Per the by-laws, church members occupied three of the nine board positions, and the pastor was president of the board. Support for Lafiya's religious nature was an unwritten expectation for the guiding leadership, as the director explained: "All board members . . . are hoping that people base their success in a relationship with Christ and the church." Youth served by Lafiya were invited to attend the church; the curriculum of youth activities included religious values such as peacemaking. If clients were willing, counselors would offer to pray and take a spiritual approach in their sessions. Funding came from client fees subsidized by the denomination, private donations, and grants from secular and religious sources, while the church supplied volunteers.

PROGRAM. The director of Tenth Presbyterian Church's outreach to international students described the basis for the program: "We are meeting international student needs, needs for cultural adjustment, friendships, learning English—we are using that as a means also to communicate our faith to them." Conversational classes in English matched small groups of students with volunteer tutors from the church. The discussions helped with acculturation as well as language skills. Though the main focus was not Christianity, tutors could ask students about their religious background and talk about their own beliefs in return. After an hour of conversation, the students would form Bible discussion groups. Students were "strongly encouraged but not required to attend," according to the program handbook; most chose to stay. Students were also invited to attend church worship services and other activities for international students with explicitly religious content. Some tutors took the additional step of becoming a "friendship partner" to a student. Friendship partners provided additional socialization and helped students with personal needs, such as finding an apartment or opening a bank account. As the handbook explains, the ministry was designed with evangelistic goals in mind; friendship partners were encouraged to engage in religious discussions with students and to invite them to make faith commitments. However, the handbook states, students' religious experiences must remain voluntary: "Being a friendship partner provides an irreplaceable foundation for sharing the Gospel with internationals. However, the friendships that are built . . . must not be conditional. Acceptance of Christianity cannot be a requirement for continuing a friendship partner relationship."

Faith-affiliated

ORGANIZATION. The Advocate Community Development Corporation (ACDC) was incorporated in 1968 as "the outlet for some of the non-spiritual, non-religious programs" of the Church of the Advocate, according to the acting director. ACDC has provided over three hundred new or rehabilitated units of housing in its impoverished North Philadelphia neighborhood, established a community park, and launched other community development projects. Founded by the wife of the rector of the Church of the Advocate, ACDC originally operated out of the church building, and many in the community still associated it with the church. A seat on the board was reserved for a member of the church. Faith was not a factor in the selection of staff, though the director was a Christian (not Episcopalian) and valued the link with the church. While the organization maintained a donor base of supporters connected with the church and denomination, its primary funding sources included HUD and local secular foundations. ACDC's programs involved no specifically religious content, though it referred people with spiritual needs to the church.

PROGRAM. In 1986, First Presbyterian Church began hosting a Thanksgiving meal open to the community. This evolved into a twice weekly Community Luncheon, serving buffet-style meals to about ninety people. The one paid staff member was a member of First Presbyterian; the program relied on a pool of volunteers, most of whom were from other churches. Anyone who wished could join in a devotional time before the meal, but there was no formal attempt to involve people in prayer or other religious elements during the program. Occasionally, church members would eat alongside beneficiaries and engage in informal conversations on spiritual topics. The primary religious impact of the program, according to the church's associate pastor for outreach, lay in giving beneficiaries a new sense of worth and well-being. Luncheon attendants were invited to Bread and Bible, a separate weekly luncheon that incorporated a worship service and Bible study and could be classified as faith-permeated. This illustrates how a church can operate various programs with different religious characteristics.

Faith-background

ORGANIZATION. At a time when many banks were redlining his impoverished North Philadelphia community, Rev. Bill Moore encouraged his congregation at Tenth Memorial Baptist Church to invest in a new financial institution owned and operated by African Americans. In April 1992, Tenth Memorial

Church hosted Governor Robert Casey to inaugurate the opening of United Bank. United Bank's assets grew to $115 million from 3,000 shareholders, many from the faith community, and it launched educational services such as workshops on credit repair, home ownership and financial planning. The bank recruited customers and investors from the faith community, though not exclusively. Although Rev. Moore, as one of the bank's founders, served on the board, United Bank had no other administrative ties with the church. Staff tended to be well-networked with African American churches, but religion was not a factor in hiring.

PROGRAM. Central Baptist Church's Outreach English program was founded by a member who learned empathy for people struggling with a foreign language during her tenure as a Peace Corps volunteer. The program offered English language classes three nights a week, primarily to Albanian immigrants living in the Philadelphia suburbs. The program received a small stipend from the church and nominal fees from the students. Apart from its location at the church and use of volunteers from the church, no religious content was involved; the director believed that would be inappropriate.

Faith-secular partnership

ORGANIZATION. Public/Private Ventures (P/PV) is a secular research and program development organization. Concerned about a persistently high homicide rate among young Philadelphians (five times higher than that of the U.S. population), and inspired by the success of a clergy-police partnership in Boston, P/PV collaborated with the City of Philadelphia in launching the Youth Violence Reduction Partnership (YVRP). YVRP brought key officials from police, probation, courts, and service organizations together with community and congregational leaders in a high-risk police district. Along with identifying and intensively monitoring at-risk youth, YVRP aimed to connect youth with the support services provided by local congregations, nonprofits, and community groups. Two years of trial and error in developing relationships with congregations (including several in our study) helped YVRP to cultivate strategies for engaging the resources of the religious community. Ten congregations, spanning two neighborhoods, entered into a formal liaison with YVRP to provide mentors and advocates for the youth.

Applying the Typology

Real organizations and programs rarely fit perfectly into ideal types. Since many entities display characteristics from more than one type, making classifications involves looking at the overall pattern of religious characteristics.

There is room, however, for variation in how individual characteristics are to be weighted in discerning this pattern. Some religious characteristics or activities may be interpreted as more significant than others for various classification purposes. Another challenge of applying the typology is deciding how to measure each characteristic. Some criteria are fairly straightforward: Is the organization affiliated with a religious entity, such as a denomination? Does the program take place in a religious setting? Other characteristics are more complex than they appear at first sight. For example, does an allusion to a biblical image or story (like the good Samaritan) in a mission statement count as a religious reference if that reference has gained coinage in the broader secular culture? Do general statements such as "Just have faith" or "God loves you" qualify as religious program content? Jeavons's (1998) approach of identifying a spectrum of possible responses is helpful in addressing these challenges.

There are also methodological issues to resolve in gathering valid data, especially in looking at program characteristics. There may be a disconnect between official policies and actual practices. Our research discovered instances in which a program's descriptive documents did not mention religion, but individual staff energetically initiated religious conversations with beneficiaries. This may particularly be the case with programs whose formal religious content is restricted by outside funding. In other cases, program literature or interviews expressed the intention that beneficiaries would experience spiritual transformation, but observations gave no indication that this happened in practice. Administrators—who typically are the ones to participate in surveys or interviews—may simply be unaware of what happens in day-to-day interactions with beneficiaries.

While this typology is inductively grounded in case studies, and was developed with input from leaders of national service and civic organizations, it has yet to be systematically tested. First, the model should be tested empirically on a representative sample to assess whether the types represent the true variety of organizations and programs and whether the characteristics prove to be analytically significant. Second, the model should be evaluated qualitatively with practitioners in diverse grassroots organizations. How do field workers assess the typology's accuracy and helpfulness? Do the given religious characteristics capture what they see as the essential elements of their organization's or program's nature?

Toward this goal, Green and Sherman's study (2002) gives an indication of the distribution of programmatic religious integration strategies and organizational types. They asked 389 faith-based organizations that had received government contracts to select the category that best described the faith dimension of their social services: *not relevant, passive, invitational, relational, integrated,* and *mandatory.* The category most selected was passive (45%), followed by not relevant (20%), integrated (15%), relational (11%), and invitational;

less than 1% selected mandatory. Among congregations, which represented 22% of the total, only 9% selected the not relevant category, and 28% selected relational; otherwise their distribution was similar to the overall sample. This highlights the overall dominance of the implicit (passive) integration strategy, but also indicates the relative importance of a relational integration strategy among congregations. Monsma's (2002) study illuminated the distinctions between *faith-based/integrated* and *faith-based/segmented* welfare-to-work programs. Similarly, Green and Sherman's research shows that service providers often draw a line between a faith-centered approach that incorporates pre-evangelistic integration strategies (invitations and relationships) and optional religious content, and a faith-permeated approach that makes this content mandatory. Chapter 9 explores this distinction further.

Green and Sherman's work also points to how organizational and program characteristics can be combined into useful categories. They factored religious characteristics into two key variables: the degree to which the organizations maintain religious distinctiveness, and the extent of religious expression in service provision. Statistical analysis of these two dimensions produced four categories, which they label *non-expressives* (comprising 27% of the sample), *quiescents* (26%), *vocal inclusives* (21%), and *fully expressives* (27%). Congregations, not surprisingly, were significantly more likely to be fully expressive (47%) and less likely to be non-expressive (15%). These findings give an estimation of the distribution of the types here described as faith-background, faith-affiliated, faith-centered, and faith-permeated, although the correspondence is not exact (the faith-permeated type is not fully represented in their study, because their sample consists of organizations that contract with government). It is clear that entities that serve the needy are divided in whether they make their faith commitments explicitly known to beneficiaries, and in whether these faith commitments play a key role in their organizational operations.

Green and Sherman's study suggests that only a small percentage of congregational programs are faith-centered or faith-permeated, at least among those that receive public funds. A congregation, by definition, is a faith-permeated organization. It is founded expressly for religious purposes, and maintains that purpose through its mission statement. A congregation depends on the faith community for support. Its staff is selected on the basis of religious criteria, and its personnel are expected to participate in extensive religious practices. Social service programs run by a congregation, on the other hand, have variable religious characteristics. Such programs may or may not incorporate explicitly religious content, or connect such content to social outcomes. Monsma's (2002) research indicates, in fact, that congregational welfare-to-work programs are less likely to integrate significant religious content than independent faith-based nonprofits, regardless of funding. Discussions of faith-based initiatives sometimes assume that the social ministries of congregations are more inherently religious than those sponsored by other entities. It may be that public policy should place the programs run by congregations in a special category for funding purposes, but it is not accurate to base this distinction on the presumption that church-based programs necessarily incorporate explicitly religious messages or activities.

As this analysis confirms, a multidimensional model is necessary to capture the religiosity of an organization or program. Classification attempts based on self-evident features such as affiliation, mission statement, or location in a church can be deceiving (Ebaugh et al. 2003). As Jeavons put it, "organizational identity . . . is only the public tip of the investigative iceberg" (1998, 82). Some nonprofits that were birthed by a congregation or denomination are now religious in their name only. For other entities, a secular-sounding name or lack of official sponsorship by a religious body belies the presence of religious staff who express their faith to beneficiaries through informal invitational and relational strategies. One church's application for city funding for its drug recovery program was rejected because the program bore the name of the church. The pastor took back the application, removed the church's name in the program title, and resubmitted it. The program was funded.

Supreme Court Justice Harry Blackmun called the task of identifying religious organizations a "vaguely defined work of art" (*Bowen v. Kendrick,* 487 U.S. at 631 [1988]). Bringing more clarity to this task does not diminish the need for artistry. With faith-based organizations now the focus of so many aspirations and apprehensions, it is critical to develop conceptual categories and descriptive language that capture their complexity. This typology of the religious characteristics of social service organizations and programs may add clarity and precision to discussions of their role. The typology may also be of practical use to nonprofits in understanding and describing their own religious character for purposes of strategic planning, fundraising, and evaluation. For these ends, further research is needed to test and refine the types. In the words of the Working Group document (2002), "We do not suggest it as a definitive work, but rather as a tool to improve understanding."

PART III

Mission Orientations

7

Defining Mission Orientations

The Relationship between Social Action and Evangelism

Defining Mission Orientations

A church's mission provides a framework for its identity, establishing the institutional boundaries of "who we are" and "how we do things." It also frames a moral order for action by the congregation corporately and its members as individuals (Becker 1999, 181). Mission in a church context has a normative and transcendent character. In most churches, mission not only describes who a congregation is and what it does, but also signifies the greater good that is intended to arise from its identity and actions. Mission models "are an 'is' that implies an 'ought'" (Becker 1999, 16). Thus mission is not just a guide for congregational life but also a core product of that life. In most churches, mission has a public dimension that designates reaching beyond the congregation as part of the purpose for the church's existence (Ammerman 1997a). A church's activities may not be consistent with its stated mission, and people in the congregation may not agree on the content of this mission, but congregants will generally agree on the rightness of having a mission that calls on them to do things that generate public good.

Moreover, unlike other voluntary associations such as book clubs or sports groups, a church's mission has a *transcendent* dimension. A characteristic feature of congregations is that even when they function like social clubs, they still think they are about something larger (Cnaan et al. 2002). This awareness of a transcendent purpose derives from several presuppositions: that people are endowed with an immortal soul that places their earthly activities into

eternal perspective (and especially the activities they do together as a worship-
ing community), that each local church in some sense is linked to churches
around the world and across time, and that the mission of the church is directed by God (mediated by the authorities of denomination and tradition) and
thus has a quality of "givenness." Each church necessarily reinterprets its mission for its own context and culture, but is constrained from inventing a mission *de novo* (Becker 1999).

A mission orientation, according to Penny Becker's (1999) analysis of congregational models, represents "ideas about core tasks of the congregation and
legitimate means of achieving them." These shared understandings are institutionally patterned, or "manifest in policies and programs, in taken-for-
granted ways of doing things" (16–17). A mission model sorts through the
complex options for church life by recognizing "bundles of things—programs,
beliefs, ways of doing things—that go together" (181). Most churches include
some form of compassionate and/or evangelistic outreach in their mission
"bundle." Mission orientation goes beyond mere program activity, however, as
Becker explains:

> In some congregations these and other activities are highly valued
> or are part of what the congregation becomes known for—they are
> part of the public identity and community reputation—while in oth-
> ers they are not. In some, they are a large part of what makes mem-
> bers loyal to this particular congregation, while in others they are
> budget items that go unnoticed and unremarked. (187)

A congregation's mission orientation is reflected in both what it does and how
it interprets and values this activity.

Our analysis of mission orientations is indebted to the work of other researchers who have developed church models centered on the church's public
role (rather than on organizational structure, leadership type, or other features
of church life). Conceptual categories in these models include whether a
church is inwardly or outwardly focused, whether it is theologically conservative or liberal, whether it gives priority to evangelism or social change, and
whether it is other-worldly or this-worldly.[1] Here, we focus on the way that
churches organize the relationship between spiritual and social dimensions of
outreach. It should be kept in mind that this is just one facet—and in many
cases not the primary one—of church mission in its broadest sense, which
includes worship, fellowship, and other internally-focused activities.

Social Action versus Evangelism? Questioning the "Two-Party" System

A study conducted by the Religion and Civic Order Project at the University of California Santa Barbara, called "Politics of the Spirit," looked at the response of the faith community to the 1992 Los Angeles riots. The report observed that the Christian social programs taking root tended to be based in evangelical and nondenominational churches, and that "many, if not most, of these programs are simultaneously directed toward the spiritual as well as the political/social transformation of individuals and of Los Angeles neighborhoods.... Religious conversion is viewed as empowering, in the broadest sense of the word." In this new holistic strategy for community revitalization, "Spiritual renewal, community organizing, personal hygiene, and entrepreneurial skills are of a piece" (Orr et al. 1994, 2, 6).

John Bartkowski and Helen Regis (2003) investigated poverty relief at thirty churches in Mississippi. They observed the intertwined nature of social and spiritual aid in these settings. "Local religious leaders commonly agree that faith-based aid provision is a holistic endeavor that—unlike public assistance programs—aims to address the material needs of the disadvantaged while simultaneously providing the means for moral development and spiritual sustenance" (64). One large African American church that they profiled offers a full complement of social service programs, including a food pantry that serves over five hundred families each month. Through its services the church aims to "offer Christ" and "teach that Jesus Christ is the answer to all of our problems," according to the pastor. "We hope that somehow, if we show enough love, [aid recipients] will come back to our services and be a part of our church" (105).

Laudarji and Livezey (2000) observed the ministry of the Revival Center Church of God in Christ, which embraces residents of a Chicago housing project. Narratives of spiritual and social transformation pervade the congregation:

> Celia, a leader of the Helping Hands Ministry, was on welfare until the pastor persuaded her to get her GED; she later became a nurse and now tithes. Alex, who came after being released from prison, has remained employed, drug free, and legal. ... One of the elders used to be "the project drunk" before he was saved, joined the church, then got a good job and kept it. (101)

Such stories illustrate what Franklin (1996, 96) calls "deliverance-oriented evangelism" in the Church of God in Christ tradition, in which social ministries represent a spiritual battle front against the oppression of addictions, family brokenness, and generational poverty.

Ten of the twenty-three congregations studied by Nancy Ammerman (1997a) had an evangelistic orientation, according to their patterns of survey responses. Most of these ten also identified "service to the needy" as a very important or essential ministry of their church. One such church was South Meridian Church of God, Anderson, a prosperous Anglo congregation whose mission statement calls it to "witness to the world through the love of Jesus Christ and in the power of the Spirit." The pastor remarked on their central purpose, "We are in the business of preparing persons for another life." Yet, the case study observes, "this emphasis on the next world does not mean that South Meridian members are indifferent to this world. . . . To that end, the church has long supported a plethora of support groups and charitable ministries" (122–130).

In a survey of clergy in Indianapolis, some respondents indicated that the Bible calls believers most clearly to provide for the poor, while others emphasized the mandate to lead people to faith. Most, however, indicated that the Bible's instructions included caring for the full range of human needs—spiritual, material, and emotional. As Arthur Farnsley (2003, 87) interprets their response, these clergy saw compassion and witness interwoven together as "part of a larger package." For many evangelical churches, he observes, social services represent an opportunity to share Christ with nonbelievers, while evangelism is intended to yield social improvements for individuals as well as the broader society.

Ram Cnaan's (et al. 2002) study of congregational outreach in seven cities similarly documents a connection between service and witness in some congregations. One minister remarked, "We have a holistic view of ministry because we believe it is important to meet spiritual and physical needs as a way of evangelism" (241). While such direct references to evangelism as a motive for social service were rare, most respondents at least hoped their congregation's social services had a religious dimension, though few thought they did this effectively.

In his study of the Four Corners neighborhood in Boston, Omar McRoberts (2003) categorizes the ways that churches in this high-poverty "black religious district" interact with their public environment. Some churches view the street as the "evil other" to be avoided, others target the street as a recruiting ground for converts, others see it as an arena for meeting social needs, while others blend the recruitment and need-response motifs. The pastor of a Pentecostal church in this latter category explained his outreach strategy:

> We deal with the total person: that means the soul, the spirit and the mind and the body. First of all, before we get a person to really understand about salvation, we must first reach the needs, whether it be homes, food, clothes, job, whatever an individual person might

need. . . . Then a relationship comes second. And then I introduce
him to salvation. (94)

McRoberts notes an "uncanny agreement about the biblical mandate to serve
the 'whole person' in all his/her social and spiritual complexity" (109).

These snapshots from other studies call attention to the question of how,
and how much, churches relate evangelistic witness—or, more broadly, spiritual nurture[2]—to their social ministry agenda. Little research has focused on
the connection between spiritual and social outreach, in part because little
connection has been imagined to exist. The analysis of mission orientations
has been dominated by the conception of American Protestantism as a "two-
party system," a metaphor first applied by Jean Schmidt and Martin Marty
(Marty 1970; see Schmidt 1991). In this system, "public" Protestants confront
this-worldly social concerns, while "private" Protestants emphasize saving
souls through evangelism.

The schema advanced by *Varieties of Religious Presence* (Roozen, McKinney,
and Carroll 1984) reinforces this conceptual division. Evangelistic churches are
other-worldly, placing stress on "salvation for a world to come," and making
"a relatively sharp distinction . . . between religious and secular affairs" (34).
They *are* publicly engaged, though "not for the purpose of social reform or
change, but to share the message of salvation with those outside the fellowship"
(36). Civic and activist churches, in contrast, are this-worldly, or take "with
considerable seriousness this present world as an important arena for religiously motivated service and action" (34). Being evangelistic, in this frame,
seems incompatible with meaningful attention to social concerns.

Another study, however, suggests that churches are springing up in the
cracks between the *Varieties* mission types. The Church and Community Project studied nearly a hundred Midwestern congregations engaged in social ministries (Dudley and Van Eck 1992). They discovered no simple correlation between theology, social ideology, and social activism. Churches with an
evangelical view of salvation, particularly black and Hispanic congregations,
were just as likely to have an activist orientation as liberal churches. Mock's
(1992) analysis of these churches challenges "the assumption that only religiously liberal congregations maintain socially activist identities and that evangelical churches see their role in the world as strictly evangelistic. Far too many
exceptions exist to support such a claim" (30). The Church and Community
Project has not been alone in suggesting that the conventional dichotomy between social action and evangelism is breaking down (e.g., Roof 1996; Ammerman 1997a). Such analyses do not imply that the public-private, social
activist-evangelistic distinctions are wholly invalid, but rather that they should
no longer be viewed as exclusive.

While old patterns are being questioned, contemporary issues are casting
the religious landscape in a new light. One corollary of the debate over chari-

table choice has been the "discovery" of faith-based ministries by policy makers and the media. In the anecdotes which typically accompany media reports on this debate, it has become apparent that the nation's most distressed communities are seeded with churches that consider spiritual transformation an inalienable part of their social mission. If evangelistic churches truly were disinterested in social affairs, the prospect of proselytizing by church-related social programs would not be an issue.[3] Since black churches are five times more likely to express an interest in public funding (Chaves 1999), faith-based initiatives have particularly highlighted the vital integration of spiritual witness with service and empowerment in some streams of the African American tradition (Loury and Loury 1997; Franklin 1997; DiIulio 1998; Billingsley 1999; Harris 2001; McRoberts 2003).

Consider, for example, the case of Life in Christ Cathedral of Faith, a socially and theologically conservative African American church. From its mission statement ("To reach our community and the world with the true message of the Gospel of Jesus Christ, proclaiming and demonstrating the love of God"), street-witnessing team, evangelism training classes, and sermons urging faith-sharing, one might conclude that this church is focused on evangelism. But observe its slate of programs—including weekly meals for homeless persons, emergency and transitional housing, budget counseling, youth mentoring, substance abuse rehabilitation, collaboration with state-funded community development projects, and a Political Action Committee—and a picture emerges of a very this-worldly, public church indeed. To which of the two "parties" does Life in Christ belong? Rather than labeling this church (and others like it) an exception, a fresh exploration of mission orientations is needed to cast new light on the relationship between evangelistic commitments and social concerns.

A Typology of Mission Orientations

To identify the mission orientations of the churches in our study, we examined both their conceptual understanding and actual practice of outreach, revealing "bundles" of beliefs and activities shared by groups of congregations. *Dominant social action* churches focus on meeting practical needs and/or working for social justice; their programs involve minimal religious elements, though they may see their good works as an implicit witness. *Dual-focus* churches include both evangelism and social action as important, but independent, aspects of their outreach mission. Churches with a *holistic* mission consider witness and service to be inseparably linked. A *holistic-complementary* sub-type conceptualizes these as congruent facets of the same seamless mission, while the *holistic-instrumental* sub-type envisions social outreach as a portal to the primary objective of winning converts. *Dominant evangelism* churches focus primarily on sharing their faith, though a this-worldly variant sees individual conversions as a pathway to social change. *Inward-focused* churches practice no significant outreach.

Congregations often lack internal consensus about their mission. This may result in a struggle over control of the church's ministry identity, or in the coexistence of more than one mission emphasis within the congregation. Leaders may espouse one orientation, members another. Principle and practice may be in tension; the congregation may identify theologically or culturally with one position while actually doing something different. Moreover, mission is not a static commodity. Congregations are continually evolving in response to changes in their constituency and context, and so a snapshot in time may capture a church in the process of migrating from one orientation to another (Ammerman 1997a). This model may thus offer observers the conceptual vocabulary to describe subgroups and evolutionary forces within congregations as well as the distinctions between them.

1. *Dominant Social Action: Addressing Social Concerns Is the Primary Mission*

> *We live the gospel. . . . I don't force myself or what I believe on people.*
> *(Soup kitchen volunteer, Church of the Advocate)*

Some churches emphasize social ministry to the exclusion of evangelism. Social action—whether relief aid, personal empowerment, community development, or advocacy—is the main mode of community outreach. In the language of *Varieties of Religious Presence* (1984), social action churches may have either an activist or civic character, depending on whether they challenge the status quo at a systemic level or empower individuals to live more wholesomely in it. Both Church of the Advocate and Central Baptist are activist: they preach about economic and racial justice, have taken controversial stands on political issues, and see themselves as advocates for the powerless. A large, prestigious Anglo church where we conducted interviews has a more civic cast; their approach is to sponsor social services to transform and empower individuals who can then build a better society.

In social action churches, the essence of Christian mission is to embody the presence of Christ through ministries of compassion and justice. Social programs may have implicit religious overtones, but they use secular methodologies. Spiritual meanings associated with social ministry in this orientation focus on the mandate for caring for the poor or the devotional aspects of activism. The faith of church members motivates and is strengthened by social outreach, but ministry is not designed to nurture faith in others. The purpose of outreach, one associate pastor said emphatically, was not to "grow the church" by converting others. Overt evangelism is rejected as foreign to the religious culture, is considered offensive or inappropriate, or is understood as incarnational witness rather than as proclamation.

An evangelistic mission may find weak support from the congregation's history or denominational affiliation. This is the case with Church of the Advocate, an Episcopal congregation. At a focus group to discuss the church's future, a church member suggested that despite a strong record of social activism, the church's outreach was "falling short" on a spiritual level. "We know that we're good on feeding and clothing and on caring and teaching and all that. We know we've accomplished that, but we don't know how to stand, first off, religiously. Or to be religious, whatever that is." This church member's struggle to put words to his sense of what was missing exemplifies the fact that, for many churches in the mainline tradition, evangelism has long been absent from the cultural vocabulary.[4] Evangelism is literally absent from the vocabulary of one suburban Presbyterian church, as a member remarked, "We don't say *evangelism* in our church. . . . You can't say the 'e-word'. We say *outreach*."

Social action churches may also avoid evangelism because of its negative connotations. Some interviewees recited unpleasant past personal experiences that led them to shy away from proselytizing. Words we commonly heard in conjunction with evangelism in a negative sense were *preachy* and *pushy*. Some interviewees considered it ethically inappropriate to interfere with others' religious beliefs, particularly adherents of other faiths. "I don't force myself or what I believe on people," insisted a member of Church of the Advocate who volunteers with the soup kitchen. Many viewed instigating spiritual conversations as intrusive and tacky, as a leader at a Presbyterian church commented: "It's a private thing—it's kind of like asking whether they've changed their underwear today to ask where they are spiritually."

Thus church ministries may lack an evangelistic dimension because bringing people to Christian faith is not a goal of outreach. On the other hand, an aversion to overt evangelism does not necessarily indicate indifference toward the spiritual needs of people outside the church. Rather, it may denote a concern for expressing spiritual care in an appropriate manner, which for this group does not include overt witnessing. The Presbyterian woman quoted above whose church avoided the "e-word" added that she thought it important to touch people's spiritual needs—but this was best done tastefully and understatedly. "It could be in a very subtle way. People can know what you believe by who you are and what you do, not necessarily by preaching to them, or putting the Bible in their face." A ministry leader at Church of the Advocate similarly observed, "You can't tell a child that God works. They got to feel. They have to see. They have to touch."

Caring for the poor thus *embodies* Christian faith, making verbal proclamation superfluous. Several interviewees quoted a saying attributed to St. Francis of Assisi: "Preach the gospel at all times; if necessary, use words." Chapter

4 introduced the idea of implicit spiritual nurture, in which service wordlessly conveys a religious message by demonstrating God's love. In the social gospel tradition, justice for the poor is not only a metaphor for God's salvation on a spiritual plane, it is itself part of that salvation. Churches with an implicit approach may thus define evangelism as doing good works in Christ's name. Isaac Miller, rector of Church of the Advocate, took this position. He hesitated before giving us his definition of evangelism, saying that it deviated from the "standard textbook definition." "There's a part of me that understands evangelism as simply the process of doing what we understand God calls us to do. . . . Hopefully we do it in such a way that we invite others to become a part of that work."

To "do it in such a way" may mean making one's own faith transparent and appealing to beneficiaries, while avoiding any appearance of coercion or judgmentalism. Beneficiaries may be encouraged to deepen whatever spiritual identity they bring to the program, even if that path diverges from the faith of the sponsoring congregation. This approach recognizes faith as a resource for beneficiaries without upholding a specific faith as an end in itself. Church of the Advocate's soup kitchen, for example, offers an optional Bible study and prayer before the meal, but avoids "proselytizing," according to a church volunteer. This would violate the ethic of the Golden Rule (see Ammerman 1997b) by doing to others what he would himself resent: "I don't like anyone to come on too strong with me when it comes to religion. Let me decide for myself."

2. Dual-Focus: Evangelism and Social Ministry Are Independent Areas of Ministry

Revitalizing the community is a way to accent the reality of the Christian witness. . . . It's Jesus, but it's also Jesus and potatoes and greens, and Jesus and a good, decent house. (Rev. Bill Moore, Tenth Memorial Baptist Church)

The mission orientation of some congregations is characterized by a dual mission focus. Such churches consider both evangelism and social ministry to be legitimate and important. But, for the most part, the two mission thrusts are not interconnected in practice and spring from different theological motivations. The mission of the congregation as a whole embraces both spiritual and social objectives, while individual programs and volunteers focus primarily on one or the other. Sharing the gospel and serving the community are the focus of separate programs, with little overlap in leadership, administration, or volunteer support.

In terms of the overall importance attached to evangelism, dual-focus churches resemble churches in the holistic category; in terms of the religious characteristics of their social programs, however, they tend to resemble dominant social action churches. Social ministries in dual-focus churches typically do not make spiritual renewal of beneficiaries an overt goal; evangelism ministries do not address substantive material needs. Religious elements in social ministries are likely to be low-key, and to take an implicit or invitational form. The lack of integration may stem from professional norms against seeking to influence the spiritual beliefs of beneficiaries, or from practical or cultural barriers to communicating with the population served by church ministries. The church pursues other forms of evangelism not connected directly to service provision, such as network evangelism among social peers. The two types of outreach programs may thus have different target audiences: a suburban church, for example, may organize social ministries in inner-city neighborhoods, while its evangelistic efforts are directed toward its local community.

In dual-focus churches, the theological grounding and desired outcomes for spiritual and social outreach are perceived to be distinct. The desire to see persons and communities experience socioeconomic restoration stands independent of the evangelistic objective of converting individuals. The two mission emphases may be mutually reinforcing—as Rev. Moore puts it, "Revitalizing the community is a way to accent the reality of the Christian witness"—but they are not interdependent. The act of social ministry has meaning in and of itself as a way of deepening one's faith or as faithful obedience to God, regardless of spiritual outcomes for others. Likewise, bringing people to faith is an end in itself, not tied to the results of social programs.

The two churches in our study that fall into the dual-focus category demonstrate different forms of this ministry model. Reverend Moore summarizes the mission of Tenth Memorial Baptist church: "The church ought to be a change agent." Tenth Memorial pursues social reform through involvement in low-income and senior housing, Empowerment Zone business development, and support for the local public school. Community development programs such as these offer limited opportunities to develop one-on-one relationships with beneficiaries, which in turn limits the possibilities for integrated evangelism. Although the church provides several social service programs that have a more individualistic orientation, such as food distribution and a GED preparatory program, volunteers do not view these as venues for sharing their faith. Rather, Rev. Moore affirms that social action has a more implicit evangelistic impact, as "it helps to bring alive what we articulate from the pulpit." Direct evangelism occurs primarily through separate programs: revivals, altar calls during church services, and a "S.W.A.T." ("Saints With A Testimony") team that organizes street outreach and tract distribution. Thus, Tenth Memorial's social and evangelistic ministry tracks promote change in its neighborhood in distinct but complementary ways.

For Media Presbyterian, the dual-focus dynamic arises in part from the geographic and cultural distance between the church and most beneficiaries of the church's social ministry. While the church responds generously to meet emergency needs in its suburban community, most of its organized social programs serve the urban centers of Chester and Philadelphia. Media also takes an annual mission trip to a rural community to build a home through Habitat for Humanity. These ministries incorporate few explicitly religious elements. The main evangelistic impact of these ministries, in Media's perception, is their appeal to unchurched observers. In chapter 4 this was introduced as *altruism evangelism*. Through these social projects the church serves as "a city on a hill" whose light draws others to God (Matthew 5:14–16).

This strategy goes hand-in-hand with a reluctance to evangelize in confrontational ways, as the chair of Media's Faith in Action committee explains: "The Bible tells us that we should witness. I frankly don't like the approach that a lot of people take to witnessing. . . . People are very turned off by people that approach them in the mall and do phone calls." A better strategy, he continues, is to spread the word about the church's social action among unchurched acquaintances and family members in hopes that this will create opportunities to share the faith commitments underlying Christian compassion. Thus the dual-focus model provides a way for members to reconcile the biblical imperative to share their faith with the prevalent cultural resistance to evangelism. On one track, church members travel to service projects that address inner-city or rural poverty. On a parallel track, this service provides a nonthreatening evangelistic opening among members' peer networks.

Social ministry and evangelism may represent either complementary specializations or competing tensions in the congregation. While Rev. Moore places evangelism and social action on equal footing, about half of survey respondents in the church were divided in prioritizing one over the other. At Tenth Memorial, this division is friendly, with members respecting one another's ministry "callings." In other cases, relations between the two camps may be more polarized. Missional tension may also spring from interpersonal conflicts or disputes over access to church resources, in which members eye rival mission ventures as a threat to their ministry "turf."

3. Holistic: Evangelism and Social Ministry Are Dynamically Interconnected

> We can't be a church in this neighborhood and not be involved in various kinds of social ministries that are meeting these needs. Nor can we countenance the possibility of that kind of ministry apart from giving the gospel. . . . [They are] inextricably related to one another. (Rev. Phil Ryken, Tenth Presbyterian Church)

A third mission orientation places evangelism and social action in dynamic interaction. Evangelism and social ministry are linked in terms of program design and administration, theological grounding, and desired outcomes. Concern for others' spiritual condition reinforces holistic churches' sense of obligation to address social needs, and the hope of inspiring spiritual renewal in others is a central meaning attached to their social activism. "For us it goes hand in hand," said a youth ministry leader at Bethel Temple. "Part of our witness is doing social action. You don't separate the two."

The methodology of holistic ministry programs assumes a connection between spiritual transformation and socioeconomic empowerment. A relationship with God, by itself, may not be sufficient or even necessary to turn a person or a community around, but it is seen as increasing the odds. Conversely, meeting people's material needs does not guarantee their openness to the gospel, but it helps. In describing the rationale behind their church's programs, interviewees sometimes talked about creating evangelistic opportunities by showing people compassion; other times they talked about improving people's social well-being by leading them to experience spiritual renewal. An outreach program may be oriented more toward social change or toward spiritual nurture, but in a holistic context both are underlying goals.

The social ministries of holistic churches provide spiritual nurture to beneficiaries in a variety of ways (introduced in chapters 4 and 5). Integrated evangelistic strategies have built-in religious activities, either optional or mandatory, such as incorporating prayer into a counseling session, leading a Bible study as part of an after-school program, or holding a worship service before a meal. Other programs employ a more informal, pre-evangelistic approach, cultivating relationships with beneficiaries and looking for opportunities to pursue a spiritual dialogue. In a two-step invitational strategy, the social ministry brings beneficiaries into the physical or relational space of the congregation, where they can be encouraged to attend other church services at which a gospel message is presented.

Such pre-evangelistic strategies rely on the implicit witness of good works and caring relationships to create an atmosphere of spiritual receptivity. Unlike the premise of dominant social action churches, however, the holistic model presumes that good deeds alone are insufficient to spread the faith. Evangelism has both an implicit and explicit component. This is clear in the assertion of the missions pastor at Tenth Presbyterian Church that the gospel "is to be communicated in both word and deed. In deed alone is not enough because it is something that has content—verbal content. . . . But the means by which we communicate it is not only verbally but in loving action." Works of service are generally intended to communicate an explicitly Christian message, whether overtly at the time of service delivery or at a later point, whether through organized evangelistic activities or informal relationships.

The holistic model has two subtypes. In both, the spiritual and social dimensions of mission are interrelated. The subtypes represent two broad ways of conceiving of this relationship.

HOLISTIC-COMPLEMENTARY SUBTYPE

> *The church has done evangelism and the church has done social ministry—*
> *but not always together. We must get excited about the whole gospel to*
> *minister to whole persons. (Rev. Jim Kraft, First Presbyterian Church)*

The first subtype is labeled *holistic-complementary*. According to this outlook, telling people about the gospel and demonstrating one's faith through social action are seen to have equal intrinsic value, and each has more value in association with the other. This package is understood as "the whole gospel."

In this model, evangelism and social ministry are interwoven but not interchangeable. Each plays an essential role in the overarching mandate to love the world in Jesus' name. When asked whether First Presbyterian incorporated evangelism into social services, the associate pastor for outreach replied:

> That's like saying, would I feel the need to split down a quarter. . . .
> Each side is distinct; we do call it the "head" and the "tail.". . . . [But]
> they are two sides of the same coin. It is twenty-five cents if I hold it
> up this way. It is twenty-five cents if I hold it up that way. It is the
> gospel whether I hold it any way. It's the gospel with both evangel-
> ism and social ministry.

This integration is inspired by Christ's example of "sharing the principles of God and meeting human need," according to a ministry leader at Germantown Church of the Brethren. Another ministry leader at Germantown explained the congruence between word and deed in public mission. Citing the church's mission statement "to make known to as many people as possible the redeeming love of God," she commented: "Love is an action word. . . . People want to see action, not [hear] so much mouth." Without social ministry, evangelism is just "so much mouth." Without verbalizing its basis for compassion, the church's social activism loses its redemptive power.

Interviewees expressed these views with varying degrees of sophistication. Some were able to articulate a conceptual or theological distinction between the evangelistic "head" and social "tail" of the gospel coin. For others, the meanings were not so much linked as blurred. In these interviews, when we posed the question of how the two dimensions of outreach were related, it was obvious from the way respondents tried to make sense of the question that they did not think of these as discrete concepts, but simply accepted them both as a given. Asked for her definition of evangelism, for example, a church member on staff with Nueva Creación's summer camp and after-school program responded, "I have no idea!" Follow-up questions revealed that she made no abstract distinction between sharing God's love through words versus actions; to her they were "both the same." In practice, she clearly did both. Helping youth improve their academic performance was important to her, but so was giving them opportunities to learn about God and to come to faith.

A member of Germantown Church of the Brethren summarized the message that church outreach is intended to convey: "We love you because God loves you." This simple mandate can be expressed through a variety of forms of evangelism and social ministry. Along with meeting the felt needs of individuals, holistic-complementary churches may engage in community development and political advocacy as more in-depth ways of substantiating God's love. The pastor of a small inner-city congregation expanded on this theme: "God is concerned that we love our neighbors as ourselves. . . . If my neighbors are hungry, I come up with creative ways to feed them. And then we've got to ask the question, Why are they hungry? And if there are structures in our society that cause them to remain hungry, then we have to unite in one voice to seek to change the structures." The underlying goal of these efforts, he said, is to draw people toward "conversion to Christ and his kingdom."

HOLISTIC-INSTRUMENTAL SUBTYPE

The church needs to be actively engaged in social ministries, but social ministries that are rooted and funneled out of the truth of the gospel. . . . Social ministry to non-Christians is the vehicle through which the gospel can flow. (Rev. Joel Van Dyke, Bethel Temple Community Bible Church)

The second subtype, *holistic-instrumental*, orders evangelism and social action in hierarchical relationship. This mission orientation places primary emphasis on evangelism, and views social ministry as a vehicle for sharing faith. While witness and compassionate action are both important functions of the church, evangelism is a decided priority. Effectively touching a person's spirit, however, entails caring for the whole person. A ministry leader at Tenth Presbyterian shared this premise: "People respond to the gospel both from what they hear but also in how they see it lived out and in people meeting needs of theirs." Churches must help meet people's material and emotional needs in order to open the door to spiritual nurture. Religious conversion, in turn, provides the anchor for effective social interventions.

In this subtype, the value of social ministry is directly linked to (though not reducible to) its function as a carrier of religious meaning. Social ministries are likely to feature spiritual objectives and overt religious elements. A ministry leader at Bethel explained, "The gospel has to be in everything we do." When the church includes evangelistic tracts in its food boxes, "there's a response. People remember—people know that they're loved and cared about." For evangelistic aid to be Christlike, this leader later qualified, it must be driven by love for people rather than "a selfish motivation to get people saved." This perspective favors programs of relief and personal development, which offer natural avenues for evangelistic interactions with beneficiaries.

The holistic-instrumental approach often incorporates the belief that people's immediate needs—whether financial, physical, relational, or emotional— may eclipse their sense of a need for God. A ministry leader at Christian Stronghold voiced this postulate: "By going out to the community and meeting their felt needs, that gives us the opportunity to spread the good news of Jesus Christ. If you are hungry, you won't hear me. If I feed you, you will listen." By helping people overcome their physical hunger, the church hopes to trigger a new awareness of their spiritual hunger. Evangelistic social ministry aims to turn a material crisis into a "religious problem-solving perspective" which can lead to conversion (Lofland and Stark 1965, 867).

Koinonia Christian Community Church, a young congregation in a poor neighborhood, made social services the cornerstone of its member recruitment strategy on the hope that people who might never visit church on a Sunday might come to church for a hot meal or a parenting seminar. Asserts pastor Jerome Simmons, "Everything we have developed in our church programs, whether methods or resources, is a tool for the purpose of winning souls." These "tools" make Christianity more attractive to potential converts than purely evangelistic methods like street preaching alone. Yet Koinoinia's passion for "winning souls" meets an equal conviction that these souls are embodied in whole persons with complex, intermeshing problems. As a ministry leader at Koinonia put it, "People aren't just suffering from one thing. So when you want to fix the person, you want to fix the person wholly." Compassion is assigned intrinsic value beyond its function as a pathway to conversions. Evangelism is the church's priority, but it is only part of how the church works toward "fixing people wholly."

4. Dominant Evangelism: Sharing the Gospel Is the Primary Mission

> Evangelism starts at the core. Once you change a person's life you can also change their social position. (New Covenant Church small group leader)

Dominant evangelism churches share the emphasis on evangelism found in holistic-instrumental churches, but without the accompanying level of involvement in social outreach. Mission is equated with sharing the gospel. Promoting conversions is considered the only way that the church can truly make a difference in this world.

Some churches clearly fit the other-worldly evangelistic mission template identified by Roozen, McKinney, and Carroll (1984). Focused on saving souls for eternal life, they consider organized social action irrelevant at best, and a dangerous diversion from more pressing spiritual concerns at worst. Social compassion is not entirely absent; the church may encourage individual church members to practice benevolence, and may provide occasional charitable aid such as holiday gift baskets. Evangelistic programs may include one-time material incentives, such as hosting a free barbeque in conjunction with an outdoor revival. Such churches may also become involved in political issues viewed as an extension of the church's theology, such as pro-family or anti-abortion legislation. In general, however, social concerns are delegated to the purview of secular entities.

Yet not all churches that prioritize evangelism lack this-worldly attention to social concerns. Just as some with a dominant social action orientation frame their activism as implicit evangelism, some dominant evangelism churches define spiritual nurture as the highest form of social compassion. A church with this orientation takes seriously its role as a social change agent, but interprets this role in terms of its capacity to effect spiritual or moral change at a personal level. A ministry leader at New Covenant declared, "We are preaching the gospel to our friends, to our community because we want to improve the social condition. There is not one without the other. . . . We want them to be safe. We want them to have an improved life. And [becoming saved] is the only way they are going to get it." Stark labeled this strategy the "miracle motif," or "the idea that if everyone were converted to Christ, social ills would disappear" (Stark 1971; quoted in C. Smith 1998, 191).

As with holistic churches, such dominant evangelism churches blur the line between sacred and secular. Their worldview "does not place a dichotomy between the spiritual and the social. It is blended into one," according to a New Covenant church leader. This leader then adds, "The spirit, of course, is primary and this is why we are led by the spirit." The church subsumes social well-being under the spiritual realm. A central assumption of this mission orientation is that a person's spiritual status has relational, physical, and socioeconomic consequences. Helping people in need thus requires getting at the root of their problems by a religious conversion and process of discipleship that produces fundamental life changes. Narratives of successful ministry commonly feature a person who becomes a Christian and consequently makes changes (quitting an addiction, reconciling with a spouse, completing a GED, gaining a new sense of self-esteem) that improve his or her socioeconomic standing. These individuals are then believed to have a ripple effect on their community, as they draw others to faith.

Since a regenerated soul is a prerequisite for a transformed life, social interventions offered by this-worldly dominant evangelism churches are typically directed toward those who are already Christians, or who are willing to hear the gospel message. Evangelism is seen to widen the scope of the church's influence on society by bringing more people into the church's circle of care.

Participants in the dominant evangelism type disagree on the value of offering aid to those who clearly reject the Christian message: some are resigned to it as an expression of Jesus' mercy toward sinners, others lament it as poor stewardship of church resources. But they agree it has small chance of doing much good in the end.

The approach of this church type, like the holistic-instrumental type above, is intensely individualistic (C. Smith 1998; Hollinger 1983). The task of the church is to redeem individuals, rather than reform social structures. As Bishop Milton Grannum of New Covenant explained, "God saves people and people make communities. We believe that programs that address communities will usually not succeed. But if you deal with individuals and change individuals, you change families all to the better and then you change communities." This view is often supported by a premillenial theology that expects the world to grow incurably worse as the apocalyptic return of Christ draws near. Given the inevitable moral decay of our culture and deficiencies of our political system, the role of the church is to enlist new believers, who are then empowered to improve their lot in a flawed and sometimes hostile society.

5. Inwardly Focused: No Significant Social Action or Evangelism

Some churches have little or no active outreach.[5] Despite an evangelistic or compassionate ministry activity here and there (such as an annual Bring-a-Friend-to-Church Day or a Thanksgiving canned food drive), such churches are not oriented toward the world outside the walls of the church. Their main focus is the internal, "priestly" ministries of worship, fellowship, and discipleship (Davidson and Koch 1998). This type most closely resembles the sanctuary type in the *Varieties of Religious Presence* model.

The exclusively inward focus of some churches arises from their identities as "protected enclaves in a hostile world" (Warner 1994, 72–73). Their concern is to shield members from the temptations and travails of society, not to change society. McRoberts discovered, however, that a lack of outreach programs does not necessarily indicate an other-worldly disinterest in social concerns. In the inner-city churches he studied, such an assumption "would be grossly out of sync with what the churches themselves believed they were doing" (2003, 102). Rather, some "priestly" congregations focus their mission on "the privileged role of the church: to be an incubator of saved souls and sane psyches, ready to face the world. . . . People 'built up' in the church community were uniquely suited to push for social transformation outside the church" (103–104). Inward-focus churches point to the socially uplifting effect of discipleship and mutual aid. Rather than sponsoring corporate ministries, the church equips members to witness, serve, and work toward social change as individuals.

The inwardly focused category also includes churches that claim a mission orientation in principle without substantiating it in practice. Ammerman's

(1997a) study, for example, noted that at two of the evangelistic congregations in their sample, "the endorsement of evangelistic emphases is not matched by actual activities in the church" (339). Similarly, there are churches that assign theological or cultural preference to social action without actually engaging in it. Although they may respond similarly to outwardly oriented churches on survey questions about mission priorities, there is a discrepancy between belief and action.

Mission Orientation and Program Activity

Ten of the fifteen churches we selected for study fall in the holistic category, evenly divided between complementary and instrumental sub-types. Two churches are dual-focus. Two are dominant social action. At the other end of the spectrum, one is dominant evangelism. (None, of course, were in the final inwardly focused category.) The assignment of mission orientations was based on a combination of survey data, interviews with clergy and ministry leaders, and field observations of actual ministry practice.[6] Table 7.1 presents the average program activity for churches in each type. Given that our sample is not representative, the number of churches in each type should not be taken as significant. However, the distribution of activity across the mission orientations suggests several patterns that warrant further investigation.

The average number of evangelism ministries predictably increases across the types, from dominant social action to dominant evangelism. The average

TABLE 7.1 Average Number of Ministry Programs per Church by Mission Orientation

	Social ministry type (average number of programs)					
Mission Orientation	Relief services	Personal development	Community development	Systemic change	All social action programs	Evangelism programs
Dominant social action (N=2)	2.5	3.0	1.5	2.5	9.5	0.5
Dual-focus (N=2)	2.5	4.0	3.5	1.5	11.5	4.0
Holistic (N=10)	3.2	4.6	2.8	0.6	11.2	6.2
Holistic-complementary (N=5)	3.4	4.4	3.4	1.0	12.2	6.0
Holistic-instrumental (N=5)	3.0	4.8	2.2	0.2	10.2	6.4
Dominant evangelism (N=1)	2.0	2.0	0	0	4.0	8.0
All churches (N=15)	2.9	4.1	2.5	0.9	10.5	5.3

number of social programs, however, peaks in the holistic-complementary category. Holistic churches averaged more social programs than the two dominant social action churches, except in the systemic change category. Dual-focus churches sponsored the most community development (reflecting Tenth Memorial's strong record in this area), holistic churches the most relief and personal development. Interestingly, the two holistic subtypes diverge in relation to structural ministries (community development and systemic change). All but one of the five holistic-complementary churches had a systemic change ministry, compared to only one of the five holistic-instrumental churches. Holistic-complementary churches also participated more substantially in community development. Within this small group of holistic churches, it is apparent that the integration of an evangelistic emphasis amplifies rather than dilutes social activity, but the way in which this emphasis is integrated can affect the kinds of social involvement.

Conclusion

We have suggested a typology of mission orientations that creates space for congregations that are both evangelistic and socially engaged. This spectrum of types indicates that the religious impulses to serve and to save are not always polarized drives. Rather, churches interrelate these two imperatives in a range of adaptable, and sometimes rather sophisticated, ways. The two-party metaphor is helpful for describing congregations that embrace the dominant poles of social action and evangelism, but the rich variety of the field demands more nuanced imagery. The dual-focus and holistic categories are more than combinations or variants of other orientations; they represent a distinct understanding of the Christian mandate and the church's public role.

The task of selecting the case studies was complicated by the difficulty of casting churches into neat categories. Church of the Advocate, for example, with its history of radical activism, leadership in community organizing, and multiple service programs, fits the archetype of a social action church. But then we found that Advocate prefaces its soup kitchen meal with a time of Bible study and prayer, that members were wrestling with how to encourage service beneficiaries to attend worship services, and that the church was forming an evangelism committee to plan recruitment activities. We selected Bethel Community Bible Church because its conservative theology, street witnessing campaigns, enterprising outreach to youth, and support for missions marked it as an evangelistic congregation. Then we discovered that the church had recently revised its mission statement to include "revitalizing our community" as one of its priorities, created the staff position of director of economic and community development, and launched several new social service programs, all of which integrated spiritual elements. We selected Media Presbyterian Church because of the holistic perspective advocated by the pastor, but then did not find evidence for the integration of evangelism within service programs. Rather, we observed that Media balanced these mission priorities in its outreach as a whole, and so we had to create a new category to represent this strategy.

Ammerman (1997a) contends that the majority of churchgoers are not bothered by such seeming departures from archetypal expectations. Ordinary people, she writes, "feel much freer than do professional ideologues to put together ideas and practices from a very large cultural tool kit. These ideas may not appear to form a coherent intellectual system, but they contribute to workable strategies of action." She argues persuasively that categorical polarities like social action versus evangelism fail to capture the "middle ground of everyday practice":

> Support for an evangelical view of Christian life is not systematically opposed by those who see social activism as more important, or vice versa. Most of the people we met have simply not learned the ideological lesson that if they believe in promoting social justice, they should place less emphasis on witnessing; or—at the other pole— that if they believe in witnessing, they should be wary of calls for social justice. (358)

Congregational studies misrepresent churches when they force them into a dichotomous mission mold that more reflects the preconceptions of traditional analyses than the shape of a congregation's own worldview. Our journey of discovery affirmed an approach of thinking about evangelism and social action not as competing parties but as strategic resources for mission that churches can opt to combine in multiple, innovative, and evolving ways.

8

Influences on Congregational Mission

Why do churches adopt a particular mission orientation? And what helps, hinders, or sways them as they put their beliefs about mission into action? Research has been accumulating on the variables that predict which congregations engage in social outreach (see Scott 2002). However, the question here is not just *whether* a church involves itself with community concerns but *what form* this involvement takes, and, in particular, how a church relates the spiritual and social facets of its mission. The factors that beckon a church to active engagement with social needs may be different from the factors associated with how the church views the spiritual dynamics of this ministry. This chapter explores some of the variables salient to mission orientation and places the development of these orientations into historical context.

Mission Orientations and Congregational Characteristics in Our Case Studies

Table 8.1 displays the mission orientation and selected characteristics for each church. (For more descriptive information on the churches and their ministries, see the tables in chapter 2 as well as appendix 1.)

Two things are immediately striking about this table. First is the consistent portrait that emerges of the churches in our study with a holistic-instrumental mission: theologically conservative congrega-

TABLE 8.1 Mission Orientations and Selected Characteristics of the Case Study Churches

Mission Orientation	Race	Location	Residency[a]	Size[b]	Education[c]	Theology[d]
Dominant social action						
Central Baptist	Anglo	suburban	semi	medium	high	liberal
Advocate	Black	inner city	local	v. small	medium	liberal
Dual focus						
Media Presbyterian	Anglo	suburban	semi	large	high	moderate
Tenth Memorial	Black	inner city	semi	large	medium	conservative
Holistic						
Holistic-complementary						
Cookman U.M.	Black	inner city	local	v. small	low	moderate
First Presbyterian	Anglo	downtown	local	large	high	moderate
Germantown C.o.B.	Black	metro[e]	local	small	medium	conservative
Life in Christ	Black	inner city	local	medium	medium	conservative
Nueva Creación	Hispanic	inner city	local	v. small	low	liberal
Holistic-instrumental						
Bethel Temple	Hispanic	inner city	local	medium	medium	conservative
Christian Stronghold	Black	inner city	semi	mega	high	conservative
Faith A.G.	Black	inner city	local	small	low	conservative
Koinonia COGIC	Black	inner city	local	v. small	low	conservative
Tenth Presbyterian	Anglo	downtown	comm.	large	high	conservative
Dominant evangelism						
New Covenant	Black	metro[e]	comm.	mega	high	conservative

a. Residence of members: local = majority live in immediate neighborhood (within fifteen minutes); semi-local = majority live in nearby neighborhoods (within half an hour); commuter = significant minority (over 15%) live more than a half hour away.

b. Size (average church attendance): very small = <100; small = 100–200; medium = 200–500; large = 500–1500; mega = >1500.

c. Education: low = less than 50% have had at least some college education; medium = 50%–75% have some college; high = over 75% have some college.

d. Theology: based on two survey questions—liberal = the Bible is not literally true, and everyone or all true believers are saved; moderate = the Bible is inspired but not literal, and only the born-again are saved; conservative = the Bible is to be taken literally, and only those who have been born again are saved.

e. *Metro* means a non-inner-city urban residential area.

tions in a distressed urban setting, most of whose members live nearby (with the exception of Tenth Presbyterian). This pattern will be explored later in the chapter.

But perhaps even more arresting is the diversity within other mission orientations. No consistent pattern for race, size, or education level emerges within the dominant social action, dual-focus, or holistic-complementary categories. Together these three categories, representing churches that give higher or equal emphasis to social action, include churches of every theological stripe, corroborating the insight from the Church and Community Project that every theological tradition contains the seeds of social ministry (Mock 1992; Dudley and Van Eck 1992). No simple linear correlation exists between a church's characteristics and its mission. This is clear from comparing churches that share a mission orientation—such as Media Presbyterian and Tenth Memorial (dual-focus), or Life in Christ and First Presbyterian Church (holistic-complimentary)—but differ considerably in terms of constituency, race, polity, and location.

Factors Affecting Mission Orientation

This diversity does not mean that contextual factors lack any relevance to mission orientation, but, rather, suggests that the patterns of relevance are complex. Analyzing these relationships entails more detailed investigation than our limited data can provide. However, the case studies offer some insights. We briefly examine several key influences on mission orientation: culture, theology, structures of authority, resources, and community context.[1]

Culture

A key cultural consideration is congregational identity. According to Carl Dudley (2002, 66), identity "gives the group coherence and a basis for making decisions. Embedded in congregational identity are the criteria for what is acceptable and the sources of energy for ministry." A church's identity encompasses key characteristics such as ethnicity and class, which can exercise a sometimes unexamined influence on a church's ministry choices. For example, middle class sensibilities at Media and First Presbyterian deem some forms of evangelism more acceptable than others. Congregational identity also derives from the congregation's unique history and store of experiences and influences. Penny Becker (1999), drawing on Gary Alan Fine (1987), uses the term *ideoculture* to describe the particularities of a given church in relation to other churches. A church's ideoculture reinforces its mission orientation through language, rituals, and symbols, such as the stunning murals in the sanctuary of Church of the Advocate that surround worshipers with images related to the themes of liberation, justice, solidarity, and pride in their African American heritage. Such "shared cultural elements" enable or constrain various forms of congregational action (Wood 1997, 603).

Cnaan and Boddie (2001) report the "power of tradition" in upholding a congregation's commitment to social ministry. A strong identification with a particular brand of mission can become a self-fulfilling prophecy. The greater the role that a given ministry motif plays in a church's self-described character, the more the congregation will be likely to selectively endorse and fund those ministries that are consistent with its heritage. This pattern was clear at Central Baptist Church. Many members chose the church because of its social justice legacy; others were socialized into the church's expectations for participation in ministry after joining. In this sense, Central suggests a liberal version of a "strict" church in the sense described by Wellman (2002; see also Iannaccone 1994), generating strong and magnetic attachments around shared norms for values and behavior. While social justice seems to provide a strong "hook" where churches can hang their identity (Wood 1994), any active mission orientation can serve the same function.

Once established, a church's mission identity becomes part of the way it carves out its niche in the religious marketplace (Ammerman 1997a; McRoberts 2003). As one Advocate member observed, "The Advocate does not get a lot of members from its soup kitchen, but it gets members because it has a soup kitchen." Similarly, Bill Borror noted, "the fact that we are doing so much in the community" has helped to fuel Media Presbyterian's growth. "We have had people join and come out because of things we have done for people that they have heard about." Jim Kraft remarks that First Presbyterian's sometimes controversial advocacy for affordable housing "has been an attractive thing to people who care about social ministry. . . . I think it goes hand in glove with the traditional evangelism of going door-to-door and delivering packets."

Race and ethnicity also can have a significant influence on mission orientation. The dichotomous paradigm of saving souls and reforming society originated with Anglo churches. Protestant Latino and African American congregations, as a generalization, have tended to start from the assumption that the ideal—or practical necessity—is to do both. This was illustrated in a discussion with Rev. Willie Richardson, pastor of Christian Stronghold Baptist Church, an African American congregation. Asked if the conservative, largely white Bible college where he was educated had influenced his commitment to serving the community, he answered emphatically, "No, no, no. . . . My interpretation of the Great Commission definitely is not their interpretation." He then described being the only minority student in a class where they were debating the social gospel. The teacher asked why he was not joining in the discussion. He recalled his response:

I don't see where I have an opportunity to participate in this, I said, because you've only got two positions here. One is arguing for the social side of things and the other one is arguing for biblical inerrancy. . . . But as I see Christ in the Bible, I see that you've got to do both. . . . I know from being a pastor you can't do either/or.

The perception that an evangelistic mission excludes social activism can have racial overtones, as Rev. Richardson's experience points out, particularly in an urban environment.

The shared preference for a both/and ministry paradigm does not mean African American churches all have the same mission orientation, however, because there are a range of ways that this ideal may be expressed. This is clear from the diversity within our small sample. New Covenant subsumes social empowerment within the mandate to make disciples; Church of the Advocate, true to its name, emphasizes that discipleship entails pursuing social change; Life in Christ values "properly balancing evangelism and social justice." Moreover, churches across racial lines may share the same mission orientation, displaying remarkable similarities in their language, values, and worldview. Racial heritage does not determine mission orientation. It does, however, provide a bounded set of options for interpreting and mobilizing the church's mission.

A similar observation may be made about the influence of Hispanic culture on mission (Aponte 1998; Maldonado 1999; Espinosa, Elizondo, and Miranda 2003). Latino Protestants tend to favor an interpersonal over an institutional approach to organizing ministry. This pattern was evident in our observations of Bethel Temple and Nueva Creación Lutheran Church. Both congregations emphasized Latino values of relationship, availability, and presence. The contribution of these cultural values to mission orientation, however, was variable. The value of presence expressed itself at Bethel via an emphasis on relational evangelism; Nueva Creación's pastor emphasized solidarity with the poor and other concepts drawn from liberation theology. Thus different ethnicities offer different cultural resources for mission, but churches may appropriate different facets of their own cultural heritage.

Theology

Mainline congregations are more likely than evangelical congregations to sponsor social programs, particularly community organizing or systemic change (Wuthnow 2004; Chaves 2004; Chaves and Tsitsos 2001; Ammerman 2001).[2] It is no accident that both dominant social action churches in our study are theologically liberal, while all six churches that prioritize evangelism over social action (in the dominant evangelism and holistic-instrumental categories) are conservative.[3] The most direct influence of theology appears to be on the emphasis a church attaches to evangelism (see Hoge, Perry, and Klever 1978). The conservative churches in our study sponsored an average of 6.3 evangelism programs (followed by moderates with an average of 5.3 programs), compared with the liberal churches' average of 2. Some beliefs associated with liberal theology are less compatible with the concept of evangelism specified in chapter 2. At Central Baptist, Jesus is not a focal point of some members' understanding of salvation; they would not find it meaningful to practice evangelism as we have defined it, with the intention of encouraging people "to accept and follow Jesus Christ."[4]

On the other hand, the case studies also reveal the limited predictive power of theological categories (as narrowly defined by views on Scripture and salvation). Conservative beliefs may predict whether church members practice evangelism, but not whether they also stress serving the poor (see Clydesdale 1999, C. Smith 1998).[5] The liberal, moderate, and conservative churches in our study averaged about the same number of social ministries (10.7, 11.3, and 10.2 respectively). Some mainline churches like Nueva Creación may not have an evangelical interpretation of the gospel, but they do engage in evangelism.[6] It cannot be assumed that conservative churches are *only* concerned about saving souls, or that liberal churches are disinterested in the spiritual needs of their community. Traditional theological categories cannot explain what the most socially active churches have in common, nor why churches in the same theological camp have different mission orientations.[7]

The lack of simple correspondence between theological orientation and mission orientation is demonstrated by Faith Assembly of God. Richard Smith recognized that his church's level of social involvement was atypical for Assembly of God churches.[8] But he did not claim to be any less theologically conservative than his denomination. "My theology is the same in terms of doctrine," he stated, noting his accordance with official Assembly of God tenets. He added, "But there's a whole lot more to theology than those five doctrines." He described the source of his mission orientation in terms of "practical theology"—"serving the poor, relocating among the poor, sacrificing." These were ideas Rev. Smith said he gained from role models like John Perkins, an evangelical African American leader who founded an extensive network of social ministries and who preaches a message of "redistribution, racial reconciliation and relocation" (Perkins 1993). Reverend Smith cited a "Justice For All" conference led by Perkins as a seminal influence on his vision for urban ministry.

Theology does matter, but the range of theological issues represented in the assignment of liberal and conservative labels is too limited. As Rev. Smith put it, "there's a whole lot more to theology" than traditional litmus tests such as the authority of Scripture and the pathway to salvation. This insight calls

for further exploration of theological or worldview questions having more direct salience for mission orientations (Moberg 1972; Hoge, Perry, and Klever
1978; Dudley and Van Eck 1992; Mock 1992). These questions include the
connection between the material and spiritual realms, the relationship of individuals to society, the sources of social problems and social change, the definition of sin as personal and/or systemic, the relationship between personal
faith and social ethics, the implications of salvation for social well-being, and
the relationship between this world and the world to come. The salience of
these beliefs should be appraised using a framework that does not box perspectives into simple either/or categories. In the end, whether a church takes
the Bible literally is not as important to its mission as what parts of the Bible
it emphasizes and how it relates those teachings to its social context.

Noting that religious conservatives and liberals engage about equally in
charitable activities, Robert Wuthnow observes that they tend to be "motivated
by different values and use different language to legitimate their activities"
(1991, 134; see also Becker and Dhingra 2001). Similarly, as a carrier of culture,
religious ideology has an indirect effect on mission by shaping how a church
defines the meaning and goals of its social ministries (see Williams 1996). A
theological orientation may thus be a guide, not so much to what churches
actually *do* in mission, but rather to what they *believe* or *say* they are doing.
Church of the Advocate (liberal), First Presbyterian (moderate), and Tenth Presbyterian (conservative) all sponsor community meals. Each church provides
essentially the same social benefit, but they bring quite different theological
perspectives to bear on their motivations for this service, and give different
accounts of the ministry's purpose. Church of the Advocate views feeding the
hungry as a way of living out one's faith; at Tenth Presbyterian, this service is
also intended as a portal to sharing one's faith. At First Presbyterian, these two
purposes are carried by two different ministries (Community Luncheon and
Bread and Bible). Each religious tradition adds its own flavor to public engagement.

A congregation's theology may interact with its identity to selectively reinforce aspects of its mission orientation. Worship services at Tenth Memorial
clearly convey the congregation's zeal for saving souls. On the Sunday the
researcher visited, the front of the bulletin urged, "EACH ONE BRING ONE
. . . WITNESS TO SOMEONE ABOUT JESUS TODAY!" Inside, a "Great Commission Report" gave the number of "total souls" for the year to date (there
were eighty-one). A note from the pastor read, "Did you share a testimony last
week? . . . Some lost soul is depending on you!" The list of church ministries
on the bulletin included the Evangelism Task Force but none of the dozen
social programs sponsored by the church. Little was visible in this or other
congregational gatherings to indicate Tenth Memorial's substantial involvement in social services and economic development.[9] As this illustrates, when

theologically conservative churches engage in social action, these efforts may not be considered part of the core bundle of activities that "are highly valued or are part of what the congregation becomes known for" (Becker 1999, 187).[10]

Authority

Denominational affiliation, a potential source of authority for mission, appears to serve as a reference point for mission orientation but not as the determining factor (Becker 1999). Churches whose mission orientation was consistent with their denomination, like Nueva Creación, saw themselves as leaders rather than followers, modeling the best elements of their heritage. Germantown Church of the Brethren's mission accords with the position expressed by the denomination: "Those churches which will make an impact on this world are those that pursue both a social gospel and a personal gospel. Some do one or the other. However, those churches from an Anabaptist tradition believe that these two parts should be integrated." Other churches were conscious of going against their denominational grain. Media Presbyterian, for example, is considered more evangelical than the average mainline congregation (Rev. Borror describes Media as "a postdenominational, postmodern orthodox church"); Rev. Smith admits that Faith's emphasis on social ministry is atypical for Assembly of God churches. Reverend Borror and Rev. Smith both turned outside their denomination for inspiration for their mission.

Church leadership is another potential source of authority for mission. We observed two basic patterns: ministry leadership may be concentrated in a pastor who sets the agenda, or else leadership is diffused among members or staff who take responsibility for various ministry programs. Neither of these patterns attaches to a particular mission orientation. This is clear by comparing two holistic-complementary churches: First Presbyterian Church and Life in Christ. In First Presbyterian's polity, the session of elders serves as the decision-making body and ministry oversight is delegated to staff. The authority of the pastoral team lies chiefly in its respected influence on the missional vision of other church leaders. Dickie Robbins, like many African American Pentecostal pastors, is a charismatic, authoritative leader who initiates and directly oversees most of the ministries. Yet even authoritative pastors can exert only limited control over the congregation's activism. "Doing what is expected by church leaders" ranks near the bottom of the list of potential motivations for outreach at every church we surveyed. The nature of congregations as voluntary organizations means that church leaders can create ministry programs but they cannot force members to support them; if pressed, dissenting members may simply leave (and at several of the churches, they did).

On the other hand, pastors do exercise considerable influence in shaping the overall direction of the church (see Day 2002). Pastors and key leaders can steer members toward evangelism and/or social action by preaching, teaching, publicizing ministry opportunities, providing literature (such as evangelism "how-to" bulletin inserts at First Presbyterian), selecting educational curriculum and guest speakers, offering specialized training (such as training in evangelism at Christian Stronghold or in community organizing at Church of the Advocate), establishing membership requirements (such as the commitment to work toward "peace, justice and the wholeness of God's creation" in Central Baptist's membership covenant), networking with compatible parachurch agencies (such as the neighborhood development organizations connected with Germantown Church of the Brethren through pastor Richard Kyerematen), and writing formal mission statements. Members often credited church leaders with inspiring—even prodding—them to step out in faith in new ministry ventures. Moreover, by shaping church structures (such as the Faith in Action Committee at Media Presbyterian), leaders privilege some forms of outreach over others, making it easier for members who already share their mission orientation to put it into action.

Given the influence of leaders on a congregation, the natural follow-up question is what shapes the leader's understanding of mission. Clearly, the formation of missional beliefs and practices begins long before a person takes a church leadership position. David Apple's prior exposure to holistic mission in an African American church, for example, helped sustain his motivation to push Tenth Presbyterian to integrate social ministry into its evangelism-dominant model. Bill Borror grew up in an evangelical church, influencing his emphasis on evangelism at Media despite the dominant social ministry orientation of other Presbyterian churches in the area. The path of mission formation in church leaders is worthy of further study.

Another prominent source of authority for mission is the Bible. All the churches we studied draw on Scripture to varying degrees as the foundation for outreach, whether or not they take Scripture literally. In general, the Bible plays a more central role in the churches that emphasize evangelism (the dominant evangelism and holistic-instrumental subtypes). Yet, in these churches, the Bible is used equally as an anchor for social ministry as for evangelism. At Christian Stronghold, social ministry leaders repeatedly echoed the assertion that "Everything is Bible based." A brochure for the church's counseling ministry explains what this means for ministry: "There is a source that deals with all of life's problems, that identifies the cause and provides the solution. That source is the Bible." Among the Christian Stronghold members surveyed, the belief that the Bible is literal correlates significantly with the belief that evangelism is an essential quality of the Christian life, but also with the belief that Christians should pursue economic and social justice (both correlations significant at the .05 level).

Resources

A congregation's size, its budget, and the social class composition of its membership have been found to correlate with its likelihood of sponsoring social ministries (Scott 2002). Resource level may also affect mission orientation. Budget squeezes in small churches can create pressure to expand the member base. While evangelism is not equivalent with new member recruitment, evangelism may be a key element of a church growth strategy. Life in Christ Cathedral of Faith built a congregation from scratch, initially by reaching out to persons with drug addictions. Dwindling numbers prompted Church of the Advocate to form an evangelism committee for the first time to explore member recruitment. At the same time, rector Isaac Miller believed Advocate's struggle for financial and human resources actually strengthened its social justice orientation, because it allowed them to identify with people on the social margins: "If we were a more prosperous church, I know we wouldn't hold these kinds of [social change] issues as close to our heart as we do." Resource pressures cannot wholly explain mission; the strong commitment to evangelism at large churches like New Covenant and Christian Stronghold is certainly not driven by survival.

The impact of resources surfaces not primarily in the direction of a church's vision for outreach, but in its ability to implement the vision. Evangelism and social ministry require different raw materials. Evangelism, particularly network evangelism, is cheap. Community development is not. Congregations with limited resources like Life in Christ have limited options for funding and staffing social ministries; lacking sufficient outside support, Life in Christ had to discontinue its resource-intensive private school. Middle-class churches can draw on the wealth and civic skills of their membership for larger community development projects. Over thirty First Presbyterian families put up their homes as collateral to fund the construction of the Samuel Miller Christian Retirement Center, for example.

Changes in resource status can accompany changes in a church's approach to mission. Bethel's growing emphasis on community development has correlated with its slow but steady growth in size and resources. Similarly, outreach at Faith Assembly of God has evolved in response to available resources. Reverend Richard Smith relates that when the church was new, "We did mostly evangelism. Then one to two years later, we realized we have to do more. . . . The desire was there, but not the money or resources before. Then we got the building and got stabilized." At different points in a church's history, different elements of its mission may have prominence, depending on what the congregation is practically able to accomplish.

One option for congregations with limited resources is to find external funding sources. Among the urban churches, funding for almost all of the community development projects came from outside the congregation. The trade-off is that these funds may come with strings attached that limit the integration of religious elements. A church's mission orientation may drive funding decisions; some churches have a policy against accepting funds that would undermine their religious message or autonomy. "I don't like money that tells us what we can do with it," asserts a Bethel Temple ministry leader. "I've watched too many places change their programs, change their ways because of grants. I believe God has given us a vision for programming and we shouldn't change it." Other congregations, however, accept what they can get and make the best of it. Several churches reported that they had altered the religious nature of a social service program because of pressure from funders (private as well as public). This can contribute to a dual-focus pattern, in which churches distinguish between social ministries that operate according to funders' rules and evangelism ministries over which they have autonomy.

Context

Churches are open systems, meaning that as they seek to change their environment through programs of evangelism and/or social action, their environment also inevitably has an impact on them. Comparing the three Presbyterian churches in the sample—Media Presbyterian (PC-U.S.A.), First Presbyterian (PC-U.S.A.), and Tenth Presbyterian (PCA)—illustrates the influence of a church's location on its mission. The three churches fall into three different categories: dual-focus, holistic-complementary, and holistic-instrumental, respectively. Both Tenth and First Presbyterian are downtown churches that made an intentional choice to identify with the city, and both started social ministries in response to being confronted with a local need (homelessness, deteriorating housing). At Tenth, the ministries that evolved to meet these concerns have a more explicit and prominent evangelistic dimension. While Media Presbyterian does respond to the needs of its suburban community, most of its activism is directed outside the immediate area. Members' exposure to social need follows, rather than motivates, their involvement.

Eight of the ten holistic congregations draw the majority of members from the neighborhood around the church. Personal proximity to needs can give evangelistic congregations pragmatic motivation to adopt social causes. Church members are more likely to know people with needs or to be needy themselves, increasing the demand for social ministry (Cnaan, Boddie, and Yancey 2003). Reverend Richardson writes that in a context of urgent need, abstract theological disputes over providing services versus saving souls assume less relevance: "We who are ministering in the city cannot afford to engage in that debate, because our people are dying" (Richardson 1992, 154). After becoming a commuting congregation, the original Bethel Temple congregation responded to the decline of the church's community by withdrawing from outreach and ultimately relocating; the new Bethel, reborn with local members, has responded to the challenges of its community by adding compassionate minis-tries to its evangelistic mission (Ammerman 1997a documents other instances of both responses). The sense of a mandate to social action has grown among church leaders who relocated into Bethel's neighborhood: "We can't sit back and watch stuff happen," said a staff member, "and not be compelled to do anything about it."

In developing their ministry niche, congregations scan the local ecology to discover which needs are not being met, and how they can work with estab-lished providers (Ammerman 1997a). A mission orientation can influence a congregation's assessment of local needs and assets, and vice versa. Evangel-istic churches take into account not only the gaps in the social safety net but the spiritual gaps as well. Ministry director David Apple explained that one reason Tenth Presbyterian's programs for addicted and homeless persons em-phasize an "evangelistic dimension" is because many traditional social work services are already available in the church's downtown area. "We don't dupli-cate what secular institutions are doing well already, but we try to set a good foundation for people so that they can take advantage of what is there."

As suggested previously, the holistic-instrumental type appears particularly compatible with an inner-city context. The case studies suggest multiple rea-sons why a distressed setting may be conducive to ministries that blend com-passion and spiritual nurture. Requests for aid bring community residents into contact with the church, expanding the opportunities for evangelism. Minis-tries of relief and personal development are more affordable forms of ministry for resource-poor churches than community development, and also offer more range for integrating explicit evangelistic elements. The church's cultural and geographic proximity presents fewer barriers for people who receive compas-sionate aid to be absorbed into the congregation. Moreover, the culture of the inner city is often more accepting of spiritual overtures. Thus, when Tenth Presbyterian sends medical students to inner-city Philadelphia for evangelism training, they typically encounter less resistance from urban residents than from their professional peers.[11] A track record of dramatic narratives of per-sonal transformation can also energize a congregation for holistic ministry. At Bethel Temple, for example, the former drug addicts evangelized by Rev. Cen-teno are now among the most active members of the church; the urgency of outreach of word and deed resonates with them because of their own experi-ence. Ironically, material poverty in a church's neighborhood can aid in the mobilization of human resources for holistic ministry.

Interviewees at several holistic-instrumental churches admitted that if their church were ministering in a wealthier community they would not engage in social ministry to the same extent, because it would not be a necessary vehicle for sharing the gospel. The key decision that such churches make is to identify with a poor community (even when, as in Christian Stronghold's case, the majority of members commute from other neighborhoods). Given their theological affirmation of concern for the poor, their commitment to evangelism, and the strategic benefits of social ministry for establishing a spiritual connection with people in need, the holistic-instrumental path makes sense. Without a connection with a distressed parish, a church's impetus for incorporating social concerns into a strong sense of evangelistic mission is diminished. New Covenant is isolated from social need, because of its primarily middle class constituency and its location on a 33-acre campus in a prosperous urban neighborhood. The ideological congruence between dominant-evangelism New Covenant and the holistic-instrumental churches suggests that New Covenant might become more involved in social ministry if it were in a needier context. On the other hand, New Covenant deliberately chose to relocate into a higher-class neighborhood as a symbol of the gospel of empowerment that it preaches, suggesting that, in this case, the mission orientation influenced context rather than the other way around.

The Mosaic of Missional Influences

Mission orientation is shaped by a mosaic of influences. A congregation's denominational identity, race or ethnicity, and assimilation of larger cultural forces such as individualism provide the palette from which a church draws in composing its missional vision. Sources of authority direct the contours of a church's understanding of the relationship between evangelism and social activism. A church's capacity to implement its vision is constrained by the resources available for ministry. Evangelism and social action are carried out in dialogue with the community context. No single factor determines the shape of a congregation's mission. Churches in the same neighborhood, denomination, or ethnic group may relate to their community context quite differently (McRoberts 2003); churches with little in common in terms of culture, polity, or congregational characteristics may nevertheless conduct their outreach in kindred ways.

Historical Perspectives on the Relationship between Evangelism and Social Action

History provides another source for understanding the influences on a church's relationship to its social context. Congregations do not invent their mission orientation afresh; they draw on established historical scripts of how to conduct outreach, while adding their own innovations. To understand the roots of these orientations, we present a brief history of the relationship between evangelism and social action in Protestant congregations, focusing on Anglo American evangelicalism.[12] Describing evangelical social action as "a long (and variegated) tradition," Clydesdale asserts, "One cannot speak of a single history of giving and caring in the evangelical tradition, for there are really several different histories" (1990, 188). These various strands are reflected in the persistence of different mission orientations.

Mission in American Protestantism through the Nineteenth Century

The Puritans brought with them to America the precept that caring for those in need is a mark of the pious Christian life. Because colonial Christians lived for the most part in religiously homogenous communities, converting unbelievers was not initially a significant theme of religious life (though preachers emphatically called "backsliders" to repentance). Charity, urged as a Christian duty and "visible sign" of genuine faith, was typically directed at members of the religious community and accompanied by moral stipulations. Influenced by growing social diversity and the Enlightenment motif of rational choice, religious expression in eighteenth-century America adopted a growing emphasis on individual religious choice. The Great Awakening of the 1730s and 1740s birthed a new form of "revival religion," which continued through the Second Great Awakening in the mid-1800s. Evangelical leaders delivered impassioned sermons intended to move crowds of listeners to a dramatic conversion experience. They also insisted that regeneration should produce, in the words of evangelist and abolitionist William Goodell, "a high type of piety and an enlarged benevolence" (quoted in Strong 1997, 2).

Revivalism thus went hand in hand with the rise of home mission agencies and voluntary societies. A "Benevolent Empire" of religiously based social services proliferated in the 1800s, driven by the social forces of immigration, industrialization, and urbanization, as well as by the earnest desires of revival-era Christians to show the "fruits of conversion." Christian activism blended relief aid, a sweeping moral agenda, and social advocacy. Protestants "poured their energies into the causes of hospitals, schools, orphanages, prison reform, temperance laws, peace activism, recreation and leisure organizations, Sunday education for working children, the outlawing of dueling, services to native Americans and the poor, and the reform of prostitutes, drunks, and other dishonorable elements" of society (C. Smith 1998, 4). The role of congregations, particularly those serving immigrant groups, expanded to include many civic and mutual aid functions, placing them at "the social center of the community" (Cnaan et al. 2002, 26). Christians generally accepted the charge laid down by the editor of *The Watchman*, a leading Baptist publication, who wrote in 1857: "It is ours, not only to fit ourselves and others for a better world, but to labor to make this world better" (quoted in T. Smith 1957, 153).

George Marsden points out that by the time of the American Civil War, with more than three-fourths of churchgoers attending revivalistic churches, "Protestant evangelicals considered their faith to be the normative American creed" (1980, 11). Evangelicals took it for granted that they should preach the gospel and reform society through charity as well as political engagement on behalf of moral causes and vulnerable social groups. One reason for the conjoining of evangelism with social action in this period was the desire to bring the poor masses within the Christian fold. "Religious benevolence had both a material and a spiritual aim—relieve suffering while growing the ranks of the faithful by spreading the Christian gospel" (Bartkowski and Regis 2003, 32). Catholic social services developed in part to counter the success of evangelization efforts among the Irish immigrants served by Protestant charities. A holistic orientation also derived from a tremendous optimism that linked the evangelical call to individual Christian "perfection" with the potential for social progress on a grand scale. The goal of many evangelicals was nothing less than to usher in the kingdom of God on earth through the blending of witness and social action. They saw it within their grasp "not merely to preach the gospel to every creature, but to reorganize human society in accordance with the law of God," as Edward Beecher proclaimed in 1835 (quoted in T. Smith 1957, 225).

One pacesetter in the combination of progressive social action and a commitment to evangelism was Charles Finney. Finney was the most famous American evangelist around the middle of the nineteenth century, but he was also one of the leading crusaders against slavery (see Dayton 1976). Oberlin College, which he helped lead for many years, was a crucial center of the abolitionist movement. Finney's Oberlin students also conducted missionary work among Native Americans while pressuring the federal government to keep the treaties that it constantly ignored. Finney preached that salvation meant turning from selfishness to benevolence (a teaching to be echoed by the later social gospelers, with a shift in emphasis). Finney joined other prominent evangelical leaders in preaching that slavery was a sin.[13] At the same time, he maintained that efforts toward social change would be most effective if accompanied by revivals. Finney believed that the best hope for social change lay in the mass conversion of individuals, though he did not depict saving souls as a substitute for social engagement. As historian Timothy Smith argues, "if evangelicals insisted upon moral solutions to social questions, they never forgot that personal sin often had communal roots" (1957, 152).

The Social Gospel and the Great Reversal

By the close of the nineteenth century, the American religious terrain had changed dramatically. Whereas Charles Finney was a postmillennialist (the belief that Christ's kingdom comes in history as the gospel progressively transforms the culture), eventually evangelicalism became associated with premillennialism (history and culture will get worse and worse until Christ's return, when all things will be made new). This more pessimistic attitude about the possibility of progress within history contributed to a loss of political engagement. The prominent evangelical leader Dwight Moody urged Christians to abandon social reform—though not personal charity—and focus on personal evangelism with his famous metaphor: "This world is a wrecked vessel. . . . God has given me a lifeboat and said, 'Moody, save all you can' " (quoted in Strong 1997, xxxi). Although John Wesley, the founder of Methodism, advocated both personal and social holiness, by the late nineteenth century Methodists tended to focus on private sanctification. Premillennialist spokesman C. I. Scofield (whose edition of the Bible is still popular among fundamentalists) led the turn inward: "The best help a pastor can bring to the social problems of the community is to humble himself before God, forsake his sins, receive the filling with the Holy Spirit, and preach a pure gospel of tender love" (quoted in Strong 1997, xxxi). This withdrawal of evangelical social commitments was accompanied by a posture of "clerical laissez-faire" that explicitly or implicitly endorsed the materialism, suppression of labor rights, and economic inequalities associated with expanding capitalism (Schmidt 1991, 23).

Meanwhile, another group of Protestants was developing what became known as the *social gospel*. In response to the growing social crisis spawned by industrialization, leaders of this movement called Christians to focus on economic justice and social reform, rooted in a theology of the kingdom of God. Initially, the social gospel movement represented, not a radical departure from evangelical faith, but an urgent charge to evangelicalism to recover the social dimension of its own heritage. "There are two types of Christianity, the old and the older," wrote Josiah Strong. "The one seeks to save individuals, the other aims at the salvation of individuals, plus the organization of society on a Christian basis" (quoted in Schmidt 1991, 140). A reclamation of this "older," more holistic vision, Strong expected, would kindle a new religious awakening. Another leader in the movement, Charles Macfarland, also asserted a holistic perspective: "We are happily discovering that the conservation of the evangelistic note is essential to an effective Social Gospel, and are no longer disposed to rend asunder what Christ has joined together" (quoted in Schmidt 1991, 134–135). Many of the early social gospel advocates insisted that their attention to the structural causes of poverty did not minimize the importance of personal salvation—but it did change their understanding of the meaning of salvation.[14]

B. Fay Mills started out as a conventional revivalist who once declared, "The one reason for our being here in this life is that we may save souls" (quoted in Schmidt 1991, 94). After discovering the social gospel, he began to preach a "new evangelism" that called people to be saved in order to work for the kingdom of God. He assured critics, "I shall not cease calling individuals to repentance and faith in the Lord Jesus Christ" (quoted in Schmidt 1991, 97). An observer at a revival in Columbus in 1895 described Mills's brand of social evangelism: "To conviction of personal sins and effort to save men from them, is added conviction and sorrow for social sins and a practical effort to improve the material, political and social environment in which the individual lives" (quoted in Schmidt 1991, 96). Mills became the target of harsh conservative criticism. His theology as well as his politics became increasingly radical, and eventually he left the evangelical fold for Unitarianism.

As the controversy over the social gospel intensified, harmonizing evangelical revivalism with social ethics grew increasingly untenable. Like Mills, many social gospel advocates came to embrace radical new theological ideas that denied or downplayed historically orthodox Christian doctrines. Influenced by the rise of scientific rationalism, followers of the social gospel questioned orthodox doctrines such as Jesus' deity and the literal interpretation of Scripture, and embraced what seemed then to be radical ideas, like evolution. Liberals introduced a new ethic that preferred right behavior over right beliefs. "Truth was not what you thought but what you did" (Webber 2002, 29; see also Wuthnow 1989). In contrast to the privatized "soul salvation" preached by conservatives, Walter Rauschenbusch asserted that a socially conscious "religious morality is the only thing God cares about" (quoted in Marsden 1980, 91–92). The social gospel movement shifted the locus of salvation from the regeneration of individuals to the redemption of the entire social order. With this shift, many organizations like the YMCA, which was originally founded in the 1850s as "a united expression of the soul-winning fervor of evangelical Protestantism" (T. Smith 1957, 76), started down a path of secularization that ultimately obscured their religious roots.

Another factor that exacerbated the division between spiritual and social work in the early twentieth century was the rise of scientific philanthropy. This systematic approach to social services separated the concept of *charity*, meaning the provision of material aid, from *correction*, which "referred to reform and conversion, the notion of inner change" (Ellor, Netting, and Thibault 1999, 24). In effect, the new approach decoupled the religious mandate for social service from the goal of engendering spiritual change in others through service. As the profession of social work organized itself under secular norms, religious presence in social services came to be seen as redundant and backward (Cnaan, Wineburg, and Boddie 1999; Glenn 2000).

Conservative evangelicals grew alarmed at what they saw as a "movement of growing hostility to the true gospel of Christ," in the words of Amzi Clarence Dixon, pastor of Moody Church in Chicago (quoted in Schmidt 1991, 126). In response, conservatives not only attacked liberal theology by reaffirming the fundamentals (hence the label *fundamentalists*) of historic Christian orthodoxy, but also completed their withdrawal from their own earlier vigorous engagement with social action. This period from 1900 to 1930 when "all progressive social concern became suspect" became known as the Great Reversal (Marsden 1980). The dynamic preacher Billy Sunday castigated the social gospelers for "trying to make a religion out of social service with Jesus Christ left out."

Sunday renounced any mission of the church outside of personal evangelism, proclaiming, "We've had enough of this godless social service nonsense" (quoted in Schmidt 1991, 151, 153; see also Marty 1980).

The result was a deep division between social gospel advocates focused largely on socioeconomic justice via political reform, and fundamentalists primarily concerned with personal conversion and private morality. American Protestantism came to be dominated by this two-party system of social-action liberals versus evangelistic conservatives, with intense suspicion on both sides (Marty 1970; Schmidt 1991).

The Reversal of the Great Reversal

In *The Uneasy Conscience of American Fundamentalism* (1947), Carl F. H. Henry deplored fundamentalism's anti-intellectualism and withdrawal from cultural and political concerns. As the founding editor of *Christianity Today*—which would become evangelicalism's flagship publication—Henry urged conservative Christians to return to the social arena.[15] Unlike liberal activists, however, Henry also returned to the emphasis shared by nineteenth-century evangelical reformers on the "spiritual dynamic for social change." Neoevangelicals like Henry presented evangelism as the path to effective social reform: "Christian social action condones no social solutions in which personal acceptance of Jesus Christ as Saviour and Lord is an optional consideration" (quoted in Schmidt 1991, 212).

The turmoil of the 1960s further polarized liberal and fundamentalist positions, but also stimulated the emergence of a moderate evangelical wing that sought to engage the pressing issues of the day (Hollinger 1983). Social concern became a point of distinction between the growing evangelical movement and fundamentalists, who for a time continued to maintain that the church's mission should focus primarily or exclusively on evangelism and selected moral issues.[16] In 1973, a circle of younger evangelicals met in Chicago and issued a ringing call for Christians to combat racism, economic justice, militarism, and discrimination against women (see Sider 1974). The next year, Billy Graham chaired a global assembly of evangelical leaders in Lausanne, Switzerland, and the ensuing Lausanne Covenant charged Christians with both personal evangelism and social responsibility. While these documents expanded the vision for Christian social action, they remained firmly within the circle of theological orthodoxy.

The National Association of Evangelicals (NAE), representing fifty-one denominations, has continued this trajectory. Rich Cizik of the NAE pronounced, "The Cold War between religious groups over the poor is over" (Evangelicals and the Poor 1999, 6). In 2002 the NAE passed a resolution, "Heeding the Call of the Poor: Let the Church Be the Church," which urged: "Through ministries of evangelism, discipleship, mercy and justice, we should serve the poor, strengthen families and transform our communities." This dynamic holistic vision has contributed to the explosion of evangelical support for church-based and parachurch relief programs such as Compassion International, an organization serving children in impoverished countries, whose literature declares: "Earlier in this century a debate over a 'Social Gospel' and a 'spiritual gospel' split the church. But we see no such dichotomy" (quoted in Clydesdale 1990, 197).

Regnerus and Smith dub the return of conservative Christians to social involvement the "reversal of the great reversal." They argue that in times of upheaval, "ideas about engagement with the broader culture are likely to change form," and that religious traditions are still regrouping from the "cultural shockwave" of the 1960s (1998, 1350). This restructuring has allowed the ascendance of a new social vision among "the younger evangelicals who are now a full century away from the debates that formed twentieth-century evangelicalism" (Webber 2002, 25). This generation appears to have inherited an emphasis on personal faith while rejecting the isolationist tendencies that previously accompanied it.[17] As Joel Van Dyke said of Bethel Temple, "In the last ten to fifteen years, conservative, evangelical churches like us have become part of a movement . . . to develop the communities they minister to without losing the centrality of the gospel of Jesus Christ." Mainline churches have been impacted by this revisioning process as well. Carl Dudley notes that many "socially sensitive liberal churches [have] recognized their need for explicit spiritual grounding" (2001, 15), and mainline congregations declared the 1990s the decade of evangelism (Wuthnow 1996).

African American Churches

Without attempting to give their history full justice, we note that, for African American congregations, the story of the relationship between evangelism and social action has followed a different path.[18] Eric Lincoln writes, "The black church *came into existence* fully committed to the private or spiritual aspects of religion as *yin* to the *yang* of public religious concern" (in Billingsley 1999, xxi; emphasis in original). The holistic stream in African American churches may be traced to its source in African religions and a "Black sacred cosmos . . . which envisaged the whole universe as sacred" (Lincoln and Mamiya 1990, 2). The split between fundamentalists and social-action liberals among Anglo churches in the early twentieth century did not find the same purchase in the African American community. The struggle for survival has instead contributed to an enduring understanding that "the church has to meet the needs of the whole man," as a church leader at Tenth Memorial put it. "In the context of racism and segregation, out of necessity, spiritual and natural concerns converged at the church door" (Calhoun-Brown 1998, 436).

For African Americans, themes of freedom, empowerment, and deliverance historically have both spiritual and social connotations. Following the Civil War, "black churches believed that destiny had bestowed upon them a special mission" to uplift their community (Paris 1985, 67). As the only indigenous African American institution, the church took on a natural role as the center of cultural life, education, and mutual aid. Black churches and religious leaders helped urban black neighborhoods cope with the flood of southern migrants, took a stand at the center of the civil rights storm, and continue to anchor growing movements of economic development and social reform. The experience of alienation from mainstream American society has fostered a sense of solidarity and responsibility, with the credo: "If the Black church doesn't do it, who will?" (Day 2002). As rates of church attendance flag, particularly among younger African Americans, while social pressures continue to mount, both evangelism and social ministry have regained new urgency (Franklin 1997). McRoberts (1999) notes in particular a surge in the social activism of conservative Pentecostal clergy.

Of course, the label "the black church" embraces a wide range of denominations and approaches to mission—including the activist legacy of political engagement and entrepreneurial innovation (Day 2002); the "deliverance-oriented evangelism" of many Pentecostal churches, stressing personal development ministries that bring empowerment through inner renewal (Franklin 1996, 96); the relief and community development ministries of neighborhood churches that leverage needed goods and services (Lincoln 1994; Jackson et al. 1997); the mutual aid tradition of group survival through shared resources and emotional support (Milsap and Taylor 1998); and the "exilic consciousness" leading many churches to a posture of evangelistic refuge, rescuing souls to be "in the world, but not of it" (McRoberts 2003, 61; Nelson 1997). Churches vary in their posture toward the racial inequities of the status quo—some equipping individuals to triumph over obstacles in their environment, others working to change the rules of access at a systemic level, and others advocating strategies for building self-sufficient African American communities (Baer 1988; Calhoun-Brown 1998). As a generalization, however, African American churches have historically understood these various goals of social change to be congruent with promoting personal conversions.

Old Themes, New Expressions

The landscape of Protestant mission is an amalgamation of past innovations that have become institutionalized patterns, a patchwork of "something old, something new." Each of the current mission orientations has historical antecedents. Churches tend to appropriate preexisting ideas about ministry when they engage in outreach, in conjunction with circumstantial factors such as congregational identity and community context. But churches also reshape these missional patterns as they inhabit them. Ideas take different forms in different contexts, and the world has changed since these missional paradigms were developed (Swidler 1986; Ammerman 1997a). When conservatives re-acted against the social gospel movement, their rejection of social action was inseparable from their antipathy toward the movement's embrace of scientific rationalism, unorthodox theology, and liberal political views. The argument between theological conservatives and liberals was in large measure a debate over modernity. While this argument continues, it has now been transposed into a postmodern era. The conservative/liberal-evangelism/social action divide should be viewed not as an unchangeable given but as a historical phenomenon that is being actively renegotiated, giving rise to new ministry patterns.

Many observers of American religion have concluded that the terms *liberal* and *conservative* are semantic shortcuts that no longer capture the spectrum of missional activity within these theological traditions (Peterson and Takyama 1984; Demerath and Williams 1989; Dudley and Van Eck 1992; Mock 1992; Roof 1996; Ammerman 1997a; Clydesdale 1999). Martin Marty's (1980, 479) image of religious traditions as a "repository of options" is helpful in under-standing the current "deprivatization" of religious conservatives (Regnerus and Smith 1998). In the first part of the twentieth century, the conservative tradition became the repository for a privatized, other-worldly faith, focused on guarding personal piety and winning souls to the exclusion of social concerns. Depri-vatized conservative churches have become open to new options for relating to their context. Orthodox beliefs about the divinity of Christ, the authority of the Bible, the centrality of the conversion experience, and the imperative of evangelism, along with cultural and policial conservatism, are being combined in new ways with a "practical theology" that animates churches' social action. While the polarized categories of dominant social action and dominant evan-gelism persist (and may in fact still represent the majority of congregations), it appears that a more inclusive vision of ministry has gained a foothold.

These developments have led Christian Smith to suggest that evangelicals today "may be the most committed carriers of a new social Gospel" (1998, 43). This shift can be explained in part by understanding American evangelicalism as an evolving dialogue between the conservative impulse to preserve inherited religious traditions and a "restless public activism" that is responsive to social forces (Smith 1998, 47). These forces include the trends described in the first chapter: the recasting of the relationship between church and state; new fund-ing opportunities for religious agencies; evolving awareness of the contribu-tions of organic religion to personal well-being; heightened expectations for faith-based approaches to social problems; and increased openness to religion's presence in public life. These trends run up against other prevailing currents: theological, organizational, and cultural limitations to the scope and scale of church-based community outreach; lingering skepticism of religion's social relevance in policy, media, and academic circles; concerns that devolution erodes government's commitment to maintaining a social safety net; political divisions over "moral values," split along religious lines; traditionally strict interpretations of church-state separation; and professional social work standards and cultural norms against evangelistic expression in the context of social services. The confluence of these currents has generated both tensions and possibilities.

Current mission orientations thus represent the intersection of old ideas with new contexts. Ministry leaders now express similar ideas and struggle with similar challenges as they did one and two centuries ago. Many churches have been reinterpreting their mission identities, drawing selectively on influences from their culture, community ecology, resource base, and theological heritage. Ironically, the reengagement of evangelical churches in social ministry has much in common with the original roots of the social gospel movement. But the current expression of this holistic theme—crossing denominational, demographic, and racial lines—also represents significant innovations. This movement is shaping the way the next generation of American Christians will put their faith into action.

9

Conversionist Churches and Social Action

When the researcher[1] arrived at Faith Assembly of God for the Peacemakers meeting, most of the twenty-five or so teens who were Peacemakers had already arrived and were setting up chairs, or milling around talking and laughing. The basement room was filled with boisterous good humor. Rose, an African American woman in her late 30s on staff with the program, was making tea and boiling hot dogs in the small kitchen toward the back of the room. Rose chatted with the researcher as teenagers flitted in and out being more or less helpful: retrieving cups from the pantry, setting out ketchup and mustard, interrupting to check whether the hot dogs were ready.

A boy approached to ask what kind of hot dogs these were. At first taken aback by the question, Rose recalled that he and his sisters were devout Muslims and on restricted diets. Later, the researcher asked the Muslim youths if it bothered them to be in a program associated with a church. They remarked that pastor Richard Smith was respectful of their faith and invited them to join in prayer but didn't make them pray to Jesus. When the Peacemakers had pizza, he made sure to order one with toppings that they could eat.

While the group was waiting for a police officer to arrive to give a presentation, they dug into the first round of hot dogs and Rev. Smith started the announcements. Peacemaker youth needed to show the staff satisfactory report cards to continue in the program. Two new tutors from a Philadelphia Bible college would be available to help youth with their homework. Then Rev. Smith asked, "How many heard someone got shot on the Avenue?" (a nearby thorough-

fare). This had occurred the previous Saturday, near a check-cashing establishment. "You all be careful walking up there," Rev. Smith admonished. "A bullet
supposed to hit someone beside you can hit you. A bullet doesn't have a name
on it."

Violence is not news to Faith's low-income, multiethnic Frankford neighborhood in northeast Philadelphia. The Peacemakers program originated in
response to a shooting on the front steps of the nearby elementary school in
1995. As students poured out of the school after dismissal, two parents picking
up their children were shot in the head by an estranged husband. The bodies
lay on the school steps for three hours before the medical examiners trans-
ported them away. In the trauma that followed, Faith Assembly of God pulled
together neighborhood groups to respond. With foundation funding, the
church organized volunteers to provide a "Safe Corridor" along the most-
traveled student routes. The program also trained Peacemaker youths in conflict resolution and neighborhood safety, helped them prepare antiviolence
presentations for other youth, and offered constructive after-school activities.
Teens received a small stipend for faithful participation. The program also paid
a stipend to about eight low-income adult supervisors, including Rose.

Unlike the faith-permeated or faith-centered character of Faith's other social ministries (including a food program that served three to four hundred
people per month, addiction recovery homes for men and women, and a parenting support group), Peacemakers fell into the faith-affiliated program type.
Since Peacemakers depended on secular foundation funding, they had to follow the funders' rules, explained Rev. Smith. They could teach values from a
Christian perspective, but without promoting Christian doctrine. Youth reported that the program taught general affirmations such as "God wants us to
get along" or "God wants us to be safe." Non-christocentric group prayers were
the only explicit religious element. At the same time, Rev. Smith expressed his
hope that the program would provide openings to share the gospel with youth.
Peacemakers were invited to attend the church, and many of them took part
in Faith's other activities for youth. Spiritually nurturing relationships were
forged between youth and their adult mentors from the church. Reverend
Smith estimated that in the past year, ten youth converted or recommitted to
Christianity as a result of their connection with the Peacemakers program.

At the Peacemakers meeting, after another round of hot dogs, it became
apparent that the police officer was not going to show up. Reverend Smith
decided to go ahead with the meeting by calling everyone to attention for a
prayer. He prayed to "creator God" for a blessing on their endeavor of peacemaking and on the families of all the youths. Afterward, they discussed arrangements for various upcoming Peacemaker presentations, and then dis-
missed. Amidst much joking around, the youth's respect for Rose and Rev.
Smith was evident.

Rose described her involvement with Peacekeepers as a spiritual calling.

When teens confided their problems to her, she would respond by encouraging them to "pray it all out and give it to the Lord." She viewed the violence, family brokenness, poverty, and drugs in Faith's neighborhood as manifestations of a spiritual battle in which "the devil is using our children," a battle that only Spirit-filled Christians could win. "I believe in this program [Peacemakers], and I believe in the church doing it, because our children gotta get strong," she said. "They need to know the Lord and how to fight this." Yet Rose accepted that Peacemakers could not overtly lead youth to resist the devil or "know the Lord," because of its funding. Many people need to see claims about Jesus demonstrated before they will believe, she explained. Peacemakers provided the church an opportunity "to show our kids God's love and that he really does exist."

Characteristics of Conversionist Social Action

Defying stereotypes, Faith Assembly of God combines zeal for sharing the gospel with an active concern for the social well-being of its community. Chapter 7 described how the dual-focus, holistic-instrumental, and holistic-complementary categories represent different ways of organizing and ordering these two mission emphases. Our research suggests that churches that promote conversions as well as social ministry are more likely to be found among minority churches in urban centers (like Faith), but not exclusively in this setting. An evangelistic orientation and theological conservatism often go hand-in-hand, particularly within the holistic-instrumental subset (like Faith), but they are not synonymous. The politics of these congregations likewise tends toward but is not limited to the right.[2] Of course, not all (or even most) conversionist churches are also engaged substantially in social ministry; moreover, this subset likely represents only a fraction of all socially active churches. Thus their contribution to the social safety net has largely been overlooked. As Chaves writes, "The congregation actively delivering social services is a rarity, but it is one worth understanding more deeply" (2004, 52). The congregation actively serving society alongside, or motivated by, a desire to save souls may be an even greater rarity, but the current political and religious climate calls for these congregations to be understood in greater depth.

Here we explore the characteristics of the social involvement of dual-focus and holistic churches. Five main dialectical qualities stand out that depict the both-and nature of their public mission. First, socially active conversionist churches are characterized by *engaged orthodoxy*, meaning they tend to balance this-worldly responsibilities and benefits of the Christian life with the urgency of saving souls for heaven. They employ a *whole-person anthropology* that impels them to tend equally to spiritual and social needs. *Invitational voluntarism* allows evangelistic churches to resolve the tension between the absolute claims of their faith with the free will of the beneficiaries with whom they share their faith. The *expressive relationalism* of socially active conversionist churches means they promote caring relationships as an effective path for both implicitly and explicitly communicating the gospel. Finally, the attribute of *expanded individualism* may lead members of conversionist churches to value personal regeneration and structural change as mutually reinforcing mission objectives.

Engaged Orthodoxy: Other-Worldly and This-Worldly Ministry

Borrowing a phrase from Christian Smith, a key phrase that describes socially active conversionist churches is *engaged orthodoxy*, or "a genuine heartfelt burden for the state of the world, a tremendous sense of personal responsibility to change society" (1998, 43, 44). While salvation secures believers a place in a heavenly afterlife, spiritual realities are also interconnected with natural realities here and now. Being saved does not mean keeping oneself pure while waiting for heaven; it means getting one's hands dirty tending this world's fields of sin and sorrow. Conversionist churches thus work to better this life while preparing people for the next one.

Lou Centeno, co-pastor of Bethel Temple, emphasized that Christians have a proactive role in the world: "I believe very strongly that if all [God] wanted me to do is to get saved and that was the end of it, he would have taken me to heaven just that quick." As long as Christians remain on earth, they have a job to do: "to introduce [people] to God" so that they can work together to create "the kind of world that he intended for us." Although Rev. Centeno believes this will only be fully accomplished in heaven, "that's no reason why we can sit around here and twiddle our thumbs and figure, well, we're just going to wait for this pie in the sky." He critiqued churches that detach themselves from the problems of their community. "They're pursuing safety, and they're pursuing protection and pursuing purity—but they've basically neglected the other command of the Lord to help your neighbor, to reach out to your neighbor." Churches must never become so heavenly minded as to be no earthly good.

But in doing earthly good, conversionist churches also remain heavenly minded. Churches in the holistic-instrumental subtype, in particular, emphasize that people's eternal destiny has priority over their temporal circumstances. Bethel Temple's director of community development placed social ministry into this perspective: "Unless salvation comes, all the good things you can do for [people] amount to nothing. . . . The spiritual side is what it's all about, ultimately. It's no good to have a nice car and live in a nice house and still be going to hell when you die." David Apple similarly remarked that all the food, tutoring, and other support services offered by Tenth Presbyterian Church ultimately had limited value unless people came to Christ. "We can offer all those things and people can go to hell." Coming from a more moderate theological position, Rev. Jim Kraft did not mention hell, but still referenced the afterlife in explaining First Presbyterian's mission: "We all talk about exercise being good for the body, but God and his kingdom are for eternity. So I think we're only doing part of the job, if we don't introduce people to Christ."

This other-worldly consciousness resists reducing faith to its social utility, but it does not negate a concern for people's quality of life here and now. A key way that these churches seek to call people's attention to their spiritual condition is by addressing felt needs in the here and now. Salvation is seen as having this-worldly implications, and social ministry bears witness to other-worldly truths.

Whole-Person Anthropology: Spiritual and Social Deliverance

Churches in our study consistently used the imagery of "wholeness" to describe the integral relationship between spiritual and social ministry (similarly observed by McRoberts 2003). The use of this motif spanned denominational, class, and ethnic boundaries, as the following interview excerpts illustrate:

> [What is the church's mission?] To minister to the whole person and bring people to saving faith in Jesus Christ. (Lay leader, Faith Assembly of God)

> We're not only taking care of the spiritual side of people, but the whole man. (Rev. Richard Kyerematen, Germantown Church of the Brethren)

> Evangelism meets the needs of the whole man, just as Christ did. . . . You cannot just tell a person that God loves them, when they're hungry. You got to feed them. And if you meet their needs then people will have more confidence in knowing that the church is concerned about them. (Ministry leader, Tenth Memorial Baptist Church)

> I want to reach the whole person. . . . Human beings don't live by bread alone, but by the word and ministry of God. (Rev. Jim Kraft, First Presbyterian Church)

> The transforming power of the gospel ought to be evident, not by looking at people on their way into church, but on their way out of church. They should be allowed to come in as broken as society has caused them to be, but leave as whole as God desires them to be. (Bishop Dickie Robbins, Life in Christ)

Sometimes in these quotes the language of wholeness is used to defend social action, other times to reinforce an evangelistic mandate. Either way, a whole-person anthropology asserts the "totality of human beings—that they are not just physical, emotional, material beings, but also spiritual beings in which all those aspects are intertwined," according to a Tenth Presbyterian church leader. A leader of health ministries at First Presbyterian put it this way: "If the body is ill then the spirit is taxed. And if the spirit is taxed, then the body is ill. These are interlocking events." Meeting people at their point of social need, in this perspective, has spiritual ramifications; conversely, spiritual re-newal has the potential to empower other areas of a person's life. A whole-person anthropology lays the groundwork for an integrative ministry strategy.

The goal of "wholeness" means that these churches are not satisfied with "only taking care of the spiritual side of people," as Rev. Kyerematen stated. People cannot be whole unless they are living the quality of life that God in-tends. On the other hand, conversionist churches tend to be skeptical of social programs that measure tangible outcomes alone, without considering people's interior condition. As a woman who counseled addicts advised: "Drugs are just a surface problem. You may have gotten rid of the surface problem, but the real source of the problem is still there."

A whole-person perspective on ministry may thus hold spiritual renewal as an assumed ministry goal, even if it is not explicitly expressed. Arthur Far-nsley (2003, 91) comments on the evangelistic agenda of many theologically conservative churches involved in social services: "It would be wrong to suggest that they were using the delivery of human services as some sort of cover for their underlying goal of evangelizing. It would be better to say that, for them, services and community development are about the whole person, and the whole person must be in right relationship to God through Jesus."

Invitational Voluntarism: Spiritual Commitment and Personal Choice

Voluntarism, as defined by Stephen Hart, is "the strand within Christian tra-dition that focuses on the direct relationship between God and each person as a centered, coherent, freely acting individual" (1992, 43). Evangelism is pred-icated on the principle of voluntarism because it presents the path of faith as a choice that each person must freely make for himself or herself. Most Chris-tians accept that conversions may be encouraged, but should not—and indeed, cannot—be forced.[3] The churches we studied drew a distinction between using social ministries to create opportunities to share faith with beneficiaries, and requiring beneficiaries to profess faith in order to receive aid. Even when pro-grams incorporated mandatory religious elements, for the most part they re-quired beneficiaries only to be present for a religious activity (such as a sermon or prayer) but not to participate personally.[4] They sought to win conversions by persuasion rather than by coercion.

"We are very careful not to push people about anything concerning their faith," said a ministry leader at Central Baptist. At a theologically liberal church where witnessing is not the norm, this sentiment is not surprising. But we heard echoes of this statement from conversionist churches as well. A youth leader at Bethel emphasized that the way to influence youth was through informal mentoring relationships, "not forcing Jesus into it but showing his love and being an example." Christians need to be explicit about their religious reasons for helping people, said a ministry leader at Tenth Presbyterian, but "I understand that you can't force it down their throat." Cookman's Donna Jones explained why the religious elements of their welfare-to-work ministry were optional: "We do have free will, and so they literally have to make a choice in the matter—they don't have to accept our kind of teaching [about] who God is, or what we believe in. . . . A lot of them are not receptive to it . . . and we don't have a problem with that. We don't try to force anybody."

On the other hand, for conversionist churches, respecting the free will of beneficiaries to make moral and religious choices does not mean taking a neutral stance with respect to those choices. Conversionist social programs typically uphold a Christian moral framework, even if they do not demand that beneficiaries conform to it. While such programs affirm the right of beneficiaries to reject the Christian message, they also assert that this decision has inalienable consequences both for this life and the life to come. Conversionist churches balance the transcendent moral and spiritual claims of their faith with the personal freedom prized by voluntarism by casting the call to spiritual commitment in the form of an invitation.[5] According to an associate pastor at First Presbyterian, evangelism means "trying to create opportunities for people to take their next logical step in their relationship with God," whether this is attending a church service, reading Christian literature, or praying with a church member. Social services provide a pre-evangelistic platform for extending these opportunities.

Invitational voluntarism often couples religious teachings with appeals to a beneficiary's self-interest. For example, a ministry leader at Faith Assembly of God concluded that issuing sympathetic warnings about the dangers of destructive behaviors such as substance abuse was more effective than moralizing: "The Lord doesn't want us doing this, but he does give us free will. And it's not like, 'You better stop doing that because God said no.' He loves me so much he knows this will destroy my body." On the positive side, a ministry leader at Christian Stronghold described the attraction of their religious message in their outreach to troubled youth: "If we can get them to accept the Lord, to start applying biblical principles to their lives, they're going to be more successful." The principle of voluntarism provides incentive for churches to frame religious invitations in terms of the practical benefits of faith rather than doctrinal content.

Expressive Relationalism: Telling and Modeling the Gospel

Given the postmodern "preference for personalized faith," conversionist churches appear to be moving away from impersonal evangelistic strategies that rely on scripted communication—such as mass revivals and organized door-to-door campaigns—toward a more organic, relational approach (Wolfe 2003, 192; Webber 2002; Woods 1996). While affirming the importance of Bethel Temple's street evangelism program, associate pastor Joel Van Dyke acknowledged that the most effective way they shared the gospel was "in the context of needs being met and relationships being formed." David Apple similarly explained why building relationships is a priority in Tenth Presbyterian's work with homeless persons: "Once there's trust, there's openness to the truth that we have to speak. Otherwise people aren't going to listen to us and the church isn't credible." *Expressive relationalism* communicates the gospel through relationships cultivated in the context of social ministry.

The ideal of "Christ living through me in relationships," as David Apple put it, has an inherently incarnational, implicit character. Christians are to be "God with skin on" to people in need (Rittenhouse 2002, i). "Before people read the Bible, they will read you first," remarked Rev. Robbins. The ideal of incarnational ministry is Jesus, who "didn't send a messenger, or didn't just put out a hand to pull us up," but "became like one of us, and lived among us," said Luisa Cabello Hansel of Nueva Creación. For conversionist churches, a relational model is also expressive in that it entails telling people about Jesus as well as being compassionately present with them in Jesus' name. Relationships forged in the context of service are intended to become the conduit for evangelistic dialogue. A Christian Stronghold leader reflected this intention in his definition of evangelism: "I can share Christ by my deeds, I can share Christ verbally. My actions can draw people to me who will say, 'Why would you do that?' and it gives me an opportunity to share my faith." At another large African American church, a ministry leader described the spiritual impact of social action: "When you exemplify love to someone, . . . it opens up the door for you to share more. And that's the evangelistic purpose . . . to open up a door." Her church's evangelistic purpose was advanced by modeling God's love through acts of service, but as a pre-evangelistic strategy it was not wholly fulfilled until church volunteers walked through the open door of these relationships to "share more."

The combination of telling and modeling the gospel is illustrated by the food ministry of Faith Assembly of God. The explicitly evangelistic intent of the program was expressed by a volunteer's prayer during the prayer circle at the start of the food distribution, that "a little part of God's Spirit will go in every bag of food, so that we might know Jesus and tell someone about Jesus today." This aim was accomplished in part through structured religious elements: group prayer, a noontime worship service, evangelistic tracts, and invitations to other church activities. But what the coordinator of Faith's food ministries talked about most in her interview was her relationships with the people who came for food. She described her conversations with one woman, a "strung-out" addict whose boyfriend abused her: "I never push. I just keep saying, 'To God, you're a beautiful baby girl. Anytime you're ready, I'm a heart-beat away. I'm glad you came today.' They need the relationship. Now she trusts me and she's almost ready." By providing a consistent, nurturing presence in her life, the coordinator hoped to help this woman connect the program's tangible aid and religious content with the possibility of personal transformation.

Expressive relationalism is closely related to what Christian Smith (1998, 187) describes as the individualistic "personal influence strategy" of social change, "which maintains that the only truly effective way to change the world is one-individual-at-a-time through the influence of interpersonal relationships." Smith notes that the social impact of the personal influence strategy is limited because it fails to take into account the complex social forces that affect individuals. As the next section will explain, a relational approach to evangelism does not *necessarily* restrict churches to a personal influence strategy for social change. However, since community development and advocacy programs present fewer opportunities for personal interactions with beneficiaries, closely linking evangelism to caring relationships may narrow the range of a church's social action.

Expanded Individualism: Personal and Social Reform

When asked about the needs in Faith Assembly of God's community, Rose replied that she was not going to give the expected answer about more jobs or other socioeconomic factors. "No. We need, what our children need is Jesus." The community's problems, as she saw it, were driven by personal failings—selfishness, pride and greed. "Ain't no government gonna work for this. Ain't no state or new law that's gonna help this. Jesus, period."

Rose's worldview accords with the thoroughly individualistic nature of mainstream evangelical social ethics (Hollinger 1983; Wuthnow 1991; C. Smith 1998; Emerson and Smith 2001). In an atomistic understanding of society, social problems are ultimately individual problems—like selfishness and greed—writ large. Thus solutions to social problems come, as Glenn Loury (1995) put it, "one by one from the inside out." The way to reform society is not to modify the social environment, or to band together to demand political change, but rather to promote the spiritual regeneration and personal development of individuals who can transform their environment by acting with integrity and compassion. Ethicist Lewis Smedes summarized Christian individualism: "The gospel makes men good. Good men make good societies" (1966, 10). In other words, ministering to the whole person is the way to build wholesome communities. Most of the holistic-instrumental and dominant-evangelism churches in our study would subscribe to this idea. As represented by Rose's comments, such Christians are either unaware of or uninvolved in possibilities for social change beyond personal transformation.

In contrast, the holistic-complementary churches we studied supported outreach to individuals in tandem with structural responses to social need. They sponsored nearly as many community development programs as personal development ministries, and four out of the five participated in systemic change activities as well. Such churches are better captured by Dennis Hollinger's description of a "new breed" of evangelicals, who "seek to incorporate an understanding of structural change within their theology and have come to view sin as both corporate and personal." They "emphatically stress the need for personal conversion and discipleship, but they simultaneously assert that the Christian message applies to social realities, which transcend the changed hearts of individuals" (1983, 138).[6] Their approach to social change acknowledges that "a good society requires not only individuals who behave well but social structures that create well-being" (Hart 1992, 150).

Personal and structural change ministries should not be "played against each other," insisted an associate pastor at First Presbyterian Church. "Yes, individuals have to be transformed. That's the only way real change happens. But transformed people transform the social environment in which they function." First Presbyterian teaches that "transformed people" produce social change not only through their individual efforts but also through organized social action. The associate pastor described their ultimate ministry focus: "There is a very clear kingdom justice goal. That is, a sense that everybody ought to at least have the opportunity for a basic life that works." This means, he later noted, that there were "times to go out and say, 'Wait a minute, enough is enough.'"

Life in Christ, like First Presbyterian, asserts that spiritually transformed individuals have a responsibility to work together for social change. "Our people are citizens as well as Christians," pastor Dickie Robbins explained. Pointing to the model of the prophets who held Israel's kings accountable, he introduced the church's new Political Involvement Ministry with this ambitious vision: "We'll put an end to evil government in the city!" Yet he also insisted that the benefits of structural activism can only be preserved by spiritually transforming a critical mass of individuals. Reverend Robbins described two community development collaboratives in which Life in Christ was involved: one funded by the state (Weed and Seed), the other sponsored by a private Christian foundation. Both projects involved similar structural improvements, such as tearing down abandoned houses, but the private initiative also recruited churches to mentor residents and to lead evangelistic activities. Reverend Robbins expected the Christian program to have a greater long-term impact:

> The Weed and Seed effort is probably going to change more the infrastructure and appearance of the community, whereas the other initiative will change the people themselves. . . . If you change the people, the people will change the community. If you change the

community and don't change the people, the people will change
the community back.

Reverend Robbins was not disparaging efforts to improve the community's
"infrastructure and appearance." Rather, he was making the case for integrating religiously based personal development into community development.

The individualism of many conversionist churches thus does not preclude
their involvement in social justice, but it does color their motivation for structural change and their interpretation of how it comes about. Their activism
cannot be explained simply either as accommodating or confronting the status
quo (Kanagy 1992), because it incorporates elements of both. A pastor of a
small, Anglo inner-city congregation emphasized this point:

> I think as individuals become Christians and then see that the word
> of God challenges them to live in different ways, that will impact
> upon the neighborhood. But I also think that the Christian must
> seek to change the structures in our society, which unbelievers have
> set up. I believe the individual has to be changed *and* the structures
> have to be changed, because they condition one another mutually.

For these churches, a focus on individuals is expanded by a sense of calling to
address the social structures that limit their God-given potential, and a concern
for justice is shaped by the belief that social reform is best promoted and
protected by spiritually regenerated individuals. God saves individuals, who
work together for social justice. This position is what we are calling expanded
individualism.

Nueva Creación Lutheran Church: A Mainline Holistic Vision

Patrick Cabello Hansel, pastor of Nueva Creación, believes the Bible is inspired
but not literal, and that "everyone is saved by God." His liberal-leaning theology
and his "unabashedly left" political views were influenced by liberation theology and his experiences living in Latin America. (Patrick is Anglo; his wife
Luisa, who also serves as associate pastor, is from Chile.) Social activism is
central to his understanding of what it means to be a Christian. Yet he also
envisions evangelism as one of the core purposes of the church. Nueva Creación's story shows how the five attributes above may be adapted outside of the
evangelical context.

In 1993 Rev. Cabello Hansel began networking in a predominantly Puerto
Rican, low-income neighborhood in preparation for planting a new bilingual
church. At its launch, one resident shared her holistic vision for the new congregation: "I see our church as helping the community out, and bringing people to God." The name Nueva Creación/New Creation was chosen, according

to Rev. Cabello Hansel, to reflect their mission "to work with God's spirit to re-create this community, both on an individual and on a community level." Themes of spiritual and social renewal are interwoven in the congregational culture. At the close of a worship service, for example, Rev. Cabello Hansel charged the congregation to spend their week "inviting others who do not know Christ and working for peace and justice." A prominently displayed banner in the church sanctuary depicts a dove surrounded by olive branches hovering over a city skyline, with an adapted quote from Luke 4:18: "The Spirit of the Lord has anointed us to preach good news to the poor."

Nueva Creación brings "good news to the poor" through sermons and liturgy about the importance of forgiveness through faith in Christ, door-to-door campaigns to invite neighborhood residents to church, and events such as street fairs featuring a religious speaker. Families served by the church's social ministries are invited to church. While Rev. Cabello Hansel does not believe that Christianity offers an exclusive path to salvation, he encourages people to become Christians. He characterizes salvation as:

> Prayer and fasting, and a confession publicly of one's wrongdoing, making amends, being forgiven, working as a servant, working for peace and justice, seeking the lost, and being humbled. That's all a part of the spiritual path of being born again. So it's not a thing that happens, it is a movement. It's like a river that you're a part of.

This understanding of salvation emphasizes the *engaged* aspect of engaged orthodoxy. The goal of sharing faith with ministry beneficiaries, Rev. Cabello Hansel says, is "to lead them into a deeper relationship with Christ. But I also think that in the Bible, salvation is more than just that, it's more than eternal life. It is salvation from oppressive systems."

At Nueva Creación, the image of wholeness is thus extended from whole persons to include all of society and the created order. As Luisa Cabello Hansel put it, "God makes us whole, and God makes us instruments to bring wholeness to the community." The message of invitational voluntarism includes not only calling people to a better life through Christ but also "a commitment to serve Christ through the church." The word Patrick Hansel uses to describe these intermeshed goals of mission is *shalom*, the Hebrew word for peace, which he says signifies "the restoration of the whole creation." True shalom "only comes from a relationship with God, and a relationship with each other." In Nueva Creación's inclusive worldview, pursuing this expansive vision entails collaboration with other community groups, who "may not share the doctrine, but they share the faith in the vision," according to a ministry leader.

The theme of expressive relationalism in Nueva Creación's mission is summed up by Luisa Cabello Hansel: "God calls us to live incarnationally."

The Hansels accepted this principle as a personal challenge to relocate into their church's neighborhood, and they believe their personal availability has enhanced the credibility of their witness. The church's greatest evangelistic impact, says Rev. Cabello Hansel, comes from church members "showing that they may be living a new life" through their relationship with Jesus and sharing their transformational experience with neighbors. Relational influence is also valued in Nueva Creación's approach to social change, as the foundation for networking and community organizing.

Reverend Cabello Hansel sounds the theme of expanded individualism in the way he defines personal regeneration: "Transformation generally takes place first within the individual, coming to an awareness of being loved and forgiven by a gracious God, and then being transformed and the evil or oppression taken away from them. . . . That individual transformation leads to involvement in justice and the building of a community." A pastoral intern at Nueva Creación who works with youth and immigrants similarly explains that evangelism empowers individuals to work for change: "I believe the kingdom of God is built here among us. In order to do that you need to do outreach and bring people into Christian faith." This perspective on the connectedness of personal and social transformation rests on an awareness of both personal and systemic causes of poverty. According to the pastoral intern, "sin is not only, . . . 'I spoke wrongly about this person or I robbed somebody or lied'— but this is also sin, to let people live in despair." The church counters this despair on multiple levels: through ministries of relief and personal development, such as a food pantry and after-school program; through community development projects; and through participation in the advocacy coalition, Philadelphia Interfaith Action.

Despite similarities with more evangelical congregations, there are also differences. Nueva Creación's style of invitational voluntarism does not stress moral absolutes. While ministries incorporate religious elements such as prayer and biblical teachings, Nueva Creación leans more on implicit strategies of religious integration; for example, Rev. Cabello Hansel describes beautification efforts in the neighborhood as a "sign" of God's salvation. The pastoral intern asserts that while spiritual and social care should be integrated, in practice the social aspect predominates: "There's not enough bread on the table. My concern might be their spiritual life, but their concern is bread on the table, so what do I address first? . . . My personal tendency is that I will address the bread issue first and then the spiritual, but hopefully my actions will express my faith." Although balancing social action and evangelism was his goal from the church's founding, Rev. Cabello Hansel admits, "I think since then we have done better at the social than we have at the evangelism."

Holistic Beliefs about the Role of the Church

Survey questions on beliefs related to the role of the church in society provide another window on the characteristics of socially active conversionist churches. Responses from three holistic churches, with a social action dominant church included for comparison, are presented in table 9.1. Tenth Presbyterian (a very large, Anglo, downtown church) and Christian Stronghold (a very large, African American, inner-city church) are among the most theologically conservative churches in our study. Both have a holistic-instrumental mission orientation. Close to 100% of respondents at each church strongly agree that salvation comes through Jesus Christ alone, and over 85% strongly agree that the Bible is to be taken literally. Holistic-complementary First Presbyterian (a large, Anglo, downtown church) occupies a more moderate theological position, with 77% of respondents strongly affirming salvation through Christ, and 80% agreeing that the Bible is literal (but with only 39% agreeing strongly). Central Baptist (a medium-sized, Anglo, suburban church), with a social action dominant mission orientation, is the most theologically liberal church in the study; only 7% believe in a literal interpretation of the Bible (62% strongly *disagree* with this position), and 32% agree that salvation comes through Christ alone (26% strongly disagree).[7]

The churches' this-worldly sense of responsibility is seen in the data reported in section A of table 9.1. The majority of respondents in the three holistic churches said that churches should focus equally on helping people in this life and preparing people for the life to come (engaged orthodoxy). The churches differed in the emphases of the remaining respondents: theologically conservative, holistic-instrumental Tenth Presbyterian and Christian Stronghold leaned toward other-worldliness, while moderate, holistic-complementary First Presbyterian leaned toward the here-and-now. Not surprisingly, Central Baptist focused emphatically on this-worldly concerns.

In section B, a slight majority (56%) of Tenth Presbyterian respondents said that the role of the church is to care for people's spiritual well-being, or "the quality of their relationship with God." The remainder affirmed a blend of spiritual care and care for people's social well-being, described as "the quality of their health, economic condition, family life, etc." At almost every other church we surveyed, the majority of respondents chose the "both" option, and the remainder leaned strongly toward spiritual care (though at Central Baptist, the remainder were about split between spiritual and social care). Consistent with the whole-person view of human nature, improving people's social and economic quality of life is a core function of the church, but not in isolation from the equally or more important role of nurturing people's spiritual needs.[8]

At each of the four churches, the percentage of respondents saying the church should focus on caring for people's spiritual well-being was greater

TABLE 9.1 Beliefs about the Role of the Church

A.	The church should focus on . . .[a]		
Church	Helping people here and now	Both	Preparing people for eternal life after death
Tenth Presbyterian (N=227)	6.4	61.0	32.6
Christian Stronghold Baptist Church (N=620)	14.2	64.6	21.1
First Presbyterian (N=193)	23.4	60.1	16.5
Central Baptist (N=142)	79.4	19.1	1.4

B.	Churches should care for people's . . .		
Church	Social and emotional well-being	Both	Spiritual well-being
Tenth Presbyterian	0.5	43.8	55.7
Christian Stronghold	5.3	64.6	30.1
First Presbyterian	3.7	59.4	36.9
Central Baptist	9.8	78.2	11.9

C.	The task of the church is to . . .		
Church	Work to change society	Both	Work to change the lives of individuals
Tenth Presbyterian	2.4	23.5	74.2
Christian Stronghold	9.1	47.1	53.0
First Presbyterian	3.2	31.9	64.9
Central Baptist	5.0	77.9	17.1

D.	The way to share God's love with people is by . . .		
Church	Telling about Jesus	Both	Demonstrating it with caring actions
Tenth Presbyterian	12.7	72.7	14.6
Christian Stronghold	18.9	66.7	14.5
First Presbyterian	8.0	63.3	28.7
Central Baptist	2.8	23.2	74.0

E.	Poverty is largely due to . . .		
Church	A person's foolish choices or immoral lifestyle	Both	Social, economic, and political factors
Tenth Presbyterian	16.5	48.5	35.0
Christian Stronghold	16.4	52.1	31.5
First Presbyterian	20.1	40.8	39.1
Central Baptist	0.0	8.1	91.9

a. The belief questions provided respondents with two statements on either side of a five-point scale. They were to circle a number indicating whether they agreed more with the statement on the left or on the right, or circle "3" to mean they agreed equally with both. The percentages in the table represent the sums of the two agree-left and the two agree-right options.

than the percentage saying it should prepare people for life after death. This indicates that a spiritual focus is not necessarily equated with other-worldliness. Rather, the data suggests that respondents sought to nurture others' faith in part for the sake of how it could help them in *this* life. Such a this-worldly spirituality was evident in a statement by an associate pastor at First Presbyterian that Christianity says "to people across the socio-economic spectrum, 'Jesus makes a difference and not just pie-in-the-sky, not just after you die. Jesus makes a difference now in your quality of life, your ability to deal with life.'" At the three holistic churches, attending to people's spiritual needs entails concern for both their earthly and eternal well-being; and helping people here and now includes both social and spiritual care.

The influence of the individualism of the broader American culture is evident in section C. None of the case study churches surveyed, even the social action dominant ones, said the task of the church was primarily to work to change society rather than individuals.[9] Most Central Baptist respondents held individual and social change as equal priorities. The majority of respondents at the three conversionist churches attached a clear priority to changing individuals. Tenth Presbyterian's strong preference for individual reform is not surprising, since all of its ministries focus on relief and personal development. The individualistic thrust at First Presbyterian is less expected, given its involvement in structural ministries. This reflects, in part, an evangelical tendency to interpret programs of social reform in terms of their impact on individuals (C. Smith 1998). It also suggests the congregation had not embraced the expanded individualism of the leadership. Overall, the African American congregations in our study were less individualistic in their responses than the Anglo congregations (see Billingsley 1999). Interestingly, a higher percentage of respondents at Christian Stronghold, which emphasizes personal empowerment, gave priority to changing society than at social justice-oriented Central Baptist.

As displayed in section D, the conversionist churches diverge strikingly from Central Baptist on the way to share God's love. Consistent with the principle of expressive relationalism, the majority of respondents in the holistic churches indicated that Christians must both model God's love through caring actions and verbally tell people about Jesus (with the remainder of respondents at First Presbyterian set apart by leaning strongly toward caring actions). In contrast, three-fourths of Central Baptist respondents stressed the implicit demonstration of spiritual nurture through caring actions. In the social action dominant framework, "embodying God's presence in service to the poor" (Ammerman 2002, 149) is the main way of conveying religious meaning; in fact, proselytizing may be viewed with suspicion (Marty 1981). For holistic churches, a complete presentation of the gospel ideally involves both word and deed.

The question on the causes of poverty in section E generated the most internal diversity within the three conversionist congregations. The largest segment of respondents at each church indicated that poverty is caused equally by social factors (elaborated on the survey, "such as racism and lack of good jobs") and by personal choices ("such as laziness or drugs"); the remainder leaned toward social causes.[10] In contrast, with near unanimity Central Baptist members pointed to social factors. No simple correlation emerged in the case studies between perceived causes of poverty and patterns of ministry. At both Christian Stronghold and Tenth Presbyterian, about a third of respondents attributed poverty to structural factors; Christian Stronghold has six community development and systemic change programs, while Tenth Presbyterian sponsors no ministries of a structural nature. It is important to note that only one of the congregations surveyed—Faith Assembly of God—highlighted personal choices as the main cause of poverty.[11]

Tenth Presbyterian, Christian Stronghold, and First Presbyterian frame the church's task as one of changing individuals, yet their members also believe that impersonal social forces are at least as responsible for poverty, if not more so, as individual choices. Even at Tenth Presbyterian, where three-fourths of respondents preferred ministering to individuals over reforming society, only 17% placed responsibility for poverty primarily on individuals. Asserting that social problems are best resolved by transforming individuals is not the same as *blaming* individuals for their social problems. Socially active conversionist churches tend to acknowledge the role of external factors in tension with a message of internal empowerment. Regardless of the root cause of the need, such churches hold individuals responsible for taking steps to improve their situation. This was illustrated by a message from Rev. Moore to the men of Tenth Memorial Baptist Church: "While it's true that circumstances beyond our control make it difficult for us to be all that God wants us to be, we must look at these as challenges and opportunities."

Table 9.2 explores the responses of these same four congregations when asked to select the three items they believed poor people need most to escape poverty. Education and employment fell in the top three at all the churches surveyed, particularly Central Baptist. Respondents in the two holistic-instrumental churches were also overwhelmingly likely to identify conversion as a solution to poverty. At Central Baptist, in contrast, conversion was considered the *least* helpful solution. In their worldview, spiritual care is important overall, but irrelevant to social outcomes. The conversionist churches were more likely than Central to select "better personal morals," but this was not in the top three items of any of the fourteen churches surveyed. This underscores that promoting spiritual transformation as a solution to poverty is not equivalent to blaming poverty on personal failings. Rather, these findings suggest that conversionist churches believe that conversion can empower poor persons

TABLE 9.2 What Poor People Need Most to Escape Poverty

| Church | Item that can help poor persons escape poverty (percent selecting each item)[a] | | | | | |
	Spiritual conversion— faith in God	A good education and a decent job	To be treated with dignity and respect	A caring church family	A more just society	Better personal morals or lifestyle
Tenth Presbyterian	*84.0*	72.0	30.7	56.0	12.0	27.6
Christian Stronghold	*91.1*	76.9	16.0	46.3	11.6	28.7
First Presbyterian	60.1	*76.2*	47.7	44.0	15.5	37.3
Central Baptist	9.2	*90.8*	66.9	28.2	59.2	9.9

a. Respondents were instructed to select the three items they believed would be most helpful. The percentage of responses for the item most selected by the congregation is in italics. The survey included an eighth item, "Adequate government support," not shown here; none of the congregations selected this in its top three responses.

indirectly, for example, by bringing them into the embrace of a caring church family, and by helping them to take advantage of economic opportunities such as a good job.

These survey data, along with case study observations, suggest some general comparisons between holistic and dominant social action orientations to ministry. Churches in both categories agree that caring for people's spiritual well-being is important, but disagree whether this can be accomplished primarily by conveying God's love implicitly through acts of social care. Both types of churches that engage in social ministry affirm that Christian faith is concerned with the affairs of this world, but conversionists insist also on the importance of the spiritual realm beyond this life. Both tend to recognize the role of structural causes of poverty, but conversionists tend to place these social factors alongside an individualistic emphasis on personal, moral factors. A holistic approach is characterized by the belief that the gospel is shared through compassionate demonstration *plus* verbal witness, and that social problems are best tackled through social interventions *plus* personal faith.

"On the Wall": The Public Face of Conversionist Social Ministry

Having a commitment to evangelism does not preclude churches from adopting social ministries that lack an overtly religious character. Nine out of the twelve dual-focus and holistic churches in our study (including five out of the eight theologically conservative churches) had ministries like Faith's Peacemakers program that did not integrate significant religious elements. As with

Peacemakers, in many of these instances the religious dynamic was constrained by an outside funder or partner. For example, a support group hosted by one church stopped praying together after being told that it would put their United Way funding in jeopardy. Even without external constraints, however, evangelistic churches often voluntarily adopt relational, invitational, nonconfrontational religious-integration strategies. These more low-key approaches to faith-sharing are preferenced by a confluence of theology and culture—the voluntarism of evangelical faith rooted in the doctrine of free will, and the pervasive relativism and "norms of polite nonjudgmentalism" noted by Wuthnow (1996, 63).

Yet ministry leaders often alleged that social programs lacking overt religious content still had an evangelistic impact, through pre-evangelistic strategies of invitations and relationships. Rose was confident that her patient mentoring of Peacemaker youth would bear spiritual fruit. She talked informally to youth about faith, but ultimately she saw her involvement in their lives as the greatest witness: "They'll look at what you do and not what you say." Bethel Temple staff contracted with the junior high school across the street to teach an audiovisual technology class in the church's Arts and Media Center. "It obviously would not be a time for proselytizing or anything of that nature," acknowledged Rev. Van Dyke, "but that's not our style, anyway. It's much more relational evangelism. By getting those kids in here and building those relationships, we earn the right to ask them to come out [to other evangelistic youth activities]." Relational and invitational strategies thus allow conversionist churches to diversify their social programs and remain faithful to their evangelistic mission, without overt proselytizing. As a Christian Stronghold member put it, "Through ministry, even if it's not evangelism, you evangelize."

Churches may also make a distinction between how they present religious messages in the public context of social programs versus their private church "turf." Christian Stronghold launched an after-school "self esteem" program for troubled boys at a nearby elementary school, which the ministry leader described as part of the church's long-term goal of evangelizing the school. Because the program involved a public school, the leader said it "must walk softly with the Muslim children in the school," and the program lacked explicitly religious content. But through this faith-affiliated self-esteem program, ministry staff invited schoolchildren to attend the church's faith-permeated summer camp. In the context of church camp, the leader explained, "any of the families that register know that their children are coming to a Christian church, so if a Muslim family registers a child, then that child is going to be evangelized."

In this model, two normative sets of integration strategies, accompanied by different styles of religious language, come into play. In the realm of public social outreach (e.g., the self-esteem program), faith-based service providers may employ the implicit or pre-evangelistic strategies of encouraging spiritual awareness and religiously derived values, but avoid making religiously specific claims; in private, explicitly religious arenas (e.g., the church summer camp), beneficiaries may fairly expect the integration of overtly evangelistic and faith-specific content. Yet it is the church's intention to share the same underlying message (e.g., that children need a relationship with God to be whole) in both arenas, translated into a format appropriate to that context.

Given the complex relationship between religious motivations and charitable involvement, Robert Wuthnow observes that individuals can become "heteroglossic, allowing them to speak with many voices, to suggest motives, but not to identify completely with any one" (1996, 62–63). Churches, too, can be "heteroglossic." Holistic churches, in particular, may present their multifaceted mission in complex, sometimes seemingly inconsistent ways. An example comes from the Christian Anti-Drug Dependency Coalition (CADDC), founded by the pastor of Germantown Church of the Brethren. A grant proposal to the city of Philadelphia uses minimal religious language, describing CADDC only as being associated "with that long-demonstrated tradition of caring and helping of the local church." But CADDC's brochure, distributed among churches, is more explicitly religious: "These initiatives are working because they are Christ centered and are dependent upon the work of the Holy Spirit." Program staff had become heteroglossic, able to translate the social dimension of their ministry in order to connect with audiences from other or no religious traditions (Bartkowski and Regis 2003).

These strategies illustrate what Ammerman, following Walter Brueggemann, calls "on the wall" versus "behind the wall" conversations. The metaphor comes from the story in 2 Kings of an assault by the Assyrians on the walled city of Jerusalem.

> Before the leaders of Israel would consent to a conversation "on the wall" in Aramaic (the language of the imperial state), they insisted on a conversation "behind the wall" in Hebrew (the language of Judah). In that language the people could recount their own primal narrative. . . . It enables Israel's leaders to enter the conversation "on the wall" with alternative proposals born of an alternative view of the world but negotiated now "on the wall" in the language of the realm. (Ammerman 1997a, 359)

To extend this metaphor, churches engaged in social ministry come to the wall not to defend their walled city against assailants, but to address the needs of the world outside the wall, or to seek resources and partners for this venture.

When churches having an evangelistic purpose for social ministry stand "on the wall" of the public arena, they may sense the need to carry on a conversation about their mission in a way that makes sense to a non-evangelical society (which may be indifferent or even hostile to this mission). On the wall of public ministry, practitioners tend to stress gentle religious themes that will find broad acceptance and connect with the felt needs of beneficiaries, such as God's love and provision. On the wall of partnerships with public or private secular entities, church leaders may make the pragmatic decision to curtail overt evangelistic activities in particular program areas in order to leverage necessary resources. On-the-wall public documents like grant proposals may highlight the values and goals that churches share with other segments of society: compassion, justice, community restoration, economic self-sufficiency, and healthy relationships. But "behind the wall," in church services, evangelistic events, and program literature designed for a religious audience, discussions of ministry include more spiritually explicit and personally engaging themes: the call to repent and follow Christ, the transforming power of the Holy Spirit, the challenge of spiritual warfare, the long road of faithful obedience and fruitful ministry.[12]

Faith Assembly's Peace Celebration was advertised to the community with an "on-the-wall" flyer that highlighted the free food and entertainment. "Behind the wall," the church calendar described this event as "a special Street Outreach Service. . . . Pray for God to deliver, heal, and break the chains of darkness." The church called for prayer "that Christ will be exalted" through the work of Peacemaker staff, and that Peacemaker youth "will come to faith in Christ through our efforts." Someone hearing this behind-the-wall language about the spiritual purpose of Peacemakers might be surprised that the program is actually carried out in such a seemingly secular way, and might even conclude that the church is not being faithful to its mission. Likewise, an observer familiar only with the program's operation and "official" descriptions might not understand Faith's confidence that the program was having a significant spiritual impact, and might suspect the church of practicing stealth evangelism. Understanding the capacity of holistic churches for heteroglossic discourse helps to make sense of this seeming incongruity.

Not all churches are heteroglossic. Some evangelistic churches carry out their on-the-wall conversations in a way consistent with their behind-the-wall language—even if this means limiting the groups with whom they engage in conversation. This was why Rev. Phil Ryken stated that Tenth Presbyterian Church could not accept public funding for its ministries (all of which had explicit religious elements): "For us, our message is everything. Our message is salvation in Jesus Christ, and that's wrapped up in all the charitable work we do. If there is any threat to that message, then that really threatens the effectiveness of what we do."[13] Churches that for various reasons are not heteroglossic, that see any variation in their evangelistic strategy as compromise and a threat to their effectiveness, may be less willing to pursue public funding for their programs.

It is worth investigating further which churches are willing to diversify their outreach strategies in order to take advantage of public funding. Black churches, for example, are significantly more likely to express an interest in public partnerships (Chaves 1999). To what extent is this related to the fact that as an anchor of the African American community, black churches have a legacy of serving multiple roles, and that their identity entails a degree of dynamic "dialectical tension" (Lincoln and Mamiya 1990, 11)? That as minority voices in a dominant Anglo culture, they have become skilled at being "bilingual" in communicating their social and spiritual mission? Or is it that their more limited access to private resources leads them by necessity toward a more "practical theology," as Rev. Smith put it? Whatever the underlying factors, it is clear that black churches and other churches may engage in public ministry while retaining a passionately evangelistic mission "behind the wall."

Conclusion

"Some who support the work of religious congregations do so because they hope to win converts to their faith. Others believe that their faith requires them to serve those in need, whether the needy convert or not. Many believe both these propositions at the same time" (Dionne and Chen 2001, 3). The ambit of churches whose mission encompasses both converting unbelievers and serving the needy appears to represent a gathering movement. Carl Dudley observes that the end of the twentieth century "witnessed a dramatic mingling of spiritual and social concerns, as if the socially sensitive liberal churches recognized their need for explicit spiritual grounding, and the biblically centered evangelicals celebrated their renewed commitment to social ministries" (Dudley 2001, 15). Other observers have similarly pointed to "a large middle ground in which people are drawing on elements from both evangelical and liberal traditions" (Ammerman 1997a, 358; Olson and Carroll 1992; Becker 1999; Dudley 2001).

The current conversation about faith-based initiatives calls for closer attention to these churches that do not dichotomize word and deed. Only a fraction of churches adopt this position, although their prevalence—or at least their public presence—appears to be growing.[14] But whatever their extent, it is helpful to get a better understanding of what they do and why. Our sample suggests that the activity and impact of such churches is likely disproportionate to their number, particularly among inner-city, minority, and theologically conservative congregations. These are the churches that will (at least compared to other evangelical churches) be most proactive in responding to community crises, partnering with government and other secular funders, and declaring to unjust systems, in the words of church leaders at First Presbyterian, "enough is enough."

PART IV

Saving Souls and Serving Society

10

Does Faith Work?

Spiritual Dynamics and Social Outcomes

On what would have been Dr. Martin Luther King's seventy-fifth birthday, President George W. Bush stood behind the podium where Dr. King had preached at Union Bethel African Methodist Episcopal (AME) Church in New Orleans, Louisiana. He used this "bully pulpit"—literally, at least, in the pulpit sense—to advocate for the expansion of federal aid to faith-based service organizations, without repressing their religious nature. "Faith–based programs are only effective because they do practice faith. It's important for our government to understand that."[1]

Researcher Byron Johnson offers a more cautious assessment (2002, 21). Existing studies, according to his review, do contain "preliminary evidence that faith-based programs can provide effective interventions," but because of their limited number and scope, these studies cannot "unequivocally certify the claim that faith-based programs are more effective than their secular counterparts." Recent scholarship has provided insight into how the religious dimension might contribute to purported outcomes (Bicknese 1999; Richard, Bell, and Carlson 2000; Lockhart 2003; C. Smith 2003), but is still a long way from endorsing the categorical affirmation of President Bush and many other supporters of the faith-based initiative that a religious approach is better at solving social problems.

Our study cannot add anything in a quantitative way to this argument. We lack systematic data to offer judgment on the outcomes of the 158 social ministries of the churches we studied, let alone to compare them to secular programs. We did, however, collect a great deal of information on how the people in the churches themselves viewed the impact of their programs. Regardless of whether their claims can be empirically verified, it is important to listen to how faith-based activists explain the role of faith in the efficacy of their ministry.

How Faith Works

Our explication of the "discourse of social utility" (Bartkowski and Regis 2003, 62) links the efficacy of social programs to their religious dimensions in five main areas: capacity, staffing, content, conversion of beneficiaries, and availability of extended social support. The arguments for efficacy can be summarized in the form of five postulates:

1. Being faith-based expands program capacity.
2. People of faith serve more effectively.
3. A religious perspective enhances program content.
4. Spiritual conversion empowers people to achieve socioeconomic goals.
5. Faith-based programs offer support from a religious community.

In other words, service providers claim that faith enhances the potential of the producers (1–2), the product (3), and the users (4–5) of social services.[2]

Being Faith-Based Expands Program Capacity

Some ministry leaders claim that their programs have an advantage in attracting and using resources. Several churches reported becoming a focal point for donors and community volunteers who were dissatisfied with the lack of spiritual depth in secular programs. Faith-based programs are "recognized as legitimate places for investment by people with social capital to expend," particularly people who want to provide services in a religious context (Ammerman 1997a, 367; also Becker and Dhingra 2001).

Ministry leaders also expressed confidence that God enabled them to stretch their ministry resources. The director of the mall ministry at First Presbyterian described how funds and volunteers dramatically appeared just when she thought they were at the end of their resource rope: "I just have this sense that God is bigger, and building this house for us. . . . As we step out in faith in these different ministries, God will provide the people that we need to do it." The director of community development at Bethel Temple stated that they did not pursue government funding, preferring to raise all their funds from within the Christian community. "It's not easy to get, but I just have no doubts that God will provide what we need for everything we do. I've seen that myself since I've been in ministry."

A different way that church-based ministry may be said to enhance capacity is by transforming aid recipients into providers of aid. As beneficiaries are converted, this expands the pool of people available to support the church's good works. Kenny, who first came to Faith Assembly of God for food, had a dramatic conversion experience and eventually overcame his drug habit. After five years of training, the pastor asked him to lead Faith's residential drug rehabilitation program. Residents in this program provide volunteer support to keep the church's food program and other ministries running—thus bringing Kenny's story full circle. At almost every church in our study, we heard narratives of people who had made the journey from beneficiary to committed Christian to volunteer worker. Kenny voiced a common motif when he insisted to the men in the rehab program: "God doesn't save us just to sit in pews— he saves us so we can go back to where we came from and pull somebody out the same way we were."

People of Faith Serve More Effectively

The second line of argument is that faith-based services are effective precisely because they are provided by people of faith. According to this argument, religious practitioners can tap into transcendent motivations and supernatural reservoirs of power and perseverance that amplify the impact of their service. Faith is also said to make a difference because it leads practitioners to treat beneficiaries with love, dignity, and high moral expectations.

Mary Nelson, director of a large nonprofit in Chicago called Bethel New Life, summarized what she sees as the "faith factor" in community development (Nelson 2001, 3):

> We say that our faith base has provided the GLUE that holds us together when racism, ageism and sexism would pull us apart. . . . The faith base is the GASOLINE for the long haul, the reminder that God doesn't give up on us, that God is with us in this effort for the long haul. The faith base is also the GUTS, to make the risky decisions, to step out in faith, to stand strong in going against the tide of doubt and hopelessness.

A fourth G-word—guidance—might be added to this list of how faith empowers providers. Jeavons describes guidance as "the potential for Divine intervention or God's providence affecting organizational performance" (1998, 89). A leader of the Grandparents as Parents support group at the Church of the Advocate attested: "I always ask Christ to allow us to do our best and to guide us in the right direction for information and being able to help those that come here. . . . Without that, I don't think we could be this successful."

The belief that God motivates, sustains, and directs their efforts gives ministry workers confidence that their work will have the intended results. This self-assurance derived from faith is particularly important in settings of lower socioeconomic opportunity, where congregants might otherwise feel they lack the skills and experience to make a contribution. A ministry leader at Faith Assembly of God, a native of the church's low-income community, credited her faith for helping her overcome self-doubt. "The pastor will say to me, 'I need you to do this,' and I think, 'I don't have a clue how to do that!'. . . . I have to believe that the Lord spoke to him, so I step out in faith." Belief in the efficacy of faith-inspired ministry can thus help to create the conditions in which people can develop the skills necessary for effective ministry, setting up a self-fulfilling prophecy.

Faith-based providers also believe they are effective because they have access to spiritual resources for problem-solving. Particularly in the Pentecostal tradition, ministry leaders stress the role of the Holy Spirit in empowering them to take a supernatural stand against evil in their community. A ministry leader at Faith Assembly of God asserted that the drug trade is a "stronghold" of malevolent spiritual powers. Church members wage spiritual warfare through "intercessory prayer," bolstering their more conventional arsenal of counseling, support groups and life skills training. But it was not only the Pentecostal interviewees who voiced this theme. The director of First Presbyterian Church's crisis pregnancy center described her ministry as "an incredible battlefield. I mean, Satan is just right there. We're right on the front lines, and you just can't go in without being equipped with prayer and the armor of God."

Ideally, at least, religious conviction impels service providers to be more loving, kind, and humble. A youth ministry leader at Bethel Temple confessed, "By myself, if I wasn't a Christian, I wouldn't care. I have a love that's greater than me." In evaluations of Cookman United Methodist Church's welfare-to-work program, clients indicated that the love and respect they received from the staff positively impacted their achievements in the program. One student shared her impression that staff are "sweeter and [more] humble than the rest of the world is. . . . They show you that they care." While these constructive qualities are not possessed only by Christians, it is generally expected that people of faith will display them.[3]

The altruism attributed to church members' faith not only enhances their capacity to serve individuals but also facilitates their organized action for justice. A member of Church of the Advocate who participates in Philadelphia Interfaith Action explained why he thought it significant that this community organizing coalition was made up of congregations. "The core basis of this is fellowship, the improvement of one another's condition. I don't know if other groups would have that in mind. Their agenda might be improving the circumstances of their group and not the others." He later noted that coming to faith helped him to transcend self-interest on a personal level: "I've been born again in the last two years. . . . I have come to love and respect and care for my fellow man, much more than I did before."

The first two premises—that being faith-based expands program capacity and staff efficacy—connect social outcomes with the faith of the providers, not with the faith of the beneficiaries. The effect on outcomes thus potentially applies to any type of program with a religious affiliation and religiously motivated staff. The discussion of the next three premises primarily concerns faith-permeated or faith-centered social programs that integrate explicitly religious elements.

A Religious Perspective Enhances Program Content

In chapter 5 we suggested that religious content can be described by its *topicality*—whether religious teachings are directly pertinent to the program's intended outcomes. In cases where the religious content is relevant to the social service, some argue that this content provides additional knowledge or skills ("religious cultural capital") that can help beneficiaries achieve their intended goal (Lockhart 2003).

A church leader at Christian Stronghold asserted, "Success comes from knowing God's word and applying it." He believed that a religious grounding was what made the church's home-ownership seminar effective: "The Lord would have us do the purchase of a home and have land. . . . Sometimes in society they give you a whole bunch of instructions and information, but when you know that this is what the Lord has in store for you, you get that sense of confidence." The seminar connects factual "instructions and information" about home ownership with biblical principles about the value of property. The added biblical perspective, this leader says, is more motivational than factual content alone.

Jobs Partnership of Philadelphia, a collaboration of businesses and churches (including Koinonia and Germantown Church of the Brethren), includes substantial religious content intended to help beneficiaries find and keep employment. A twelve-week class presents religious teachings on work-related topics such as respecting authority and workplace integrity, illustrated by this excerpt from the final lesson, "Excellence in All": "It is our responsibility to be diligent and skillful in our work (Proverbs 10:4, 5). Whatever we do, in word or deed, we should do all for God's glory (1 Corinthians 10:31 and Colossians 3:17). . . . God will hold you accountable for how you use the resources He has given you."[4] Many Jobs Partnership students come with a scattered work history and minimal job training. The Bible offers a solid foundation for the "soft skills" necessary for successful employment, said the director. Beneficiaries do not need to be religious themselves to be informed and motivated by this religious program content.

Spiritual Conversion Empowers People to Achieve
Socioeconomic Goals

The fourth and perhaps most controversial premise links social outcomes with religious conversion. At ten out of the fourteen congregations we surveyed, "conversion—faith in God" was the item that respondents most often identified as a solution to poverty (in seven of these congregations, conversion was selected by over three-fourths of the members). Bethel Temple's director of community development asserts:

> Salvation changes people's lives. It's the only way that people change. People that are saved make better use of the social programs. People that are saved can go through drug programs a lot better, usually. People that are saved and in prison come out better. People who are saved get a better job. It's proven by our members who were in really bad situations—most of them would say they would either be dead or in prison by now. . . . Those people are making a lot of money, . . . living better, providing for their family better, all because of the gospel.

In this perspective, spiritual transformation is at the heart of personal change, and, it is assumed, this personal change provides a pathway to a better life.[5] Based on the anthropological premise that "we are spiritual beings, our spirituality is what holds us together," Rev. Donna Jones asserts that social change ministries must address the "spiritual issues that keep people from full empowerment." According to this perspective, without inner renewal, people's circumstances may change but their root problems will re-manifest themselves in other forms. People who have experienced spiritual empowerment can change from the inside out.

The interviews revealed three main ways that ministry leaders believe personal faith has transformational power: it fosters new moral values and behaviors, it alters one's attitude toward oneself and the world, and it gives access to supernatural empowerment. It should be kept in mind that in the context of the churches we studied, these faith functions work in tandem with social aid. The Bethel leader quoted above sounded the common motif that becoming a Christian does not substitute for social interventions, but that "people that are saved make better use of the social programs." At the same time, the experience of salvation, in and of itself, is believed to have an effect independent of other forms of aid.

CHANGES IN BEHAVIOR AND MORAL VALUES. Advocates for faith-based service laud its potential to transmit values and shape moral behavior (e.g., Olasky 1992). Underlying the faith-based initiative is a "fervently held" assumption that congregations "bring moral teachings and strong core values to bear on whatever service or community-building activities they undertake" (Farnsley 2003, 11–12). Many religious social service practitioners do not see behavior as morally neutral. There is a wrong way to live and a right way to live, and right living reaps positive socioeconomic consequences. The assumption is that when one becomes a Christian, or at least follows the moral directives of the Christian faith, one will adopt new values, develop new habits, and abandon risky behaviors, which in turn will improve one's overall well-being (C. Smith 2003).

Values-based ministry is particularly evident in churches' work with youth. For example, the summer "enrichment camp" sponsored by Lafiya, a nonprofit center associated with Germantown Church of the Brethren, promised to teach "social manners and etiquette, character-building virtues, spiritual values from a Christian perspective, conflict resolution and caring for and maintaining a healthy body and our environment." The day care located at the Germantown church stated on its brochure: "Church of the Brethren is a 'peace church'. . . . We do work in cooperation with the values of the church. . . . Nonviolent conflict resolution is taught and encouraged." One of the objectives of Germantown's Friday night youth group, according to a promotional flyer, was "to contribute to the cultural, moral and social enrichment of the participants." The flyer quoted Proverbs 22:6: "Train a child in the way he should go, and when he is older he will not depart from it." The spiritual character of churches' youth ministries is intertwined with their efforts to mold the moral character of a new generation.

Fulfilling the potential of value-based ministry sometimes requires ministry leaders to function as disciplinarians. After seventeen years of dealing with tenants who destroyed the property or failed to pay rent, the director of a church-affiliated housing ministry said his role had evolved into that of a "first sergeant" in enforcing residency rules. He commented, "Most of our people who are in need of affordable housing are probably also lacking discipline in many areas of their lives." In one case, a family was on the verge of eviction because of unpaid rent. The estranged husband refused to contribute, accusing the wife of drug use and prostitution. The board of the housing ministry decided to accept partial payment with the stipulation that the mother attend drug counseling and possibly parenting training as well. "You have to be tough" with difficult residents, remarked the program director. Yet he admitted that his ministry experiences had actually challenged his original stereotype that "poor people were poor because they wanted to be poor." He now traced the behavioral problems of residents not to personal depravity but to life-skill deficiencies inherited through generations of poverty. The moral teachings of the church provide a necessary corrective to these deficiencies. Faith-based programs thus succeed by offering a combination of personal development and discipline.

CHANGES IN ATTITUDE. Many practitioners in faith-based ministries see God's movement within the soul as the catalyst for a transformation that works from the inside out. A new orientation to God is said to result in changes in bene-ficiaries' attitudes toward self and others, which in turn enhance their ability to set constructive goals and to succeed in the struggle to achieve them. As Lockhart (2003, drawing on Milner 1994) puts it, faith-based social ministries can facilitate a religiously grounded internal status transformation that has implications for external status.

This argument begins with the assumption that the root cause of many individuals' social problems is a distorted view of the self, a view twisted by a negative environment, racism, abuse, destructive habits, and satanic forces. Having internalized the false message that their lives lack value, marginalized persons need to hear the good news that they are created in the image of God. An elder at Life in Christ expounded on this theme at the church's Drug Free support group meeting. "God wants to prosper you," the elder, himself a former addict, told the room full of substance abusers. "God did not want you to be a homeless, hungry alcoholic—the devil tricked you, but God's grace and mercy has been there for you and will help you out." His message was that God's transforming work starts as addicts begin to appropriate a positive image of their destiny.

The idea that faith in Christ offers a transcendent source of self-esteem (Lockhart 2003) is a core premise of Christian Stronghold's ministries. One outreach leader assessed the main issue facing African American ex-prisoners: "They will not have finished high school and will have a poor self-image and a lack of hope. . . . So what I'm looking at with them is to help them to define themselves as God sees them." Another Christian Stronghold member simi-larly described how "using the promises in the Scriptures" can help women end their dependence on public assistance by correcting a faulty self-image. Discovering God's assurances of their worth can lead women "to say to them-selves, 'I'm better than this and I can do more for myself and my family,'" thus galvanizing a new resolve to achieve their potential.

At another program for women on welfare, at Cookman United Methodist Church, pastor Donna Jones stressed the theme of hope: "When you're talking about people restoration, without the hope that comes from faith, I don't see that it's possible." Staff described how women on welfare were trapped in a downward spiral of failure and despair, exacerbated by the relentless bureau-cratic demands and looming cut-off deadlines for benefits. Their goal in shar-ing the gospel with its themes of liberation and love was to break the spiral, allowing women to focus on the road to self-sufficiency. At the same time, staff members were realistic about the ongoing challenges faced by low-income women that would not be dissipated by an optimistic outlook on life. Thus, one of the chief roles of faith, according to Rev. Jones, is to build the inner resilience needed to persevere despite obstacles. In her view, becoming a Christian does not eliminate the barriers to socioeconomic development, but enables people to deal with them in a healthy way.

Personal faith is also said to empower personal responsibility. A ministry leader at Germantown Church of the Brethren identified a posture of entitlement as one of the primary obstacles to community development. "If we have the mentality that somebody owes it to me, then we're not going to have the motivation to learn what's available." The realization that " 'I *can* make a difference' starts with knowing Christ." David Apple of Tenth Presbyterian Church shared this perspective. "It's so easy to blame others, but it's only when I accept responsibility for myself that I can do something. . . . I'm not saying that people need to pull themselves up by their own bootstraps because many people don't have the straps or the boots. But people need to get to the point of saying 'I need help' and then try to access what resources are available." Spiritual support braces people to work toward their own recovery, Dr. Apple explained. In a twist on the familiar adage, God helps people to help themselves.

ACCESS TO SUPERNATURAL POWER. One of the central messages of many faith-based programs is that once people discover their value and potential in God's eyes, they can begin to take responsibility for improving their status. A second theme is that people are incapable on their own of breaking destructive habits, but that God is able and willing to transform their lives. Nueva Creación's Rev. Cabello Hansel referred to the intersection between these two messages as "a creative tension between empowering people and the power of the cross." The therapeutic perspective on the role of faith subjectivizes the source of social need as a disempowering crisis in self-identity. A supernatural perspective points to spiritual realities beyond the self that can either sabotage or salvage human potential. Evangelistic social ministries encourage people to yield their lives to the "power of the cross," a power that is greater than people's ability to bring about change in themselves.

Some practitioners believe that God can intervene to extend the impact of social ministry by defeating evil spiritual forces that ensnare both persons and communities. "We are dealing with a spiritual battle," asserted a ministry leader at Germantown Church of the Brethren, manifested as "a system that's intended to keep people in poverty." Salvation brings individuals into the realm of God's protection and emboldens them to resist the evil at work in the surrounding society. References to supernatural change emerged most often in the context of stories about deliverance from addictions or other deep-seated problems. For a drug counselor at Bethel Temple, the process of recovery is a spiritual struggle. "If we can present Christ and if they can grasp the truths of who they are and what they have in Christ, then they'll be set free. . . . We always look at it as a one-step program, just new life in Christ." The essential "one step"—a depreciative reference to twelve-step programs that call on a nonspecific "higher power"—is freedom from "bondage to sin" through Christian faith.

The unique role of faith-based social ministry, in this perspective, is to provide an opening for God to do what God alone can do. "Only God can take certain things out," affirmed one ministry leader at Faith Assembly of God. "He takes it out by the root." The religious disciplines structured into Faith's drug recovery program are an invitation to supernatural deliverance from the "root cause" of addiction. Residents are supposed to spend over an hour each day reading the Bible and praying, and to fast until evening three days each week. "If you don't fast, you don't last," the ministry leader would recite to the residents, "and if you don't pray, you don't stay." Many interviewees echoed this emphasis on prayer as a portal to God's transforming power.

Faith-Based Programs Offer Support from a Religious Community

A *Philadelphia Inquirer* article (John–Hall 1999a) reports the story of Tyrone Thomas, who came to Faith Assembly of God needing assistance for himself and his daughter as he recovered from addiction. They were embraced by the congregation: "When he gets low on groceries at the end of the month, his church feeds him. . . . When Thomas is running late picking up Jovonna from day care, a member of the church always comes through." The church also helped him cope with the stress of diminishing income due to changes in public assistance by providing counseling, prayer, and emotional support. Thomas remarked, "The biggest thing is they've taught me to live by faith. Just being around people who are Spirit-filled is what has kept me going." With his life stabilized, Thomas eventually became active in leading the church's youth club and rehabilitation program.

Social ministry practitioners point to this kind of informal support from the sponsoring faith community as a contributing factor in their programs' efficacy. While urging beneficiaries to take responsibility for their own lives, many practitioners also recognize that individual efforts can falter unless one's life is enmeshed with those of others in a healthy way. More often than not, realizing the social benefits of spiritual transformation involves years of patient support through the ups and downs of rebuilding a life. The theme that belonging to a faith community yields socioeconomic advantages thus offers a counterbalance to the individualistic orientation of many faith-based ministries. Relationships with other Christians via mentoring, church membership, or discipleship programs can help to sustain personal empowerment.

Ongoing socialization from others in the faith makes people less likely to revert to negative attitudes and behavior. Mentoring is one formal way that this socialization may take place. Several of the churches used mentors in conjunction with social programs: Cookman United Methodist Church recruited female Christian mentors for the women in its welfare-to-work program, Life in Christ's Generation of Destiny program matched at-risk youth with responsible adults, Media Presbyterian paired children of single moms with male church members who could take them under their wing, Tenth Presbyterian organized Christian "friendship partners" for international students, and First Presbyterian mobilized church members to help residents in their affordable housing units with budgeting and other life skills.

Another way that faith-based social ministries can increase the support available to beneficiaries is by inviting them to join a church. Marginalized persons who join a church gain more access to the social and spiritual resources of a "caring community" (Wuthnow 2004). Congregants have more opportunities to learn about one another's needs and to respond in personalized ways, and the inclination to share resources is greater when there is a shared community identity and trust born of mutual association (Smidt 2003). Some churches also give attenders formal preference for particular benefits; for example, Bethel Temple's holiday baskets are distributed first to low-income families in the congregation. Congregations offer an alternative relational network and links that facilitate "flows of information, resources, and opportunities" as well as socialization (C. Smith 2003, 26). Moreover, church services are likely to reinforce the spiritual dynamics of social ministries by instilling moral values,[6] admonishing attitudinal and lifestyle changes, inspiring hope and perseverance in the face of obstacles, cultivating religious cultural capital, and providing opportunities for experiences of supernatural deliverance.

Will It Work without Faith?

We asked interviewees if it was possible for people to escape poverty *without* Christian faith. Practitioners in evangelism-dominant churches and faith-permeated programs typically responded with skepticism. Asked what the chances were that someone could experience a significant life transformation without becoming a Christian, one ministry leader replied wryly, "Slim to none, and as they say, Slim just got on a bus." New Covenant members believed that social programs would be ineffective if they did not change people's hearts. One small group leader likened such programs to "putting a Band-Aid on a severe cut." In contrast, "evangelism starts at the core. And once you change a person's life you can change their social position."

Among ministry leaders at holistic churches, a more typical response was a qualified "yes, but . . ." Yes, secular services can certainly meet people's material needs, impart skills, and provide economic opportunities. But, many interviewees told us, there are limits to what secular aid alone can accomplish. In Richard Smith's words, without faith, "empowerment or transformation is possible," but it "has not seemed sustainable." A main theme of these qualified explanations was that spiritual renewal does not substitute for conventional methodologies but rather helps make secular aid more effective. David Apple observed that the main challenge faced by the homeless people he worked with at Tenth Presbyterian Church was not lack of resources but lack of the self-love, confidence, motivation, or discipline necessary to benefit from them. People were more likely to use the available resources effectively if they had God in their lives, he asserted: "It's only in Christ that people finally possess the freedom to finally look beyond themselves for a source of healing."

Another "yes, but . . ." theme relates to a whole-person anthropology that widens the goals of social ministry. Yes, persons on welfare can become self-sufficient without becoming a Christian, stated Bishop Dickie Robbins. But if the goal is to "change their quality of life in every sense, then the power of God is essential." The director of Jobs Partnership, a faith-permeated job training and placement program, similarly argued that students can achieve employment objectives without an experience of spiritual transformation, but "real change only happens if they know Christ." The goal of Jobs Partnership is "holistic change—not just in their job status but in their relationships at home, their self-confidence." A Baptist pastor described the biblical principles related to poverty and wealth taught in his church's job training program as "universal principles . . . that will better the lives of people," whether or not they are Christians. He added, "But the principles hopefully lead us to Christ. I mean, that's the bottom line."

Can religions other than Christianity serve the same function? In his speech at Union Bethel, President Bush affirmed a content-neutral understanding of faith: "Miracles happen as a result of the love of the Almighty," imparted "by religions from all walks of life, whether it be Christian, Jewish, Muslim, Hindu." But a ministry leader at Tenth Presbyterian questioned whether other religions could satisfy the broader aims of ministry in a holistic sense:

> I've known people who have become Muslim and have changed
> their lifestyle and have recognized that it's God's will that they
> should support themselves and be faithful to their families—they
> become good people, so to speak. . . . The point to me is that there
> has not been a change in their heart, there has just been a shift of
> their way of thinking about what is right, and I don't see that from
> the heart they're really doing these things.

Ironically, despite the emphasis in the faith-based initiative on religion's role in teaching moral behavior, this practitioner shifted the focus from behavior to matters of the heart. To him, only Christianity could satisfy the ultimate goal of ministry because it would lead a beneficiary not just to do the right thing but to be a new person.

At Nueva Creación, pastor Patrick Cabello Hansel takes a broader view of the relationship between faith and social change. When asked whether the youth in the church's job skills development program could incorporate values and make constructive choices without faith, he responded, "I do not think that you can do that without a personal commitment to faith." But, he added, "God works in transforming ways through faith that is not specifically Christian as well . . . even if it's just faith in life or in the community." As an example, he cited Alcoholics Anonymous members who "have a hard time with the church and with Christian theology" but have a meaningful faith in a "higher power." He allowed that faith itself—not the object of faith—can act as the transforming power.

Interviewees in dominant social action churches and faith-affiliated programs offered the contrasting view that spiritual condition and socioeconomic status are distinct and unrelated. According to a ministry leader at a dominant social action church, if a faith-based program "helps to lead people to Christ, that is okay, that is good," but as for the impact of this spiritual nurture on effectiveness, "I'm not sure that that is very important at all." What matters is "the job that is being done." People need God for their spiritual well-being, but social outcomes like overcoming drug addiction or welfare dependency are best achieved through secular methodologies. "Faith is not a rehabilitation issue," insisted a member of Church of the Advocate who is a professional social worker. "Should I say to the junkie, 'I'm going to pray for you?' No! You find him a bed in rehab. You do something that's reality-based. . . . From what I know about addiction, the issue is the drug. . . . It has nothing to do with whether you believe in God."

Regardless of whether practitioners held that Christian faith was *necessary* to the aims of social ministry, seldom did they claim that it was *sufficient*. "The gospel is the vital tool," said a woman who works with substance abusers, "but there are other things they need to be a whole person." The same ministry leader at Tenth Presbyterian Church who questioned whether personal change was possible without conversion cautioned against seeing faith as a panacea. He criticized Christians who say to people in distress, " 'Well, your problem is you need to get saved and then God will take care of everything.' " David Apple summed up the value-added quality of holistic faith-based ministry: "It should be doing everything that the world is doing, plus recognizing our need for salvation in Christ."

Limitations of the Argument for the Efficacy of Spiritual Nurture

Our study has brought the arguments for the efficacy of faith-based approaches into sharper relief, but it cannot offer a rigorous evaluation of their veracity. Within the context of our case studies, however, challenges to these claims— particularly to the premise that outcomes are linked to spiritual transformation and affiliation with a faith community—emerge on two fronts. First, there are cases where the evidence seems to contradict the anticipated results of faith-based approaches. Second, even if the argument for integrating spiritual nurture has merit, our observations point to lapses in how it is applied in practice.

When Spiritual Nurture Doesn't Seem to Work

How do interviewees account for the stories of people who have an experience of spiritual transformation but find themselves still addicted, jobless, or poor?

A Bethel Temple ministry leader acknowledged, "I've heard a lot of people confess Christ that are now out there doing drugs or in prison." Often the youths he thought most likely to succeed were the ones who ended up back in the streets. He mused sadly, "I don't know the answer to why some kids make it and some kids don't." His first tentative response to this question was of a theological nature. "I think it comes back to what's salvation . . . Is every seed that grows, even a little bit, saved? Or is it only the ones that fully grow that are really saved?" His answer suggests that those who don't "make it" may have claimed to be Christian, but their behavior calls into question the authenticity of their salvation or the faithfulness of their Christian life. This line of reflection preserves the link between spiritual and social well-being.

But later this leader offered another explanation as well. He observed that people's potential is often limited by various external obstacles.

> This country offers opportunity so that if you can get that boost up
> to the table, you can do things, but if you can't get the boost up you
> keep eating the scraps. . . . There are some single mothers who are
> strong believers . . . who are on welfare and have no opportunity,
> just have too many kids, or different things. They're probably gonna
> be poor for the rest of their life. There's very little they can do about
> it. . . . There are just some phenomenal injustices that people just
> can't crawl out of.

He critiqued conservative economic policies for making people "keep eating the scraps." Becoming a Christian does not guarantee a change in socioeconomic status, he allowed, unless society provides a "boost up" to allow people access to opportunity. Structural limitations may set the boundaries for what transformed people can accomplish for themselves. A leader of prison ministries at Christian Stronghold similarly observed that although education has been demonstrated to reduce recidivism, the prison system works against educating prisoners. In a capitalist society with institutionalized racism, he noted, prisons are "a fast growing business." Even when faith leads prisoners "to define themselves as God sees them" and to take steps toward becoming responsible citizens, their potential is limited by structural incentives to keep them in prison.

Sometimes ministry practitioners deal with the discrepancy between the way things should work and the way they do work by redefining the goals of social ministry. Escaping poverty is not necessarily the highest goal, said the Bethel leader quoted above, because Christianity teaches people to be content with what they have. "Christians should be able to be poor and be happy." When asked whether he knew people who had experienced a change in their economic status as a result of accepting Christ, he answered half-jestingly, "Well, I went from being wealthy to being poor." He and other staff chose a lifestyle of downward mobility in order to minister in Bethel Temple's community. Thus the church challenged the materialism of American culture as the measure of success for its ministries.[7]

In a similar vein, David Apple drew a distinction between *spiritual* poverty and *material* poverty. Spiritual poverty, according to Dr. Apple, is a depressed state of being that "sucks the life blood" out of people; it has more to do with attitude than assets. "When people are in Christ, they no longer have that spirit of poverty." Knowing that they are on the right road, embraced by a supportive church community, gives people hope that transcends their circumstances. Even if they are still "poor in terms of dollars and cents," he argued, they are not *really* poor. By subjectivizing outcomes in this way, practitioners can maintain the argument for efficacy despite tangible evidence to the contrary.

Confidence in the ultimate potency of faith can yield a different standard and timetable for evaluating program outcomes. Donna Jones judged the impact of Cookman's welfare-to-work program not only by whether a student obtained immediate employment, but by her chances for long-term success: "If the first thing that she received was faith, before anything else, then we feel as though we've provided a good foundation on which to build for her life skills, job development, and other issues that plague her and her family." Dr. Apple told the story of one homeless man with a long-time addiction to alcohol and crack, who was befriended by Tenth Presbyterian members. At the urging of church volunteers, he entered a faith-permeated rehab program. He eventually found a job, married the mother of his children, bought a home, cleared his criminal record, and now volunteers through the church to reach other addicts. While his story has had a happy ending, Dr. Apple noted that it took him six years and multiple relapses to get there. At various points along the road, his case might have looked like a failure.

Finally, practitioners may address the discrepancy between hoped-for and actual results by stressing the role of faith in coping with life's disappointments. Conversion may allow people to experience personal peace in the midst of ongoing struggle. When asked how salvation is related to empowerment, a leader at Nueva Creación paused before saying she did not have an easy answer.

"Faith is something that helps you hold on even if things don't change. This is not a recipe for success. It's just the assurance that you're not alone."

Shortcomings of Faith-Based Ministry in Practice

To what extent do arguments for the empowering impact of faith-based social ministry represent an idealized portrait of this ministry? Field observations provided a window into how the potential of faith-based social service sometimes failed to translate into practice.

Being faith-based did enhance the capacity of some programs in our study by making them more attractive to some volunteers and funding sources, but it closed other doors. In a few instances, church-based programs were told their religious nature made them ineligible for city and state funds not covered by charitable choice. Businesses and secular foundations like United Way in some cases were even less faith-friendly than government. Program capacity was also constrained by shortages of volunteers, funds, and leadership from within the faith community. Recruitment of beneficiaries to serve as volunteers has its advantages, but it can also leave programs vulnerable to the vicissitudes of an unstable and resource-poor community. Nueva Creación's volunteer base was slashed, for example, when welfare reform sent many of the mothers in the community back to work.

Although the altruistic caring of faith-based practitioners is presumed to promote constructive relationships with beneficiaries, church program staff did not always treat people with dignity or cultivate their self-esteem. For example, volunteers with a mobile medical clinic used beaded bracelets as evangelistic aids, in which each color symbolized a theological idea associated with the gospel message. The bracelets' color scheme reinforced the racist association of *black* with *sin*, a particularly insensitive gesture in a neighborhood populated by African Americans. Another example comes from an observation of a faith-affiliated homeless shelter. An interview with one of the residents was abruptly interrupted by the overnight monitor, a volunteer from a local church. "She should be getting ready for bed. If she stays up too late it will be hard to get going in the morning," the volunteer said brusquely, addressing herself only to the researcher as if the resident were not in the room. At this snub, the resident's expression and posture visibly slumped.

Faith-based ministries may serve an important role by reinforcing moral behaviors and teaching values, but not everyone may appreciate all the values that are taught or how the desired behaviors are enforced (Farnsley 2003). For example, the regimentation of some faith-based drug rehabilitation programs, designed to bring structure and discipline into lives dominated by addictions, struck some beneficiaries as overly-controlling. Faith-based programs walk a fine line between repudiating immoral or destructive behaviors in the name of a holy God, and, in the name of a loving God, accepting and empowering the people who do these behaviors.

Although the congregations that sponsor ministries offer a potential source of social support for beneficiaries, the power differential between servers and those served makes it difficult to encourage church attendance without raising thorny ethical issues. Moreover, the social utility of this support network is limited by the obstacles to incorporating marginalized persons into church life, including barriers of race, class, and socialization into appropriate church behavior (Laudarji and Livezey 2000; R. Smith 2001; Chaves 2004). In most of the churches, we heard about and observed the difficulty of moving from hierarchical ministry *to* the poor to ministry *alongside* poor people that authentically embraces them as equals. At Tenth Presbyterian Church, the Sunday evening worship service offered in association with a free dinner attracted "people who are homeless, economically disadvantaged, substance abusers, etc.," according to a ministry leader. While the evening service met a spiritual need for this population, building connections with the rest of the middle-class Tenth congregation proved a challenge. He noted an incident in which some scruffy-looking people who showed up at the regular morning service were told by a church member to come back that evening, because it was assumed that they belonged in the alternative service.

Another obstacle to extending social support to recipients of social aid is resistance from unsympathetic congregational gatekeepers. Church members may be prejudiced against certain groups, protective of the building, or wary of people they consider undeserving. When a woman came to a church office looking for help with a water bill, a man on church staff later identified her to the researcher as a greedy person who "was there with her hand out" whenever she thought she could get something from the church. This assessment made them less disposed (rightly or wrongly) to bring the resources of the congregation to bear in her case. Church culture can also act as an implicit gatekeeper. For example, the tradition observed in some African American churches of bringing offerings to the front of the church in a public display may communicate to poor visitors that they are less welcome than those who have more to give.

Efforts to connect beneficiaries and the sponsoring congregation may also be limited by the concern that social ministries will appear driven by a selfish desire for church growth. A Media Presbyterian member stated that if the church's outreach served "as a vehicle for bringing people to God, that's fine. ... If we are doing this [ministry] just to bring new members to the church, that's scary." While most survey respondents in the conversionist churches said bringing people to Christ was a strong motivation for outreach, they were significantly more reluctant to say their ministry was motivated by the desire for new members.[8]

Finally, there is often a gap between principle and practice in the evangelistic rhetoric of faith-based ministry. In one instance our researcher had joined
a group of volunteers renovating a home in the inner city. A sign in front
identified it as a church-sponsored project. While taking a break they were
approached by a woman who lived next door, who queried: Why were they
doing this project? This was the moment that ministry leaders had said they
were waiting for—a natural opening to turn the conversation to spiritual topics.
But the volunteer simply told her they were helping out a local family, and
provided some details about the logistical arrangements. This was the same
volunteer who had said in an interview that doing service projects provides
church members with "a good opportunity to witness." As this illustrates, ministries do not always follow through on their intentions to encourage spiritual
renewal. The evangelistic impulse is often muted in practice by the norms
governing social interactions.[9] Moreover, when church volunteers do present
a religious message in the context of social ministry, they do not always do so
in a culturally relevant or personally sensitive way. If social ministries are not
providing meaningful spiritual nurture, then the discussion of whether spiritual transformation enhances outcomes is largely moot.

On the other hand, we also discovered many instances in which the ministries did precisely what they said they were going to do, with the result they
hoped to achieve. Here is one success story from Cookman's welfare-to-work
program, related by Rev. Jones:

> We have one woman who came to us through the shelter system,
> the mother of four or five children. She was very distraught, because
> she was concerned about her welfare being cut off. . . . She really de-
> sired to work and had tried, and just didn't have a GED and so
> forth, and had a lot of barriers to employment. She was not
> churched, didn't have a church family, didn't have family support,
> was really out there on a limb by herself. The program offered her,
> in addition to life skills, faith development. Ultimately she was one
> of our first students to get a job. Also she got wonderful housing.
> She continues to work toward her GED. Her self-esteem has just
> gone up tremendously. And she called about a month ago to say that
> she had found a church family. She's active with our mentoring pro-
> gram, and she's really made full use of everything that we've had to
> offer.

Each of the evangelistic churches we studied had similar stories to tell. Of
course, such anecdotal evidence alone cannot prove or disprove the claims set
forth by these churches about the relationship between faith development and
social outcomes. However, it suggests that the arguments are worth taking
seriously.

Conclusion: Studying Faith-Based Efficacy

The perceived linkage between the effectiveness of social ministries and their religious characteristics takes various forms. Religious programs may attract caring, morally discerning volunteers whose activism is divinely inspired and empowered. Faith-based programs can add the insight and authority of Scripture to the information and skills they impart. Personal faith may transform beneficiaries from the inside out by fostering virtuous behavior; by promoting attitudes conducive to success like self-esteem, responsibility, and hope; and by offering supernatural liberation from destructive forces. Faith-based programs may draw beneficiaries into supportive, accountable relationships within a "caring community" of Christians. According to these claims, spiritual nurture in the context of social service plays a critical role in the restoration of persons and communities.

Many of the people we interviewed would simply take these arguments for the efficacy of religiously based social services on faith, so to speak. They introduce spiritual elements into service not because of a calculated effort to maximize outcomes, but simply because they believe it is the right way to do things. But researchers, policymakers, and others tracking the course of faith-based initiatives will be interested in testing the validity of these claims. While our study lacks the quantitative evidence necessary for an objective verdict, it may help in the development of testable hypotheses that are relevant to what the providers themselves believe is taking place.

Johnson's (2002) careful review of the literature on religion and social outcomes distinguishes between *organic religion* (personal religious beliefs and practices) and *intentional religion* (interventions by faith-based organizations). The research on intentional religion is too thin to arrive at any sound conclusions on comparative efficacy, but evidence has been mounting regarding the social impact of organic religion. Johnson's review finds that personal faith consistently correlates with decreased high-risk behaviors, increased educational attainment, and increased levels of subjective well-being, hope, and purpose. "Other things being equal," the report states, the effect of religious commitments is to "measurably beget significantly better health and greater social well-being" (2002, 6; see also Fagan 1996; Larson and Johnson 1998; Levin and Taylor 1998). This data would seem to support the claim of faith-permeated and faith-centered programs that promoting religious commitments contributes to positive social outcomes. Intentional religion may be effective precisely by encouraging organic religion. However, more research is needed to winnow out the exceptions to "other things being equal"; that is, to identify confounding variables or selection biases that might suggest alternative explanations.

It is not clear whether the effect ascribed to organic religion favors Christianity, or whether, as Rev. Cabello Hansel suggested, the transformational agent is faith itself rather than the content of the faith. Moreover, correlations between religion and social outcomes beg the question of whether there is anything *inherently* potent about religion. Are any of the effects ascribed to religion attributable to underlying psycho-social forces and thus replicable in a secular setting? Lockhart (2003), for example, describes "secular conversions" in non-faith-based programs that encourage beneficiaries to internalize a new positive self-image, attitude, and work ethic, without calling on God as the source of this change. Similarly, other kinds of small groups (such as a community-based drug recovery group) may offer support and accountability comparable to a congregation. Are religious service providers simply more likely, for whatever reason, to harness these social forces (e.g., to promote internal status transformations, to offer social networks)? Or are spiritual dynamics an independent causal factor?

Explorations of these questions should take into account that, except in some faith-permeated programs, practitioners do not generally claim that salvation alone is sufficient to transform persons or communities. Rather, they assert that spiritual renewal enhances and enlarges the impact of other interventions. Faith *plus* skills and opportunity are viewed as the pathway to success. To test the validity of this understanding, researchers will need to compare three types of programs: programs that offer conventional social services; compatible programs that offer similar services with an integrated religious component; and programs whose methodology consists only of religious elements.

Studies of faith-based organizations have remarked on a tension between efficacy and witness (see Jeavons 1994; Coleman 2003; Queen 2000). Religious practitioners often have different standards of success than those who study the success of their ministries. Many ministry leaders profess an interest not just in particular quantifiable social outcomes, but in the "whole person"— a unit of assessment that is difficult to define, let alone measure. In fact, a holistic perspective may distract program resources from the specific outcomes in which funders and researchers have an interest. Given that transformation is a fuzzy, long-term process, some practitioners resist the notion of tracking outcomes at all. They measure the effectiveness of ministry not by quantifiable results but by the faithfulness of those who serve (see Jeavons 1994).

Wuthnow (2004) distinguishes between a service-provider model and a congregational model as the basis for assessing the potential impact of faith-based programs. In the service-provider model, found in the great majority of faith-based organizations, the success of the program can be measured by the effective and efficient transfer of goods and services. Religious dynamics are peripheral to "a professional staff and a rationally organized program devoted to serving clients with specific needs" (173). The congregational model, exemplified by Teen Challenge, adopts a more relational, holistic approach. The effectiveness of such programs is based on "their ability to forge encompassing whole-person, personally transforming relationships with clients" (159). In this model, "faith is essential . . . as the basis for communal interaction and life-transforming experiences" (309).

The fundamentally different goals and methods of these two models suggest that the religious dynamics that contribute to effectiveness may be quite different for relief services (e.g., soup kitchens), which typically "involve only short-term or fleeting kinds of contact with the needy," versus personal-development ministries (e.g., counseling), which "involve more intensive or long-term, face-to-face interaction" (Chaves 2004, 59). On the other hand, churches may project a holistic impact onto programs that organizationally fit the service-provider model. The potential of social ministry for "drawing clients into long-term social relationships . . . that effect some sort of personal transformation through new friendships and explicit exposure to religious teachings" (Wuthnow 2004, 173) resides not only in the program type, but also in the quality and depth of social interactions with ministry staff, and the extent to which the ministry draws beneficiaries into a supportive community beyond the program. Through pre-evangelistic strategies of relationships and invitations, short-term social aid may thus become the conduit to longer-term, spiritually transformative social connections. For example, Dickie Robbins described his objective for offering homeless-shelter residents a meal shared by members of Life in Christ: "The strategy is to establish relationship. The relationship will usher them into the local church setting. Once they are in the local church setting, we can do the intensive ministry" that is hoped to result in lasting personal change. The effectiveness of an aid program must be viewed in light of this larger package of congregational interactions.

The good intentions of faith-based providers, however, do not always translate into effective practice. Our research leads us to caution religious practitioners against a disconnect between the rhetoric and praxis of faithful service. As Chaves (2004, 63) points out, "Even when congregations set out to provide more holistic care, those efforts often flounder on the rocky shore of social boundaries and complex realities." Religious factors are only relevant to outcomes if social ministries do in fact serve as the channel for religiously inspired caring or as the catalyst for spiritual experiences. If faith is like yeast in the dough of social ministry—to paraphrase one of Jesus' parables—then its efficacy depends on being included in proper measure.

Finally, the controversy over whether conversion helps people escape poverty should not distract critical attention from the broader social forces that help to make and keep people poor. The premise that personal faith produces social change "from the inside out as people are changed, one by one," as articulated by one ministry leader, too often fails to challenge a status quo of systemic injustice (C. Smith 1998). Yet this is not inevitable. The staff of the welfare-to-work ministry at Cookman, for example, nurtured the spiritual re-sources of women to help empower their economic potential, but were also outspoken in their critique of the disempowering impact of the government's welfare policies. Even as faith helps individuals take responsibility for their own destiny, faith may also inspire advocacy for government to take respon-sibility for making society more just.

II

Social Capital and
Spiritual Capital

In 1994, two Philadelphia neighborhoods were designated Empowerment Zones, under a federal initiative to revitalize distressed communities through entrepreneurial incentives. The mayor appointed
Rev. Bill Moore, pastor of Tenth Memorial Baptist Church and respected community organizer, to serve as chair of the North Central
Community Trust Board, which had the task of allocating funds
among local economic development projects. Tenth Memorial
hosted Empowerment Zone elections, as well as several city-sponsored
workshops and training seminars. According to a city employee and
North Central Philadelphia resident who worked with Rev. Moore on
the Empowerment Zone, Tenth Memorial "understands their role
and responsibility for outreach and lifting up their neighbor."
Through its programs and networks, the church provides aid and
outside referrals to residents with critical needs. More intangibly,
Tenth "has served as a beacon of hope there, a symbol of access to
resources and assistance and possibilities—a symbol of caring."

Asked about other ways that local churches supported the goals
of the Empowerment Zone, this city employee answered: "I see a
great role for churches in terms of keeping residents informed. I
mean, you have a consistent forum that meets every Sunday, and
sometimes the pastor will make announcements of something that
has social or political impact." Churches can also disseminate information through bulletins and training workshops, she added. The
interviewer asked how effective she thought churches could be in
community development. "Very much so," she replied. She explained her answer:

They have a stable constituency which is mostly, or primarily, from the neighborhood, so they have a collective voice. They have the resources that are created by their nonprofit status, so that means access to federal and state dollars. And I guess most importantly, they have a God-given mission to meet the needs of the whole man. So they're not going anywhere. . . . [And] there's a relationship of trust, of implied trust. I think biblically, churches are supposed to be a storehouse for a community of believers. And I think ministers' interpretation of that is expanding.

From this public employee's observations, a portrait of the church emerges as a place with the potential to share information, moderate public discussions of community concerns, connect people in need with resources, channel public capital, recruit participation in civic activities, assume responsibility for outreach, foster relationships of trust, invoke an ethos of caring, and serve as a symbolic beacon of hope. And because these activities are rooted in a "God-given mission," they have a durable quality that lends stability to the community. Her assessment ends on a hopeful note that ministers are increasingly seeing the role of the church in this light. Yet in this comment is the implied critique that many churches do not now fulfill this potential role.

Congregational Social Capital

The concept of *social capital* offers a way of talking about this potential role of churches and other voluntary associations in promoting vital communities and a healthy democracy. James Coleman (1988) originally defined social capital as a resource embedded in social structures for achieving personal or corporate goals. Collective action is made possible through social networks that build "connections of communication and trust" (Ammerman 1997a, 362). The definition of social capital has evolved somewhat to include "attributes of individuals which favor their civic engagement" (Foley and Edwards 1997, 551). In other analyses, it has been extended further to include the ways that people access the resources of a group (Lockhart 2003; Schneider 1999). As Schneider clarifies, social capital is not a commodity, but rather a process abiding in social networks that represents the potential for goal-oriented action.

James Coleman (1988) identifies three main elements of social capital: social patterns of obligation and reciprocity, grounded in trust; norms and sanctions that promote some behaviors and inhibit others; and social networks that facilitate the flow of information. Voluntary associations have a special capacity to generate social capital because they typically promote relational networks, enforce norms and sanctions, and foster social trust. As Corwin Smidt writes in the helpful volume *Religion as Social Capital,* associational life tends "to bind together autonomous individuals into communal relationships," creating the awareness, motivation and solidarity necessary for collective public action (2003, 5). Political observers since Tocqueville have argued that healthy voluntary associations are critical to a functional democracy because they counter the impersonal self-interest of the market and the state.

A church,[1] in particular, can serve as a repository of social capital (Wuthnow 2004; Putnam 2000; Ammerman 1997a), or, as the city employee quoted above put it, as "a storehouse for a community of believers." The benefits of membership in a religious community do not derive from any single member but from the structured relationships that facilitate exchanges of valued services within a congregation (religious instruction, care of youth, emotional support, etc.). Congregational life thus reinforces thick webs of social ties and trust (Cnaan, Boddie, and Yancey 2003). One study finds that people are more likely to trust fellow congregants than any other group except their own family (cited in Baggett 2001). This high level of trust strengthens, and draws strength from, norms that direct the church's actions—including the norms of altruism, compassion, and civic-mindedness (Cnaan, Wineburg, and Boddie 1999). Churches also promote reciprocity through the expectation that, as people benefit from membership, they should become more committed and active members. Congregational social capital can thus be self-replenishing. For these reasons, religious communities provide a uniquely favorable setting for social capital to flourish (Smidt 2003).

The social capital of churches translates into civic benefits in three main ways: by empowering corporate social action, encouraging the civic engagement of individual members, and facilitating the sharing of resources within and beyond their relational network.

Corporate Social Action

Applying the marketplace metaphor,[2] as repositories of social capital churches are able to multiply the investments of resources (time, finances, and skills) of individual members through collective endeavors, analogous to a corporation that uses investment funds for enterprises that benefit shareholders. These collective actions include internal functions—such as worship, education, and fellowship—that return a direct value to members. But a church may also channel its resources into externally-oriented social projects, analogous to a corporation's community improvement grants that indirectly serve shareholder interests. Involvement in social action may serve the collective interests of congregational "shareholders" by enhancing a church's reputation and thus its ability to attract and retain members, by fulfilling members' sense of purpose by creating opportunities for them to live out their values, or by meeting the needs of people in congregants' extended social networks (e.g., their neighbors or ethnic group) (Cnaan et al. 2002). The nature of congregational social capital is that expending resources beyond the congregation can enhance the value of belonging to the congregation.

Another way that churches enable collective action is by serving as a focal point for community organizing and neighborhood development (Wood 2002). A Nueva Creación member who works as a community organizer likened this function of the church to a transistor that transfers energy among parts of an electrical system. Through collaborations, churches can lend social capital to other organizations. The director of a community development corporation remarked on the value of its relationship with Church of the Advocate: "It's our link with some of the people in the community, because of the social services they provide." Advocate serves as the dynamic "transistor" between local residents and other organizations. Churches have also historically served as meetinghouses for public gatherings to share information, debate issues and plan collaborative action. Congregations' community leadership is enabled by trust in their presumptive legitimacy. Whether or not they attend church services, people often regard churches as legitimate brokers of the community's interests, based on their "recognized moral character" (Ammerman 1997a, 367; Warner 1994).

Individual Civic Action

Independent of what the church does collectively, congregational social capital equips and motivates individual members to participate constructively in public life. Through their association with a church, members acquire "loans" of information, skills, and connections that they can expend in the civic arena. The relationship between church attendance and volunteering, as well as informal altruism, has been well documented.[3] The function of churches as an "incubator for civic skills" contributes particularly to the human capital development of those who are otherwise resource-poor (Verba, Schlozman, and Brady 1995, 320; Harris 2003). An example comes from Nueva Creación, which taught youth in the Pre-Work program how to report abandoned cars to the police station. Churches also provide an arena for discussing and enacting higher-order values such as compassion and social justice, grounded in a shared heritage of religious teachings (Wuthnow 2003; Cnaan, Wineburg, and Boddie 1999). Churches often teach their members that they have an obligation to society in general, and to needy neighbors in particular. The social organization of a church thus imparts structural and relational resources for volunteerism together with a disposition for civic action.

Sharing of Resources

Lockhart (2003, 505) defines social capital as "the resources available for a person or organization through social networks." Participation in a congregation increases a person's access to the church's material and human resources (Wuthnow 2004). This effect derives in part from a preference for dispensing aid and information along established channels of trust and reciprocity. Mutual aid is a "safe" investment for members of a church because they can trust that similar help will be available to them, too, should they ever need it. One church leader described what attracts people to New Covenant: "They have seen a level of love demonstrated among the membership that has been a real drawing card, and it has given them a sense of lifelong safety." In addition, the thick ties of congregational life give members greater confidence that mutual aid is being used appropriately. Mutual aid thus depends on the "enforceable trust" made possible by a norm-laden social network (Portes and Sensenbrenner 1993, cited in Schneider 1999, 273; Bartkowski and Regis 2003). This solidarity is particularly critical in inner cities, where the church may be one of the few viable institutions remaining (Cnaan, Boddie, and Yancey 2003; Milsap and Taylor 1998). The flip side of this aspect of congregational social capital is that a church may sanction those in its network who are deemed unworthy. This point is illustrated by a woman in a faith-based homeless shelter who told us that after she was kicked out of her home, she had first gone to her own church for help, but was told by the pastor that she was being punished for not paying enough tithes to the church.

Church networks may offer vertical relational ties to people in higher-status positions. Wuthnow (2002) calls this *status-bridging capital*, showing that affiliation with a church increases the likelihood of friendships with people in positions of influence such as public officials and corporate executives. These connections in turn increase the likelihood of access to information about jobs and other economic opportunities (Lin, Ensel, and Vaughn 1981). Vertical bridging can occur through a church's institutional ties or the extended personal and professional networks of its members. For example, based on the recommendation of the pastor of Nueva Creación, a former drug addict and ex-prisoner obtained a seminary scholarship and a ministry position within the Lutheran denomination. Denominational staff were willing to extend their trust in the pastor to someone who was unknown to them.

Churches may also offer lateral or identity-bridging capital that extends social ties across different organizations or cultures, expanding the pool of accessible resources for congregants and other actors (Schneider 2001; Lockhart 2003; Wuthnow 2002). At its best, this kind of bridging capital helps a group rethink how it defines *us* in relation to *them*. Lateral bridging is illustrated by the partnership between two very different churches, Media Presbyterian Church and Life in Christ Cathedral of Faith. Across denominational, racial, and socioeconomic divides, the pastors struck up a friendship. Volunteers from both churches teamed up for service projects, including the renovation of a home for a low-income family from Life in Christ. The work might not have been completed without the funds and skills supplied by the volunteers from Media. Yet Media's project coordinator insisted that both groups benefited equally from their collaboration, pointing to the sense of spiritual meaning and connectedness to God that church volunteers gained from the experience. The bonds of reciprocity that had been forged between the churches proved as important an asset in securing a needy family a new home as the material and human resources used in the actual construction.

Social Capital and Religious Cultural Capital

The social capital of congregations derives in part from their role as concentrations of cultural resources. Cultural resources include the "symbolic, linguistic, and interpretive elements" through which people make sense of their social environment, and which together "help enable or constrain people's efforts to engage together in social action" (Wood 1997, 603; C. Smith 1996). Culture shapes the ways that a group forms bonds of trust, assesses reciprocal obligations, and conducts its social relationships. Williams (2003, 172) thus describes culture as a "symbolic currency" which influences how social capital may be generated and invested into collective social endeavors. Congregations are rich in this symbolic currency (Hopewell 1987).

Religious language, in particular, serves as a cultural resource for public affairs (Williams 2003). Among the churches in our study, efforts to mobilize the charitable resources of a congregation were typically couched in religious ideas and images. For example, a notice in a First Presbyterian newsletter solicited support for the Evangelical Environmental Network (EEN), a program to promote environmental conservation:

> Experiencing the joys of nature will result in an enriched worship
> life and a growing desire to serve God by caring for creation. The
> EEN is an organization of Christians committed to honoring the
> Creator through care of his glorious creation. The EEN seeks to edu-
> cate and equip Christians to share in the responsibility of creation
> care as a part of faithful discipleship.

By framing the environment as "God's creation," care for the environment as "honoring the Creator" through "faithful discipleship," and the rewards of environmental activism as "an enriched worship life and a growing desire to serve God," this text helped to connect a social concern stereotypically associated with secular liberals (e.g., Greenpeace) with the First Presbyterian Church subculture. Application of this symbolic currency enabled the environmental issue to better capture the church's social capital.

Religious cultural capital can also facilitate lateral bridging (Warren 2003, Wood 2002). This is evident in the critical role of religious language at meetings of Philadelphia Interfaith Action (PIA). While shared social concerns bring over fifty member congregations to the PIA table, it is religious culture that enables the delegates from diverse faiths, ethnicities, and social locations to speak to these concerns with one voice. For example, at a gathering of PIA delegates, one speaker reported on PIA's efforts to stem job losses and promote a living wage. He related this work to the biblical story of Jonah, who was sent by God to Ninevah to "tell the city what time it was." He aroused cheers from the audience by declaring, "PIA says [to Philadelphia political leaders], 'Time is running out!'" Religious imagery provided a bridge between the diverse interests and social worlds of the participating congregations and their common sense of mission.

Religious culture also helps to shape the vision that translates social capital into social action. If social capital describes the capacity of a group to achieve collective goals, then *vision* may be defined as the purposeful momentum of a group toward a particular set of goals. Social capital and vision are interdependent. As Curry notes, the potential of social capital to foster the well-being of a community "can only be appropriated by individuals in the context of a shared vision; without such a shared vision this capacity of social capital remains dormant." As "communities of commitment," congregations may overtly link this vision to religious worldviews that "are reflections of ultimate commitments" (Curry 2003, 142, 152, 141). A church's religious culture serves as a lens for what members "see" in their social landscape, which in turn shapes their visionary response.

From a social capital perspective, the vision of church leaders is particularly valuable if it can serve as a rallying point for other community stakeholders. The task of creating and sustaining a unifying vision is particularly difficult in communities that are low in capital of every kind.

> The social isolation that increasingly characterizes the lives of inner city poor, impoverishes their vision as well. Creating an effective vision faces the challenge of trying to break through this isolation, especially by connecting isolated individuals with people who have already experienced success in remaking their own communities. (Wallis and Koziol 1996, 33–34, quoted in Potapchuk, Crocker, and Schechter 1997, 139n12)

Because of their presumptive legitimacy and internal bonding, churches may have an advantage in articulating this unifying vision. Engaged churches can break cycles of social isolation by embodying "a vision of what constitutes a healthy community based on strong social capital" (Potapchuk, Crocker, and Schechter 1997, 137). *Hope* is the word that Rev. Bill Moore uses to describe this fruit of Tenth Memorial's social commitments: "This congregation has given this community hope, hope that things can be better and will be better, because they've seen it, and they've been a part of it." Hope elevates the community's trust in the congregation, increasing the likelihood of future collaborative projects.

An example of how religious culture facilitates connections and trust around a shared vision comes from a monthly Mission Leadership Prayer Breakfast, initiated by a pastor in the inner-city Philadelphia neighborhood of Kensington. The invitational letter, sent to area churches and Christian organizations, lays out the rationale for the meetings:

> One of the corollaries to hopelessness is fragmentation. . . . Today, Kensington is still a vast array of disconnected people living in seemingly isolated blocks, with little strategic collaboration of resources. Wholeness will come when we leverage assets and build capacity in our residents and churches.

Common religious beliefs, language, and practices bring the participants in these prayer breakfasts together as they seek "to become visible signs of hope in their neighborhoods," according to the group's mission statement. Although the meetings have no specific practical agenda, the organizers recognize that simply gathering to eat, converse, and pray with other community leaders is a community-building act. Such gatherings create social capital. The application of that capital is guided by the group's vision for "wholeness."

Evangelism and Social Capital

The concept of social capital thus offers a way of describing churches' inherent potential for coordinating corporate social action; for encouraging volunteerism and other forms of civic engagement by individual members; for giving resource-poor persons access to the resources of the congregation and its extended social networks; and for connecting groups in the community with one another and with a unifying, hopeful vision. It is important to note that none of these social benefits are the *primary* functions of churches. The main reason that members of a church form a trusting, norm-laden social network is not to generate social action programs or to enhance the access of marginalized persons to information and resources. Rather, this occurs as people choose to associate to meet needs that are uniquely met in a religious group, such as spiritual meaning, love and identity (Cnaan, Boddie, and Yancey 2003). As James Coleman notes, "Most forms of social capital are created or destroyed as by-products of other activities" (1988, S118).

We examine here the question of whether evangelism is one of those "other activities" of a church that can generate (or destroy) social capital. The recent interest in congregational social capital has focused on how it translates into support for social action or strengthens the civic inclinations of its members, in the context of a broader debate about the trajectory of civic life in America (e.g., DiIulio 1997; Greeley 1997b; Dionne 1998; Bartkowski and Regis 2001; Baggett 2002; Smidt 2003). Churches' evangelistic functions are typically either ignored as irrelevant to the discussion of social capital, or counted as a negative civic force because of their associations with intolerance, anti-intellectualism and militant conservative politics (Marty 1981; Wuthnow 1996). The purpose of exploring the relationship between social capital and evangelism is not to argue antithetically that evangelism is an inherently positive social force. Rather, we seek to apply a social capital perspective to the claims of some of the churches in this study (in the dual-focus, holistic, and dominant evangelism categories) that their attention to spiritual needs strengthens their social impact.

It is helpful first to note that harnessing congregational resources for evangelistic purposes also involves the expenditure of social capital. Church-based evangelism draws on a norm-laden social network characterized by trust and reciprocity. The mandate to witness, like the values of compassion and social justice, is a norm with deep roots in Christian history, reinforced and translated into action through the religious culture of the church. Members are socialized into this expectation through ties with others in the congregation. An ethos of reciprocity helps to motivate evangelism, as members may seek to attract new church members out of gratitude to God or to the congregation.[4] Achieving collective evangelistic objectives depends on the church's capacity to mobilize the support of its network, comparable to what it takes to organize social service programs. Moreover, as with social ministry, evangelistic action can be deterred if the bonds between members "implode," overwhelming the impulse to reach out (Olson 1989; Coleman 2003).

Does expending social capital on evangelism mean that a church has less to apply to social concerns? Or does investment in evangelistic outreach generate a return that can then fuel social ministry? Below we examine ways that an evangelistic orientation may foster the formation of social capital, which may then potentially be available for social action. Having defined social capital in terms of social trust, norms, and networks, we consider each of these elements in turn.

Trust

Collaborative action is built on a foundation of social trust, buttressed by "sturdy norms of generalized reciprocity" (Putnam 1995, 67). Evangelism seeks to foster a trusting relationship between those sharing their faith and recipients of the message. People are more likely to respond to a religious invitation from someone they trust; but they are also more likely to trust someone with whom an evangelistic experience has forged a religious bond. A ministry leader at Bethel Temple explained, "People listen to you more if they have a relationship with you. It's about [our] being in the community for a long time, winning people's trust. . . . They'll see that there's something different about us." As people accept the message of faith and form an attachment to the church and its mission, the ethos of reciprocity can be extended beyond the congregation. The experience of spiritual renewal may foster a sense of obligation to give back to God in the form of service.

This pattern is illustrated by Cassie, a former addict and ex-prisoner in a transitional housing program located in the parsonage of Cookman United Methodist Church (but run by a secular agency). The church maintained an informal "open-door policy" with the residents, welcoming them into the congregation. According to Cassie, church staff would pray for residents, invite them to church, take them to Bible study, "treat us with a respectful attitude," and "let us know the importance of having God in our lives." She came to think of the female staff at the church as her surrogate "mothers," an indication of the high level of bonding forged through these supportive evangelistic exchanges. Through these encounters she became a "renewed believer," she said, and her life significantly changed. One evidence of that change was her extensive volunteer support of "God's work." Cassie served four days per week with Cookman's meal program for children, and generally made herself useful around the church. She was also helping to start a Christian drug abuse support group at the church. By meeting her spiritual needs, Cookman had gained her trust as a channel for serving God and helping others.

Norms

Another feature of social capital is the presence of strong norms that support some courses of action while sanctioning others. As Baggett notes, congregations "assist people in interpreting their lives in terms of what Charles Taylor refers to as a 'horizon of strong evaluation'" (2002, 436). An evangelistic emphasis directs members to extend their energies into the world beyond the church, an expectation that counters the natural centripetal force of group bonding. This outward focus sets evangelistic churches apart from those with an inward, sanctuary orientation (Roozen, McKinney, and Carroll 1984). Thus an emphasis on personal salvation does not necessarily denote "private" religion, as Ammerman (1997a) argues. The belief that the church ought to exist for the sake of others potentially creates common ground with churches oriented to social causes. Moreover, the training programs that churches develop to reinforce these evangelistic norms also serve to impart skills with potentially transferable civic value—how to communicate, how to cultivate social connections, how to build consensus around new ideas. The skills relevant for faith-sharing overlap with those essential to effective social activism.

Refusal to participate in evangelism may be chastised as a form of selfishness, of hoarding one's spiritual blessings. On the other hand, those who faithfully share their faith are promised an eternal reward. Thus the viability of evangelistic norms is not dependent on immediate, tangible outcomes. "We want to be able to bring the gospel to as many as possible, but all we can do is our best," remarked David Apple of Tenth Presbyterian Church. "We have no control over the fruit, but God does. He only asks us to be faithful." Similarly, many Christians uphold the norm of social compassion regardless of tangible results. This observation leads Smidt to suggest that "social capital generated through religious means may well have a more durable quality to it, because the motivation to remain faithful may well sustain such efforts" (2003, 217). The emphasis on faithfulness in many conversionist churches may reinforce the durability of their social capital.

Networks

Social capital inheres in "dense networks of social interaction" (Putnam 1995, 67). A strongly held norm such as the evangelistic mandate can promote internal bonding. Since many evangelism programs involve teamwork, participation can foster a heightened sense of closeness among church members, similar to the "heartfelt sense of togetherness" that often accompanies short-term mission trips (Bartkowski and Regis 2003, 168). The negative reaction that evangelism often provokes from people outside the group tends to strengthen, rather than undermine, the "subcultural distinctiveness" that energizes evangelical groups (C. Smith 1998, 178).

An evangelistic emphasis can also extend the congregation's social network beyond the church. A shared evangelistic vision can serve as the span for the bridging capital that Putnam (2000, 23) likens to "sociological WD-40" (in contrast to the "sociological superglue" of inward-looking bonding capital). A concern for saving souls can forge relationships between otherwise disparate organizations and individuals. The Summer Medical Institute sponsored by Tenth Presbyterian Church, for example, brought together medical students and professionals from around the country seeking field experience in medical evangelism, in collaboration with inner-city Latino and African American churches. The bridging capital generated by shared evangelistic interests can lead to the sharing of social resources. At a "Take the City for Christ" prayer meeting, Koinonia pastor Jerome Simmons met the coordinator of a relief ministry called Love Links. As a result of their meeting, Pastor Simmons organized other churches in his community to distribute a large-scale delivery by Love Links of donated food and clothing. This relationship then led to collaboration between Love Links and the ministry of Jobs Partnership, where Pastor Simmons served as president of the steering committee.

Churches also potentially extend their social network to the individuals they are seeking to evangelize. As discussed above, socioeconomic benefits often accrue to individuals who attach themselves to a church, and evangelistic outreach aims to connect people with churches (though not necessarily the sponsoring church). Different types of evangelism have different social implications. Outreach among members' existing relationships—family, friends, and co-workers—does not significantly diversify a church's social network. Target group evangelism, one of the most prevalent evangelism types in the case studies, often provides opportunities for members to form relationships with people in another demographic, cultural, or social status group, with whom they might not otherwise interact.

One of Tenth Presbyterian's seven target group evangelism ministries is a connection with We the People, a secular residential and drop-in center for people with HIV/AIDS, many of whom are also homeless. Tenth Presbyterian volunteers lead a weekly Bible study and worship service on-site. The worship leader described the alienation of people with HIV from "normal" church folk: "There's a stigma attached. . . . They feel uncomfortable in a regular church because of that or how they dress or because they may be economically disadvantaged." Many of the people associated with We the People would not feel comfortable attending a regular church service—and many Tenth Church members would feel uncomfortable having such people worship in their midst. Ministry volunteers' commitment to evangelism has made them more willing and able to bridge the two worlds.[5] Further evidence of this bridging is that some church members involved with religious services at We the People also volunteer with HOPE, a nonprofit that "provides spiritual, emotional and physical support to people affected by AIDS."

The bridging capital facilitated by evangelistic involvement has a limited capacity to be transferred to other kinds of public goods. This may happen in three ways. First, creating ties to persons for evangelistic purposes can beget awareness of their material needs, which may lead the church to mobilize resources on their behalf. When Bethel Temple's pastor went to visit a girl who had recently become a Christian through Bethel's youth ministry, he discovered that the family had just been evicted from their home and had nowhere to go. He invited them to stay in a building owned by the church that was unused at the time. Second, evangelistic experiences can also help raise consciousness of broader social issues. One woman described a mission trip to Latin America that opened her eyes to the Hispanic population in her own city. "There is significant need," she confessed, "but we've been insulated from it." The mission trip helped to erode this insularity.

Third, as people who have been evangelized become incorporated into a congregation, they can become advocates for their own concerns. Reverend Moore related the story of Irene, a success story of the church's evangelism:

> Irene came to our church . . . right off the streets of Philadelphia.
> She accepted Christ and got off of drugs. She hadn't finished high
> school. . . . The church really embraced Irene. She has gotten her

GED, gotten off of welfare, she got an apartment. She had a son out of wedlock.. . . .The church did not ostracize her for it; as a matter of fact, they helped her. . . . She's helped us a lot with our street ministry, and helped the whole congregation a lot in understanding addiction.

Irene has been instrumental in encouraging Tenth Memorial's involvement in drug and alcohol recovery. She is a regular participant at the Narcotics Anonymous meetings hosted by Tenth Memorial, and helps other recovering addicts become integrated into the life of the church. She brings substance abuse concerns to the attention of the congregation. Irene tried to start her own drug ministry through the church, but, she told the researcher, "the church wasn't ready to deal with the issues of the people."

Irene's story thus points to both the potential and the limitation of evangelistic social capital. Her success story illustrates on a micro level Putnam's observation that "Networks of civic engagement embody past success at collaboration, which can serve as a cultural template for future collaboration" (1995, 67). In embracing Irene, Tenth Memorial gained access to a rehabilitation network, as well as a "cultural template" for dealing with substance abuse. Tenth Memorial maintains relationships with two recovery homes in the neighborhood. The church welcomes recovering addicts into its social network and incorporates their spiritual and emotional needs into sermons, prayers, and other features of church life. Yet the church was not prepared to "deal with the issues" raised by the kind of organized substance abuse ministry that Irene proposed. Nevertheless, the social attachment between Irene and the congregation has endured any tensions in their relationship.

Network Boundaries

The formation of social capital through networks entails "patterns of defining boundaries among small groups against others outside of their social networks" (Schneider 1999, 274). Churches reinforce boundaries by preferring formal membership over loose affiliation, by making a distinction between "active" and "inactive" members, and by teaching new members the meaning of belonging to their particular denomination and church. Congregational identity is also delineated by cultural cues that may be subtle, such as dress, modes of discourse, and orientation to authority. These formal and informal boundaries help to motivate and organize the flow of resources, by creating an environment of trust and reciprocity.

Evangelism reinforces congregational boundaries while at the same time making them permeable. An evangelical understanding of the gospel sets forth boundaries between who is saved and who is not. One of Christian Stronghold's evangelistic programs is a door-to-door community survey in which members ask neighborhood residents a set of diagnostic questions: Are you a member of any religious group or church? At present, how often do you attend services? If you were to die today, where would you spend eternity? The evangelistic narrative of churches like Christian Stronghold stresses the moral divide between a Christian versus non-Christian lifestyle, and presents the prospect of heaven versus hell as the ultimate boundary. Evangelism represents entering the world of the nonbeliever or "backslidden" believer in order to issue an invitation to cross over.

Crossing religious boundaries often entails crossing cultural boundaries as well. While some people testify to dramatic solo meetings with God, in general "religious experiences tend not to float down from the sky as autonomous or self-generating encounters" (C. Smith 2003). Spiritual transformation, while intensely private, is also usually embedded in social relationships. Evangelistic encounters offer an entrance to the culture and identity of the sponsoring religious group. The process of discipleship socializes new converts into the religious rituals, values, and lingo of congregational life that will help to identify them as group insiders. For example, on a Sunday morning at Koinonia, Rev. Simmons gave an impromptu speech to the congregation about the importance of showing respect to God and others during worship; after this admonition, the researcher noticed that two people sitting beside her put away the paper-and-pencil game they had secretly been playing during the service. Reverend Simmons explained later that most of the congregation were not from a churched background and had to learn how to behave during services.

Those who display "appropriate cultural capital behaviors" are more likely to be granted access to the internal resources of the church (Schneider 1999, 270).[6] Lockhart's study of faith-based welfare-to-work programs observes the role of religious cultural capital (2003, 508):

> These skills provide clients an opportunity to better "fit in" to religious congregations where they might gain additional resources such as material goods and services, job information, and the like. Religious language, particularly the language of conversion, also gives participants words and images to describe the changes going on in their lives and how they must make different choices than they have made before. This language can reinforce any internal status transformations occurring in the lives of the clients.

The role of cultural access may be particularly significant in churches whose mission philosophy focuses on empowering Christians rather than reforming society. New Covenant Church members can point to numerous "success stories" in their midst of people who followed the progression of salvation, church membership, and discipleship, followed by improvements in their health, economic status, and family relationships. Such narratives provide evidence for the religious logic of evangelism and fuel the church's continued investment into outreach.

To summarize, there are several ways that a church's evangelistic activities can contribute to the formation of social capital. Faith sharing can build bonds of trust between members of the congregation and those whom they evangelize, and encourage an ethos of reciprocity in which service is offered in response to spiritual blessings. As a strongly held norm, the mandate to witness can bind members of the congregation together in a shared mission, while at the same time providing a centrifugal force that directs the church to invest its capital outward into the world. An evangelistic orientation may serve as a bridge between the social network of the congregation and diverse individuals and groups, with the possible result of enlarging the church's awareness of social needs and motivation for action. Evangelistic activity reinforces a congregation's group identity by highlighting its religious and cultural network boundaries, but can also provide an entry point for socializing individuals into the "appropriate cultural capital behaviors" needed to fit into the congregation and gain access to its resources.

Limitations of Evangelistic Church-Based Social Capital

It must be emphasized that church-based social capital creates only the *potential* for constructive public outcomes. John Coleman (2003) reminds us that the notion of capital represents the capacity for productivity, not the product itself:

> Like capital in wealth, human and social capital can lie dormant. . . .
> Some religious units either pay scant attention to the social capital
> they generate or do not know how to turn it into politically or civically
> relevant social movements, service, and volunteerism. As a result,
> much of the social capital of some congregations remains frozen
> within the local unit, or it becomes isolated in separate pockets of
> friendship cliques within the congregation, failing to spill out into
> the larger society. (38)

When churches do tap into their social capital potential, the challenges of lateral bridging tend to limit their investment in collective social action that is truly representative of the community (Ammerman 2001; Schneider 2001; Day 2002; Chaves 2004). Incompatible organizational cultures and racial, cultural, or economic divides can present hurdles to authentic cooperation despite shared social goals. The parochialism of many congregations erodes community trust, as Bethel Temple pastor Lou Centeno observed: "People can get kind of possessive. People can get into a period of competition and working against the kingdom of God, instead of working together in the kingdom of God." Such churches tend to prefer programs closely linked with their own congregation to collaborative projects over which they have less control (Wuthnow 1997).

These limitations lead John Coleman to conclude that "those who hope to renew American social capital only, or even primarily, on religious social capital may rest their hopes on too thin a reed" (2001, 292). Evangelistic commitments may further undermine the civic utility of religious social capital. It is fairly obvious that even if an evangelistic orientation does have the potential to strengthen the stock of social capital available for social action, churches do not always (and many would say they *rarely*) fulfill this potential. Either an evangelistic orientation may fail to generate—or may even weaken—social capital, or the capital associated with evangelistic activity may not be used for social action.

A strong sense of evangelistic mission can discourage networking with secular organizations or religious groups with a different mission orientation. Churches with an evangelistic orientation tend to form fewer partnerships than activist congregations (Ammerman 2001). Evangelism can also strain the quality of the church's relationship with individuals or with the community as a whole if it is perceived as too pushy or out of touch with the needs of the community. For example, some residents in the area around Germantown Church of the Brethren complained about the noise of its evangelistic street services. Asked their opinion of Bethel Temple's outdoor worship service, members of a neighborhood watch team affirmed that it was a "good idea to have some kind of event on Friday night that shut down these drug corners." However, they felt that this particular event was "too preachy" and would not affect local youth. Negative impressions of evangelistic activities can diminish residents' trust in church members and make community groups less likely to cooperate with the church.

Evangelism may fail to create a bridge between the church and evangelistic targets who might benefit from access to the church's resources. Churches that focus their evangelistic energies on overseas missions, for example, have no contact with converts except through financial giving. For local missions, differences in race, class, household composition, and geographic residency often function as a barrier between faith and church affiliation. The main mode of evangelism for many churches is network evangelism that capitalizes on existing social relationships, like friends or family members (Woods 1996). This is the kind of outreach that has been promoted by recent church growth movements such as the "purpose driven church" (Warren 1995). Network evangelism tends to reinforce the demographic and cultural homogeneity of the congregation because it brings in people who are already like "us." While homogeneity arguably enhances a church's bonding capital by making it easier for members to understand and trust one another (Cnaan, Boddie, and Yancey 2003), it does not foster the bridging capital that can connect a church to a more diverse field of social concerns. Rather, the congregational boundaries

heightened by an evangelistic orientation may entrench social patterns of segregation and inequality (Wuthnow 2004).

Bartkowski and Regis describe faith-based social capital as "Janus-faced"
because of the inherent tension between "consensual and coercive elements
of religious belonging." The same religiously-grounded norms that propel
members to invite others into the faith also bolster the "moral strictures and
behavioral standards" that may serve to exclude people deemed "undeserving"
from congregational participation (2003, 21). The stronger the moral imperative to expand the congregational network through evangelism, the higher the
bar of religious cultural capital typically needed to access congregational resources. This tension was present in an interview with a Cuban immigrant
who had left Bethel Temple to attend Nueva Creación Lutheran Church because
she found Bethel too morally constrictive. "At Bethel it was like you had to
change a lot of your lifestyle to be baptized. . . . There are things that maybe
you *want* to change, and there are things that they were just forcing on you."
She preferred Rev. Patrick Cabello Hansel's approach to lifestyle issues in
terms of personal choice rather than absolute moral laws. "He explains why
things could be bad, or could be not good for you. . . . Instead of isolating you,
that sort of makes you feel like you want to be there." On the one hand, Bethel's
strong moral code helps drive its substantive investment in community outreach. On the other, this woman resented what she felt to be the church's
"forcing" its code on her, and found it "isolating."

While the presence of capital implies the capacity for action, it does not
specify the content of that action. Churches may channel the social capital
generated through evangelistic means into outcomes that others would not
consider conducive to building civil society. Evangelism by sects that advocate
a retreat from society, for example, may result in a net loss of social connections. Converted individuals may be socialized into ideas that create alienation
from others outside the group, like the assertion that God hates homosexuals,
or into uncivil forms of political activism.

Finally, the social capital generated by conversionist churches may not
translate into social action. Evangelism may enhance trust, strengthen bonds,
create bridges, raise awareness, impart cultural and social skills, and facilitate
access to resources, and yet not produce a substantial increase in civic engagement. This is mainly due to a lack of either the inclination or the organization to engage meaningfully in social ministry. As explored in chapter 7,
many evangelism dominant churches see their mission as "reforming the nation by reforming the individual" (Schmidt 1991, 1). They do not see a need to
participate in programs of economic development or community organizing
because they believe that the church is best suited to make a social contribution
through individual conversions. Other dominant evangelism churches subscribe to a "lifeboat" interpretation of evangelism, with a mission of rescuing
eternal souls from a world doomed to self-destruction. These churches may

view social action as a distraction from the church's primary soul-saving objective.

On the other hand, an evangelistic church may have the inclination to participate in social ministry but lack the organizational capacity. Like a factory that turns out a specific product, a church is set up to "produce" a particular mission. Shifting gears requires substantial motivation, energy, and leadership skills. The more efficiently a church specializes in one type of mission, the more difficulties it is likely to encounter in trying to change direction. One church where we interviewed tried unsuccessfully for several years to launch a mentoring program for women on welfare. Although the resources and the "heart" for compassionate outreach were present, the leadership was unable to overcome the hurdle of inertia, as church volunteers and dollars were already committed to evangelistic projects. This example highlights Becker's (1999) point that congregations are institutionally embodied (see also Wuthnow 2003). The trust, reciprocity, and shared norms that characterize a church's social network are developed in a specific organizational and cultural context. This context may render a church's social capital more or less pliable in terms of the range of projects to which it may be applied.

Despite these obstacles to organized social action, as "incubators for civic skills," evangelistic congregations can still foster civic engagement among their membership. None of the above caveats limit the capacity, or the inclination, of individual members to volunteer for nonprofit organizations, donate to charities, exercise their political rights as citizens, or participate in other civic activities. In fact, evangelistic churches may encourage such behavior as the way that Christians "leaven" the social order.[7]

Social Capital and Holistic Ministry

Some evangelistic churches may be better able than others to overcome the limitations described above. A holistic mission orientation (see chapter 7) gives churches both the inclination and the organization to capitalize on the social potential of evangelism. "Jesus Christ did two things" for people, asserted a church leader at Christian Stronghold. "He met their felt needs and their spiritual needs." This normative example provides holistic churches the basis for organizing their energies and resources. A whole-person anthropology, in combination with engaged orthodoxy, drives churches to be aware of and responsive to the material, emotional, and educational needs in their community. The perception that addressing felt needs makes spiritual overtures more winsome also increases the likelihood that the capital generated by evangelistic commitments will be channeled into social concerns.

An emphasis on the whole person may encourage churches to enlist beneficiaries of evangelism as human resources for social ministry. Bishop Dickie

Robbins spoke in a sermon about the hidden talents of residents of his inner-city community: "Some of the most gifted people you'll ever meet are those you pass by on Third Street" (a street notorious for drug trade). Life in Christ Cathedral of Faith affirms to marginalized people that they have worth in God's eyes, and validates this evangelistic message by engaging them in worthwhile service. Asserted Bishop Robbins, "You can't wait until they are healthy to start saying, 'Now give back.' You tell them the whole time so that part of the motivation becomes that they can use their experience to help somebody else." Many of Life in Christ's current ministry leaders are former addicts who came to the church through its Drug Free program. The evangelistic nature of the church's social outreach reinforces the norm of reciprocity that binds converts to the congregation and to its work in the community.

The production of bridging capital may be enhanced by expressive relationalism, defined previously as the understanding that the gospel is best communicated in the context of caring relationships. Churches that value relationalism as a pathway to religious expression are more likely to persist in forging connections with people in their ministry target group. The leader of a ministry affiliated with New Covenant Church to residents of a public housing complex asserted that reaping the evangelistic potential of social ministry required long-term investments in people:

> You cannot go in and be with these people for a few weeks and then leave. They do not trust anybody. If you go in and give them clothes or something, they will come in and take it. But they still will not trust you. You have to be there for them week after week, and month after month. Then they will finally start trusting you.

This commitment to relationship is echoed in David Apple's description of Tenth Presbyterian Church's outreach to homeless persons: "The first goal is that each worker be a friend to each guest in order to establish trust. If there is no trust then there can be no ministry" (Apple 1994). Richard Kyerematen reported that his emphasis on evangelism led to a shift in Germantown Church of the Brethren's approach to serving homeless persons, from "just going downtown and feeding them" to more intentional efforts "to take them into the life of the church." A neighborhood resident who came to Faith Assembly of God for food testified that the main way the church helped him was "not so much in giving or in stuff, but through prayer, hope, and encouragement." The desire to develop a spiritual connection with beneficiaries may lead ministry participants to move beyond disbursing material aid to establishing the trusting bonds that are essential to social capital.

The expanded individualism of some holistic churches nurtures a vision of how spiritually transformed individuals can together promote social change. Without this vision, the social capital of evangelistic churches may be invested exclusively in services to individuals without promoting collective action to challenge institutionalized injustice. Structural and personal factors create a disempowering spiral in Nueva Creación's community, noted Patrick Cabello Hansel: "We don't get the services because we don't have the political power, because we don't have the economic power, because we're discouraged, so we don't vote." Spiritual renewal provides hope in the midst of despair and alienation, creating new possibilities for cooperative action. Salvation, said Rev. Cabello Hansel, is "the foundation of the community that enables you to work for justice, while at the same time living together as sinful beings in a sinful world."

In his most recent book, Robert Putnam calls for "social capitalists" to strengthen the connections within and among social networks in order to build up civil society. He cites Henry Ward Beecher's advice from a century ago: to foster connectedness, "multiply picnics" (2000, 414). Life in Christ has followed this advice literally. On a muggy July day, church vans picked up about 45 residents from local homeless shelters to join members of the congregation for their annual all-day picnic in the park, with games, music, and free food. Shelter residents came, according to pastor Dickie Robbins, both because they were spiritually hungry, and because they knew they would be fed lunch. While the picnic included a time of worship and brief evangelistic devotional, the focus of the outreach was not to convert the homeless guests. Rather, Rev. Robbins said, the point was that church members "began to draw people into the fellowship. They began to seek out people who were not regulars and find ways to involve them in what is going on." Reverend Robbins noted that if shelter guests got involved in the church's Drug Free program, they were particularly likely to continue attending the church. "If we use [social ministry] to build right relationship, they will keep coming. If they keep coming then we will have the opportunity in a more traditional worship setting to both share the gospel and give the altar call."

Reverend Robbins may be considered both an evangelistic entrepreneur and a social capitalist. His holistic understanding of the church's mission draws a path from softball to altar call, highlighted by success stories of homeless shelter residents who "have gotten off of drugs and gotten jobs" along the way.

Conclusion: From Spiritual Capital to Social Capital

Congregations represent a significant source of energy for social action because of their unique capacity to motivate and mobilize a constituent network for public ends. Congregations translate their social capital into social well-being by taking collective action, by empowering the civic involvement of members, by uplifting individuals by incorporating them into the church's caring community, and by harnessing religious cultural capital to social concerns. An evangelistic mission may strengthen a church's social capital, particularly if the church adopts a holistic approach to ministry, sharing faith both in word and deed, grounded in relationships of trust and reciprocity. This potential may be limited, however, by the challenges of connecting constructively with people across racial, cultural, or socioeconomic lines, and by the lack of a social vision.

Into this guardedly optimistic analysis of churches' social capital potential, Don Browning sounds a cautionary note (quoted in Coleman 2003, 45):

> It is dangerous to think of churches in terms of social capital. Churches are carriers of religious stories that reveal God's will and grace. Salvation, not the increase of social capital, is the primary purpose of churches and their narratives. . . . Christians do not live the Christian life to produce social capital but it appears that increased social capital is a long-term, secondary consequence of Christian life.

This suggests that social responsibility and evangelism are not necessarily in zero-sum relationship, whereby increasing one entails suppressing the other. Enervating a church's evangelistic commitments may squelch their capacity to generate social capital as a "secondary consequence" of their mission. The way to encourage evangelistic churches to become more invested in social causes is not by diverting their drive to lead people to salvation. Rather, evangelistic churches can be encouraged and equipped to carry out this core purpose in ways that amplify the church's beneficial impact on individuals and communities.

I2

Conclusion

New Understandings, New Questions,
New Opportunities

What makes a pastor work sixty-hour weeks to turn a former bar
into a day care? Why do some churches insist on having a Bible
study before providing a hot meal for homeless persons? Does it
make a difference when an after-school program teaches children
about God along with math? How does a faith-based program help a
cocaine addict to come clean, get a job, reunite with his family, and
volunteer to reach out to other addicts?

In light of such questions, this book was written to provide a
clearer view of religion's public role from the frontlines of church-
based community involvement. We offer a conceptual framework for
understanding the spiritual dynamics of social ministry and, in particular, the relationship between witness and service. We close with
recommendations for public policy and research concerning faith-
based social action. This starts with a more careful definition of
faith.

What Is the *Faith* in Faith-Based Social Action?

The word *faith* has become common in discussions of social policy,
yet it is rarely defined. We note at least six different senses in which
faith may be understood in the context of social action programs:

1) *Organizational attributes:* A social ministry may be faith-based
in terms of the ways that it is organizationally connected with religion (see Smith and Sosin 2001 and Jeavons 1998). For programs
directly sponsored by a congregation or denomination, the connec-

tion is obvious. Other ties to a faith community come in the form of informal affiliations, formal partnerships, sources of funds and volunteers, referral networks, professional associations, or client constituency. A religious identity may also be evident in the organizational culture. Examples include direct religious references in the mission statement, the requirement that staff belong to a church or sign a doctrinal statement, the governing board's reliance on prayer or theological principles in decision-making, and a policy against staff drinking or other behavior considered immoral.

2) *Religious practices:* A service program may be faith-based in reference to its integration of religious elements. Faith may be communicated and cultivated through explicitly religious activities such as corporate worship, prayer, references to Scripture, and invitations to evangelistic events. The program may formally incorporate religious content, or foster informal conversations on spiritual topics. Beneficiaries may be encouraged or required to participate in religious practices or to make personal faith commitments. Religious practices such as biblically based training sessions or chapel services may also form part of the ministry experience of program staff and volunteers.

3) *Personal meanings:* In contrast to the public character of religious practices, faith can also denote the private, subjective beliefs and meanings that individuals bring to, and derive from, acts of service. Compassionate ministry may be interpreted as an act of worship, for example, in which the volunteer symbolically serves Christ. Advocacy for environmental concerns may be motivated by a belief in God's sovereignty over creation. Community development may be intended as a demonstration of God's love and justice for "the least of these." In this sense, ministry is faith-based to the extent that it enriches and expresses one's own spiritual life.

4) *Values and vision:* To paraphrase Farnsley (2003, 12), one "value-added" that faith-based programs bring is that they "add values" to social action. The ideals of love, service, compassion, and justice that undergird church-based social action have deep roots in the Judeo-Christian heritage, and indeed are shared by many different religions. Calls for social change ring in harmony with the prophetic tradition of the Bible. Moreover, social ministries often seek to reinforce responsibility, frugality, integrity, chastity, and other qualities grounded in transcendent standards for moral behavior. To speak of programs as being faith-based in the values sense is to refer to the core religious principles that frame a vision of how the world ought to be and how people ought to behave in it.

5) *Relationships:* Faith may be said to shape the relationships among social activists and beneficiaries in a service program. Ideally, the faith of volunteers makes them more kind, loving, empathetic, and other-directed. The principle that people are created in the image of God may inspire religious providers to respect the dignity of all persons, however marginalized by society. Faith-based

programs may also promote "relational benevolence" (Sherman 2000, 33) that fosters personal connections between givers and receivers of service rather than maintaining an impersonal, objective distance. This relational approach promotes opportunities for faith-sharing and cultivates beneficiaries' God-given potential as community assets.

6) *Connection with outcomes:* Faith may be viewed as an active ingredient in the production of social outcomes. A faith-based methodology may focus on the connection between personal spiritual transformation and socioeconomic status, on the relevance of religiously grounded principles to social goals such as employment or marital health, or on the empowering effect of kindness and moral guidance offered in a religious context. Community organizing efforts may additionally draw on the bond of fellowship among people of faith to achieve collective social goals. Program personnel may rely on spiritual inputs such as prayer, Scripture, and the guidance of the Holy Spirit for the efficacy of their interventions.

The definition of *faith-based* is thus multifaceted. Faith influences the organizational attributes of service programs and links these programs with the larger community of the faithful. Faith is affirmed and expressed through devotional acts that bind social activists with one another and with God. Faith motivates involvement in social action and imparts personal meaning to this involvement. Faith anchors social change in values for individuals to live by and a vision for their larger social context. Faith inspires people to love sacrificially and to serve with humility, honoring the God-given dignity of all people. Faith invokes the transcendent power of God to transform the whole person from the inside out. Each of these facets of faith has different implications for practicing, studying, and developing policies concerning church-based outreach.

Clearly, faith-based ministries are not all based on the same faith, or related to faith in the same way. What makes a social ministry "faith"-ful in one instance may not apply in the next. Fruitful discourse thus requires teasing out the various meanings of faith that apply. The debate over charitable choice provides an example. When people discuss the merits of government partnerships with faith-based organizations, do they mean any program with a religious mission statement or affiliation? Or programs in which staff are motivated by beliefs about the religious significance of caring for the poor? Or programs that incorporate religious elements and nurture spiritual transformation as part of their treatment methodology? People may be using the same language and yet mean different things.

Without a clear and objective definition, the term *faith-based* often becomes a symbolic token in public discourse, with connotations that invoke the prejudices, both positive and negative, of the speaker. This subjective and politicized usage has created roadblocks to understanding the reality of faith-based action itself, in all its variety and complexity. More precisely nuanced under-standings—such as the organizational and program types described in chapter 6—are thus essential to sound policymaking and valid scholarship.

Faith-Based Social Action and Public Policy

Martin Marty (1980, 464–65) related the story of a Chicago Lutheran church in the 1960s that accepted government funds to expand its social ministry. On a Sunday morning, the minister informed the congregation: "I know that this may violate your sense of devotion to the traditional doctrine of the separation of church and state, but in that case I advise you to go out and get a *new* traditional doctrine of church and state."

Since the passage of charitable choice in 1996, America has found itself in the contentious process of "getting a new doctrine of church and state"—rethinking the meaning and application of the First Amendment. We draw on our research to offer the following observations and recommendations for public-private partnerships involving faith-based entities (we use this term in the broadest sense of any organization or program type with a connection to religion).

Churches' Mission and Charitable Choice

The challenges related to public funding are not the same for all congregations. The variety of mission orientations suggests that each type is likely to respond to faith-based initiatives in a different way. Dominant social action churches are likely to have the least reservations about the restrictions on religious ac-tivities associated with government funding (see Chaves 1999), because their programs already incorporate little explicitly religious content. However, they may oppose faith-based initiatives on other grounds (see Eilperin 2001). In Philadelphia, a group of activist congregations took a principled stand against charitable choice as part of their protest against welfare reform. Dual-focus congregations are likely to be open to public partnerships, unless they see this hindering a strategy of altruism evangelism. If one reason that a church en-gages in social ministry is to gain a reputation for being "salt and light" in the world, the church may not want to share the credit with the government.

Holistic churches are likely to have a mixed response to the prospect of collaborating with government. On a practical level, they may welcome the additional source of funds for meeting urgent needs, particularly churches whose membership base is resource-poor. But they will also appraise funding opportunities in light of their effect on their religious autonomy and evangel-istic witness (see Farnsley 2003). Several of the holistic churches in our study declined to pursue funding opportunities because they came with too many strings. Holistic-instrumental churches in particular are cautious of restrictions against integrating explicitly religious elements or "sharing a moral message," as Faith Assembly of God's Richard Smith put it. A ministry leader at Bethel Temple asserted: "We're willing to work with anybody, but we're not willing to compromise what we believe. . . . I wouldn't want to take government funding if it meant we couldn't do what we want to do. If they want to give us money to do what we want to do, then that's great." Dominant-evangelism churches are more likely to have scruples or policies against using public funds. One church leader reportedly spurned government funding as the "devil's money." (In contrast, another pastor explained his openness to government funding with the biblical proverb, "The wealth of the wicked is laid up for the just.")

Publicly supporting the social ministry of a conversionist church—a church where evangelism is one of the mission activities that is "highly valued or [is] part of what the congregation becomes known for" (Becker 1999, 187)—does not inevitably entail government-funded religious indoctrination. Conversionist churches may draw on a range of evangelistic strategies, not all of which involve overt proselytizing. Evangelism, in the words of one African American Baptist pastor we interviewed, "involves being flexible." A nonprofit affiliated with his inner-city church used state funds to provide welfare-to-work services. He emphasized that "in the classroom we do not proselytize." The program curriculum was entirely secular. But he also asserted that their program had a spiritually transforming impact on beneficiaries—not because of religious teachings but "because of the personal relationships that are developed between student and staff." The church offered a free lunch to beneficiaries, accompanied by a Bible study, giving the pastor "a chance to share with them what our whole mission is all about." Program staff also invited the mothers in the program to take advantage of church activities such as youth nights and a women's group. Through these voluntary channels, several women had joined the church.

According to the pastor, these invitational and relational strategies derive from Jesus' holistic example: "Jesus had many ministries, but he had one overriding dominant mission." The pastor listed his church's many ministries: "Clothing, food, job training, job development, small business development, community development credit union, community development bank, school. . . . These ministries are very important, but the overriding dominant mission is to win many people to Christ." Thus the *meaning* of this church's welfare-to-work program is evangelistic, but the *methodology* is consistent with secular programs. Spiritual nurture is a "value added" component that enhances but does not replace conventional social interventions.

In contrast to this holistic-complementary approach, most dominant evangelistic and some holistic-instrumental churches do not separate the meaning from the methods. "We see evangelism taking place in all of the other ministries. It is not a separate thing," said Phil Ryken of Tenth Presbyterian Church, explaining that evangelism was "part of the ultimate purpose" of their services to homeless persons and international students. "I don't think we can imagine a social ministry apart from the giving of the gospel." He was wary of partnering with government, because to compartmentalize the explicitly religious components of social ministry would limit the church's potential to nurture the spiritual transformation that they considered essential to effective social outcomes.

Many critics of faith-based initiatives worry that accepting public funds will compromise a church's mission and diminish its religious autonomy. Cookman's experience illustrates the reality of these dangers. In the early stages of Cookman's welfare-to-work contract with the state, Rev. Donna Jones discouraged other churches from following their path, saying, "The state is not ready to partner with churches." Transitional Journey staff criticized the state's bureaucracy, its welfare policies, and its motives for working with churches. They also spoke ruefully of their own naivete in pursuing the contract and the mistakes they had made in its implementation. But in the end, Rev. Jones extended her sense of public mission to encompass the church's influence on government:

> I believe the church is here to enable government to do a better job by incorporating and infusing Christian principles and Christian values of hope, of personhood. Because the government sometimes loses sight of persons, whereas the church, our whole focus and mission is on the soul, is on the person. . . . We can work cooperatively. The danger that we have is that the church will take on everything, and abdicate the government from any responsibility in social service; but the church can, at least, begin a dialogue with the government . . . to ensure that the whole person is dealt with in our society in a way that brings life.

Each church must assess the risks and potential benefits of a government partnership in relation to its own unique mission, ministry context, and store of experiences. "Our congregation has counted the cost of our decisions," said Rev. Jones. Religious entities need information, training, and technical assistance to help them make wise decisions regarding funding opportunities. The decision, however, should be theirs to make.

Redefine the Question: From Whether to How

The debate over faith-based initiatives often gets posed along these lines: Should government support the social service work of the faith community? But this is asking the wrong question, or at least, asking a question that has already been answered definitively. Government has for decades been committed to "government by proxy," carrying out its public agenda through private institutions. Religious agencies are now too integral to the fabric of the public social safety net to excise all forms of collaboration with government. Few opponents of faith-based initiatives would insist that Koinonia and Faith Assembly of God should no longer distribute free USDA food products or city-funded food bank items; or that Christian Stronghold's day care may no longer accept state subsidies for children in low-income families; or that state universities must stop co-sponsoring men's health fairs at New Covenant and nutrition programs at Nueva Creación; or that Homes of Hope, a separately incorporated nonprofit founded by First Presbyterian, should be ineligible for HUD funds to provide Mt. Holly residents with affordable housing. On the other hand, many would question whether the state should have entered into a contract with Cookman United Methodist Church to provide welfare-to-work services.[1]

Thus, the policy question should be restated as not *whether* government should partner with faith-based groups, but *which ones* and *how*. Our categories help to define this question more precisely. Most people, even critics of charitable choice, have few objections to government's funding of faith-background and faith-affiliated entities, in which organizational ties to religion are loose and religious dynamics are only implicitly present. Even before the passage of charitable choice in 1996, millions of public dollars flowed to these types of organizations. Should faith-permeated and/or faith-centered entities be equally eligible for funding, and under what conditions? By what criteria should government draw the line? Using a common language to describe the varieties of faith-based organizations may not make it easier for all parties to come to an agreement on these questions, but it will at least help to clarify and narrow down the areas of disagreement.

The question of which entities government may support is refocused by the distinction between organizations and programs. Should access to funds be determined by institutional features (like staffing or affiliation), or the actual religious content of social programs, or some combination of the two? What eligibility rules should apply to faith-affiliated programs sponsored by faith-permeated organizations, such as a church-run program with minimal religious content? Or to a faith-affiliated nonprofit that runs a faith-centered program?[2] Policy discussions should untangle which constitutional concerns address the sponsoring organization versus the specific program to be funded. We believe that the religious elements and integration strategies of a social service program should have more bearing on its eligibility for direct public funding than the religious characteristics of the sponsoring organization. Government funding should take into account whether a program requires beneficiaries to participate in worship services, but not whether the organization uses religious criteria for selecting its staff and governing board.

Shifting the focus from *whether* to *how* government should partner with the faith community also opens the possibility that different forms of collaboration with government may be more appropriate for different faith-based types. The policy discussion ought to look beyond direct funding. Whereas faith-permeated programs may be ineligible for direct grants or contracts, it is possible to support their work through indirect means, such as the subsidies used by low-income families at Christian Stronghold's day care. Government support may take a wide range of forms—including vouchers, nonfinancial partnerships (such as in-kind aid, referral networks, staff training, and shared space), tax incentives for private charitable donations, and funding channeled through intermediary institutions. Continued innovation in the funding mechanisms and structures for service delivery will allow a wider range of faith-based agencies to expand their programs.

Guidelines for Religious Activity

The charitable choice statute aims to protect service providers' "religious character and freedom" and assures that an agency that receives government funds shall not be forced to alter the "definition, development, practice, and expression of its religious beliefs."[3] Charitable choice also bans the use of federal funds for "sectarian worship, instruction, or proselytization." Other pieces of legislation passed as part of faith-based initiatives carry similar language. What is protected under an organization's "religious character"? How can a government-funded religious agency exercise its freedom to maintain the "practice and expression of its religious beliefs" without violating the ban on worship, instruction, or proselytization using public funds? Faith-based service providers need clear guidelines for what they can and cannot do with government funds. In 2003 the White House released a set of guidelines, which are currently being tested by legal challenges as well as by the exigencies of actual practice.[4]

Our research observed several examples of how churches have been negotiating the boundaries of appropriate religious expression in the context of public services (see Sinha 2000; Unruh and Sinha 2001). For example, the welfare department determined that Cookman's Transitional Journey could present itself to beneficiaries as a "Christ-centered job development program" (*yes* to expressing its religious character), but that it could not require beneficiaries to take part in religious activities (*no* to worship, instruction, and proselytization). It could include Bibles as an optional resource in its literacy curriculum, but it could not use state money to buy them. It could include content of a general spiritual nature in its self-esteem class (such as affirmations of women's worth in God's eyes), but must reserve specifically Christian or Methodist teachings for the optional spiritual development class.

Cookman's example illustrates that it is possible for government-funded faith-based programs both to honor the First Amendment and to care for the spiritual needs of clients. Doing so includes using exclusively private funds to pay for any religious activity; making clear distinctions in time and place between the mandatory, government-funded components of the program and the voluntary, privately-funded religious components; disclosing the religious affiliation and activities of the program to prospective clients so that they can make an informed choice about participation; ensuring that clients can receive the social services of the program without participating in its religious elements; notifying clients of their right to choose an alternative provider and their right to opt out of religious activities; and, for churches, setting up a separate bank account or establishing a separate non-profit entity to run the program (Sider and Unruh 2000; Sider and Unruh 2001; Unruh and Sinha 2005). Together these measures maximize the values of personal choice, religious freedom, and social efficacy.

The purpose of such guidelines is not to sanitize publicly funded programs from religious activities and messages. While clients must be protected from religious coercion, this does not mean shielding them from any form of religious expression. As James Reichley warned, a society "that seems to regard religion as something against which public life must be protected, is bound to foster the impression that religion is either irrelevant or harmful" (1985, 165). The ban against the use of government funds for religious proselytizing, instruction, and worship is wise, not because there is something sinister about these religious elements, but solely because they are religious. The guarantee of a secular alternative is a good policy, not because government must protect clients from religion, but because clients must have the right to choose the religious character of their environment. Neither the ideals of the Constitution nor the interests of the public are served by policies that seek to blunt the evangelistic commitments of government-funded organizations—though the public certainly has an interest in ensuring that these religious energies are appropriately expressed and privately funded.

Charitable choice guidelines should also take into account the fact that many service beneficiaries are themselves religious (Wuthnow 2004). One Muslim woman specifically chose Transitional Journey because it provided her with a safe environment to practice her own faith. "I come here and get the benefits without compromising myself," she said. "They respect me and I respect them" (John-Hall 1999a). In our conversations with beneficiaries, many talked about the importance of their faith in giving them strength and hope despite the obstacles they faced. Such people may perceive the spiritual character of faith-based programs not as a threat, but as a refuge from the secular nature of government social services. Secularism—which can in fact function as a religion—can also be coerced. This was illustrated in our interview with one Christian homeless woman in a transitional housing program who was threatened with expulsion from the program if she did not stop talking about her faith with other clients.

Religious Control over Staff Selection

One of the most politically explosive objections to charitable choice has been the charge of employment discrimination using government funds. Title VII of the 1964 Civil Rights Act safeguards the right of religious organizations to use religious criteria in hiring employees with religious duties. In 1972, Congress expanded this right to cover all employees of religious organizations.[5] At issue is whether religious organizations forfeit this right when they receive public money, which brings with it a prohibition against discrimination on the basis of religion.[6]

The ability of faith-based programs to provide social services without compromising their religious mission depends in large measure on having staff who share their beliefs and values. Nueva Creación's youth development program did not incorporate explicitly religious teachings. Yet its most important religious aspect, according to a ministry leader, was the participation of "church members with a strong knowledge of the Bible, and Christian life, because sooner or later children will come to you with tough questions," and only people of faith could respond appropriately with "Christian content." Many holistic providers place a strong value on expressive relationalism (defined in chapter 9), which means that program personnel not only do the works of service required by their faith but they seek to express that faith through caring relationships. Among faith-based organizations contracting with government in Green and Sherman's (2002) 15-state study, 72% of organizations agree that their staff is available to discuss spiritual matters with clients. "People get converted based on relationships. They don't get converted based on putting the Ten Commandments on the wall," remarked Rev. Jones. Charitable choice's guarantee that organizations do not have to remove religious symbols from the program environment or otherwise obscure their religious identity is a helpful step, but does not go far enough in protecting religious organizations' control over their mission.

Another factor is that staff often play multiple roles in small, faith-based organizations that receive public funds. The director of Lafiya Family Services Center was also an "urban missionary" with Germantown Church of the Brethren, heading several church programs including the food pantry, youth ministry, and outreach to families of prisoners. One of the Transitional Journey instructors also helped lead Cookman's Kid's Café, providing a weekly meal, Bible story, and recreation for children. The director of the after-school program at Nueva Creación's community center was also the church secretary, and another staff member at the community center was a pastoral intern who led the church's immigration assistance program. Disallowing organizations to consider religion as a factor in hiring would have a stifling effect on the capacity of these organizations and their sponsoring churches to generate the needed human resources for their full range of programs.

Ministry leaders pointed to control over staff and board selection as a key factor in preventing the secularization of their programs. This is particularly the case for ministries whose religious character is informal and organic rather than formally structured. Lafiya Family Services Center provides counseling and youth services with a blend of public and private funds. Although spiritual nurture is absent from the mission statement, the director explained that support for evangelistic goals was an assumed requirement for the staff and board, "because it is so much a part of who we are as the guiding leadership." In the relationalism of Lafiya's religious culture, mission is ultimately defined by the people who make up a ministry, not by documents or policies. The organic nature of their mission made them vulnerable to secularization, the director acknowledged, pointing to the YMCA as an example. Lafiya's ability to sustain its religious character depends on its ability to select leaders who share the church's vision.

Some interviewees considered the ability to hire other Christians to be essential to their program's effectiveness, believing that a divine agency works uniquely through people of faith. The director of one publicly funded, faith-affiliated after-school program asserted that he preferred hiring "born again" people to work with the youth, even though their position did not entail overt religious elements. A non-Christian may be a "good person," but if they are not born again, he said, "the program suffers. . . . They can only establish a good, moral environment, but the Spirit of God isn't there." From a secular point of view, "a good, moral environment" might be a sufficient platform for a successful after-school program. From the director's perspective, however, a spiritual dynamic was missing that would diminish the quality of the program. While such assertions are factually untested, they represent a stumbling block to collaboration if program leaders are unwilling to sacrifice perceived efficacy for public funding.

Control over personnel is also important because this provides a foundation for other aspects of an agency's "religious character and freedom" protected by charitable choice. Personnel are responsible for the presence of religious objects in program space and for the use of religious language in self-descriptive materials. Personnel can help to sustain, or undermine, an affiliation with a religious entity such as a sponsoring denomination. Personnel bring with them a network of contacts and cultural capital that can enhance the organization's effectiveness in generating funds from the faith community. The religiosity of personnel, especially in leadership positions, shapes an organizational culture in which religious speech and values are either welcomed or stifled. This may have a significant influence on the *self*-selection of religious staff and volunteers. Affinity with the religious practices and mission of a program is thus a legitimate qualification for a staff position along with other criteria related to skills and experience.

As Wuthnow (2004, 175) writes, "Faith is principally about community, a community of belonging and identity that involves deep friendships and caring and that puts religious teachings into practice." In many faith-based programs, staff selection is not merely a matter of performing a function but of cultivating a community. According to Green and Sherman's (2002) study, 67% of faith-based organizations contracting with government say allowing faith-based groups to hire staff based on faith commitments is very or somewhat important. In another study (Ebaugh et al. 2003), 72% of faith-based agencies providing services to the homeless in Houston assert that having religious staff members promotes their mission. If the right to a hiring preference is not preserved, some faith-based social service programs may choose not to participate in faith-based initiatives. Others will still participate but at a potential cost to their religious identity, mission, and program capacity.

If the right to a hiring preference is not preserved, some faith-based social service programs may choose not to participate in faith-based initiatives. Others will still participate but at a potential cost to their religious identity, mission, and program capacity.

A Case for Charitable Choice

Rep. Robert C. Scott (DVa.), one of the leading Congressional critics of charitable choice, argued that the policy is either unconstitutional or unnecessary. "Can you proselytize during the programs and can you discriminate in hiring? That's the whole controversy," he said. "If it's 'no, you can't,' you don't need charitable choice. If it's 'yes, you can,' you're funding religion" (Eilperin 2001).

Our case studies suggest that his premises are flawed. First, faith-based programs may make a distinction between witnessing to their faith through social services and proselytizing. Many conversionist ministry leaders are savvy about adapting the presentation of their message in contextually appropriate ways. While their "overriding mission" may be "to win many people to Christ," in the words of the inner-city Baptist pastor quoted above, they have options for pursuing this mission without violating the guidelines for direct government funding—through implicit witness, pre-evangelistic strategies of invitations and informal relationships, or privately funded, optional activities. Because beneficiaries in such programs are able to receive the services in an essentially secular manner, and because no government funds are expended for religious activities, such arrangements do not constitute "funding religion." For the programs that are unwilling to separate their Christian message from their service methodology in this way, the option of funding through vouchers or other indirect means should be available.

Moreover, even if programs do not proselytize and do not use religious criteria in hiring, there is still a need for the protections and guidelines afforded by charitable choice. The religious character of an entity is broader than the question of whether it is explicitly evangelistic. Nueva Creación's youth development program, for example, was supported with a government grant. Making converts or attracting church members was not a goal of the program, according to a member of the staff. However, the program had an unmistakably religious character: it taught religiously based values, led youth in prayer, offered an optional Bible study, and created opportunities for informal dialogue on religious topics between youth and staff. Through these program dynamics, said the staff member, the youth were able "to see what it is to be a Christian." She doubted she would choose to make the program more explicitly evangelistic, even if it were privately funded. But if the government restrictions were such that they would have to renounce their religious character altogether, she said she would rather refuse the public money.

We must be realistic about our expectations for faith-based initiatives. The great majority of congregations will probably never apply for public funds for their social services (Chaves 1999) (though a greater number will be involved indirectly by supporting nonprofits that partner with government). Faith-based programs that apply for funding may not have the capacity to carry out their intended outcomes on a competitive basis (Farnsley 2001). Faith-based programs that receive public funds may fail to comply with government regulations; some may, either unintentionally or purposely, exercise an evangelistic agenda in a way that violates the religious freedom of their clients. Government funding and its attendant bureaucratic pressures may lead some religious entities to stray from their core mission. And even when religious organizations do collaborate successfully with government, the potential scale of their contribution is less than conjectured by some advocates (see Kennedy and Bielefeld 2003).

Despite these limitations, among those congregations and related religious organizations that do opt to engage in public partnerships, we believe that most are willing and able to provide services in a manner that is faithful both to the Constitution and to their religious identity, if given the proper guidance.[7] Even if only a small percentage of all religious organizations expand their social ministries through faith-based initiatives, the local impact of these efforts will be significant. Faith-based initiatives thus have the potential to amplify the resources available for social compassion. The needs are urgent. Public policy should make room at the table for the civic contributions of all who have something to offer, including conversionist Christians with a mission to serve society.

Implications and Recommendations for the Study of Faith-Based Social Action

If researchers do not grasp the uniqueness and complexity of the faith community, their findings may be muddled, and consequent social policy recommendations will be flawed. To gain a full picture of the contributions and limitations of faith-based social action, researchers must pay attention to the spiritual dynamics of social ministry, and not divorce social outcomes from the religious methodologies and meanings invested in them. This entails continuing the work toward operationalizing the "faith factor" of faith-based organizations (Goggin and Orth 2002). It also involves recognizing the features that distinguish specifically church-based outreach from other private and public sector social activism.

Below we consider several ways that our study may open up new areas of research or shed new light on old inquiries concerning church-based ministries and religious social activism more broadly.

Faith-Based Social Outcomes

One particularly pressing question to explore is what works and why. Much attention has been focused on the question of whether faith-based services are more effective than secular ones. But it is not meaningful to pose this question about faith-based services in general, because, as our typology indicates, so much variety exists in the religious characteristics of faith-based organizations and programs.

A more fruitful approach may be to investigate what *kinds* of faith-based programs can be most effective, and under what conditions. Which religious elements (prayer, religious teachings, invitations to conversion) contribute to efficacy, and how? Does the way that religious content is integrated into the program (mandatory, integrated-optional, relational, invitational, or implicit) make a difference? What organizational religious characteristics (such as the religious practices of personnel, reliance on religious funding sources, or religious criteria for staff selection) are significant for program outcomes? Does the relationship between religious characteristics and outcomes vary depending on the type of service provided—relief services, personal development, community development, and systemic change?[8] How are each of these relationships affected by other organizational factors such as resource level and degree of professionalization?

Corresponding to the claims described in chapter 10 related to the users, producers, and content of social services, there are several pathways by which a faith-based social service program might be efficacious. Looking at the role of religious dynamics in substance abuse interventions, for example, it may be that spiritual renewal can trigger positive changes in a person's self-image, attitudes, and behavior that enhance rehabilitation outcomes. Congregational social networks may aid this transformational process by offering beneficiaries added support and socialization. Alternatively, faith-based recovery ministries may attract volunteers and staff whose religious convictions make them more apt or better able to form relational bridges across barriers of race and class, to provide beneficiaries the right balance of affirmation and accountability, or to stick with beneficiaries through the ups and downs of the recovery process. Another explanation is that the religious tradition of a faith-based program offers insights and information about how to overcome an addiction that is absent from secular program content.

None of these explanations, of course, is mutually exclusive; when a faith-based program achieves successful outcomes, it is likely to represent a combination of these factors in addition to other variables that have nothing to do with religion. Moreover, faith-based programs may be subject to particular influences that negatively affect outcomes as well, such as a narrower range of institutional linkages, or more limited access to certain funding streams and to professionally trained social work staff (Smith and Sosin 2001; Kennedy and Bielefeld 2003). Sorting out all these influences is a remarkably complex task, requiring attention to the nuances of the meanings of faith outlined at the beginning of this chapter.

A different sort of question related to outcomes concerns knowing whether the religious integration strategies employed by faith-based programs are having the intended spiritual impact. Are beneficiaries in programs with an implicitly religious character spiritually nurtured by the love demonstrated through acts of compassion? To what extent do beneficiaries respond to invitations to participate in religious activities outside of the service program? Do programs that emphasize a relational strategy succeed in drawing beneficiaries into informal religious dialogue? And do these invitations and relationships ultimately lead to spiritual renewal or incorporation into a faith community? Does the integration of religious elements into program content engender spiritually transforming experiences, and does it matter whether these elements are optional or mandatory? Are beneficiaries and unchurched members of the community sufficiently impressed by religious social activists or curious about their motivations that someone will eventually ask, as a ministry leader at Bethel Temple predicted, " 'Why are you here?' . . . Then you can share."

Although the churches in our study provided many accounts of evangelistic success stories, evidence from other studies suggests that such anecdotes are the exception rather than the rule, and that religious strategies are not, in general, as effective as religious providers would like to think they are (Chaves 2004; Wuthnow 2004). An evangelistic orientation may do more to motivate churches to serve the needy than to equip churches to reap a spiritual harvest from this service.

Assaying the Field

Reliable conclusions about the role of the faith factor in achieving social outcomes depends on valid categorizations of organizations and programs. We invite refinements on our typology of religious characteristics in order to capture the diversity of the field of social action in the most factual and useful ways, particularly beyond the Protestant Christian tradition. These types can then be used to discover patterns of financial and nonfinancial support, institutional linkages, professionalization, capacity, and other organizational attributes in relation to religious characteristics (Working Group 2002). Hopefully this research will help replace the generic lumping of faith-based organizations with a more richly textured portrait of the entities working to address our most pressing problems.

The conceptual models in this book related to religious elements and strategies may also be helpful to the task of gathering data on the spiritual dimensions of social care. What manifestations of religion are most common in the context of social services? What is the prevalence of programs that involve overt proselytizing or mandatory religious practices? What factors—theological, organizational, cultural and environmental—best predict differences in religious program dynamics? Are different kinds of social needs (food, employment, substance abuse counseling) typically associated with different integration strategies? How do external pressures (such as licensing requirements) and opportunities (such as charitable choice) affect the amount, type, or integration strategy of religious elements?

Finally, we need a more detailed picture of churches' mission orientations. A more representative sample is needed to confirm or refine the mission categories proposed here and to discover the distribution of churches among the types. Viewing social action in the context of its relationship to evangelism casts a new light on the ongoing research on which churches are most likely to be engaged in social ministries, and what form those ministries take (relief, personal development, community development, systemic change). The comparative range and extent of social and evangelistic activity within each mission orientation needs to be determined. Given that some churches evangelize, not as an alternative to social service, but *through* social services, we need more precise ways of capturing this activity. It is important to learn whether conversionist, socially engaged churches represent a growing middle-ground movement, and if so to chart where and how this movement is taking place.

Toward a both/and Paradigm

In 1915, Harry Ward cautioned in his book *Social Evangelism* against turning the social gospel into a false dichotomy, critiquing those who opposed the movement:

> [Their] favorite antithesis is whether the Church is to save the social order or to save souls from hell, whether we need the arousing of a new social conscience or a revival of religion, whether the world is

to be saved by perfect laws or by redemption, by a new industrial system or by individual regeneration. The answer of course is *"By both."* These things are not in antithesis but are inseparable complements. (Quoted in Schmidt 1991, 148, emphasis in original)

Ironically, we return to this point made by an advocate of the social gospel almost a century ago in order to gain a better perspective on evangelistic social action today. Ward viewed supposedly antithetical facets of the church's mission as "inseparable complements." One hears echoes of this position from a member of Germantown Church of the Brethren, who asserts that church members should simply try to communicate Christ's love to people and "not necessarily think about 'We're doing evangelism' and 'We're doing social ministry.' I think that here we just are so strongly committed to both, that they seem to be simultaneous." Sociological models of mission orientations that force (and reinforce) dualistic paradigms do not accurately capture the role of congregations like Germantown Church of the Brethren in public life. We need to adopt models that make room for the more holistic response, "by both."

A dualistic paradigm is evident in surveys that ask congregants to choose between presumably opposing statements—"The church should focus on helping people here and now" versus "The church should focus on preparing people for eternal life after death." This way of asking questions may distort the shape and practical influence of members' theology. Our survey allowed respondents to state that they agreed equally with both. At Christian Stronghold and Media Presbyterian, about two-thirds of respondents selected this "both" option. At Christian Stronghold, however, the remaining respondents leaned slightly toward preparing people for life after death (21% versus 14%), and at Media the remainder leaned toward helping people here and now (20% versus 13%). Had respondents been forced to choose, Christian Stronghold would likely have been labeled other-worldly, masking the church's significant investment in people's lives here and now; while Media would likely have been identified as this-worldly, despite the church's emphasis on "getting the word out," as one member put it, that Jesus "died for our sins and went to heaven, and if we believe in Him we'll have eternal life." Most congregants at both churches did not view other-worldly and this-worldly concerns as exclusive but integrated both into their concept of mission. Thus as a framework for understanding how faith calls people to live in the world, "a dichotomy disguises reality" (Ammerman 1997b, 357).

The division between social action and evangelism into "two contrasting civil religions" (Wuthnow 1989) coincided with the rise of sociology as an academic discipline. It is thus perhaps no coincidence that dualistic paradigms have dominated the scholarly imagination in the study of religion. Nancy Ammerman writes that "Our theoretical models have too often been unidirectional and unilinear. More of one meant less of the other." She notes the failure of this "persistent positing of dichotomies" to explain contemporary realities in terms of individualism versus community, public versus private religion, particularism versus the common good, evangelical versus liberal, and evangelism versus social justice. "Either/or theories too often exclude and obscure realities that do not fit the 'positive' end of the theoretical continuum" (1997b, 350–351).

We suggest that holistic congregations—those that value and practice an integrated understanding of evangelistic witness and social action—are among the realities that these polarizations have obscured. Their motivation and capacity for social action is inseparable from their commitment to nurturing faith in others. Their social and spiritual vision are intertwined. For these churches, evangelistic energies may drive, not diminish, their stock of social capital available for social projects, and vice versa. More of one means more, not less, of the other. While the polarization of evangelism and social action attended the birth of modernity, assumptions about mission orientations need to be revisited in light of the postmodern axiom that "Life is much more a both/and proposition than an either/or one" (Ammerman 1997, 351).

Taking a both-and approach does not negate the existence of divisions in American Christianity, but it does change how we interpret these divisions. In 1969 Schmidt observed that Protestantism was split "between those who see the church's task as the transformation of society, and those who see its mission as individual salvation; in brief, between the advocates of social Christianity and the spokespersons for individualistic evangelicalism" (Schmidt 1991, xxxv). Evangelicalism is still largely individualistic, but it can no longer be generalized as disinterested in social change. There are, indeed, many churches that focus on evangelism to the exclusion of social concerns, but evangelistic churches are also included in the mix of churches that see their mission as the transformation of society.

It may be more accurate to speak of a three-way division in terms of how this mission is expressed: churches that view social change taking place *primarily* by improving people's socioeconomic environment (dominant social action); those that view social change taking place *primarily* through the "miracle motif" of spiritual regeneration (dominant evangelism); and those that pursue social change through a combination of these approaches (dual-focus and holistic). Illustrating these different approaches, Church of the Advocate sees itself as "champion of the poorest among us" by meeting needs and advocating on behalf of its community; New Covenant empowers individuals "to fulfill God's victorious and prosperous plan for their lives, their families and their community" through personal conversions; and Life in Christ seeks "to transform a community" by "proclaiming and demonstrating the love of God."

Another kind of division lies in the focus on systemic reform relative to compassionate relief. Is the purpose of social ministry to redistribute resources to the poor, or to challenge the structural causes of poverty, or both? The great majority of churches offers relief services to needy individuals, but a segment goes further to engage in ministries to develop communities at the institutional level or to confront political injustices. Moreover, some churches take a third way by focusing on personal development—neither endorsing the status quo nor confronting it directly, but empowering individuals to be agents of personal and community change. While a primarily evangelistic orientation may predispose a church to focus on individuals, a dominant social action orientation does not necessarily correspond with an emphasis on social justice.

Looking at this division reveals the changing social framework in which church-based social involvement has been studied and discussed. In the 1960s and 1970s, research on Christian social action tended to focus on churches' divisive positions on broad social issues, such as racism, welfare, and foreign policy (Johnson 1967; Rokeach 1969; Broughton 1978; Hoge, Perry, and Klever 1978). One effect of the movement toward devolution has been to shift the locus of social policy onto community-level concerns such as drug abuse, single parenthood, and affordable housing. From this perspective, churches tend to be unified by "a pragmatic ethic of compassionate outreach and service that informs congregational practices more than explicit ideology does" (Becker 1999, 219). Churches that see the world very differently can end up with ministries that look similar in practice. Equating social activism with particular ideological positions highlights political polarities while obscuring these more functional commonalities.

A third important division lies in the perceived relationship between social ministry and spiritual meanings. For some, the spiritual meaning of social ministry is primarily implicit; acts of compassion and justice represent a faithful response to God's will, an expression of devotion, and a tangible demonstration of God's love. Many in this group consider it inappropriate to seek to influence the beliefs of beneficiaries. As a Central Baptist member serving with the Interfaith Hospitality Network (IHN) put it, "We show our faith in God through our kindness to others. . . . We are very careful not to push people about anything concerning their faith." In faith-background or faith-affiliated programs like IHN, service shows the fruits of conversion. In contrast, faith-centered and faith-permeated programs hope for conversions as a fruit of service. Social action has additional meaning as an evangelistic instrument for providing spiritual nurture and attracting people to the faith. Joel Van Dyke of Bethel Temple summarized this perspective: "Social ministry to non-Christians is the vehicle through which the gospel can flow." This group may consider the ability to explicitly communicate the gospel as essential to the purpose and effectiveness of their ministry. Some religious providers take up a middle ground: while maintaining an underlying evangelistic intent, they adapt their religious integration strategy to situations that call for a more implicit approach. Without overtly sharing their faith, they focus on making themselves spiritually transparent and relationally available to the people they serve, hoping that beneficiaries will respond to this compassion by initiating spiritual conversations or responding to invitations to outside religious activities. All three groups enact their religious beliefs through social ministry, but they disagree over whether and how these beliefs ought to be expressed.

To discern these new paradigms, scholarship will have to acknowledge the ways that the dualistic model of evangelism and social ministry has been shaped by a focus on the white, middle-class church majority (Becker 1999; Day 2002). Moving toward a both/and perspective on the public role of congregations calls for a more inclusive vision. Our own analysis has been significantly influenced by our selection of case studies: some of the most active churches in a city and region of active churches (Cnaan 2002 and Cnaan, Boddie, and Yancey 2003). Nearly two-thirds of our churches are in minority inner-city communities. This is the population at the heart of the controversy over faith-based initiatives. Our sample is not representative of all congregations—or even necessarily of all churches that are active in community outreach—but it does provide a window into a segment of the faith community that has disproportionate significance to the larger society.

Conclusion: The Faith Factor and the Public Good

Sherri Heller, as Deputy Secretary of the Pennsylvania Department of Public Welfare, pointed to the faith factor in explaining the state's overtures toward collaboration with religious service providers:[9]

> We learned that no matter what laws you pass, no matter what deadlines you set, what does it really take for a young single mother to get up at 6:00 in the morning and put a toddler in a snow suit and stand at the bus, and go to an entry level job? The answer is they have to be inspired by something, by someone. For some people, it's a vision of a better future; for some people, it's caring about their children's future; for some people, it's faith in God.

Her comments presume that religious groups have an efficacious spiritual *something* unmatched by secular approaches to aid. While charitable choice represents a new direction in public policy, the underlying ascription of instrumental social value to "faith in God" is not a new insight. As Alexis de Tocqueville observed in 1835, "I do not know if all Americans have faith in their religion—for who can read the secrets of the heart?—but I am sure that they think it necessary for the maintenance of republican institutions."

But with the interest in the public role of faith-based institutions comes the temptation to reduce churches to instruments of social work, to make religion a tool of social progress. Dean Trulear (1999, 25) warns against valuing religious organizations "more for what they can do than for what they essentially are. . . . Their outreach, their service delivery, their helping ministries flow from their very being as faith-based institutions." If public policy is to encourage the civic potential of the faith community, it must also accommodate the commitment to spiritual nurture that flows from the same source. Assessments of congregations' civic value must increasingly recognize their role in nurturing faith, instilling religious values, and fostering spiritual community alongside their role as providers of social services. Further, respect for the intrinsic value of religion, "even when not all religion is—at first glance—socially utilitarian" (Coleman 2001, 303), is necessary to guard against the subtle establishment of religious traditions that appear to have more civic utility than others.

Another danger is that public policy may exploit religion's social contributions to mask the deconstruction of public responsibility for society's most vulnerable. While faith communities may promote the values and civic habits that sustain political institutions, they bear this role in tension with their prophetic calling to hold these institutions accountable to transcendent standards of justice. The charitable work of religious institutions cannot substitute for government funding of the social safety net or for public policies that empower people to provide for themselves. The prophetic voice of the church must insist that government not abandon its proper role.

We close with a word to faith-based practitioners. One reason for the eruption of the fundamentalist-liberal divide is that conservatives neglected the challenge laid down by advocates of the social gospel to respond to the urgent cry of the poor, beyond basic charity. The growing radicalism of the social gospel followed, in part, the failure of evangelical churches to "awaken to their social task in time to lead and direct the social movement already under way" (Schmidt 1991, 107). For its part, the social gospel movement failed to heed the warning of one of its own advocates, Josiah Strong, that "if the pendulum should now swing to the other extreme," liberal churches could lose their center by emphasizing love of neighbor over love of God (quoted in Schmidt 1991, 104). The liberal shift in focus from individual to social salvation helped to provoke conservatives' withdrawal into the realm of soul-winning.

A confluence of theological, social, and cultural factors appear to be giving churches today a second chance. Mainline churches are experiencing, by some accounts, a resurgence of personal spirituality; many evangelicals appear to be reclaiming their social responsibilities. Yet each strand of American public religion retains its particular cultural voice. Evangelical social ministry does not look the same as activism in the mainline tradition. And when theologically moderate and liberal churches share the gospel, the message and their manner of sharing it is distinct from the evangelism of conservative churches. Churches that find a way to blend the best of both traditions—saving souls and serving society—in the context of their own unique legacy offer the best hope for maintaining the integrity and dynamism of the faith community in an era of government by proxy. Such churches share the good news of Christ in both word and deed. They bring their spiritual and social resources to bear on the urgent needs of individuals while at the same time seeking to establish the justice of God's kingdom. If this both/and mission paradigm took widespread root it could radically alter the course of American Christianity.

The greatest challenge to this vision is represented not by either/or polarities but by a neither-nor orientation—neither socially active nor evangelistically inclined. From almost a century ago, social gospel advocate Harry Ward again speaks to us today. Ward criticized both sides of the social gospel debate for doing less than they claimed: "The terms social service and evangelism are both overworked. One has long been and the other is fast becoming a house of refuge for the crowd that cry 'Lord, Lord, but do not the things that I say.' The shibboleth is shouted but the deed remains undone" (quoted in Schmidt 1991, 147). Let it not be said by future generations that we carried forward a debate about Christian mission while leaving words of good news unspoken and deeds of compassion and justice undone.

Appendix 1

Profiles of the Case-Study Churches

The following profiles list the social ministries sponsored by each church along with their mission statement or logo. Each church and pastor as well as several key informants signed a confidentiality waiver permitting us to share their name. Leaders who are no longer with the church at the time of this writing are marked with an asterisk. The profiles also indicate the name of the researcher assigned to each church. Most of our information about each case-study church comes from the researcher's field notes, recorded interviews, and summary reports.

BETHEL TEMPLE COMMUNITY BIBLE CHURCH (PHILADELPHIA)

Rev. Joel Van Dyke* and Rev. Luis Centeno* *(both left the pastorate to become missionaries)*
Researcher: Paula McCosh
"Discipling our members, evangelizing our community, and revitalizing our neighborhood in the name of Jesus Christ."
Ministries:

> Food/clothing pantry
> Christmas store (thrift)
> Summer Medical Institute (mobile clinic)
> Proclaimers of Hope (substance abuse recovery house)
> Youth center/youth recreation activities
> Youth Violence Reduction Coalition
> Summer camp
> After-school program
> God's Gym (handicap-accessible gym)
> Economic development initiative

School adoption
Arts and Media Center
Housing rehabilitation

CENTRAL BAPTIST CHURCH (WAYNE, PENN.)

Rev. Marcus Pomeroy and Rev. Marcia Bailey*
Researcher: Gaynor Yancey
"A Caring, Concerned, and Questioning Congregation."

Interfaith Hospitality Network
Global Residence (temporary housing for immigrant families)
English as a Second Language tutoring
Mainline Youth Alliance (services for homosexual youth)
Habitat for Humanity
Undoing Racism Mission Group
Ecology Mission Group
Economic Justice Group
Central Baptist Church Concerned (education and advocacy for homosexuals)

CHRISTIAN STRONGHOLD BAPTIST CHURCH (PHILADELPHIA)

Rev. Dr. Willie Richardson
Researcher: Averil Clarke
"Glorifying Christ, Amplifying the Bible, and Edifying People."

Food pantry
Health fair
Counseling
Youth self-esteem program
GED preparation
Literacy program
Youth tutoring
Summer camp
Creative World day care
Community development initiatives
Housing construction collaboratives
School adoption
Community newspaper
Community Action Council (lobbying activities)

CHURCH OF THE ADVOCATE (PHILADELPHIA)

Fr. Isaac Miller
Researcher: Averil Clarke
"An investment in the health, welfare, and spirit of our community."

Hot meal program
Food/clothing pantry
Staff social worker
Summer camp
LIFE (after-school program)
Grandparents As Parents (GAP) support group
Madeira Family Center
Art Sanctuary
Advocate Community Development Corporation
Philadelphia Interfaith Action (PIA)

COOKMAN UNITED METHODIST CHURCH (PHILADELPHIA)

Rev. Donna Jones
Researcher: Jill Witmer Sinha
"Christians Responding to Opportunities to Witness, Nurture, and Serve."

Community Family Dinner
Kid's Café
Food/clothing pantry
Life on Life's Terms (emergency housing)
Transitional Journey Ministry (welfare-to-work program)
Women's substance abuse recovery/post-prison transitional housing
Overcomers (substance abuse support group)

FAITH ASSEMBLY OF GOD (PHILADELPHIA)

Rev. Richard Smith
Researcher: Jill Witmer Sinha
"To live out the gospel in our community."

Food/clothing pantry
Hot lunch program
Flea market
Parenting support group
Men's recovery home
Women's recovery home
Youth Violence Reduction Coalition
Peacemakers
Safe Corridors (supervision of school routes)

FIRST PRESBYTERIAN CHURCH (MT. HOLLY, N.J.)

Rev. James H. Kraft* *(retired)*
Researcher: Averil Clarke
"Loved, Served, and Sent by Christ, We Share Life at Its Very Best!"

Community Luncheon
New Life Pregnancy Center
Interfaith Hospitality Network
Health services
Summer camp
First Focus (educational seminars)
The Well (counseling center)
Mall ministry (seminars and support groups)
Support groups
School partnership
Habitat for Humanity
Homes of Hope (low-income housing rental and rehabilitation)
Samuel Miller Christian Retirement Center
Mt. Holly 2000 (community development coalition)
Continuing the Dream (racial reconciliation collaborative)
Affordable Housing Coalition

GERMANTOWN CHURCH OF THE BRETHREN (PHILADELPHIA)

Rev. Richard Kyerematen
Researcher: Joan Hoppe-Spink
"To proclaim the Good News of our Lord and Savior Jesus Christ throughout the whole world, and more particularly to the residents of the city of Philadelphia; . . . To be a light of love, hope, peace and service in our homes, church, community, and world."

Outreach to homeless persons
Food pantry
Transitional housing
Germantown Ave. Crisis Ministry
Ministry to families of prisoners/Angel Tree
Summer camp
Germantown Ecumenical Ministries after-school program
Lafiya Family Counseling Services
Friday youth night/youth recreation activities
Jobs Partnership (job readiness, mentoring, and placement)
Christian Anti-Drug Dependency Coalition
South Mount Airy Task Force
Sunflowers Pre-School Program
Dignity Housing (low-income rental and rehabilitation)
Congregations Organized for Public Engagement (COPE)

KOINONIA CHRISTIAN COMMUNITY CHURCH (PHILADELPHIA)

Pastor Jerome Simmons
Researcher: Kesha Moore

"To fulfill the will of God for this ministry by letting our Christian light shine before men so they may see our good works and glorify our Father in heaven. (Matthew 5:16)"

  Thrift store
  Love Links (bulk food/clothing distribution)
  Hot meal program
  Food pantry
  Youth mentoring/recreation activities
  Overcomers/Christian Anti-Drug Dependency Coalition
  Jobs Partnership

LIFE IN CHRIST CATHEDRAL OF FAITH (CHESTER, PENN.)

Bishop Dickie Robbins
Researcher: Kesha Moore
"To reach our community and the world with the true message of the Gospel of Jesus Christ. We will not only proclaim the love God has for humanity, but we will demonstrate that love through a holistic approach to ministry."

  LIFE hot meal program
  Emergency housing
  Educational seminars
  Budget counseling
  Drug Free
  Community Economic Development Ministry
  Eagle's Nest Academy
  Affordable housing rental and rehabilitation
  Public boards/revitalization initiatives
  Political Involvement Ministry

MEDIA PRESBYTERIAN CHURCH (MEDIA, PENN.)

Rev. Bill Borror, Senior Pastor
Researcher: Paula McCosh
"Using time, talents, and treasures to embrace our world in the name of our Lord and Savior."

  Food cupboard
  City Team (meals for homeless persons)
  Sew 'n Sew (donation of items for shelters and other nonprofits)
  Carpenter's Club (housing rehabilitation)
  Second Time Around (support group for grandparents as parents)
  Summer camp/youth activities
  Tutoring with World Impact private school
  Support groups
  Housing rehabilitation (in partnership with Life in Christ)

Habitat for Humanity
Environmental Committee

NEW COVENANT CHURCH OF PHILADELPHIA

Bishop Milton Grannum
Researcher: Tim Nelson
"Touching Philadelphia and the World by Reaching and Empowering Individuals."

Men's health fair
Richard Allen Ministries (outreach to housing project residents)
Christians United Against Addictions
Covenant International Institute (business training)

IGLESIA LUTERANA NUEVA CREACIÓN/NEW CREATION LUTHERAN CHURCH (PHILADELPHIA)

Rev. Patrick Cabello Hansel
Luisa Cabello Hansel, associate pastor
Researcher: Paula McCosh
"Celebration, Transformation, Education, to All the Nations."

Food pantry
Immigration assistance
Summer camp
After-school program
Computer lab
Pre-Work program (job readiness for preteens)
Nutrition education
Youth basketball/youth recreation activities
School adoption
Community garden
Community beautification
Job developer
Philadelphia Interfaith Action (PIA)

TENTH MEMORIAL BAPTIST CHURCH (PHILADELPHIA)

Rev. William B. Moore
Researcher: Kesha Moore
"United in the belief of what Jesus Christ taught, covenanting to do what He commanded and cooperating with other like bodies in kingdom movements."

Food pantry
Youth basketball/youth recreation activities
Urban/suburban summer camp
GED program

Drug recovery program
Moore Manor (senior housing)
10th Memorial Community Development Corp. (housing construction)
Master Street 2000 (home-ownership promotion)
Economic development initiatives
School adoption/School-based Family Center
Civil rights activism (Urban League and PUSH)
Black Clergy (education and advocacy)

TENTH PRESBYTERIAN CHURCH (PHILADELPHIA)

Rev. Dr. James Montgomery Boice* *(deceased)*
Rev. Dr. Philip Ryken, Associate Minister
Dr. David Apple, director of mercy ministries
Researcher: Tim Nelson
"To all who are spiritually weary and seek rest; to all who mourn and long for comfort; to all who struggle and desire victory; to all who sin and need a Savior; . . . this church opens wide her doors and offers her welcome in the name of the Lord Jesus Christ."

Summer Medical Institute (mobile clinic)
Community Dinner
Alpha Pregnancy Center
Outreach to homeless persons
English as a Second Language tutoring/friendship partners
Divorced/single-parent support group
HOPE (AIDS ministry)
Advance youth tutoring

Appendix 2

Pastoral Interview Guide (excerpt)

The object of this interview is to talk about the church's outreach ministries and about the pastor's understanding of the relationship between the spiritual and social aspects of ministry.

The Church's Mission and Ministry

1. How would you describe this church's mission? Does the church have a mission statement?
   a. What is the church's role or mission in relation to this community?
   b. Which of the church's outreach ministries do you consider to be the most important, or the most central to the church's mission?
2. Considering overall the ministries of your church that reach out to the community:
   a. About how many people would you estimate have become Christians or been restored to active faith through the church's ministries over the last year?
   b. Can you give an example of someone who became a Christian through outreach?
3. How would you describe the overall impact or outcome of the church's outreach ministries on the community?
   a. How effective would you say your church's outreach efforts have been? By what method or standard do you evaluate effectiveness?
   b. Do you have specific goals for what you hope your outreach ministries will achieve?

4. On the questionnaire, you answered that your church gives a [higher priority to members OR outreach to non-members OR to both] Can you say anything more about why this is your priority? Has this always been the priority of the church throughout its history?

5. How does involvement in outreach affect the people who serve with the ministry?

   a. How does the church's involvement in outreach affect the congregation as a whole? What are the benefits and what are the drawbacks for the congregation?

6. Considering all your church's ministries that are aimed at trying to improve the quality of life of individuals or the community as a whole, would you say that, overall, your church emphasizes meeting people's needs through providing social services *(such as food, clothing, emergency shelter, etc.)*, participating in economic or community development *(such as job training, education, youth mentoring, health programs, day care, etc.)*, or working towards political change *(e.g., political action groups, community organizing, voter registration, etc.)*?

   a. Why does the church focus on this/these area(s) of ministry rather than the other(s)?

   b. What are the theological foundations for the way you approach social ministry? What biblical texts are important?

   c. Is the concept of social justice important to this church's ministry? What does this concept mean to you?

7. Have you ever addressed social or political issues in sermons or study groups? Which issues?

8. Do you receive any funding from the government for your ministries? From private foundations?

   a. What are the conditions, if any, under which you would accept government funding to support your community ministries?

9. Do you have a sense of the extent to which people in the church meet each other's needs, or the needs of people outside the church, on an informal, one-on-one basis, outside of the church's social ministry programs? What kinds of needs are met in this way?

   a. How do you motivate and train people in the church to meet the needs of others?

Evangelism

1. Different people and churches have different understandings of what *evangelism* means. How would you define evangelism?

   a. What does it mean to become a Christian? To be saved? *(If other specific terms are used, such as* witness *or* gospel, *ask for further definitions)*

   b. What are the theological foundations for your church's evangelism? What biblical texts are important?

   c. What are the various ways your church practices evangelism?

   d. How do you train people in the congregation to evangelize?

2. Do you think of becoming a Christian as a one-time decision, or as a more gradual process?

   a. In the cases you have witnessed, are the changes that result from becoming a Christian usually dramatic or subtle? Can you give an example?

3. How is God's love usually best shared—by telling someone verbally about the gospel, or by demonstrating God's love through caring actions, or both?

Relationship between evangelism and social ministry

1. Which should be the focus of Christian ministry: people's social and emotional well-being, such as the quality of their health, living conditions, family life, etc.; or people's spiritual well-being, the quality of their relationship with God; or both?

   a. *(If both are important:)* How are these concerns related?

2. On the questionnaire, you answered that, overall, your church gives [priority to evangelism OR to social ministries OR to both equally.] Can you say more about why this is your priority?

   a. Has this priority been about the same over the history of the church?

   b. Is the present amount and balance of evangelism and social ministries right for this church, in your opinion, or would you like to see more or less of one or the other?

   c. How much agreement is there in the congregation over what the church's priority should be in this area? Has this question ever caused any tension in the church?

3. Does the church actively and consciously seek to combine its work in evangelism and social ministry? How does this work in practice? Please give examples.

   a. Are there any social ministries that do not explicitly involve evangelism?

   b. *(If little or no integration:)* Do you believe that outreach to the needy should *not* be accompanied by trying to introduce people to Christianity? Why?

4. In a more general or theoretical sense, how would you describe the relationship between evangelism and social ministry—between sharing the gospel message, and helping people improve their social situation?

   a. In what ways are these two aspects of ministry related, and how are they distinct? Are they ever in conflict?

   b. Are there other churches or programs that you look to as models for this relationship?

   c. What is the theological or biblical basis for your understanding of the relationship between evangelism and social ministry?

5. How does your [denominational AND/OR ethnic] heritage influence your church's approach to outreach?

   a. Are there any factors in the community that influence your church's approach to outreach?

6. What do you see as the connection between salvation and social empowerment or improvement in a person's living situation?

    a. How would you describe the relationship between a person's spiritual commitment, lifestyle choices, and socioeconomic well-being?

    b. To what extent do poverty and other social problems reflect a spiritual need?

7. What are the key factors that are needed to help a poor person to become economically stable?

    a. If someone becomes a Christian and is a faithful disciple, what is the likelihood that their social status will improve? Or is it likely that they might stay poor?

    b. Is it possible for someone who is not a Christian to experience empowerment?

8. If a non-Christian who has a basic need wants to be helped through the church, but is not interested in hearing the message of the gospel or getting involved in the church, how would you respond or encourage members of the church to respond? Should the church continue to provide them with help?

9. When you think of people who now live changed, better lives because of the work of your church, what do you think it is that is responsible for this long-term change? What are the factors that help this to happen?

    a. Can you tell me about one or two people who have experienced significant life changes through the ministry of the church?

10. What is it that distinguishes your social programs from similar secular programs? Could a secular agency providing the same services as you do, without the spiritual dimension, be as effective as your ministries, and why?

11. Can you think of changes for the better in the community or in society in general that the church may have had some part in helping to bring about?

    a. What do you consider the agents or factors most responsible for this change?

12. What are the main obstacles to your church's ministry in the community? Is there anything that you think the church needs that would help your ministries to be more effective?

Notes

1. Pastors and several key informants gave us permission to use their real, full names. All first names given without surnames are pseudonyms.

2. Here we use the more inclusive terms *congregations*. Later, in reference to our research, we narrow our terminology to speak of *churches*, since our study was limited to Protestant churches. Some of the analysis, however, may transfer to other faith traditions.

3. Four major national congregational surveys—the Independent Sector study (Hodgkinson and Weitzman 1993; Saxon-Harrold et al. 2000), the National Congregations Study (Chaves 1999), the Organizing Religious Work Project (Ammerman 2001), and the Faith Communities Today (FACT) Study (Roozen and Dudley 2001)—paint complementary portraits of congregations' ministry priorities and charitable activities. Alongside these national surveys are many regional and local studies examining congregational civic involvement, including the seminal *Varieties of Religious Presence* which analyzed congregations in Hartford, Conn. (Roozen, McKinney, and Carroll 1984); analysis of the use of space among of Chicago congregations by the Community Workshop on Economic Development (1991); Wineburg's longitudinal research in Greensboro, N.C. (1992, 1994); Ammerman's study of twenty-three congregations in nine communities undergoing significant change (1997); the Urban Institute's survey of D.C. congregations (Printz 1998); a report on congregational social services in Indiana (Polis Center 2001); Stone's appraisal of congregation-sponsored services in Minnesota (2000); Amato-von Hemert's examination of rural church responses to poverty (2000); a capacity study of congregations in California (Anderson, Orr, and Silverman 2000); Wuthnow's portrait of congregational linkages with nonprofits in Lehigh Valley, Penn. (2000); Bartkowski and Regis's studies of the relief efforts of congregations in Mississippi (2001);

McRoberts's analysis of congregations in Four Corners, a Boston neighborhood (2003); a census of the community-serving activities of Philadelphia congregations (Cnaan and Boddie 2001), and a seven-city study of congregational activity (Cnaan et al. 2002).

Other sectors of the "big picture" of congregation-based social activism have been illuminated in greater detail by denominational studies, such as the Presbyterian Panel (1997) and a United Methodist church survey (Grettenberger 2001), and by studies focusing on congregations from particular racial or ethnic groups, such as black churches (Lincoln and Mamiya 1990; Ward et al. 1994; Jackson et al. 1997; Billingsley 1999; ITC 2000), Hispanic Protestant churches (Maldonado 1999; Mata 1999; Sherman 2003), and immigrant congregations (Warner and Wittner 1998).

Studies (such as our own) focusing on congregations that are active in community ministry, while having limited generalizability, highlight the unique attributes of particular forms of faith-based social outreach. These include the Church and Community Project involving 111 churches in the process of developing social ministries (Dudley and Van Eck 1992), Sherman's research on congregations involved in welfare-to-work partnerships (2000 and 2002), Harper's investigation of twenty-eight churches doing model community development work around the country (1999), and Day's case studies of ten African American Philadelphia churches engaged in economic development (2002).

For helpful bibliographies, see Scott (2002), Johnson (2002), Admiraal and Vander Kooi (2000), and Harvard Divinity School (1999).

4. The difference in range may be attributed to the sampling methods and to differing definitions of social ministries. The lower figure comes from the National Congregations Study, which used hypernetwork sampling. This method, Chaves asserts, corrects a bias toward larger, urban congregations in traditional sampling methodologies that leads to an overestimation of congregational participation in formal social service activities, since larger congregations are more likely to sponsor projects. This is evident in the NCS data: While only 57% of congregations in the NCS sponsored social service activities, 75% of respondents attended a congregation that sponsored such activities. NCS also used a stricter definition of what qualified as a social ministry.

5. Cnaan (et al. 2002) notes that this figure does not include salaries for church staff that oversee programs, utility costs for building space dedicated to social programs, and other indirect expenditures. Taking all related expenses into account, the congregations in Cnaan's seven-city study spent an average of 22.6% of their budget on social ministry.

6. The broader picture of faith-based activism—including the work of denominations, ecumenical coalitions, local nonprofits, and national service networks—complements this portrait of congregation-based social ministry (see Cnaan and Milofsky 1997; Wolpert 1997; Cnaan, Wineburg, and Boddie 1999; Pipes and Ebaugh 2002; Seley and Wolpert 2003; Wuthnow 2004). Castelli and McCarthy (1998) estimate that this broader organizational field expends between $15 and $20 billion in private funds per year on social services. Much of this faith-based activity is linked to congregations in some way, such as through their initial charter, formal affiliation, funding, volun-

teers, referral networks, etc. (Twombly and De Vita 1998; Wuthnow 2000; Ammerman 2001).

7. Sources on the social contributions of African American churches include Jones (1982); Sawyer (1988); Lincoln and Mamiya (1990); Lincoln (1994); Ward et al. (1994); Billingsley and Caldwell (1994); Kostarelos (1995); Franklin (1997); Loury (1997); Milsap and Taylor (1998); Billingsley (1998); DiIulio (1998); and Harris (2001).

8. The literature on the charitable involvement of church members is considerable. Helpful sources include Wuthnow, Hodgkinson, and associates (1990); Wuthnow (1991); Cnaan, Kasternakis, and Wineburg (1993); Wald, Kellstedt, and Leege (1993); Verba, Schlozman, and Brady (1995); Jackson et al. (1995); Chambré (1997); Greeley (1997a and b); Hoge et al. (1998); Park and Smith (2000); Becker and Dhingra (2001); Cnaan (2002); Smidt (2003); and Wuthnow (1991, 2004).

9. For more on the value of congregations as sources of mutual aid, see Taylor and Chatters (1988); Maton (1989); Ellison and George (1994); Milsap and Taylor (1998); Bell and Bell (1999); Ellor, Netting, and Thibault (1999); Krause et al. (2001); and Wuthnow (2004).

10. For a critical analysis of the assumptions underlying devolution and remoralization, see Skocpol and Fiorina (1999); Bane, Coffin, and Thiemann (2000); McConkey and Lawler (2001); Wineburg (2001); Farnsley (2003); and Chaves (2004).

11. While charitable choice originally applied only to federal funds in the Temporary Assistance to Needy Families (TANF) program, several other legislative initiatives subsequently adopted variations of the language of the 1996 provision. Many now use the term charitable choice to mean the concept of government funding for faith-based social service programs more broadly.

12. We use the word *ostensibly* because Monsma (1996) shows that the situation in practice was actually rather more complex. Application of the "pervasively sectarian" standard lacked clarity and consistency. For example, Monsma documented that two-thirds of the child welfare agencies ranked most religious on his survey received some public funding, and that faith-based child welfare agencies had greater freedom in incorporating religious components than religious schools working with the same population.

13. For more information on faith-based initiatives, see the Web sites:

http://www.whitehouse.gov/government/fbci
http://www.religionandsocialpolicy.org
http://cpjustice.org/charitablechoice
http://www.financeprojectinfo.org/FCBO/index2.asp

14. For an overview of the conflict and movement toward common ground, see the two reports issued by the Working Group on Human Needs and Faith-Based and Community Initiatives (2002 and 2003), and the document "In Good Faith" (Breger et al. 2001). See also the following helpful analyses: Davis and Hankins (1999); Dionne and Chen (2001); McConkey and Lawler (2001); and Walsh (2001). Montiel (2003) provides a review of the literature.

15. We support faith-based initiatives in principle, and, in fact, have been calling for expanded church-state cooperation in the human service arena since before charitable choice (see Sider and Rolland 1996). However, we object to some aspects of how

these initiatives have played out in the larger political context, particularly in conjunction with deep cuts in social service spending at the federal and state levels. See two editorials by Ron Sider: "At a Time of Growing Poverty, New Tax Cut Plan Is an Outrage," *Philadelphia Inquirer* (12 February 2003, A23); and "Compassionate Conservatism or Blatant Injustice? Evaluating the New Bush Tax Proposals," *PRISM* (March/April 2003, 36).

16. In contrast to the minimal aid to congregations, it is important to note that independent faith-based *nonprofits* (sometimes affiliated with congregations) received significantly higher levels of government funding even prior to charitable choice, as Monsma (1996) documents.

17. The extent of this impact is bounded by the fact that charitable choice and the directives of President Bush's faith-based initiative affect only *federal* funds, as they are distributed through five federal departments or channeled through the states. Some states have instituted their own version of charitable choice, expanding access to state resources; others have policies against funding religious groups. Counties and municipalities likewise vary in their willingness to collaborate with faith-based organizations.

18. Among the fifteen churches profiled in our study, one (Cookman United Methodist Church) had a state contract for welfare-to-work services. (Cookman was, in fact, the first church in the state of Pennsylvania—and one of the first in the country—to receive direct government funds under charitable choice. See Sinha 2000 and Unruh and Sinha 2005 for a more detailed description of the program.) Six churches (Advocate, Faith Assembly of God, Germantown Church of the Brethren, Koinonia, Nueva Creación, and Tenth Memorial) sponsored food programs that operated with city or state support. Separately incorporated nonprofits (primarily associated with services for children and housing) founded by five of the churches (Advocate, First Presbyterian, Germantown Church of the Brethren, Nueva Creación, and Tenth Memorial) received public funding of some sort. Three churches were actively seeking public funding at the time of the study (the City of Philadelphia had actually approved a grant for Germantown Church of the Brethren's substance abuse ministry, but ran out of funds before it was disbursed). Pastors from these churches attended seminars and requested information from the state on public funding, and submitted or planned to submit grant applications.

A majority of the churches we studied also cooperated with governmental entities in more indirect ways. Christian Stronghold's day care accepted state subsidies for low-income children; Bethel Temple's staff participated in the police-clergy ridearound program; Bishop Dickie Robbins of Life in Christ served on the board of the Chester Educational Foundation, which administered funding from the state for a major economic development initiative; the University of Pennsylvania co-sponsored a Men's Health Program at New Covenant; two churches participated in planning meetings for the Youth Violence Reduction Partnership (YVRP), a project sponsored by a secular nonprofit in collaboration with the City of Philadelphia; and six churches "adopted" local schools, providing support services to students and making their facilities available for school needs.

19. Our investigation of church-based outreach follows Bartkowski and Regis (2003, 191) in taking an *emic* rather than *etic* approach, emphasizing the perspective of faith-based practitioners on their activities:

In anthroplogical parlance, etic accounts are imposed on cultural groups by outsiders. They are often ethnocentric inasmuch as they show an insensitivity to the stated motivations of the persons whose life experiences are scrutinized by social scientists. Emic accounts take seriously the vocabularies that actors themselves use to describe their own social practices and underlying motivations. The account we provide engages the stated motivations of religious leaders and benevolence workers, while striving to relate their experiences to the theoretical perspectives.

For this study, we were "insiders" both in the sense of sharing the Christian faith and commitment to social activism of the churches we studied, as well as in taking church members' worldviews at face value rather than looking for underlying explanations. By letting these worldviews speak for themselves, we hope to bring them into dialogue with theories of religion and public life. (See also Becker and Eiesland 1997.)

CHAPTER 2

1. For various reasons, only one of these five—Church of the Advocate—became a case study. For a more detailed description of the study's methods, see the Web site http://hirr.hartsem.edu/research/research_churchoutreachindex.html.

2. Just how remarkable Philadelphia's tradition of church-based social service is depends on where you look. Studies of some major cities such as Washington, D.C. (Printz 1998) and Chicago (Community Workshop on Economic Development 1991) show comparable levels of congregational activity, but other cities like Indianapolis and Mobile (Cnaan et al. 2002) seem to have notably lower involvement.

3. The Philadelphia census gathered data from key informants at 1,376 congregations, out of a master list of 2,095 congregations generated through intensive detective work. While the study's sampling methodology was not representative, statistical analyses of interim data at several points indicate that the unreported congregations would only marginally change the results (Cnaan and Boddie 2001). It should be noted that their survey included all congregations, not only Christian churches.

4. The number of programs reported by Cnaan and Boddie is likely an underestimate, since the census only recorded information on the first five programs. Their criteria for defining social programs counted any "organized activity to help people in need" that is recognized by the congregation with a name and an identity, exists beyond a one-time response, and is open to the community (2001).

5. In addition to the initial questionnaire sent to the pastor, congregational surveys generated a total of 2,044 usable surveys from fourteen of the fifteen case-study congregations. We were unable to implement the survey at Cookman, but the congregation was small enough to allow us to extrapolate the basic demographic information. For more information on the survey, see http://hirr.hartsem.edu/research/research_churchoutreachindex.html and http://network935.org/resources/pdfs/cq.pdf.

6. Congregational response patterns on similar survey questions for the most part followed the pastor's appraisal, with a few exceptions. In these, members were more conservative than the pastor.

7. It is also helpful to compare these case-study churches with our larger sample of churches in the Philadelphia area with a reputation for activism, from which these

cases were drawn. Based on analysis of the first 70 surveys returned from this list of 126 churches, the main denominational affiliations in our referential sample were Baptists (27%), Presbyterians (20%), and Episcopalians (9%), along with independents (18%). (Baptists and Presbyterians may have been over-represented due to our project's affiliation with Eastern Seminary, which has ties to both denominations.) Referred churches were located mainly in the inner city (29 churches, or 41%); about a fourth of the churches were in other urban locations, and a fifth were in the Philadelphia suburbs. The major ethnicity (37%) of the responding churches was African American; 27% were predominantly Anglo; 13% were predominantly Hispanic or mixed Hispanic/Anglo. Church size was distributed fairly evenly across the spectrum. Nearly 40% identified themselves as community churches, with most members living in the surrounding neighborhood; less than 10% were commuter churches. Theological moderates and conservatives dominated among responding churches, again potentially reflecting the study's sponsorship.

8. We acknowledge that *social action* has connotations for some of politically oriented ministry, but we use it in the broader sense of organized action with intended social impact.

9. In many cases, we discovered that a particular ministry was "on hold" or was "in the works," even though it was cited as a program on church documents or on our initial survey. We counted ministries only if we saw evidence of actual activity.

10. All of the churches were generous in responding to informal requests for emergency assistance. We did count emergency aid ministries when the church carried them out in a regular, organized manner with assigned staff. For more information on how ministries were counted, see http://hirr.hartsem.edu/research/research _churchoutreachindex.html.

11. Admittedly, the task of classification involves an element of subjectivity. Some programs fall into two or more categories. Pregnancy centers, for example, meet one-time urgent needs such as for pregnancy tests and baby supplies (relief services), but they also often provide counseling and education (personal development). Here we have opted to classify pregnancy centers as relief services, as their main purpose is oriented toward individuals with a particular short-term need. As another example, Bethel Temple's Arts and Media Center trains youth in marketable graphic arts and music production skills (personal development), but it also serves as an economic development initiative, bringing capital and entrepreneurial opportunities into a depressed neighborhood (community development). Based on our knowledge of the program and the church's intentions, we have included it under the latter category.

Classifying programs for youth is particularly difficult, because youth work almost by definition has a developmental quality to it (personal development) but also often involves the establishment of institutions such as day care centers or recreational facilities (community development). To place a program, we asked: Is the primary goal to guide, mentor, empower, transform, or enhance the skills of youth, or does the program exist to fill an institutional gap or provide a basic service necessary for the health of the general community (such as child care or education)? In many cases after-school and summer camp programs exist to serve the needs of working parents as much as their children. However, we classified these programs along with recreational and tutoring services as personal development. We classified private schools and day care programs, because of their more institutionalized nature, as community development.

12. While we believe the same four categories of social action would extend to all types of faith-based organizations, the patterns of distribution may be different for congregations than other FBOs.

13. Our count of sanctuary evangelism programs does not include altar calls or other evangelistic components of regular worship services, but only special Bible studies or church services that are designed to include spiritual "seekers." Also uncounted (though important) was small group outreach. Four of the churches (Bethel Temple, Christian Stronghold, New Covenant, and Tenth Presbyterian) had or were launching cell groups with evangelistic overtones.

14. Although some of the churches described visitation outreach to nursing homes, prisoners, and other needy populations as social ministry, we counted them only as evangelism because of the primarily spiritual nature of these activities.

CHAPTER 3

1. Elsewhere in the book we use past tense to describe the churches and their ministries, reflecting the fact that our research captured the churches at a set time frame and many of the details of their situation have since changed (including the relocation of some pastors and key informants). In this chapter we bring their stories into present tense to give them more immediacy.

2. In the independent Pentecostal church tradition, it is not unusual for the founding pastor to be titled Bishop, with their wives given the honorary title of Lady. Most of the congregants at Life in Christ refer to their pastor simply as "Bishop," out of both respect and affection.

3. Unfortunately, the school closed within a few years from financial pressures.

4. For the story of another Presbyterian church that resisted relocation to serve its urban context, see *Downtown Church: The Heart of the City* (Edington 1996; see also Bakke and Roberts 1998).

5. Not all ACTS ministries are counted as social programs for the purpose of our study. The nursing home visitation and worship service for people with HIV/AIDS are counted as evangelism; the racial reconciliation group primarily attracts members of Tenth Presbyterian, and thus does not fall under our definition of outreach.

6. Unlike Tenth Presbyterian, Media and First Presbyterian belong to the Presbyterian Church U.S.A., which is considered a mainline denomination. Tenth Presbyterian withdrew from the Presbyterian Church U.S.A. in the 1970s over theological controversies, including the ordination of women, and joined the newly formed Presbyterian Church in America (PCA). Tenth Presbyterian continues to uphold its legacy of staunch adherence to traditional Calvinist theology and opposition to any theologically liberalizing influence.

7. Since the end of the research project, which Bishop Grannum called a "transforming experience," New Covenant has significantly expanded its social involvement. New ventures include supporting a ministry to battered and addicted women, building a senior housing complex on the church campus, adopting several public schools,

mentoring children of prisoners through the Amachi program, providing financial counseling, and launching a youth job training program.

CHAPTER 4

1. From this definition, it is clear that one may take a broad view of faith which embraces anything that gives one a sense of meaning—an indeterminate higher power, a general ideal of love, even one's own best self (as in the famous example of "Sheilaism" described by Bellah et al. 1985). In our analysis we are concerned with meaning that is grounded in the existence of a supernatural being, and more specifically the Christian deity, who—according to Christian doctrine—relates personally to humans. A broader view of faith might expand the range of meanings but would not shed as much light on the churches in our range of vision.

2. Admittedly, these four themes do not exhaust the religious meanings available to volunteers (especially to those outside the Protestant Christian tradition), much less the broader range of meanings that are not specifically religious. We acknowledge our indebtedness to others who have elucidated the motives and meanings behind Christian charitable work, particularly Clydesdale (1990), Davidson, Johnson and Mock (1990), Wuthnow (1991), Hart (1992), C. Smith (1996), Jeavons (1994 and 1998), Cnaan et al. (2002), and Hugen et al. (2003).

3. Jim McDonald, "Life Transformed," in the April 2004 newsletter *Bread*.

CHAPTER 5

1. This chapter is adapted from its original publication as a journal article: Heidi Rolland Unruh, "Religious Elements of Church-Based Social Service Programs," *Review of Religious Research* 45 (4):317–335. June 2004. © Religious Research Association, Inc. All rights reserved.

2. It is important to note that there is no single interfaith canon of activities that may be considered specifically religious. Since our study draws on Protestant Christianity, not all of the elements identified here will apply to every religious tradition. However, future studies may identify a core set of elements that intersect with social service provision across various faiths (see Goggin and Orth 2002).

3. The first church-based program to receive state funding in Pennsylvania under Charitable Choice, Transitional Journey provided life skills training, GED instruction, computer classes, and job placement and follow-up services to about thirty women on welfare per year for the three years of the grant. It should be noted that all of the religious elements were privately funded. After the original state funding ended (and after the period of our case study), the program significantly changed its clientele and curriculum, though it retained a religious character.

4. This quote is from the transcript of an interview with Rev. Jones in a segment on Charitable Choice on the *Leher News Hour* television program, "Faith-Based Welfare," 11 November 1999.

5. This table and the discussion of integration strategies was originally published in Sider, Olson and Unruh (2002), with some subsequent modifications. The table also appeared in the Working Group reports (2002 and 2003) and Sider and Unruh (2004).

6. Because our analysis evolved over the course of our research, we lack consistent data across the case studies for an empirical validation of this model. We acknowledge the need for further testing, and point to studies such as Goggin and Orth (2002) and Ebaugh and Pipes (2003) as sound steps toward operationalizing religious elements. The role of ethnographic insight and inductive model-building such as ours in this ongoing, collaborative process of mapping unknown terrain is suggested by the classic work of Glaser and Strauss (1967: 23): "In generating theory it is not the act upon which we stand, but the *conceptual category* (or a *conceptual property* of the category) that was generated from it. . . . One generates conceptual categories over their properties from evidence; then the evidence from which the category emerged is used to illustrate the concept." See also Denzin and Lincoln (1994) and Corbin and Strauss (1998).

7. As an example of the influence of professional norms, the National Association of Social Workers 1996 *Code of Ethics* (naswdc.org/pubs/code/code.asp) emphasizes that social workers are to "promote the right of clients to self-determination," which precludes religious persuasion. Interaction outside the bounds of the social work contract carries "a risk of exploitation or potential harm to the client." Professional social work principles thus discourage integrated and relational evangelistic strategies, though they leave room for an implicit spirituality that refrains from passing religious judgments. (See Cnaan, Wineburg, and Boddie 1999.)

CHAPTER 6

1. This chapter is adapted from its original publication as a journal article: Ronald J. Sider and Heidi Rolland Unruh, "Typology of Religious Characteristics of Social Service and Educational Organizations and Programs," *Nonprofit and Voluntary Sector Quarterly* 33 (1): 109–134. © 2004 Association for Research on Nonprofit Organizations and Voluntary Action.

2. The Working Group on Human Needs and Faith-Based and Community Initiatives, initiated by Senator Santorum and originally chaired by former senator Harris Wofford, brought together leaders from religious, civic, and policy advocacy organizations with a diverse range of views on faith-based initiatives. Ron Sider participated in and in 2003 co-chaired this group. Through a series of monthly meetings, the group revised the typology of organizations and programs we had drafted, and included the typology in its two published reports (Working Group 2002 and 2003). The second report includes several revisions to the first published version that refined but did not change the basic categories. The revised version, with some additional modifications, is presented here.

3. Our literature review is indebted to Goggin and Orth (2002) and Scott (2002).

CHAPTER 7

1. The seminal work *Varieties of Religious Presence* (Roozen, McKinney, and Carroll 1984) identified four mission types: *sanctuary congregations* provide a refuge to members from the temptations and tempests of the world; *civic congregations* help members make moral decisions and participate responsibly in the social order; *activist congregations* challenge the status quo and work toward social justice; and *evangelistic*

congregations emphasize converting the unchurched (see also Carroll and Roozen 1990). Mock (1992) proposed a nine-celled typology based on the interaction between sanctuary-civic-activist orientations to society and evangelical-moderate-liberal religious identities. The five congregational self-images identified by Carl Dudley and Sally Johnson (1993) include *pillar churches* that assume civic leadership, *pilgrim churches* that shepherd a particular people group, *survivor churches* that weather storms of crisis, *prophet churches* that challenge the world, and *servant churches* that help people in need with a "quiet faithfulness." Nancy Ammerman (1997b) proposed sorting churches into evangelical, activist, and "Golden Rule" categories.

2. As defined in chapter 2, *spiritual nurture* includes any form of activity or discourse related to deepening a person's faith. *Evangelism* refers more specifically to efforts to connect people who do not consider themselves Christians, or who have become estranged from the church, with salvific faith and a church community.

3. It should be acknowledged that politically and theologically conservative congregations, which presumably are more prone to evangelize, are less likely to express an interest in applying for public funds than are liberal and moderate congregations (Chaves 1999). Often, such faith-permeated groups are included in media reports as examples of faith-based programs that do *not* plan to take advantage of charitable choice. However, that does not change the observation that evangelistic congregations with a significant (and mainly privately funded) investment in social ministry are not accounted for by traditional mission orientation categories.

4. For example, the index to a recent book on mainline faith-based activism (Wuthnow and Evans 2002) lacks any reference to evangelism or proselytizing.

5. Because all of our case studies had an active outreach orientation, we cannot say much about this group. However, we have encountered many inward-focused congregations through church consulting and networking.

6. Living entities, as we pointed out previously, rarely fit perfectly into ideal types. Some of the churches have a borderline or blended mission orientation, displaying characteristics from more than one type. Whether First Presbyterian Church should be considered a holistic or dual-focus church depends on which church members you talk to (we selected holistic because of the pastoral team's strong identification with this orientation). Tenth Presbyterian Church had staff and members whose views were closer to dominant evangelism. The director of mercy ministry, David Apple, has pushed the church toward a holistic approach. While some leaders at New Covenant describe having a holistic-instrumental approach, the actual ministries reflect a pattern of dominant (but this-worldly) evangelism. (Since the study ended, New Covenant has become holistic-instrumental in practice.) Bethel Temple has experienced a recent shift from dominant evangelism to a holistic-instrumental mission.

CHAPTER 8

1. Our analysis is indebted to the framework used by Nancy Ammerman (1997a) to analyze congregational responses to community change.

2. On the other hand, conservative Christians are as likely as liberal Christians, if not more, to volunteer for charitable activities or to be involved in political advocacy as individuals (C. Smith 1998; Regnerus and Smith 1998; Clydesdale 1990).

3. Assignment of theological orientation was based on survey questions.

Churches were identified as liberal if the pastor and majority of the congregation held that the Bible is not literally true, and that everyone or all true believers are saved. Moderates believed that the Bible is inspired but not literal, and that only the born-again are saved. Conservative theology was defined as holding a literal view of the Bible and a born-again understanding of salvation. This discussion uses *religious conservative* and *evangelical* interchangeably, even though these terms are not strictly synonymous. We also recognize that *liberal* is not the same as *mainline*, though mainline Protestants are typically more liberal leaning. Moreover, while this analysis focuses on the theological poles, we agree with Ammerman (1997b) that many, if not most, churches live somewhere in between, and that this middle ground represents not merely weak versions of liberal and conservative, but stands in its own unique religious tradition.

4. It should be noted that Catholic teaching rejects proselytizing altogether, describing it as "a manner of behaving contrary to the spirit of the Gospel, which makes use of dishonest methods to attract [persons] to a community—for example, by exploiting their ignorance and poverty" (cited in Wilson 2000, 3). Catholics detach social ministry from evangelistic purposes, following the principle that "actions of aid relief and assistance should be conducted in a spirit of service and free giving for the benefit of all persons without the ulterior motive of eventual tutelage or proselytism."

5. Clydesdale's (1999, 103) review of the evidence suggests "a weak to moderately positive relationship exists between conservative religion and support for the poor." African Americans, it should be noted, tend to show greater support for the poor regardless of theological tradition.

6. At Nueva Creación, for example, Rev. Cabello Hansel believes that everyone is in the process of being saved. He preaches faith in Christ as *a* way rather than *the* way to this salvation.

7. This assessment is further corroborated by Katie Day's (2002) analysis of African American churches in Philadelphia engaged in economic development. Her ten case studies (which overlapped with our own sample) included five churches involved with the community organizing coalition Philadelphia Interfaith Action and five that employed less confrontational, more individualistic strategies. She found "there were no discernible relationships leading from socio-economic status to conservative (or liberal) theology to conservative (or progressive) politics to affiliation with PIA" (189); in fact, members of churches affiliated with PI A believed more in spiritual conversion as strategy for social change than in non-PIA churches.

8. This now appears to be changing, at least in terms of the denominational leadership's attention to social concerns. The Spring 2004 issue of the Assembly of God's journal, *Enrichment,* was dedicated to compassion ministries, including articles by both of this book's authors (see http://enrichmentjournal.ag.org/200402/index .cfm).

9. This absence of social action markers in the culture of the congregation is particularly striking in Tenth Memorial's case, considering the church's well-known association with several major community development initiatives and its reputation in the neighborhood as a "symbol of caring," as one civic leader described it. Outside the congregation, Tenth Memorial is best known for its prophetic function; but within the congregation, priestly themes predominate (Lincoln and Mamiya 1990).

10. These theological and cultural influences on how churches perceive and

present their mission call into question the self-reported rates of social activity among some theologically conservative churches. Liberal churches tend to have a greater investment of their identity in their social action programs, and may therefore have a greater interest in reporting them; conservative churches may think of their outreach programs in terms of evangelism, and may not recognize or have an aversion to terms such as *social reform* or *social justice*. This was the case with Joel Van Dyke, whose initial reaction when asked to define the term *social ministry* was "humanistically-based things devoid of the gospel"—despite Bethel Temple's quite active involvement in what we call social ministries.

11. When asked whether he thought their church would still conduct street evangelism if it were located in a wealthier neighborhood, a ministry leader at Tenth Memorial Baptist Church responded: "There might be a need [for street evangelism], but I don't think you will have a Bill Gates that would stand on a street corner. So the environment helps to shape in a sense what we do."

12. Sources for this section include T. Smith (1957); Moberg (1972); Hengel (1974); Dayton (1976); Marsden (1980); Marty (1980); Bremner (1988); Clydesdale (1990); Schmidt (1991); Jeavons (1994); Strong (1997); C. Smith (1998); Ellor, Netting, and Thibault (1999); Hall (2001); Thuesen (2002); and Wuthnow and Evans (2002).

13. Not all evangelicals adopted this abolitionist stance. In slaveholding states, many agreed with the retreatist position of theologian John Holt Rice that "it never has fared well with either church or state, when the church meddled with temporal affairs" and that the role of the church was to "go on minding [its] own business, and endeavoring to make as many good Christians as possible among masters and servants" (quoted in Strong 1997, xxvi).

14. Walter Rauschenbusch led the way in challenging an exclusively other-worldly understanding of salvation by asking, "If we are converted, what are we converted to?" He asserted, "Salvation must be a change which turns a man from self to God and humanity. . . . A salvation confined to the soul and its personal interests is an imperfect and only partly effective salvation" (quoted in Strong 1997: xxxiii). He also extended salvation to include social structures: "It is not enough to Christianize individuals; we must Christianize societies, organizations, nations, for they too have a life of their own" (quoted in Wood 1990, 167).

15. Dennis Hollinger (1983) documented *Christianity Today*'s role in calling evangelical attention to social and political issues in the last half of the twentieth century. He found, for example, that in a sampling of five years of the magazine drawn from the period of 1958 to 1976, 141 articles dealt with social issues compared to twenty-five on personal moral themes.

16. Fundamentalism's self-imposed isolation from the political arena changed dramatically when Jerry Falwell launched the Moral Majority in 1979–1980.

17. In the book *Compassion Evangelism*, Thomas Nees (1996) documents this change within one conservative denomination, the Church of the Nazarene. "Until very recently, compassionate ministries needed an explanation if not a defense. Now it is the reverse. Nazarenes expect the church to respond to the poor and the needy" (63). Only a handful of denominationally sponsored "compassionate ministry centers" existed in the mid-1980s, when the denomination began to respond to a growing interest in social ministry from local churches. By 1996, the number of nonprofit cen-

ters had jumped to eighty-five, and the national office additionally recognized nearly 400 "Good Samaritan churches," or congregations that were responding to needs in the community. (See also the chapter on the Nazarenes in Davidson, Johnson, and Mock 1990).

18. The mission trajectory of Hispanic churches, with their diverse national origins, is also influenced by but distinct from Anglo religious history. Unfortunately we cannot do justice to a full description of missional emphases in Hispanic religious traditions (see Aponte 1998; Maldonado 1999; Mata 1999; Cnaan, Hernandez, and McGrew 2003; Espinosa, Elizondo, and Miranda 2003).

CHAPTER 9

1. Jill Witmer Sinha provided the field notes for this narrative.

2. Out of the twelve dual-focus and holistic churches in our study, eight are theologically conservative, and seven are denominationally evangelical or independent. As might be expected, the theologically liberal-leaning holistic congregation (Nueva Creación) was politically liberal as well, but not all the theologically conservative churches were also politically conservative (see Petersen and Takayama 1984; Dixon, Lowery, and Jones 1992). Tenth Memorial Baptist Church, like many African American congregations, is theologically conservative while oriented politically to the left; particular leaders at theologically conservative churches—like David Apple at Tenth Presbyterian and the director of community development at Bethel Temple—described their politics as left-leaning.

3. Unfortunately, this conviction does not always preclude evangelistic ministries from using manipulative or subtly coercive tactics to encourage conversions. For a discussion of proselytizing and coercion, see Sider and Unruh (2001).

4. Three of the holistic-complementary churches and all of the holistic-instrumental churches integrated mandatory religious elements in at least one of their ministries (typically in programs for children or substance abusers, or in food aid attached to a worship service). Only two of these programs discriminated against beneficiaries on the basis of personal faith: the residential addiction rehabilitation programs at Bethel Temple and Faith Assembly of God. The intensive religious approach of these programs screened out beneficiaries who were not Christians or willing to participate in spiritual activities. The purpose of Faith's Recovery Home, for example, was to enable recovering substance abusers to "maintain Christian life through the Bible as instruction for life," while a staff member with Bethel's Proclaimers of Hope described the rehabilitation program as "a one-step program, just new life in Christ."

5. This was observed in action one Sunday at Cookman United Methodist Church, when Rev. Donna Jones concluded the sermon, as she often did, with an altar call: "The doors of the church are open with an invitation to become a disciple by giving everything up. There is no greater joy." On this Sunday, one woman went forward. She happened to be a client in the church's welfare-to-work program who had responded to the invitation of program staff to attend church services, and was now responding to the call to personal faith. Rev. Jones prayed, "May she put her hand into your hand, may she put her heart into your heart."

6. One of the "new-breed" evangelicals that Hollinger documented is Ron Sider,

whose 1977 book *Rich Christians in an Age of Hunger* and other subsequent writings argued these points—thus putting us in the somewhat delicate position of describing a social context that the author participated in shaping.

7. Nueva Creación would have provided another helpful comparison, but unfortunately, their congregational survey generated insufficient responses to include their data. For more information on survey methodology, see http://hirr.hartsem.edu/research/research_churchoutreachindex.html.

8. It should be noted that the question did not identify *who* is the object of the church's care. It is likely that Central interpreted this in terms of caring for the social and spiritual well-being of the membership, rather than people outside the church. Nurturing a spiritually, socially, and emotionally supportive community is an important part of Central's mission.

9. As another example of the dominance of the individualistic social ethic, more Central Baptist respondents selected "showing compassion to individuals in need" as a very important motivation for outreach (67%) than "helping make society more just" (57%), even though Central sponsored more ministries of a structural nature than ministries targeting individuals.

10. This finding is in harmony with Clydesdale's observation that religious conservatives have a "dichotomous understanding of poverty in the world," which allows that some are poor "because of their own sin" and others are poor "because of the sin of others and/or the evil of this world" (1999, 114).

11. At Faith, 45% of respondents selected personal choices, while 35% said poverty was caused equally by personal and social factors. (However, with only twenty-three survey respondents, these results are not very reliable.) Aside from Faith, the shared tendency among the case study congregations to point to social causes of poverty alone, or social causes in combination with personal causes, could be a feature of their shared commitment to community outreach. It is possible that in this respect, churches that are focused outward have more in common with one another—regardless of whether that mission is expressed as social action and/or evangelism—than with congregations that are focused inward on member care.

12. Our status as evangelical "insiders" helped give us access to this behind-the-wall language. At one theologically conservative church, the pastor complained about a university-sponsored survey about social activism he had just completed because he did not think its questions were relevant to his church, despite the fact that they ran several social programs. He said he had a better rapport with our researcher who, as a seminary student, understood the way his church did things. We heard similar comments from other church leaders, implying that because the study was sponsored by a seminary and led by Christians, they could talk more freely about spiritual matters because they were more confident of being understood.

13. This quote is from the transcript of an interview with Phil Ryken in a segment on charitable choice in the television program *Religion and Ethics Newsweekly*, 6 April 2001.

14. This is supported by Green and Sherman's (2002) 15-state study of faith-based organizations that have received government contracts. Among "fully expressive" organizations (those with the highest level of religious integration), three-quarters are new to working with government. Evangelical groups and African American congregations represent the highest proportion of fully expressive organiza-

tions. Among all congregations with government contracts, 77% say spiritual transformation of clients is very or somewhat important.

CHAPTER 10

1. From a White House press release, 15 January 2004.

2. For our conceptualization we are indebted to Jeavons (1998), who organizes the faith dimension according to its role in the organization, including its influence on a program's selection of staff, sources of resources, products, and technologies.

3. In a Pew Forum (2002) survey, nearly three-quarters (72%) said that the care and compassion of religious practitioners is an important reason for supporting faith-based programs. A majority also cited the power of religion in changing people's lives (62%) and the superior efficiency of faith-based programs (60%) as reasons for supporting faith-based initiatives. This suggests that the assumptions held by many faith-based practitioners about the efficacy of their ministry are shared by most Americans.

4. "Keys to Personal and Professional Success" (Germantown, Md.: Jobs Partnership, Inc., 1998).

5. Interviewees in holistic churches exhibited mixed responses to the question of the relationship between personal and structural change. Some thought exclusively in terms of aiding individuals; many recognized the existence of structural injustice but thought that the way to challenge it was by changing individuals; others believed that churches should work on both fronts, the personal and the structural, simultaneously—though they had more hope for change at the personal level. While the relationship between individual- and structural-level change is too complex to parse here, it may be generalized that these ministry leaders see personal reform as *a* pathway to better social conditions, but disagree on whether it is *the* pathway.

6. For example, Rev. Jerome Simmons of Koinonia offered money to any youth in the church who brought him a good test score or homework paper from school, saying, "We need to reward our young people for excelling."

7. This attitude toward wealth, we should note, was by no means universally shared. At Christian Stronghold, for example, an associate pastor suggested that a way to evangelize students might be to have a church member with a good career speak to them and "give a testimony of how God has impacted his life to make him successful." A statement of beliefs printed in the bulletin at Life in Christ, read aloud by the congregation, included this affirmation: "I am meant to prosper and not be in poverty." Bishop Dickie Robbins sported a sharp wardrobe in order to model the rewards of faithful obedience to God.

8. At Life in Christ, for example, 65% said that bringing people to Christ was a very important reason for their outreach; in contrast, only 31% claimed bringing people to the church as potential members was a very important factor.

9. Wuthnow describes the effect of the norm of professional distance: "It is acceptable to be friendly and to express interest in clients' problems, but not acceptable to talk candidly with clients about why one became involved in caregiving and how that relates to one's deeper values" (2004, 264). He also suggests that beneficiaries may be less interested in the religious motives of caregivers than religious providers might hope. Wuthnow concludes that "faith-based organizations seem not to be any more effective than other service organizations in communicating ideas about faith in

general or about unconditional love in particular" (285; Chaves 2004 makes a similar point).

On the other hand, another volunteer from the same church related a story when the "ask-me" evangelism strategy did work out as intended. The resident of a trailer home asked the church volunteers who were building a ramp for his disabled wife, "Why would you want to do this?" One of the volunteers answered, "Because Christ directs us to." At first the resident had been resistant to anything having to do with religion, but by the end of the week of work, he allowed the volunteers to pray with him, and even prayed himself. "I never really knew what or who Christians were before," he was reported to have said, "but now I do." Wuthnow suggests that such results are more likely to follow from services associated directly with a congregation than those performed by a faith-based nonprofit.

CHAPTER 11

1. Although we focus on the social capital of churches in this chapter, most points apply to congregations more broadly as well.

2. Bartkowski and Regis (2003) point out the limits of the economic or rational choice framework to describe social capital in relation to religious life, in that it "lacks a language for analyzing moral motivations for social action" such as compassion and altruism (170). We borrow entrepreneurial language for this overview, without endorsing all the philosophical ramifications of rational choice theory.

3. For references, see chapter 1, note 8. However, while church attendance increases the likelihood of volunteering overall, there is evidence that attenders are less likely to volunteer for activities outside of the church (see Wilson and Janoski 1995; Park and Smith 2000; and Campbell and Yonish 2003).

4. Among the churches we surveyed, the likelihood of citing "showing thanks for what God has done for you" as an extremely important motivation for outreach increased among respondents who were actively involved in evangelism (measured by their acts of evangelism score) and who said seeking to bring others to Christ is an "essential" quality of the Christian life. A higher sense of belonging also correlates significantly with a higher acts of evangelism score.

5. Given the general resistance to associating with people with HIV/AIDS, as Grettenberger (2001) documents, Tenth Presbyterian is unusual in its willingness to reach out to this population over the objections of some members of the congregation. When transvestites from We the People showed up at the church for a Bible study, the question arose over which bathroom—men's or women's—they should use. Tenth Presbyterian ministry leader David Apple chuckled as he recalled assigning them a private bathroom: "That's not something you normally have to think about at church." He added that this is why he sees these programs as ministries, not only to the street people who attend, but also to the volunteers who are learning to love everyone unconditionally.

6. Note that we are talking here only about access to mutual aid, not about access to social service outreach programs; the great majority of the programs we studied were open to people regardless of their religious beliefs and behaviors.

7. At New Covenant, for example, believing that bringing others to faith is an essential quality of the good Christian life correlates with the belief that it is essential

for Christians to be a good citizen (Pearson's R = .351), and to care for the sick and needy (Pearson's R = .189). Both are significant at the .01 level.

CHAPTER 12

1. Although the state contract was made directly with the church, Cookman initially intended to establish Neighborhood Joy Ministries (including Transitional Journey) as a separately incorporated nonprofit. Later, Cookman decided not to pursue separate incorporation for its social ministries. Staff felt that keeping the welfare-to-work program officially under the church's wing would send a message to the congregation as well as to the community about the social mission of the church, as one program leader explained, "We wanted to make a statement. We wanted to let them know that the church still cares and is very much involved."

2. Monsma's (2002) study of welfare-to-work ministries in four cities found that the correlation between the religious characteristics of the organization and of the program ran counter to expectations: "The more holistic providers—those that integrate religious elements into their welfare-to-work programming—were *less* likely to be run by a congregation than by a separate agency, and the less integrally religious programs were slightly *more* likely to be run directly by a congregation" (11).

3. Section 104 of the Personal Responsibility and Work Opportunity Reconciliation Act of 1996, subsection (d).

4. See www.whitehouse.gov/government/fbci/guidance/partners/html for the federal guidelines (and Lupu and Tuttle 2002 for a critical analysis). The situation is complicated by the fact that laws concerning government-funded religious social service programs are still in transition, and different streams of federal funding—as well as state and local funding—are covered by different laws.

5. In 1987, the U.S. Supreme Court unanimously declared this provision constitutional. With one exception (*Dodge v. Salvation Army*, 1989), federal and state court decisions have ruled that this hiring right is not lost when a religious organization receives government funds.

6. For more on the authors' perspective on this question, see Sider (2002), Esbeck, Carlson-Thies, and Sider (2004), and Unruh and Sinha (2005).

7. The need for guidance is indicated by a "constitutional competence" survey by Kennedy and Bielefeld (2003), in which 70% of clergy in South Bend, Indiana, did not know that religious instruction or prayer could not be included in the social services funded by government. On the other hand, among congregations that contracted with government in Green and Sherman's 15-state study (2002), 84% agreed that prohibiting the use of public funds for inherently religious activities was very important or somewhat important. This suggests that once educated about the rules, the great majority of congregations that partner with government will be willing to abide by them.

8. This line of questioning can also draw on Wuthnow's (2004) description of service-provider and congregational models of social aid; Bartkowski and Regis's (2003) categories of intensive assistance, intermittent direct assistance, parachurch assistance, and distant missions; and Sherman's (2000) distinction between commodity-based and relational benevolence.

9. This quote is from the transcript of a segment on charitable choice on *The NewsHour with Jim Lehrer*, "Faith-Based Welfare," 11 November 1999.

References

Adams, Lawrence E. 2000. Christians and Public Culture in an Age of Ambivalence. *Christian Scholars Review* 30 (1):11–36.

Admiraal, Kristen, and Stacy Vander Kooi. 2000. *Coming Full Circle: Devolution of State Delivery of Human Services to Faith-Based Human Service Organizations: A Pilot Study*. Grand Rapids, Mich.: Calvin College.

Amato-von Hemert, Katherine. 2000. Between Imprisonment and Integrity: Rural Churches Respond to Poverty and Policy. *Social Work and Christianity* 27 (2):188–217.

Ammerman, Nancy. 1994. Telling Congregational Stories, *Review of Religious Research*, 35 (4):289–301.

———. 1997a. *Congregations and Community*. New Brunswick, N.J.: Rutgers University Press.

———. 1997b. Golden Rule Christianity. In *Lived Religion in America*, ed. David Hall, 196–216. Princeton, N.J.: Princeton University Press.

———. 1997c. Organized Religion in a Voluntaristic Society. *Sociology of Religion* 58 (3):203–15.

———. 2001. Doing Good in American Communities: Congregations and Service Organizations Working Together. Research report from the Organizing Religious Work Project, Hartford Institute for Religion Research. Hartford, Conn.: Hartford Seminary.

———. 2002. Connecting Mainline Protestant Churches with Public Life. In *The Quiet Hand of God: Faith-Based Activism and the Public Role of Mainline Protestantism*, ed. Robert Wuthnow and John H. Evans, 129–158. Berkeley and Los Angeles: University of California Press.

Ammerman, Nancy T., Jackson W. Carroll, Carl S. Dudley, and William McKinney, ed. 1998. *Studying Congregations: A New Handbook*. Nashville: Abingdon.

Anderson, Scott D., John Orr, and Carol Silverman. 2000. Can We Make Welfare Reform Work? The California Religious Community Capacity Study: Final Report. Sacramento, Calif.: California Council of Churches.

Aponte, Edwin. 1998. Latino Protestant Identity and Empowerment: Hispanic Religion, Community, Rhetoric and Action in a Philadelphia Case Study. PhD diss., Temple University.

Apple, David S. 1994. Wholistic Ministries at Tenth Presbyterian Church. Master's thesis, Eastern Baptist Theological Seminary.

Baer, Hans A. 1988. Black Mainstream Churches: Emancapitory or Accommodative Responses to Racism and Social Stratification in American Society? *Review of Religious Research* 30 (2):162–176.

Baggett, Jerome P. 2002. Congregations and Civil Society: A Double-Edged Connection. *Journal of Church and State* 44 (3):425–454.

Bakke, Ray, and Sam Roberts. 1998. *The Expanded Mission of City Center Churches.* Chicago: International Urban Associates.

Bane, Mary Jo, Brent Coffin, and Ronald Thiemann, eds. 2000. *Who Will Provide? The Changing Role of Religion in American Social Welfare.* Boulder, Colo.: Westview.

Barna, George. 1995. *Evangelism That Works: How to Reach Changing Generations with the Unchanging Gospel.* Ventura, Calif.: Regal.

Bartkowski, John P., and Helen A. Regis. 2001. Religious Civility, Civil Society, and Charitable Choice: Faith-Based Poverty Relief in the Post-Welfare Era. In *Faith, Morality, and Civil Society,* ed. Dale McConkey and Peter Lawler, 132–148. Lanham, Md.: Lexington.

———. 2003. *Charitable Choices: Religion, Race, and Poverty in the Post-Welfare Era.* New York: New York University Press.

Beck, Carolyn. 1990. Entrepreneurs in God's Economy: Christian Stronghold Baptist Church. *Urban Mission* 7 (5):7–19.

Becker, Penny Edgell. 1999. *Congregations in Conflict: Cultural Models of Local Religious Life* (Cambridge: Cambridge University Press).

Becker, Penny Edgell, and Pawan H. Dhingra. 2001. Religious Involvement and Volunteering: Implications for Civil Society. *Sociology of Religion* 62 (3):315–335.

Becker, Penny Edgell, and Nancy L. Eiesland. 1997. Developing Interpretations. In *Contemporary American Religion: An Ethnographic Reader,* ed. Penny Becker and Nancy Eiesland, 15–23. Walnut Creek, Calif.: AltaMira.

Bell, Tenolian R., Sr., and Janice Lester Bell. 1999. Help-Seeking in the Black Church: An Important Connection for Social Work to Make. *Social Work and Christianity* 26 (2):144–154.

Bellah, Robert N., Richard Madsen, William M. Sullivan, Ann Swidler, and Steven M. Tipton. 1985. *Habits of the Heart: Individualism and Commitment in American Life.* New York: Perennial Library.

Berger, Peter L. 1967. *The Sacred Canopy: Elements of a Sociological Theory of Religion.* Garden City, N.Y.: Doubleday.

Berrien, Jenny, Omar McRoberts, and Christopher Winship. 2000. Religion and the Boston Miracle: The Effect of Black Ministry on Youth Violence. In *Who Will Provide,* ed. Mary Jo Bane, Brent Coffin, and Ronald Thiemann, 266–285. Boulder, Col.: Westview.

Bicknese, Aaron. 1999. *The Teen Challenge Drug Treatment Program in Comparative Perspective*. PhD diss., Northwestern University.

Billingsley, Andrew. 1999. *Mighty Like a River: The Black Church and Social Reform*. New York: Oxford University Press.

Billingsley, Andrew, and C. H. Caldwell, 1994. The Social Relevance of the Contemporary Black Church. *National Journal of Sociology* 8:1–23.

Boddie, Stephanie C. 2003. Faith-Based Organizations and the Distribution of Social Responsibility: A Look at Black Congregations. Paper presented at the Spring 2003 meeting of The Roundtable on Religion and Social Welfare Policy, Washington, D.C.

Boris, Elizabeth T. 1998. Myths about the Nonprofit Sector. Center on Nonprofits and Philanthropy, Charting Civil Society Series Brief. Washington, D.C.: The Urban Institute.

Bradley, Don E. 1995. Religious Involvement and Social Resources: Evidence from the Data Set "Americans' Changing Lives." *Journal for the Scientific Study of Religion* 34 (2):259–267.

Breger, Marshall, Stanley Carlson-Thies, Robert A. Destro, Richard Foltin, Murray Friedman, Nancy Isserman, John A. Liekweg, Forest D. Montgomery, Melissa Rogers, Duane Shank, Julie Segal, Jeffrey Sinensky, Stephen Steinlight, Heidi Unruh. 2001. *In Good Faith: A Dialogue on Government Funding of Faith-Based Social Services*. Philadelphia: The Feinstein Center for American Jewish History.

Bremner, Robert H. 1988. *American Philanthropy*. 2nd ed. Chicago: University of Chicago Press.

Broughton, Walter. 1978. Religiosity and Opposition to Church Social Action: Test of the Weberian Hypothesis. *Review of Religious Research* 19:154–166.

Calhoun-Brown, Allison. 1998. While Marching to Zion: Otherworldliness and Racial Empowerment in the Black Community. *Journal for the Scientific Study of Religion* 37 (3):427–439.

Campbell, David E., and Steven J. Yonish. 2003. Religion and Volunteering in America. In *Religion as Social Capital*, ed. Corwin Smidt, 87–106. Waco, Tex.: Baylor University Press.

Canda, Edward R. 1998. Afterword: Linking Spirituality and Social Work: Five Themes for Innovation. *Social Thought* 18 (2):97–106.

Carroll, Jackson W., and David A. Roozen. 1990. Congregational Identities in the Presbyterian Church. *Review of Religious Research* 31:351–369.

Carter, Stephen. 1993. *The Culture of Disbelief: How American Law and Politics Trivialize Religious Devotion*. New York: Anchor.

Case, Anne C., and Lawrence F. Katz. 1991. The Company You Keep: The Effects of Family and Neighborhood on Disadvantaged Youths. NBER Working Paper 3705, National Bureau of Economic Research, Cambridge, Mass.

Castelli, Jim, and John D. McCarthy. 1998. Religion-Sponsored Social Services: The Not-so-independent Sector. Aspen Institute Nonprofit Sector Research Fund Report.

Chambré, Susan M. 1997. The Spirituality Factor: Exploring the Link between Volunteering and Faith. *Leadership* (April–June):19–21.

———. 2001. The Changing Nature of "Faith" in Faith-Based Organizations: Secularization and Ecumenicism in Four AIDS Organizations in New York City. *Social Service Review* 75 (3):435–455.

Chang, Patricia Mei Yin, David R. Williams, Ezra E. H. Griffith, and John Young. 1994. Church-Agency Relationships in the Black Community. *Nonprofit and Voluntary Sector Quarterly* 23 (2):91–105.

Chaves, Mark. 1999. Religious Congregations and Welfare Reform: Who Will Take Advantage of "Charitable Choice"? *American Sociological Review* 64:836–846.

———. 2001. Religious Congregations and Welfare Reform: Assessing the Potential. In *Can Charitable Choice Work?* ed. Andrew Walsh, 121–139. Hartford, Conn.: The Pew Program on Religion and the News Media.

———. 2004. *Congregations in America.* Cambridge: Harvard University Press.

Chaves, Mark, and Lynn M. Higgins. 1992. Comparing the Community Involvement of Black and White Congregations. *Journal for the Scientific Study of Religion* 31 (4):425–440.

Chaves, Mark, and William Tsitsos. 2001. Congregations and Social Services: What They Do, How They Do It, and With Whom. *Nonprofit and Voluntary Sector Quarterly* 30 (4):660–683.

Chong, Beryl, Dean Curtis, Ryan Hasler, and Christina Dicken. 2003. Some Worry Separation of Church and State Imperiled. *Springfield (Mo.) News-Leader,* 5 January.

Claman, Victor, and David Butler, with Jessica Boyatt. 1994. *Acting on Your Faith: Congregations Making a Difference: A Guide to Success in Service and Social Action.* Boston: Insights.

Clerkin, Richard, and Kirsten Grønbjerg. 2003. The Role of Congregations in Delivering Human Services. Paper presented at the meeting of the 2003 Spring Research Conference of The Roundtable on Religion and Social Welfare Policy.

Clydesdale, Timothy. 1990. Soul-Winning and Social Work: Giving and Caring in the Evangelical Tradition. In *Faith and Philanthropy in America: Exploring the Role of Religion in America's Voluntary Sector,* ed. Robert Wuthnow and Virginia A. Hodgkinson, 187–209. San Francisco: Jossey-Bass.

———. 1999. Toward Understanding the Role of Bible Beliefs and Higher Education in American Attitudes toward Eradicating Poverty, 1964–1996. *Journal for the Scientific Study of Religion* 38 (1):103–118.

Cnaan, Ram, and Carl Milofsky. 1997. Small Religious Nonprofits: A Neglected Topic. *Nonprofit and Voluntary Sector Quarterly.* Suppl. no. S3–S13.

Cnaan, Ram A., and Stephanie C. Boddie. 2001. Philadelphia Census of Congregations and Their Involvement in Social Service Delivery. *Social Service Review* 75 (4):559–580.

Cnaan, Ram A., Stephanie C. Boddie, Femida Handy, Gaynor Yancey, and Richard Schneider. 2002. *The Invisible Caring Hand: American Congregations and the Provision of Welfare.* New York: New York University Press.

Cnaan, Ram A., Stephanie C. Boddie, and Gaynor I. Yancey. 2003. Bowling Alone but Serving Together: The Congregational Norm of Community Involvement. In *Religionas Social Capital,* ed. Corwin Smidt, 19–31. Waco, Tex.: Baylor University Press.

Cnaan, Ram A., Edwin Hernandez, and Charlene C. McGrew. 2003. Latino Congregations in Philadelphia: Understanding the Organized Religion of Immigrants.

Emerson, Michael, and Christian Smith. 2001. *Divided by Faith*. New York: Oxford University Press.

Espinosa, G., V. Elizondo, and J. Miranda. 2003. Hispanic Churches in American Public Life: Summary of Findings. Interim report, vol. 2003–2. Institute of Latino Studies, Notre Dame University. South Bend, Indiana.

Esbeck, Carl H. 1997. A Constitutional Case for Governmental Cooperation with Faith-Based Social Service Providers. *Emory Law Journal* 46 (1):1–42.

Esbeck, Carl H., Stanley W. Carlson-Thies, and Ronald J. Sider. 2004. *The Freedom of Faith-Based Organizations to Staff on a Religious Basis*. Washington, D.C.: Center for Public Justice.

Evangelicals and the Poor: A Prism Forum. 1999. *Prism* 6 (6):6–9.

Fagan, Patrick F. 1996. Why Religion Matters: The Impact of Religious Practice on Social Stability. Washington, D.C.: The Heritage Foundation Backgrounder, no. 1064.

Farnsley, Arthur E., II. 2001. Can Faith-Based Organizations Compete? *Nonprofit and Voluntary Sector Quarterly* 30 (1):99–111.

———. 2003. *Rising Expectations: Urban Congregations, Welfare Reform, and Civic Life*. Bloomington, Indiana University Press.

Farris, Anne. 2005. President Reaffirms His Commitment to Faith-Based Initiative. Albany, N.Y.: The Roundtable on Religion and Social Welfare Policy. http://www .religionandsocialpolicy.org/news/article.cfm?id=2441.

Fine, Gary Alan. 1987. *With the Boys*. Chicago: University of Chicago Press.

Finke, Roger, and Rodney Stark. 1988. Religious Economies and Sacred Canopies: Religious Mobilization in American Cities. *American Sociological Review* 53:41–49.

Foley, Michael W., and Bob Edwards. 1997. Escape from Politics? Social Theory and the Social Capital Debate. *American Behavioral Scientist* 40 (5):550–561.

Foley, Michael W., John D. McCarthy, and Mark Chaves. 2001. Social Capital, Religious Institutions, and Poor Communities. In *Social Capital and Poor Communities*, ed. Susan Saegert, J. Phillip Thompson, and Mark R. Warren. Ford Foundation Series on Asset Building. New York: Russell Sage Foundation.

Forest, Jim. 1995. What I Learned about Justice from Dorothy Day. *Salt of the Earth* 15 (4):22–26.

Fowler, James W. 1991. *Weaving the New Creation: Stages of Faith and the Public Church*. San Francisco: HarperSanFrancisco.

Franklin, Robert M. 1996. "My Soul Says Yes": The Urban Ministry of the Church of God in Christ. In *Churches, Cities, and Human Community: Urban Ministry in the United States 1945–1985*, ed. Clifford Green, 77–96. Grand Rapids, Mich.: Eerdmans.

———. 1997. *Another Day's Journey: Black Churches Confronting the American Crisis*. Minneapolis: Fortress.

Freeman, Richard B. 1986. "Who Escapes? The Relation of Churchgoing and Other Background Factors to the Socioeconomic Performance of Black Male Youths from Inner-City Poverty Tracts." In *The Black Youth Employment Crisis*, ed. Richard B. Freeman and Harry J. Holzer. Chicago: University of Chicago Press.

Frenchak, David J. 1996. "Visionary Leadership in Launching Social Ministries." In *Next Steps in Community Ministry*, ed. Carl S. Dudley. Bethesda, Md.: Alban Institute.

Galloway, Paul. 1994. Spiritual Hunger Is All Over the News, But It's No Media Invention. *Chicago Tribune*, 9 December.

Garland, Diana S. Richmond, ed. 1992. *Church Social Work: Helping the Whole Person in the Context of the Church*. St. Davids, Pa.: North American Association of Christians in Social Work.

Garret, William Reace, ed. 1989. *Social Consequences of Religious Belief*. New York: Paragon House.

Glaser, Barney G., and Anselm L. Strauss. 1967. *Discovery of Grounded Theory: Strategies for Qualitative Research*. New York: Aldine de Gruyter.

Glenn, Charles L. 2000. *The Ambiguous Embrace: Government and Faith-Based Schools and Social Agencies*. Princeton: Princeton University Press.

Goggin, Malcolm L., and Deborah A. Orth. 2002. How Faith-Based and Secular Organizations Tackle Housing for the Homeless. Albany, N.Y.: The Roundtable on Religion and Social Welfare Policy.

Goldsmith, Stephen. 2002. *Putting Faith in Neighborhoods: Making Cities Work through Grassroots Citizenship*. Washington, D.C.: Hudson Institute.

Granovetter, Mark S. 1973. The Strength of Weak Ties. *American Journal of Sociology* 78:1360–1380.

Greeley, Andrew. 1997a. Coleman Revisited: Religious Structures as a Source of Social Capital. *American Behavioral Scientist* 40 (5):587–594.

———. May–June 1997b. The Other Civic America: Religion and Social Capital. *The American Prospect* 32:68–73.

Green, John C., and Amy L. Sherman. 2002. *Fruitful Collaborations: A Survey of Government-Funded Faith-Based Programs in 15 States*. Charlottesville, Va.: Hudson Institute.

Grettenberger, Susan. 2001. Churches as a Community Resource and Source of Funding for Human Services. Working Paper Series, Aspen Institute Nonprofit Sector Research Fund.

Griener, Gretchen M. 2000. Charitable Choice and Welfare Reform: Collaboration between State and Local Governments and Faith-Based Organizations. Issue Notes 4 (12), http://www.welfareinfo.org/issuenotecharitablechoice.htm.

Hadden, Jeffery K. 1995. Religion and the Quest for Meaning and Order: Old Paradigms, New Realities. *Sociological Focus*. 28 (1):83–100.

Hall, Peter Dobkin. 2001. Historical Perspectives on Religion, Government and Social Welfare in America. In *Can Charitable Choice Work?* ed. Andrew Walsh, 78–113. Hartford, Conn.: The Pew Program on Religion and the News Media.

Hardy, Dan. 2001. "Media Church Lends a Hand to Spruce up Chester." *Philadelphia Inquirer*, 25 October.

Harper, Nile. 1999. *Urban Churches, Vital Signs: Beyond Charity toward Justice*. Grand Rapids, Mich.: Eerdmans.

Harris, Fredrick C. 2001. Black Churches and Civic Traditions. In *Can Charitable Choice Work?* ed. Andrew Walsh, 140–156. Hartford, Conn.: The Pew Program on Religion and the News Media.

Harris, Margaret. 1995. Quiet Care: Welfare Work and Religious Congregations. *Journal of Social Policy*. 24 (1):53–71.

Hart, Stephen. 1992. *What Does the Lord Require? How American Christians Think about Economic Justice*. New York: Oxford University Press.

Harvard Divinity School Center for the Study of Values in Public Life. 1999. Research Report on Faith-Based Organizations and Social Service Provision. Boston: Harvard Divinity School Center for the Study of Values in Public Life.

Hengel, Martin. 1974. *Property and Riches in the Early Church*. Philadelphia: Fortress.

Henry, Carl F. H. 1947. *The Uneasy Conscience of American Fundamentalism*. Grand Rapids, Mich.: Eerdmans.

Hessel, Dieter. 1992. *Social Ministry*. 2nd ed. Louisville: Westminster/John Knox.

Hodge, David. 2000. Spirituality: Towards a Theoretical Framework. *Social Thought* 19 (4):1–20.

———. 2001. Spiritual Assessment: A Review of Major Qualitative Methods and a New Framework for Assessing Spirituality. *Social Work* 46 (3):203–14.

Hodgkinson, Virginia, and Murray Weitzman. 1993. *From Belief to Commitment: The Community Service Activities and Finances of Religious Congregations in the United States*. Washington, D.C.: Independent Sector.

Hoge, Dean R., Everett L. Perry, and Gerald L. Klever. 1978. Theology as a Source of Disagreement about Protestant Church Goals and Priorities. *Review of Religious Research* 19 (2):116–138.

Hoge, Dean R., Charles Zech, Patrick McNamara, and Michael J. Donahue. 1998. The Value of Volunteers as Resources for Congregations. *Journal for the Scientific Study of Religion* 37 (3):470–480.

Hollinger, Dennis. 1983. *Individualism and Social Ethics: An Evangelical Syncretism*. Lanham, Md.: University Press of America.

Hopewell, James F. 1987. *Congregation: Stories and Structures*. Philadelphia: Fortress.

Hugen, Beryl. 1994. The Secularization of Social Work. *Social Work and Christianity* 21 (1):83–101.

Hugen, Beryl, and T. Laine Scales, eds. 2002. *Christianity and Social Work*. Botsford, Conn.: National Association of Christians in Social Work.

Hugen, Beryl, Terry Wolfer, Diana Garland, Dennis Myers, David Sherwood, and Paula Sheridan. 2003. Reconceptualizing Faith and Its Relation to Community Ministry: A Model of Christian Faith Practices. *Social Work and Christianity* 30: 234–255.

Iannaccone, Laurence. 1994. Why Strict Churches Are Strong. *American Journal of Sociology* 99 (5):1180–1211.

ITC/Faith Factor Project 2000 Study of Black Churches. 2000. Atlanta: ITC/Faith Factor Project 2000, in conjunction with Faith Communities Today.

Jackson, Elton F., Mark D. Bachmeier, James R. Wood, and Elizabeth A. Craft. 1995. Volunteering and Charitable Giving: Do Religious and Associational Ties Promote Helping Behavior? *Nonprofit and Voluntary Sector Quarterly* 24:59–78.

Jackson, Maxie C., Jr., John H. Schweitzer, Marvin T. Cato, and Reynard N. Blake, Jr. 1997. Faith-Based Institutions' Community and Economic Development Programs Serving Black Communities in Michigan. Research report. Urban Affairs Program, Michigan State University.

James, William. 1902. *The Varieties of Religious Experience*. Longdon: Longmans, Green & Co.

Jeavons, Thomas H. 1994. *When the Bottom Line Is Faithfulness: Management of Christian Service Organizations*. Bloomington: Indiana University Press.

———. 1998. Identifying Characteristics of "Religious" Organizations: An Exploratory Proposal. In *Sacred Companies: Organizational Aspects of Religion and Religious Aspects of Organizations*, ed. Demerath III, Peter Dobkin Hall, Terry Schmitt, and Rhys H. Williams, 79–95. New York: Oxford University Press.

———. 2003. Public Services? Private Faith? What Should the Role of Religion Be in the Provision of Social Services? Paper presented at the Independent Sector Spring Research Forum, Bethesda, Md., March 7, 2003.

John-Hall, Annette. 1999a. Pondering the Welfare Gap: Faith-based Organizations Try to Assess Their Role as Public Assistance Is Cut Back. *Philadelphia Inquirer*, 7 March.

———. 1999b. A Pooling of Resources. *Philadelphia Inquirer*, 25 April.

Johnson, Benton. 1967. Theology and the Position of Pastors on Public Issues. *American Sociological Review* 32:433–442.

Johnson, Byron. 2000. A Better Kind of High: How Religious Commitment Reduces Drug Use among Poor Urban Teens. CRRUCS Report 2000–2. Philadelphia: Center for Research on Religion and Urban Civil Society, University of Pennsylvania.

———. 2002. Objective Hope: Assessing the Effectiveness of Faith-Based Organizations: A Review of the Literature. Philadelphia: Center for Research on Religion and Urban Civil Society, University of Pennsylvania.

Johnson, Byron R., David B. Larson, Spencer De Li, and Sung Joon Jang. 2000. Escaping from the Crime of Inner Cities: Church Attendance and Religious Salience among Disadvantaged Youths. *Justice Quarterly* 17 (2):377–391.

Jones, S. K. 1982. Urban Black Churches: Conservators of Value and Sustainers of Community. *Journal of Religious Thought* 39:41–50.

Kanagy, Conrad L. 1992. Social Action, Evangelism, and Ecumenism: The Impact of Community, Theological, and Church Structural Variables. *Review of Religious Research* 34:34–47.

Kelley, Dean M. 1984. Religion and Justice: The Volcano and the Terrace. *Review of Religious Research*. 26:3–14.

Kennedy, Sheila Suess, and Wolfgang Bielefeld. 2003. *Charitable Choice: First Results from Three States*. Indianapolis: Center for Urban Policy and the Environment.

Kostarelos, Francis. 1995. *Feeling the Spirit: Faith and Hope in an Evangelical Black Storefront Church*. Columbia: University of South Carolina Press.

Krause, Neal, Christopher G. Ellison, Benjamin A. Shaw, John P. Marcum, and Jason D. Boardman. 2001. Church-Based Social Support and Religious Coping. *Journal for the Scientific Study of Religion* 40 (4):637–656.

Lampkin, Linda, Sheryl Romeo, and Emily Finnin. 2001. Introducing the Nonprofit Program Classification System: The Taxonomy We've Been Waiting For. *Nonprofit and Voluntary Sector Quarterly* 30 (4):781–793.

Larson, David B., and Byron R. Johnson. 1998. Religion: The Forgotten Factor in Cutting Youth Crime and Saving At-Risk Urban Youth. Report 98–2. New York: The Manhattan Institute.

Laudarji, Isaac B., and Livezey, Lowell W. 2000. The Churches and the Poor in a "Ghetto Underclass" Neighborhood. *Public Religion and Urban Transformation: Faith in the City*, ed. Lowell W. Livezey, 83–105. New York: New York University Press.

Leonard, Mary. 2001. Faith Bill Advances amid Religious Mood: Administration Yields on Expanding Grants. *Boston Globe,* 18 November.

Levin, Jeffrey S., and Robert Joseph Taylor. 1998. Panel Analyses of Religious Involvement and Well-Being in African Americans: Contemporaneous vs. Longitudinal Effects. Journal for the Scientific Study of Religion 37 (4):695–709.

Lewis, James W. 1994. Going Downtown: Historical Resources for Urban Ministry. *Word and World* 14:402–408.

Lin, Nan, Walter M. Ensel, and John C. Vaughn. 1981. Social Resources and Strength of Ties: Structural Factors in Occupational Status Attainment. *American Sociological Review* 46:393–405.

Lincoln, C. Eric. 1994. Foreword: The Progressive Mission of the Black Church. In *Economic Empowerment through the Church: A Blueprint for Progressive Community Development,* ed. Gregory Reed, 11–17. Grand Rapids, Mich.: Zondervan.

Lincoln, Eric C., and Lawrence H. Mamiya. 1990. *The Black Church in the African American Experience.* Durham, N.C.: Duke University Press.

Linder, William J. 2001. Faith as the Foundation for the New Community Corporation. In *Sacred Places, Civic Purposes: Should Government Help Faith-Based Charity?* ed. E. J. Dionne Jr., and Ming Hsu Chen, 155–157. Washington, D.C.: Brookings Institution Press.

Livezey, Lowell W., ed. 2000. *Public Religion and Urban Transformation: Faith in the City.* New York: New York University Press.

Lockhart, William. 2003. The Added Value of Religion in Poverty-to-Work Programs: A Framework for Analysis:. The Journal of Markets and Morality 6 (2):497–524.

Loconte, Joe. 1998. The Bully and the Pulpit: A New Model for Church-State Partnerships. *Policy Review,* November/December, 28–37.

———. 2001. *God, Government and the Good Samaritan: The Promise and the Peril of the President's Faith-Based Agenda.* Washington, D.C.: The Heritage Foundation.

Lofland, John, and Rodney Stark. 1965. Becoming a World-Saver: A Theory of Conversion to a Deviant Perspective. *American Sociological Review* 30:862–875.

Loury, Glenn C. 1995. *One by One from the Inside Out: Essays and Reviews on Race and Responsibility in America.* New York: Free Press.

Loury, Glenn C., and Linda Datcher Loury. 1997. Not by Bread Alone: The Role of the African-American Church in Inner City Development. *The Brookings Review* 15 (1):10–13.

Lupu, Ira, and Robert Tuttle. 2002. Legal Analysis of Final Rules and Notices of Proposed Rulemaking Concerning the Faith-Based Initiative. Albany, N.Y.: The Roundtable on Religion and Social Welfare Policy.

Maldonado, David, Jr. 1999. *Protestantes/Protestants: Hispanic Christianity within Mainline Traditions.* Nashville: Abingdon.

Marsden, George M. 1980. *Fundamentalism and American Culture.* New York: Oxford University Press.

Marty, Martin. 1970. *Righteous Empire: The Protestant Experience in America.* New York: Dial.

———. 1980. Social Service: Godly and Godless. *Social Service Review* 54 (4):463–481.

————. 1981. *The Public Church*. New York: Crossroad.

Mata, Michael. 1999. Protestant Hispanics Serving the Community: A Research Project. Report to the Pew Charitable Trusts. Claremont, Calif.: Urban Leadership Institute, Claremont School of Theology.

Maton, Kenneth I. 1989. Community Settings as Buffers of Life Stress? Highly Supportive Churches, Mutual Help Groups, and Senior Centers. *American Journal of Community Psychology* 17:203–232.

Maynard, Roy, and Bob Jones. 1998. Fighting Poverty in Jesus' Name. *World*, 15 August.

McConkey, Dale, and Peter Lawler, eds. 2001. *Faith, Morality, and Civil Society*. Lanham, Md.: Lexington.

McRoberts, Omar. 1999. Understanding the "New" Black Pentecostal Activism: Lessons from Boston Ecumenical Ministries. *Sociology of Religion* 60:47–70.

————. 2003. *Streets of Glory: Church and Community in a Black Urban Neighborhood*. Chicago: University of Chicago Press.

Milbank, Dana, and Thomas B. Edsall. 2001. Faith Initiative May Be Revised; Criticism Surprises Administration. *Washington Post*, 12 March.

Milner, Murray, Jr. 1994. Status and Sacredness: Worship and Salvation as Forms of Status Transformation. *Journal for the Scientific Study of Religion* 33:99–109.

Milofsky, Carl. 1997. Organization from Community: A Case Study of Congregational Renewal. *Nonprofit and Voluntary Sector Quarterly*. Suppl. S139–S160.

Milsap, Cynthia, and Bernice Taylor. 1998. The Black Storefront Church: Building Community One Soul at a Time. *Pragmatics: The Journal of Community-Based Research* 1 (3):13–16.

Moberg, David O. 1972. *The Great Reversal: Evangelism Versus Social Concern*. Philadelphia: J. B. Lippincott.

Mock, Alan K. 1992. Congregational Religious Styles and Orientation to Society: Exploring Our Linear Assumptions. *Review of Religious Research* 34:20–33.

Monsma, Stephen V. 1996. *When Sacred and Secular Mix: Religious Nonprofit Organizations and Public Money*. Lanham, Md.: Rowman & Littlefield.

————. 2002. Working Faith: How Religious Organizations Provide Welfare-to-Work Services. Philadelphia: University of Pennsylvania, Center for Research on Religion and Urban Civil Society.

Montiel, Lisa. 2003. The Use of Public Funds For Delivery of Faith-Based Human Services. Albany, N.Y.: The Roundtable on Religion and Social Welfare Policy.

Moyers, Bill. 1996. Religion Is Breaking Out All Over. *USA Today*, 13 October.

Nees, Thomas. 1996. *Compassion Evangelism: Meeting Human Needs*. Kansas City, Mo.: Beacon Hill.

Nelsen, Hart M. 1975. Why Do Pastors Preach on Social Issues? *Theology Today* 32:56–73.

Nelson, Mary. 2001. The Faith Factor in Community Building. *Christian Community Development Association Restorer*, vol. 10.

Nelson, Timothy J. 1997a. He Made a Way Out of No Way: Religious Experience in an African-American Congregation. *Review of Religious Research* 39 (1):22.

————. 1997b. The Church and the Street: Race, Class and Congregation. *Contemporary American Religion: An Ethnographic Reader*, ed. Penny Edgell Becker and Nancy Eisland. Walnut Creek, Calif.: Alta Mira.

Neuhaus, Richard John. 1984. *The Naked Public Square: Religion and Democracy in America*. Grand Rapids, Mich.: Eerdmans.

Nolan, Clare. 1999. Charitable Choice: Welfare Money and the First Amendment. *Stateline.org*.

O' Keefe, Mark. 2001. Civil Religion Burgeoning in Public Square after Terror Attacks. *Religion News Service*, 22 October.

———. 2002. Federal, State Agencies Quietly Foster Faith-Based Initiatives. *Religion News Service*, 7 March.

Olasky, Marvin. 1992. *The Tragedy of American Compassion*. Washington, D.C.: Regnery.

———. 2000. *Compassionate Conservatism*. New York: Free Press.

Olson, Daniel. 1989. Church Friendships: Boon or Barrier to Church Growth? *Journal for the Scientific Study of Religion* 28:432–447.

Olson, V. A. Daniel, and Jackson W. Carroll. 1992. Religiously Based Politics: Religious Elites and the Public. *Social Forces* 70:765–786.

Orr, John, Donald Miller, Wade Clark Roof, and Gordon Melton. 1994. *Politics of the Spirit: Religion and Multiethnicity in Los Angeles*. Los Angeles: University of Southern California.

Paris, Peter J. 1985. *The Social Teaching of the Black Churches*. Philadelphia: Fortress.

Park, Jerry, and Christian Smith. 2000. "To Whom Much Has Been Given . . .": Religious Capital and Community Voluntarism among Churchgoing Protestants. *Journal for the Scientific Study of Religion* 39 (3):272–286.

Parker, Richard. 2000. Progressive Politics and, Uh, . . . God. *The American Prospect* 11 (5):32–37.

Parks, Dawn L., and Susanna R. Quern. 2001. An Analysis of Congregational Programs. *Research Notes from the Project on Religion and Urban Culture* 3 (1).

Pellebon, Dwain A. 2000. Perceptions of Conflict between Christianity and Social Work: A Preliminary Study. *Social Work and Christianity* 27 (1):30–39.

Perkins, John. 1993. *Beyond Charity: The Call to Christian Community Development*. Grand Rapids, Mich.: Baker.

Petersen, Jim. 1980. *Evangelism as a Lifestyle*. Colorado Springs: NavPress.

Peterson, Larry R., and K. Peter Takayama. 1984. Religious Commitment and Conservatism: Toward Understanding an Elusive Relationship. *Sociological Analysis* 45 (4):355–371.

Pew Forum on Religion and Public Life. 2002. Lift Every Voice: A Report on Religion in American Public Life. Pew Forum on Religion and Public Life. Washington, D.C.

Pipes, Paula F., and Helen Rose Ebaugh. 2002. Faith-Based Coalitions, Social Services, and Government Funding. *Sociology of Religion* 63 (1):49–68.

Polis Center. 2001. Indiana Congregations' Human Services Programs: A Report of a Statewide Survey. Indianapolis: Faith Works.

Portes, Alejandro, and Julia Sensenbrenner. 1993. Embeddedness, and Immigration: Notes on the Social Determinants of Economic Action. *American Journal of Sociology* 98 (6):1320–1350.

Potapchuk, William R., Jarle P. Crocker, and William H. Schechter. 1997. Building Community with Social Capital: Chits and Chums or Chats with Change. *National Civic Review* 86 (2):129–140.

Presbyterian Panel. 1997. Social Justice and Social Welfare. Louisville: Presbyterian Panel Research Services, Presbyterian Church (U.S.A.).

Price, Matthew. 2000. Place, Race, and History: The Social Mission of Downtown Churches. In *Public Religion and Urban Transformation: Faith in the City,* ed. Lowell W. Livezey, 83–105. New York: New York University Press.

Printz, Tobi Jennifer. 1998. Faith-Based Service Providers in the Nation's Capital: Can They Do More? Center on Nonprofits and Philanthropy, Charting Civil Society Series, no. 2. Washington, D.C.: The Urban Institute.

Putnam, Robert D. 1995. Bowling Alone: America's Declining Social Capital. *Journal of Democracy* 6 (1):65–78.

———. 2000. *Bowling Alone: The Collapse and Revival of American Community.* New York: Simon & Schuster.

Queen, Edward L., II, ed. 2000. *Serving Those in Need: A Handbook for Managing Faith-Based Human Services Organizations.* San Francisco: Jossey-Bass.

Reese, Laura A. 2000. Faith-Based Economic Development. *Policy Studies Review* 17 (2/3): 84–103.

Regnerus, Mark, and Christian Smith. 1998. Selective Deprivatization among American Religious Traditions: The Reversal of the Great Reversal. *Social Forces* 76 (4):1347–1372.

Reichley, A. James. 1985. *Religion in American Public Life.* Washington, D.C.: Brookings Institution Press.

Ressler, Lawrence. 2002. When Social Work and Christianity Conflict. In *Christianity and Social Work,* ed. Beryl Hugenand Laine Scales, 93–118. Botsford, Conn.: National Association of Christians in Social Work.

Richard, Alan J., David C. Bell, and Jerry W. Carlson. 2000. Individual Religiosity, Moral Community, and Drug User Treatment. *Journal for the Scientific Study of Religion* 39 (2): 240–246.

Richardson, Willie. 1992. Empowering Lay Leadership in an African-American Urban Church: A Case Study. In *Discipling the City: A Comprehensive Approach to Urban Mission,* ed. Roger S. Greenway, 149–157. Grand Rapids, Mich.: Baker.

———. 1996. *Reclaiming the Urban Family: How to Mobilize the Church as a Family Center.* Grand Rapids, Mich.: Zondervan.

Rittenhouse, Andy, ed. 2002. *Salt and Light: Saturating Knoxville with the Love of Christ.* 2nd ed. Knoxville, Tenn.: Compassion Coalition.

Rivers, Eugene F., III. 2001. Effectiveness over Ideology: Church-Based Partnerships in Crime Prevention. In *Sacred Places, Civic Purposes: Should Government Help Faith-Based Charity?* ed. E. J. Dionne Jr., and Ming Hsu Chen, 94–95. Washington, D.C.: Brookings Institution Press.

Rogers, Barbara W., and Douglas Ronsheim. 1998. Interfacing African American Churches with Agencies and Institutions: An Expanding Continuum of Care with Partial Answers to Welfare Reform. *Journal of Sociology and Social Welfare* 25 (1):105–120.

Rogers, Melissa. 1999. The Wrong Way to Do Right: Charitable Choice and Churches. In *Welfare Reform and Faith-Based Organizations,* ed. Derek Davis and Barry Hankins, 61–88. Waco, Tex.: J. M. Dawson Institute of Church-State Studies.

Rokeach, Milton. 1969. Religious Values and Social Compassion. *Review of Religious Research* 11:24–39.

Roof, Wade Clark. 1993. Religion and Narrative. *Review of Religious Research* 34: (4): 297–310.

———. 1996. God Is in the Details: Reflections on Religion's Public Presence in the United States in the Mid-1990s. *Sociology of Religion* 57 (2):149–162.

Roozen, David, and Carl Dudley. 2001. Faith Communities Today: A Report on Religion in the United States Today. Report from the Faith Communities Today (FACT) Study.

Roozen, David, William McKinney, and Wade Clark Roof. 1995. Fifty Years of Religious Change in the United States. In *The Post-War Generation and Establishment Religion*, ed. Wade Clark Roof et al., 59–85. Boulder, Colo.: Westview.

Roozen, David A., William McKinney, and Jackson Carroll. 1984. *Varieties of Religious Presence: Mission in the Public Life.* New York: Pilgrim.

Sawyer, Mary R. 1988. Black Ecumenical Movements: Proponents of Social Change. *Review of Religious Research* 30:151–161.

Saxon-Harrold, Susan K. E., Susan J. Wiener, Michael T. Mccormack, and Michelle A. Weber. 2000. *America's Congregations: Measuring Their Contribution to Society.* Washington, D.C.: Independent Sector.

Schmalzbauer, John. 1993. Evangelicals in the New Class: Class Versus Subcultural Predictors of Ideology. *Journal for the Scientific Study of Religion* 32:330–342.

Schmidt, Jean Miller. 1991. *Souls or the Social Order: The Two-Party System in American Protestantism.* Brooklyn, N.Y.: Carlson.

Schneider, Jo Anne. 1999. Trusting That of God in Everyone: Three Examples of Quaker-Based Social Service in Disadvantaged Communities. *Nonprofit and Voluntary Sector Quarterly* 28 (3):269–295.

———. 2001. *The Kenosha Social Capital Study: Churches, Nonprofits and Community.* Indiana, Pa.: Indiana University of Pennsylvania.

Scott, Jason D. 2002. *The Scope and Scale of Faith-Based Social Services.* Albany, N.Y.: The Roundtable on Religion and Social Welfare Policy.

Scott, Julia M. 2004. Groups Take Advantage of Government Funding to Increase Social Services. *Jersey Journal,* 20 March.

Seley, John E., and Julian Wolpert. 2003. Secular and Faith-Based Human Services: Complementarities or Competition. Paper presented at the Independent Sector Spring Research Forum, Bethesda, Md., March 7, 2003.

Sherman, Amy L. 2000. A Survey of Church-Government Anti-Poverty Partnerships. *American Enterprise* 11 (4):32–33.

———. 2003. The Community Serving Activities of Hispanic Protestant Congregations. Preliminary report submitted to the Center for the Study of Latino Religion, Notre Dame University, South Bend, Ind.

Sherwood, David. 1998. Spiritual Assessment as a Normal Part of Social Work Practice: Power to Help and Power to Harm. *Social Work and Christianity* 25 (2):80–99.

Sider, Ronald J. 1994. *Cup of Water, Bread of Life.* Grand Rapids, Mich.: Zondervan.

———. 2002. The Case for "Discrimination." *First Things* 124:19–22. www.firstthings.com/ftissues/ft0206/opinion/sider.html.

————, ed. 1974. *The Chicago Declaration*. Carol Stream, Ill.: Creation House.

Sider, Ronald J., Philip N. Olson, and Heidi Rolland Unruh. 2002. *Churches That Make a Difference: Reaching Your Community with Good News and Good Works*. Grand Rapids, Mich.: Baker.

Sider, Ronald J., and Heidi Rolland. 1996. Correcting the Welfare Tragedy: Toward a New Model for Church/State Partnership. In *Welfare in America: Christian Perspectives on a Policy in Crisis*, ed. Stanley Carlson-Thies and James Skillen, 454–479. Grand Rapids, Mich.: Eerdmans.

Sider, Ronald J., and Heidi Rolland Unruh. 2000. No Aid to Religion? Charitable Choice and the First Amendment. In *What's God Got to Do with the American Experiment?* ed. E. J. Dionne Jr., and John J. DiIulio Jr., 128–137. Washington, D.C.: Brookings Institution Press.

————. 2001. Evangelism and Church-State Partnerships. *Journal of Church and State* 43 (2):267–295.

————. 2004. Typology of Religious Characteristics of Social Service and Educational Organizations and Programs. *Nonprofit and Voluntary Sector Quarterly* 33 (1):109–134.

Sinha, Jill Witmer. 2000. *Cookman United Methodist Church and Transitional Journey: A Case Study in Charitable Choice*. Washington, D.C.: The Center for Public Justice.

Sjogren, Steve. 1993. *Conspiracy of Kindness*. Ann Arbor, Mich.: Vine.

Skocpol, Theda, and Morris Fiorina, eds. 1999. *Civic Engagement in American Democracy*. Washington, D.C.: Brookings Institution Press.

Smedes, Lewis. 1966. The Evangelicals and the Social Question. *The Reformed Journal* 16 (February):9–13.

Smidt, Corwin, ed. 2003. *Religionas Social Capital*. Waco, Tex.: Baylor University Press.

Smith, Christian. 1996. Correcting a Curious Neglect, or Bringing Religion Back In. In *Disruptive Religion: The Force of Faith in Social Movement Activism*, ed. Christian Smith, 1–25. New York: Routledge.

————. 1998. *American Evangelicalism: Embattled and Thriving*. Chicago: University of Chicago Press.

————. 2003. Theorizing Religious Effects among American Adolescents. *Journal for the Scientific Study of Religion* 42 (1):17–30.

Smith, D. H. 1983. Churches Are Generally Ignored in Contemporary Voluntary Action Research: Causes and Consequences. *Review of Religious Research* 24 (4):295–303.

Smith, R. Drew. 2001. Churches and the Urban Poor: Interaction and Social Distance. *Sociology of Religion* 62 (3):301–313.

Smith, Steven Rathgeb, and Michael R. Sosin. 2001. The Varieties of Faith-Related Agencies. *Public Administration Review* 61 (6):651–670.

Smith, Timothy L. 1957. *Revivalism and Social Reform: American Protestantism on the Eve of the Civil War*. New York: Harper.

Stark, Rodney. 1971. *Wayward Shepherds: Prejudice and the Protestant Clergy*. New York: Harper & Row.

————. 2000. Religious Effects: In Praise of "Idealistic Humbug." *Review of Religious Research* 41 (3):289–310.

Stark, Rodney, and William Sibs Bainbridge. 1979. Of Churches, Sects, and Cults: Preliminary Concepts for a Theory of Religious Movement. *Journal for the Scientific Study of Religion,* 18:117–131.

Steinfels, Peter. 2004. Religious Organizations Have Long Had a Role in Providing Social Services to the Needy. Does a New California Law Threaten It? *The New York Times,* 13 March.

Stone, Melissa M. 2000. Scope and Scale: An Assessment of Human Service Delivery by Congregations in Minnesota. Paper presented at the annual meeting of the Association for Research on Nonprofit Organizations and Voluntary Action, New Orleans.

Streeter, Ryan, ed. 2001. Religion and the Public Square in the 21st Century. Proceedings from the Conference: The Future of Government Partnerships with the Faith Community. Indianapolis: Hudson Institute.

Strong, Douglas M. 1997. *They Walked in the Spirit.* Louisville: Westminster/John Knox.

Stronks, Julia K. 1995. *The First Amendment, Employment Law, and Governmental Regulation of Religious Institutions.* Philadelphia: The Crossroads Monograph Series on Faith and Public Policy, vol. 1, no. 4.

Swindler, Ann. 1986. Culture in Action: Symbols and Strategies. *American Sociological Review* 51:273–286.

Tamney, Joseph B. 1991. Social Class Composition of Congregations and Pastoral Support for Liberal Activism. *Review of Religious Research* 33:18–30.

Taylor, Robert J, and Linda M. Chatters. 1988. Church Members as a Source of Informal Social Support. *Review of Religious Research* 30 (2):193–201.

Thornburgh, Georgianne, and Terry A. Wolfer. 2000. Megachurch Involvement in Community Social Ministry: Extent and Effects in Three Congregations. *Social Work and Christianity* 27 (2):130–149.

Thuesen, Peter J. 2002. The Logic of Mainline Churchliness: Historical Background since the Reformation. In *The Quiet Hand of God: Faith-Based Activism and the Public Role of Mainline Protestantism,* ed. Robert Wuthnow and John Evans, 27–53. Berkeley and Los Angeles: University of California Press.

Tocqueville, Alexis de. 1835. *Democracy in America.* London: Saunders and Otley.

Trulear, Harold D. 1985. A Critique of Functionalism: Toward a More Holistic Sociology of Afro-American Religion. *Journal of Religious Thought* 42:38–50.

———. 1999. Prophecy and Presence. *Missing Connections.* Auburn Studies 6:24–28.

Tsitsos, William. 2003. Race Differences in Congregational Social Service Activity. *Journal for the Scientific Study of Religion* 42 (2):205–215.

Twombly, Eric C., and Carol J. De Vita. 1998. D.C.-Area Ties to Religious Congregations. Center on Nonprofits and Philanthropy, Charting Civil Society Series, no. 3. Washington, D.C.: The Urban Institute.

Unruh, Heidi Rolland. 2002. Choosing Partners. *Christian Century* 119 (25):8–9.

———. 2004. Religious Elements of Church-Based Social Service Programs. *Review of Religious Research* 45 (4):317–335.

Unruh, Heidi Rolland, and Jill Witmer Sinha. 2001. Churches and Public Funds: Risks or Rewards? *Prism* 8 (3):11–13.

———. 2005. Transitional Journey Ministry: A Church-Based Welfare-to-Work Partnership Model. In *Sanctioning Religion?: The Constitution and Faith-Based Public Services,* ed. David K. Ryden and Jeffrey Polet, and Lynn Rienner.

Verba, Sidney, Kay Lehman Schlozman, and Henry Brady. 1995. *Voice and Equality: Civic Voluntarism in American Politics.* Cambridge: Harvard University Press.

Vidal, Avis C. 2001. Faith-Based Organizations in Community Development. Washington, D.C.: U.S. Department of Housing and Community Development, Office of Policy Development and Research.

Wald, Kenneth D., Lyman A. Kellstedt, and David C. Leege. 1993. Church Involvement and Political Behavior. In *Rediscovering the Religious Factor in American Politics,* ed. David C. Leege and Lyman A. Kellstedt, 121–138. Armonk, N.Y.: M. E. Sharpe.

Wallis, Allan Dennis, and C. Koziol. 1996. *Toward a Paradigm of Community-Making.* Denver: National Civic League.

Wallis, Jim. 2001. *Faith Works: How Faith Based Organizations Are Changing Lives, Neighborhoods, and America.* Berkeley, Calif.: Page Mill.

———. 2005. *God's Politics: Why the Right Gets It Wrong and the Left Doesn't Get It.* San Francisco: HarperSanFrancisco.

Walsh, Andrew, ed. 2001. *Can Charitable Choice Work?* Hartford, Conn.: The Pew Program on Religion and the News Media.

Ward, Harry. 1915. *Social Evangelism.* New York: Missionary Education Movement of the United States and Canada.

Ward, Naomi, Andrew Billingsley, Alicia Simon, and Judith Crocker Burris. 1994. Black Churches in Atlanta Reach Out to the Community. *National Journal of Sociology* 8 (Summer/Winter):49–74.

Warner, R. Stephen. 1993. Work in Progress toward a New Paradigm for the Sociological Study of Religion in the United States. *American Journal of Sociology* 98:1044–1093.

———. 1994. The Place of the Congregation in the Contemporary American Religious Configuration. In *New Perspectives in the Study of Congregations.* Vol. 2 of *American Congregations,* ed. James Wind and James Lewis, 54–99. Chicago: University of Chicago Press.

Warner, R. Stephen, and Judith G. Wittner, eds. 1998. *Gatherings in Diaspora: Religious Communities and the New Immigration.* Philadelphia: Temple University Press.

Warren, Mark R. 2003. Faith and Leadership in the Inner City: How Social Capital Contributes to Democratic Renewal. In *Religionas Social Capital,* ed. Corwin Smidt, 49–68. Waco, Tex.: Baylor University Press.

Warren, Mark R., and Richard L. Wood. 2001. *Faith-Based Community Organizing: The State of the Field.* Jericho, N.Y.: Interfaith Funders.

Warren, Rick. 1995. *The Purpose-Driven Church: Growth without Compromising Your Message and Mission.* Grand Rapids, Mich.: Zondervan.

Webber, Robert E. 2002. *The Younger Evangelicals: Facing the Challenges of the New World.* Grand Rapids, Mich.: Baker.

Weber, Max. 1963. *The Sociology of Religion.* Trans. Ephraim Fischoff. Boston: Beacon.

Wellman, James. 2002. Religion without a Net: Strictness in the Religious Practices of West Coast Urban Liberal Christian Congregations. *Review of Religious Research* 44 (2):184–199.

White House Office for Faith-Based and Community Initiatives. 2003. Partnering with the Federal Government: Some Do's and Don'ts for Faith-Based Organizations. http://www.whitehouse.gov/government/fbci/guidance/partnering.html (accessed 19 July 2003).

Williams, Rhys H. 1996. Religion as Political Resource: Culture or Ideology? *Journal for the Scientific Study of Religion* 35 (4):368–378.

———. 2003. The Language of God in the City of Man: Religious Discourse and Public Politics in America. In *Religionas Social Capital,* edited by Corwin Smidt, 171–189. Waco, Tex.: Baylor University Press.

Wilson, John. 2000. "Proselytizers." *Books and Culture: A Christian Review,* May/June, 3.

Wilson, John, and Thomas Janoski. 1995. The Contribution of Religion to Volunteer Work. *Sociology of Religion* 56 (2):137–152.

Wineburg, Robert J. 1992. Local Human Services Provision by Religious Congregations: A Community Analysis. *Nonprofit and Voluntary Sector Quarterly* 21 (2):107–118.

———. 1994. A Longitudinal Case Study of Religious Congregations in Local Human Services. *Nonprofit and Voluntary Sector Quarterly* 23 (2):159–169.

———. 1996. Relationships between Religion and Social Services: An Arranged Marriage or a Renewal of Vows? *Social Work and Christianity: An International Journal* 23 (1):9–27.

———. 2001. *A Limited Partnership: The Politics of Religion, Welfare, and Social Service.* New York: Columbia University Press.

Wolfe, Alan. 1998. *One Nation After All.* New York: Viking.

———. 2003. *The Transformation of American Religion: How We Actually Live Our Faith.* New York: Free Press.

Wolpert, Julian. 1997. The Role of Small Religious Nonprofits in Changing Urban Neighborhoods. *Nonprofit and Voluntary Sector Quarterly.* Suppl. S14–S28.

Wood, James R. 1981. *Leadership in Voluntary Organizations: The Controversy over Social Action in Protestant Churches.* New Brunswick, N,J,: Rutgers University Press.

———. 1990. Liberal Protestant Social Action in a Period of Decline. In *Faith and Philanthropy in America,* ed. Robert Wuthnow and Virginia Hodgkinson, 165–186. San Francisco: Jossey-Bass.

Wood, Richard L. 1994. Faith in Action: Religious Resources for Political Success in Three Congregations. *Sociology of Religion* 55:397–417.

———. 1997. Social Capital and Political Culture: God Meets Politics in the Inner City. *American Behavioral Scientist* 40 (5):595–605.

———. 2002. *Faith in Action: Religion, Race and Democratic Organizing in America.* Chicago: University of Chicago Press.

Woods, C. Jeff. 1996. *Congregational Megatrends.* New York: Alban Institute.

Woodson, Robert L., Sr. 1998. *The Triumphs of Joseph.* New York: Free Press.

Working Group on Human Needs and Faith-Based and Community Initiatives. 2002. *Finding Common Ground: 29 Recommendations of the Working Group on Human Needs and Faith-Based and Community Initiatives.* Washington, D.C.: Search for Common Ground.

———. 2003. *Harnessing Civic and Faith-Based Power to Fight Poverty*. Washington, D.C.: Search for Common Ground.

Wuthnow, Robert. 1989. *The Struggle for America's Soul: Evangelicals, Liberals, and Secularism*. Grand Rapids, Mich.: Eerdmans.

———. 1991. *Acts of Compassion: Caring for Others and Helping Ourselves*. Princeton, N.J.: Princeton University Press.

———. 1996. *Christianity and Civil Society: The Contemporary Debate*. Valley Forge, Pa.: Trinity.

———. 1997. *The Crisis in the Churches: Spiritual Malaise, Fiscal Woe*. New York: Oxford University Press.

———. 2000. Linkages between Churches and Faith-based Nonprofits. Report to the Aspen Institute.

———. 2002. Religious Involvement and Status-Bridging Social Capital. *Journal for the Scientific Study of Religion* 41 (4).

———. 2003. Can Religion Revitalize Civil Society? An Institutional Perspective. In *Religion as Social Capital*, ed. Corwin Smidt, 191–209. Waco, Tex.: Baylor University Press.

———. 2004. *Saving America? Faith-Based Services and the Future of Civil Society*. Princeton, N.J.: Princeton University Press.

Wuthnow, Robert, Virginia Hodgkinson et al., eds. 1990. *Faith and Philanthropy in America*. San Francisco: Jossey-Bass.

Wuthnow, Robert, and John H. Evans. 2002. *The Quiet Hand of God: Faith-Based Activism and the Public Role of Mainline Protestantism*. Berkeley and Los Angeles: University of California Press.

Yanay, Uri. 1985. Toward a Taxonomy of Social Service Programmes. *International Journal of Sociology and Social Policy* 5 (2):45–57.

Index

and social capital, 224–37
types of, 36–38
See also altruism evangelism; implicit
   spiritual nurture; integrated
   evangelism; pre-evangelism
Evangelistic congregations as a mission
   type, 21
Evangelistic ministry as a spiritual
   meaning of social action, 69, 77–80,
   82–86, 133, 257–58, 281 n.1
See also spiritual meanings of social
   action
Expanded individualism, 174, 179–81,
   183, 235–36
Explicit religious elements. *See* religious
   elements of faith-based social
   programs
Expressive relationalism, 174, 177–79,
   183, 235, 248

Faith
   charity as an expression of, 75–76,
      162, 257
   and efficacy of social ministry, 196–
      207, 213–216, 252
   See also outcomes of faith-based
      ministry
   socioeconomic corollaries of, 9, 82,
      200–204, 213–14, 230, 252–53
   as a source of meaning for social
      action, 67–69
   specificity of, 95
   transformational powers of, 200–04
   understandings of in the context of
      social action programs, 20, 84, 239–
      42
   See also salvation
Faith Assembly of God
   and conversionist social action, 173,
      177–79, 187–89, 191
   ministries of, 31, 70, 94, 119, 158, 171–
      73, 178–79, 197, 235, 245, 276 n.18,
      285 n.4
   and mission orientation, 154, 243, 286
      n.11
   Peacemakers, 171–73, 188–89, 191
   perspectives on ministry efficacy, 197–
      98, 204–05
   profile of, 25–26, 32, 263

See also Smith, Richard
Faith Communities Today (FACT) Study,
   32, 273 n.3
Faith Integration Scale, 106
Faith-affiliated organizations/programs,
   109–13, 114–17, 121
Faith-background organizations/
   programs, 109–13, 114–17, 121–22
Faith-based initiatives
   arguments for, 13, 250–51
   concerns regarding, 13, 19, 244, 251,
      275 n.15
   congregations' responses to, 14, 18–19,
      134, 191–92, 242–44
   description of, 12–14, 275 nn.11–14,
      276 n.17
   and effectiveness of faith-based
      programs, 13, 195
   and guidelines for religious activity,
      244–47
   impact on faith-based social services,
      14–15, 276 nn. 16–18, 286 n.14
   and Transitional Journey, 88, 92–93,
      95, 280 n.3
   and use of religious criteria in staff
      selection, 248–250 (*see also* staff of
      social ministry)
   Web sites for, 275 n.13
   See also faith-based programs; funding
      of faith-based programs
Faith-based organizations
   and classification efforts, 105–07, 125,
      254
   defining, 104–05, 241–42
   distinct from faith-based programs,
      107–08, 245
   religious characteristics of, 114–17
   types of, 109–11
Faith-based programs
   and classification efforts, 105–07
   religious characteristics of, 117–18
   religious integration strategies of, 96–
      100
   types of, 109, 112–14
   See also religious elements of faith-
      based social programs; social
      ministry
Faith-centered organizations/programs,
   109–17, 120–21, 199